T0291228

THE POWER OF ORGANIZATIONS

The Power of Organizations

A NEW APPROACH TO
ORGANIZATIONAL THEORY

HEATHER A. HAVEMAN

PRINCETON UNIVERSITY PRESS
PRINCETON & OXFORD

Published by Princeton University Press
41 William Street, Princeton, New Jersey 08540
99 Banbury Road, Oxford OX2 6JX

press.princeton.edu

ISBN 9780691238043
ISBN (pbk.) 9780691241807
ISBN (e-book) 9780691238050

British Library Cataloging-in-Publication Data is available

Editorial: Meagan Levinson & Jaqueline Delaney
Production Editorial: Jaden Young & Natalie Baan
Jacket/Cover Design: Heather Hansen
Production: Erin Suydam
Publicity: Kate Hensley & Charlotte Coyne

This book has been composed in Arno

10 9 8 7 6 5 4 3 2 1

To my teachers and my students.
I have learned so much from all of you.

TABLE OF CONTENTS

PREFACE

ORGANIZATIONS ARE THE MOST UBIQUITOUS and powerful agents in modern society. One example will make this clear. Ponder this question: *Why is American public opinion about climate change so polarized, with Democrats and liberals overwhelmingly believing in human-induced climate change, and Republicans and conservatives generally doubting it, despite scientific consensus and mounting evidence?* Your first instinct might be to study individual-level factors like age, gender, race, and education because my question highlighted two individual-level factors, political affiliation and political leaning. But focusing on individual-level factors shows you just a small piece of the answer. To see the full picture, you have to consider organizations. Over four decades, ExxonMobil and the Koch Family Foundation (KFF) have funded advocacy groups, think tanks, and trade associations that spread misinformation about climate science (Farrell 2016). Organizations funded by ExxonMobil and KFF have exerted immense influence on what other organizations wrote and what their leaders said about climate change. They sowed doubts about scientific evidence, cast scorn over government policies seeking to mitigate emissions of CO_2 (carbon dioxide, whose emissions raise atmospheric temperatures), and raised alarms about the economic costs of enacting and enforcing those policies. Instead, they reported that CO_2 is good for the environment and that any observed change in climate is just part of a long-term cycle. This misinformation was picked up by news sites seeking "balanced" reporting on this issue. Republican politicians who depend heavily on energy companies for their campaigns (more heavily than most Democratic politicians) began to preach the same message. Over time, misinformation from news media and Republican politicians increasingly appealed to Republican and conservative voters. Thus public opinion on climate change became polarized through the actions of many organizations: energy companies, foundations, advocacy groups, think thanks, trade associations, news media, and political parties.

If this is the kind of thing that intrigues, enrages, excites, or terrifies you, then this is the book for you. It will give you an organizational lens through which to look at the world, a lens that will bring into focus many things that may be puzzling you. Using an organizational lens makes it possible to bring into focus just the right level of analysis: not so micro as to assume that all human activity can be explained in terms of individual intentions and actions, and not so macro as to require the high abstractions of many grand theories about states, markets, or societies.

The book will also make you aware of the limits of organizations by revealing when and where they arose, and how they drove modernization. Although organizations today are powerful and ubiquitous, that was not always the case. As late as 1750, you would be hard pressed to find any large organizations, except for the state, the armed forces, and the church. Beyond these, organizations were small, weak, and rare. Most people relied on face-to-face interactions with people they knew, so they didn't need formal rules or structures to achieve their goals. It took great effort to form organizations. But in western Europe over the next century, this changed as organizations spread to almost every corner of human life: economic, political, social, and cultural. Entrepreneurs founded large trading, mining, manufacturing, and financial enterprises. State authorities centralized power over economic life in government bureaucracies. And people came together in clubs, societies, and associations to bargain for better wages and working conditions, discuss political and economic issues, mobilize for social and moral reform, and pursue common leisure and intellectual activities. Driven by European colonization and the rise of Europe as the global hegemon, organizations spread around the world. People who lived through these changes recognized them as opening a new phase in human history. And as I explain in chapter 3, thinkers who were puzzled and alarmed by the rise of large organizations in business and government galvanized much of the earliest research in sociology and management.

Many people today take the power of organizations for granted because, like the air we breathe, organizations are everywhere. Unless something goes very wrong with or because of organizations, we ignore them—just like I ignored the air in the San Francisco Bay Area until the 2017 wildfires generated so much smoke that it was unsafe to spend time outdoors. Many academics are also unaware of the power of organizations. I recall one conversation with a colleague—a political sociologist—who said she had been forced to study organizations for her comprehensive exams, but she found it boring and not applicable to her own research interests. Several years later, she has discovered that understanding the people and events she is studying hinges on understanding organizations, so she and her students need to know more about how organizations work. I hope that many faculty and students will find this book the guide they need to assimilate the accumulated knowledge of why organizations are created, how they operate, and what impact they have on local communities and wider societies and import this knowledge into fields like education, environmental studies, gender and sexuality, health and medicine, immigration, inequality, politics, race and ethnicity, religion, the family, and urban studies.

I came to study organizations in a roundabout way. I started my undergraduate studies in the rigorous engineering science program at the University of Toronto because I was a feminist who loved math, physics, and chemistry as much as English, history, and French, and because I wanted to get a well paying job to support my parents in their old age. (The pragmatism of the student from a poor family!) In my second year, I switched to chemical engineering—it turns out that I am a mediocre physics student—and immersed myself in the world of Erlenmeyer flasks, Bunsen burners, pipettes, heat exchangers, and distillation columns. But near the end of my third year, I dropped out because I didn't feel like I excelled at applying science to the real world, although my grades were well above average. Enraptured by my encounters with medieval and early modern European history during my only summer working as an engineer (in Paris of all places!), I returned as a history major and had to learn a brand new set of skills: reading long, often arcane texts quickly and deeply; composing clear narratives and compelling arguments; and summarizing qualitative evidence—so much harder than counting, taking averages, and calculating correlations. Upon graduation, I discovered that there are no jobs for people who had concentrated on medieval and early modern European history (doh!). I needed credentials that would improve my job prospects, so I entered an MBA program. There, I discovered the social sciences— economics, finance, psychology, and sociology. Because I was in business school, my courses were focused on for-profit business firms, although some courses covered business–government interactions and the non-profit sector. This training revealed to me the power of organizations, so that's what I decided to study.

I entered the Organizational Behavior and Industrial Relations PhD program at UC Berkeley School of Business (now the Management of Organizations PhD program at the Haas School of Business). The faculty there—Glenn Carroll, Charles O'Reilly, Barry Staw, Jim Lincoln, Trond Petersen, Jonathon Leonard, and George Strauss in particular—taught us that the study of organizations was grounded in labor and industrial-organization economics, sociology, and industrial-organization and social psychology, with a smattering of insights from political science and law. I did not perceive any distinction between management studies and the social science disciplines. In my view, management scholars just used ideas, tools, and techniques from these disciplines and contributed new theoretical and substantive insights to them.

As a result of my convoluted intellectual journey, I approach the study of organizations with a deep appreciation of how the past casts a long shadow and an interest in a wide variety of perspectives. As it turns out, that eclectic appreciation suits the study of organizations, which has long been interdisciplinary—not just developed by people working in multiple academic fields, but often developed by *conversations between fields*. Insights into organizations come from across the social sciences: anthropology, economics, geography, history, political science, social psychology, and sociology. They also come from scholars in professional schools, including business, education, engineering, labor relations, law, public health, and public policy. Despite this breadth, two fields lie at the core of academic research on organizations: sociology and management. Accordingly, my review of the field focuses primarily but not exclusively on organizations research in those fields.

I do not discuss economic theories that are prominent in some areas of research in business and law, such as agency theory and transaction-cost economics. I omitted them because their underlying assumptions are different from those made by most organizational scholars, and they are primarily used by economists and economics-oriented strategy and legal scholars. That is not to say that these theories are not valuable—indeed, Oliver Williamson's 2009 Nobel Prize alone demonstrates the importance of assessing transaction costs as well as production costs. I had to draw boundaries somewhere and, while I am quite well versed in these two theories, I could not include them without considering including all of applied microeconomics, which I have studied, as well as behavioral economics, which I have not.

In writing this book, I had three primary groups of people in mind: graduate students, junior faculty who study organizations, and other faculty who find that they need to understand organizations in order to answer their research questions. Among graduate students, I am aiming not only at those who are in sociology and management PhD programs, who constitute the bulk of young scholars of organizations, but also those who are in a wide array of social science departments and professional schools, including political science, geography, history, public health, public policy, and law. I want this book to be not just a guide to a very large interdisciplinary field of study, but also a tool to motivate and inspire new research. For junior faculty who study organizations, I want it to be a reference book that gives them starting points for expanding their research from their own particular niches. For faculty in other fields—strategy researchers and sociologists who do not normally think of themselves as organizational scholars, as well as political scientists, geographers, historians, and public health, public policy, and legal scholars—I intend this book to be a useful introduction that will complement their expertise in their chosen research areas. I hope it will make clear to them how to think about many phenomena through an organizational lens, since organizations have such tremendous power. I also hope that the book will be useful for ambitious undergraduates.

ACKNOWLEDGMENTS

I WANT TO THANK the current and former PhD students who worked with me on papers that relate to sections of chapters 2 through 7 (Haveman and David 2008; Haveman and Gualtieri 2017; Haveman and Wetts 2019a, 2019b; Haveman and Nedzhvetskaya 2022). Robert J. David is a professor at McGill, Gillian Gualtieri is a post-doctoral fellow at Vanderbilt, Rachel Wetts is an assistant professor at Brown, and Nataliya Nedzhvetskaya is a doctoral student at Berkeley. In addition, Joel A. C. Baum and I wrote a "from the editors" essay for the *Academy of Management Review* on the future of organizational theory (Baum and Haveman 2020) from which I drew some material for chapter 9. Finally, I greatly revised some material that appeared in an old review essay (Haveman 2000).

I also thank several colleagues for their suggestions on the manuscript. Sameer Srivastava gave me very helpful comments on chapters 1 and 3, helping me restructure the front end of the book. Brandy Aven gave me comments on chapter 5 and appendix B, increasing my confidence about the technical aspects of network analysis. Lisa Cohen and Brayden King heroically read the entire manuscript and gave me the benefit of their particular knowledge bases, which greatly improved the it. Jennifer Nelson's PhD students at the University of Illinois read the book in their seminar on organizations and provided very helpful comments. It was great to see how the intended audience receives the message. And seminar participants at the University of Toronto and Rice University helped me workshop two sections of chapter 9. Mark Mizruchi offered excellent advice about research on organizations and politics, while Rourke O'Brien gave me valuable insights into how governments create inequality. Finally, Brendan Mackie did some editing of the front end to make this book more accessible and engaging. His suggestions for enlivening that material and integrating across chapters were clever and compelling.

I owe a debt to two reviewers for Princeton University Press. Both gave me excellent constructively critical comments and both held me to a very high standard. I hope I have met that standard. Reviewer 1 reassured me about my vision of the existing books on organizations. Mark Mizruchi (Reviewer 2) was extremely careful, seeing not just many, many details but also the big

picture. He pushed me to work harder to draw more people—especially sociologists who aren't already convinced they should study organizations—into
this field, and to bring passion into my narrative by explaining what motivated
different scholars to develop new theories of organizations—what was wrong
with existing theories and what issues in society they wanted to understand
through studying organizations. I have tried, but my natural inclination is
toward calm, emotion-free prose, so I am not sure I have done enough. We will
have to wait for readers' reactions to judge my success. Mark, I am enormously
grateful for your painstaking efforts, as well as your many ideas and suggestions. I'm sure you'll let me know how good the end result is.

To better understand the state of organizational research from the 1940s
onward, and to dig into the theoretical discontents and pressing empirical issues
that drove innovations in research from the 1970s onward, I had conversations and conducted extended email correspondence with Deborah Ancona,
Al Bergesen, Bill Bielby, Ron Breiger, Ron Burt, Glenn Carroll, Neil Fligstein,
Roger Friedland, Joe Galaskiewicz, Mike Hannan, Paul Hirsch, Rosabeth
Moss Kanter, John Meyer, Charles O'Reilly, Jeff Pfeffer, Woody Powell, Cecilia
Ridgeway, Henry Walker, and John Van Maanen. I thank those kind and generous scholars for taking the time to mull over what motivated them and how to
make sense of the field's evolution. I also had very helpful discussions with two
young scholars, Douglas Guilbeault and Weiyi Ng, about organizations and
organizational theory in the digital age.

Several figures in the book come from data gathered by other scholars. Paul
Johnson, author of *Making the Market: Victorian Origins of Corporate Capitalism* (Cambridge University Press, 2010), kindly shared his data on the number
of companies registered in the United Kingdom from 1844 to 1913. Tim Guinnane, Ron Harris, Naomi Lamoreaux, and Jean-Laurent Rosenthal, authors of
"Pouvoir et propriété dans l'entreprise: Pour une histoire internationale des
sociétés à responsabilité limitée" (*Annales: Histoire, Sciences Sociales*, 2008),
generously shared their data on different forms of business organization in
Britain, France, and Germany.

A closing note for the graduate students and young faculty who are reading
this book: you are the future of organizational studies. I hope what I have written here is helpful to you as you begin your own research on organizations. I'm
sure you will surprise and impress me.

THE POWER OF ORGANIZATIONS

1

Introduction

ORGANIZATIONS ARE STUDIED by many social scientists (sociologists, psychologists, political scientists, historians, geographers, and anthropologists) and scholars in professional schools (business, education, engineering, industrial relations, law, public health, and public policy). Organizations are of interest to scholars in so many different fields because they have an enormous impact on social life, wielding tremendous power, distributing innumerable benefits, and inflicting enormous damage. All interests—economic, political, social, and cultural—are pursued through organizations. It is only through organizations that large-scale planning and coordination in modern societies—for the state, economy, and civil society—become possible. To understand the world we inhabit, then, we must appreciate the power and scope of organizations. This book defines the features of organizations, traces their rise in history, and explains how research on organizations has evolved. It also offers constructive criticism of existing research and provides "pivots" to direct future research in more fruitful ways.

What Are Organizations?

Organizations are *bounded collections of people and material, financial, and information resources*. Note, however, that the boundaries of organizations can be fuzzy, as many organizations have many part-time or temporary members. Organizations are also *sovereign actors*, with legal powers bestowed by the state (Coleman 1974, 1982). This gives them autonomy, allowing them to influence individuals inside and outside their boundaries, the communities in which they operate, other organizations, and society at large (King, Felin, and Whetten 2010). And organizational members have *common goals*, which they *cooperate* to pursue *over an extended period of time*.

Organizational goals are highly heterogeneous because organizations themselves are highly heterogeneous. In business firms and professional partnerships, the goals are typically good financial performance, operational stability, and survival. In government agencies, the goals are usually peace and national defense, public service, and regulation of the private sector. In educational and scientific institutions, the goals are to teach students and advance knowledge. In non-profit organizations, the goals might involve social improvement, culture, politics, socializing, or professional development. In sports teams and political parties, the primary goal is to win, although there may be secondary goals such as learning how to work as a team or how to be a gracious loser. In religious organizations, the goals might include preaching to and teaching congregants, creating community, spreading the faith, and helping the unfortunate.

Yet organizational members' goals often conflict. Consider, for example, the classic case of hostile workers and uncaring, rapacious managers. Workers want respect, security, safe working conditions, and good compensation. Managers want to control workers, hire them and let them go at will, invest the least possible in safety measures, and pay the least possible. But both groups have to cooperate to some extent to make whatever the organization is supposed to produce. Conflict also arises between people in different functions and subgroups, who generally have different preferences and goals. For example, people in product engineering and manufacturing prefer product designs that are easy to scale up with existing staff and equipment, while marketing staff want to dazzle customers with many options and new bells and whistles, and financial analysts want to keep costs down. Although ease of production, optional and novel product features, and low costs are almost impossible to jointly optimize, all of these groups have to work together to best meet demand and beat rival firms' offerings. Despite conflict, organizational members have to cooperate to achieve their goals.

Why Do Organizations Exist?

The answer is simple. People create organizations when they cannot achieve their goals by working alone, in small informal groups, in families, or in dispersed social movements. People create organizations when the actions they must undertake to achieve their goals require the joint, sustained, and coordinated efforts of many people, often with specialized skills. Biotechnology firms, for example, need many different kinds of people to finance, develop, manufacture, and sell their human therapeutic and diagnostic products:

- medical specialists, biochemists, and molecular biologists to refine new compounds and discover new processes to produce novel products;
- patent attorneys and other specialists to steer new compounds through the legal approval and patent processes;

- biochemists, organic chemists, and engineers to figure out how to ramp up laboratory-sized production processes to commercial scale;
- sales people conversant in human biology and biochemistry to explain the benefits of new compounds to physicians and to the functionaries of the insurance companies and health-maintenance organizations that oversee physicians' prescription decisions;
- experts in managerial accounting and capital budgeting to keep the whole enterprise from spiraling out of control;
- strategists to plot future moves; and
- human-resources staff to find, hire, train, socialize, and evaluate everyone above.

In biotech firms, no single person could accomplish all of these tasks alone. Coordinating the actions of all of these people requires structure to yield agreed-upon patterns of behavior: defined roles, decision-making processes, and rules.

In this chapter, I explain why organizations are important. Then, I provide a general description of organizations' features and their environments. After that, I outline the rest of the book.

Why Are Organizations Important?

Organizations are the basic building blocks of modern societies (Boulding 1953; Coleman 1974, 1982; Perrow 1991). From birth to death, the lives of people in modern societies play out in organizations. U.S. President Rutherford B. Hayes (1922 [entry for May 11, 1888]) recognized this over a century ago (May 11, 1888) when he wrote in his diary, "This is a government of the people, by the people, and for the people no longer. It is a government of corporations, by corporations, and for corporations." Four decades earlier, the French observer Alexis de Tocqueville marveled at the ubiquity of civic and social organizations: "Americans of all ages, all conditions, and all minds constantly unite. . . . [I]f it is a question of bringing to light a truth or developing a sentiment with the support of a great example, they associate" ([1848] 2000: 489).

Sociology operates at the intersection of biography and history in social structure (Mills 1959). This means that your life story is not just the product of your individual choices, but also of larger structures (like school systems, laws and regulations, employment relations, and social welfare systems) that have their own histories. For this reason, sociologists are concerned about the tension between structure and agency, between the "thingness" of societies that make them powerful forces in our lives and the power of people to alter societies through individual and collective action (Friedland and Alford 1991;

Sewell 1992; Emirbayer and Mische 1998). Organizations are the keys to unlocking how social structures relate to individual agency and choice. Organizations are both products of society and powerful actors that shape modern societies. Yet, at the same time, organizations are small enough that individuals—such as founders, leaders, and members of activist groups—can and do influence them.

Organizations are ubiquitous. Everyone becomes enmeshed in many different organizations over their life. Consider your own experiences:[1]

- You are most likely born in a hospital, attended to by doctors, nurses, and/or midwives who are trained in colleges and universities.
- Your birth is registered in a government bureau of records.
- You are educated in a school system, assigned to a variety of teachers as you progress through elementary and secondary school.
- If you aspire to more than a semi-skilled job, you must earn a college or university degree—increasingly, multiple degrees.
- You are likely to work in a long series of organizations, variously for-profits, non-profits, or government agencies.
- You will buy home furnishings, food, and clothing from retailers whose owners you probably won't know personally.
- If you marry, the ceremony will be performed in a religious congregation or government bureau and conducted by a religious or government official, and then be registered by a government bureau of records.
- It is quite likely that you or someone you know will be granted a divorce by a court, often with the aid of a law firm.
- Many of you will participate in worship services at a religious congregation.
- Some of you will join social movement organizations to protest societal wrongs and push for political, social, or economic change.
- At your death, most of you will be ministered to by representatives of up to three organizations—a law firm, a religious congregation, and an undertaker.

Organizations wield tremendous power and distribute innumerable benefits. They can do this for several reasons. Most organizations are larger than individuals, in three respects (Coleman 1974, 1982). First, they have more money because they are usually funded by multiple people or other organizations.

---

1. This list was inspired by Howard Aldrich's (1979: 3) list in his book on organizational evolution.

Second, they have more capacity to act because they can draw on the energy of multiple people (members or employees). Third, they can have an impact over longer periods of time because they have potentially infinite lifespans.

Organizations also generally have more power than individuals because they have more alternative exchange partners (Emerson 1962; Pfeffer 1981). For example, you usually have only a few options for internet-service providers, while those providers serve many, many customers. In the U.S., the power of organizations is especially formidable thanks to a long series of judicial decisions that gradually gave official imprimatur to the rights of corporations (Winkler 2018). In the nineteenth century, the courts there bestowed on corporations property rights, including the right to sue, the right of freedom of association (for non-profit corporations only), and the (limited) right against unreasonable search and seizure. Then came rights of personal liberty, including equal protection, due process, freedom of speech, and, most recently, freedom of religion. The legal rights of organizations, including corporations, have been extended in other countries—however, not as far as in the U.S.

Finally, organizations are powerful because they have become fully institutionalized (Zucker 1983). This means that they usually operate in the background, with most people, including government officials, paying little attention to them. Instead, we accept organizations as natural features of the social fabric. As a result of their institutionalization, organizations can persist without substantial effort or mobilization, and without much resistance or contestation (Jepperson 1991). As institutions, organizations create a social order that appears objective and exterior, meaning that it is perceived as shared by you and the others around you (Berger and Luckmann 1967). For example, schools create a social order in which students expect to learn from teachers, not from other students. Classrooms are often arranged so that students' desks face those of teachers. Even simple organizations consisting of two or three people can be perceived as objective and exterior (e.g., creating a perception of a hierarchy, with newcomers subordinate to old-timers); thus even simple organizations have strong effects on people's behavior (Zucker 1977). It is true that not all organizations are accepted and uncontested all the time; rather, to paraphrase P. T. Barnum, almost all organizations are accepted some of the time and most organizations are accepted all the time.

Yet there are limits on organizational power. Individuals and small informal groups can mount resistance to organizational actions, with varying degrees of success. The classic example is "goldbricking," meaning workers slacking off while appearing to work diligently (Roy 1952). Such productivity restrictions are intended to prevent managers from setting ever-higher production standards—a fear that was not unreasonable, based as it was on experience. Today, many workers routinely slack off by surfing the web and sending personal email and text messages during what is supposed to be productive time (Lim, Teo, and Loo 2002). Effective resistance to organizations usually comes from other organizations, especially social movement organizations. Three important American examples are the anti-slavery, civil rights, and women's rights movements (Tyler 1944; Anstey 1975; Morris 1984; Rendall 1984; McAdam 1988; Drescher 2010). Other social movement organizations resisted the dominant form of economic organization, the corporation, by promoting labor unions (Webb and Webb 1920) and cooperatives (van der Linden 1996; Schneiberg, King, and Smith 2008).

The Features of Organizations

If organizations are so powerful, then to counter or support them, we need to understand how they operate. Organizations have both formal and informal features. Formally, organizational structures divide people into work groups and link them together so their efforts will yield more than their individual capacities. Informally, organizations' cultures and patterns of social relations both reflect and often transcend their formal structures. I discuss each aspect of organizations in turn.

Formal Features

If organizations are the basic building blocks of modern societies, people are the basic building blocks of organizations. But organizations are far more than simple aggregates of individuals; instead, they are complexly structured. To understand organizations' formal structures, you need to consider several nested levels of analysis: the individual (social, psychological, and economic experiences), the job (task composition, title, status, and autonomy), the work group (goals, composition, structure), the organization (goals, division of labor and formal authority, culture, informal social relations, growth, and performance), the industry (composition, size distribution, and growth or contraction), and the field (composition, underlying logics, and power relations). Figure 1.1 illustrates these levels of analysis.

Organizations need to be organized. To produce things like cars, medical services, or software systems involves the efforts of multiple people. Who should do what? How should tasks be divided into person-sized pieces (jobs)? Both managers and workers are involved in dividing up work into discrete jobs; they "assemble" jobs by applying their technical expertise and work experience, interacting on a daily basis to negotiate who does what and when, and tackling problems as they arise (Barley 1990; Miner 1990; Bechky 2006; Cohen 2013). Over time, stable jobs emerge as tasks are reinforced through repetition.

Individuals (in a job)

Group/organizational subunit

Organization

Industry

Interorganizational field

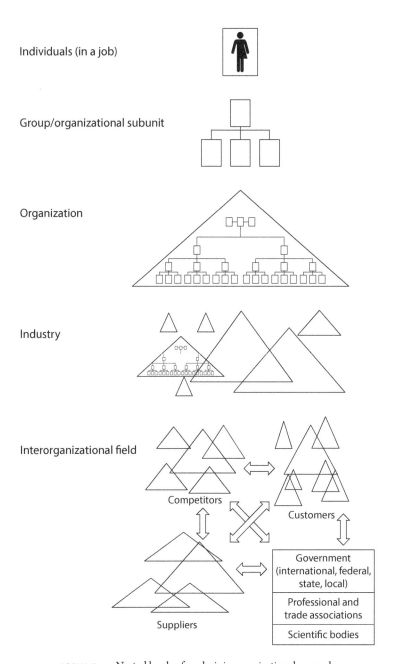

FIGURE 1.1. Nested levels of analysis in organizational research

Workers and managers reconcile information, advice, and demands with their own experiences, and interpret what people in different jobs are doing. The job-assembly process is shaped by forces both inside and outside employing organizations (Cohen 2013). Inside, interactions between people holding different jobs affect the set of tasks (task composition) associated with each job and how much status, autonomy, and rewards are associated with each job (Chan and Anteby 2016; Wilmers 2020). Outside, government regulations, occupational norms and rules, unions, and educational institutions all constrain how tasks are bundled into jobs and people are assigned to jobs. Moreover, some jobs involve interacting with people outside job holders' own organizations, which also constrains those jobs' status and autonomy.

Once jobs have been assembled, organizations must coordinate employees' actions to achieve collective goals by managing *task interdependencies*, meaning the connections between the inputs (money, information, symbols, or material objects) people need to perform their assigned tasks and the outputs they create by performing those tasks (Thompson 1967). Even short-lived organizations like film-production companies have to coordinate shared tasks (Bechky 2006). Task interdependencies are contingent on organizational goals and thus the production, distribution, and administrative technologies used to accomplish those goals. For instance, task interdependencies between workers in a manufacturing firm differ from those between workers in a service firm because the output of manufacturing firms (and therefore of their workers) can generally be stored while the output of service firms generally cannot. Even within the manufacturing sector, there are basic technological differences. Firms in petroleum refining (which uses large-scale, continuous-process technologies like distillation and filtration to move petroleum derivatives through stages of refinement) are subject to very different task interdependencies from firms in automobile manufacturing (which use mass-production technologies like the assembly line to move metals, plastics, electronics, and rubber into place to make vehicles) or firms crafting fine furniture (which use small-batch production technologies involving a combination of manual and mechanical labor to move wood, stone, metals, fabric, and plastics into place to make chairs, desks, beds, tables, etc.).

Organizations handle task interdependencies by grouping workers into units and authorizing managers to supervise them. The manager's role combines responsibility for making decisions about how to integrate the tasks of the work unit's members with formal authority and reward or sanctioning power. This is generally an effective combination: the person who is charged with making decisions about how to manage task interdependencies is both held accountable for those decisions *and* empowered to offer carrots and sticks to motivate people to implement those decisions. But in many organizations, conflict arises over how to handle task interdependencies, due to ambiguity or uncertainty inherent in the tasks, or to different people's preferences and interests concerning who gets to do what and who gets to have power over whom (Pfeffer 1981). Chapter 5 discusses how such conflicts are resolved through the use of power.

Decisions about how to group people together have fundamental impacts on people's attitudes and behavior. First and foremost, grouping necessarily puts some people together and splits other people apart. Grouping creates boundaries *around* groups and distinctions *between* groups, thus fostering strong in-group and out-group identities ("us" vs. "them"). This creates an essential paradox in group attitudes and behaviors: the mere act of people categorizing themselves as group members is enough to lead them to favor members of their group over others (Tajfel and Turner 1979, 1986; Tajfel 1982). Therefore, putting people into work groups encourages the coordination of tasks *within* work groups and discourages the coordination of tasks *between* work groups.

People in the same work group have a common supervisor and therefore have recourse to someone who can adjudicate difficulties or conflicts that arise from within-group task interdependencies. Being in the same group encourages informal coordination of tasks because members share resources. It is sometimes possible to align group members' goals by creating group standards and group rewards. All these effects of grouping decisions reinforce the development of strong group identities.

Any task interdependencies that remain after building primary work groups can be managed with other linking mechanisms, such as rules, policies, and standard operating procedures, all of which coordinate and integrate tasks among work units in predictable and stable ways. One rule-based linking mechanism familiar to us all is the set of policies governing who does and does not graduate with an academic degree—how many courses must be taken inside and outside the major field, in what order, and at what level of achievement. These policies require that academic departments, schools, and colleges cooperate and coordinate with each other, to ensure that the courses students need to earn degrees are available. Organizations can also assign individuals and groups to act as connectors between work units (e.g., liaisons and task forces), which is common when work units need substantial contact to make sure their actions mesh successfully.

Finally, there are structures larger than the single organization. First, there is the industry, meaning the set of organizations within some geographic area doing things similar to the focal organization. Second, there is the interorganizational field, meaning the set of all organizations that are connected to the focal organization and its industry, including governmental agencies; professional, scientific, and trade associations; suppliers; customers; and potential employees

(DiMaggio and Powell 1983). Industries and fields are structured through interactions (networks), ideas (logics), and numbers (distributions of organizations along salient dimensions such as size and target market), which jointly create constraints on and opportunities for individual organizations.

Organizational size and formal features. As organizations get bigger, their capacity for action increases: with more people and more money, organizations can do more things. Consider entrepreneurial ventures. When they are first founded, they are likely to be small and the founders/owners do much of the work, assisted by family members or a few paid workers. If new ventures grow—and there is no guarantee that they will, since bringing in more employees requires resources to pay them, as well as entrepreneurs' desire for and capacity to manage growth (Aldrich and Auster 1986)—the owners will delegate to others some tasks they previously did themselves, beginning with core tasks, then moving to supervisory and planning tasks. The more new ventures grow, the more their owners will rely on employees to get things done.

As organizations grow, their structures will change in many related ways (Blau and Schoenherr 1971). First and most basically, as the number of workers increases, so will the number of work groups, because supervisors have limited capacities to oversee workers. This will increase horizontal complexity, because the larger the number of work groups, the more managers you need—call them first-level managers. In turn, first-level managers require managers themselves—second-level managers. If organizations grow large enough, they will need third-level managers, and so on. You can see the result in Figure 1.1, which shows four layers of authority, from the top-level manager (with two staff subordinates on the side), a middle and lower level of managers, and front-line workers. Second, as the number of managers increases, power is increasingly decentralized, delegated down the managerial ranks. Third, jobs and work groups will become more specialized, and work groups will become more internally homogeneous (group members will do more similar tasks) but more externally heterogeneous (different groups will do more different tasks). Fourth, organizational structures will become more formally bureaucratic, with the development of standard procedures for managing people, finding and securing inputs, developing new products, seeking new markets for existing products, and dealing with oversight authorities.

Informal Features: Social Relations and Culture

What happens on the ground in most organizations differs from what you would expect if you were to consider only their formal structures. Unofficial practices, rituals, and symbolic objects abound; people in lower-level positions may be shown deference by people higher up; and people often ignore

formally prescribed lines of communication and authority. To fully understand how organizations operate, then, we must consider their informal features. First are the *social relations* that form not just inside but also outside the
formally defined lines of authority (not just who is supposed to interact with
whom, but also who really interacts with whom). Second is *culture*, the set of
shared understandings of how things do and should work in the organization,
which guides employees' actual activities (what people really do every day), and
informal norms and practices (what is expected and valued). Both social relations and cultures develop through social interaction, as people work together to
complete their assigned tasks and achieve their goals (Blau [1955] 1963). But
the formal and informal features of organizations are often only loosely coupled,
as social relationships, understandings, norms, and practices often deviate from
what is dictated by formal procedures and rules (Weick 1976).

Social relations are ties among individuals and groups in organizations. Two
main kinds of ties arise in organizations, formal and informal.[2] I discuss each
in turn.

The division of labor in organizations, meaning how tasks are assembled
into jobs, how people doing those jobs are grouped together in work units
reporting to the same manager, and how work units are linked to each other,
creates *formal social relations*, which are based on task interdependencies and
formal lines of authority. The task interdependencies that generate formal social relations in organizations can be divided into three categories (Thompson
1967) as illustrated by Figure 1.2. The simplest are *pooled task interdependencies*,
which occur when people or subunit share a common resource. At the micro
level, employees might obtain supplies from a common storeroom, use common equipment (e.g., networked computers or high-speed printers), or depend on a single person or group to process their expense reports. On a more
macro scale, the many units of a hotel chain may depend on central staff departments for marketing campaigns and for funding to renovate facilities.

More complicated are *sequential task interdependencies*, which occur when
goods or services produced by one group are passed along to a second. The classic example is employees on an assembly line. For example, teams assembling
wooden frames for chairs pass their work to teams coating frames with a protec-
tive finish, who pass their work to teams attaching cushions and padding to the
frames, who pass their work to teams covering the chairs with fabric or leather.

2. These are often augmented by *semi-formal* (or *quasi-formal*) *social relations*, meaning ties
that organizations foster but do not mandate. Semi-formal social relations include task forces,
working groups, committees, and interest groups. People usually, but not always, enter into
them voluntarily (Biancini, McFarland, and Dahlander 2014).

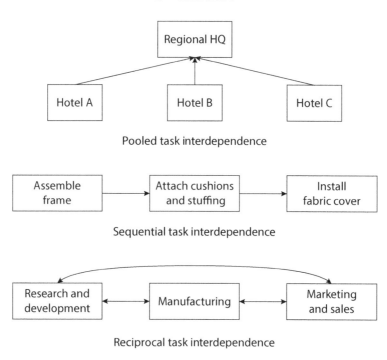

FIGURE 1.2. Forms of task interdependence

Most complicated are *reciprocal task interdependencies,* which occur when people work with each other in the production of common outputs, and in doing so pass work products back and forth. For example, take product development: people in research and development (R&D), product engineering, manufacturing, and marketing and sales depend on each other's efforts in complex ways. Marketing and sales inform R&D what customers want and R&D tells marketing and sales what is technically feasible. Product engineering figures out how to make what R&D comes up with on a large scale and asks R&D to return to the drawing board when product designs are infeasible. Product engineering also communicates with manufacturing, which may return with concerns about how to implement engineering plans. Manufacturing delivers products to marketing and sales. Finally, marketing and sales give feedback on customer (dis)satisfaction to manufacturing and R&D.

Along with social relations comes power, because (as I explain in chapter 5), power is an inherently relational construct. Much power in organizations derives from the formal authority conferred on individuals and groups by the formal structure. People at higher levels usually have more power because their positions are formally designed to have authority over lower-level positions. But that is not always the case. Maintenance workers are low-level employees invested with little formal power, but in a French cigarette manufacturer, they had a great deal of informal power because they were the only people who knew how to keep the complex, creaky equipment functioning (Crozier 1964). Thus, people in lower-level positions can acquire power if others depend on them for critical tasks and have no alternatives (Mechanic 1962).

Task interdependencies also generate horizontal power distributions, meaning differences in the capacity to overcome another's resistance and get something you want done, which overlay the vertical power distributions created by the formal hierarchy. The greater the dependence of one person or group on another, the greater the power that other person or group has over the first (Emerson 1962; Pfeffer 1981). Thus, power is never equitably distributed in organizations, but rather is associated with a person, group, or organization's relational position. Even organizations that avow radical equality develop unequal authority systems, as Robert Michels discovered through his analysis of the German Social Democratic Party, leading him to proclaim, "He who says organization says oligarchy" (Michels [1915] 1958: 365).

In addition to formal social relations, interacting to manage task interdependencies also generates *informal social relations*: for example, when people develop friendships that extend their interactions outside the workplace or when they engage in political maneuvering inside the workplace. Such informal social relations are often created when people cut through formal lines of authority to communicate with those they are not instructed to interact with. For example, in a state law-enforcement agency, business inspectors were supposed to communicate only with their supervisors, not with each other (Blau [1955] 1963). Yet inspectors often consulted each other, creating informal social ties that obviated the need to consult their supervisor; they were driven to consult with peers because they wanted to avoid earning "black marks" from supervisors for any demonstration of ignorance. Moreover, the informal social ties created by these consultations created group solidarity and a cohesive professional culture, which reduced inspectors' social isolation.

Informal social relations are also created when people interact because they work near each other or have social interests, activities, and memberships outside the focal organization. For example, scientists who more frequently encountered each other face-to-face, due to overlaps between their walking paths around their workplace, were more likely to collaborate on research projects (Kabo et al. 2014). Spatial overlaps also increased the likelihood of receiving funding for research projects, thus increasing their chance of success.

Culture consists of underlying assumptions (existential statements about how things work), values (shared understandings of what is good and bad), norms (shared understandings of what is normal and abnormal, of what we do and how we do it), and symbols (tangible artifacts like clothing and office

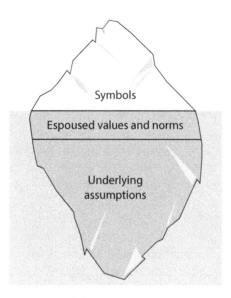

FIGURE 1.3. The (in)visibility of organizational culture

décor, intangible elements like stories and ceremonies) (Selznick 1957; Geertz 1973; Pettigrew 1979; Smircich 1983; Schein 1996). Different aspects of organizational culture vary in their visibility, like different parts of an iceberg (Schein 1996). Figure 1.3 illustrates the varying visibility of elements of organizational culture. Symbols are highly visible, while values and norms are harder to observe—although they may be made observable through analysis of formal statements of goals or missions, or informal speech. Underlying assumptions are usually invisible because they are either unconscious or taken for granted. They are the most difficult for scholars to discover.

Culture cannot be learned by organizational newcomers by poring over rule books or manuals; instead, it must be learned through direct experience. Old-timers regale newcomers with stories that reflect organizational values and norms. Language, especially organization- or occupation-specific jargon and slang, has shadings of value baked into it (Barley 1983; Van Maanen 1991). Job titles and other labels demarcate what is valued and despised. Ceremonies, rituals, and rites of passage vividly enact central cultural elements. How organizational members act every day—their interaction styles, etiquette, and dress—reveals behavioral expectations. Finally, physical structures and their layout teach silent lessons about what is (not) important. Slowly, as they encounter these symbolic elements and interact with other organizational members, organizational outsiders are transformed into insiders: they come to understand and accept an organization's culture; they may even internalize that culture, meaning they adopt the organization's values as their own, making individual and organizational values congruent. This process creates a new, shared identity, and a sense of belonging that differentiates organizational insiders from outsiders. Insiders' shared identity, in turn, generates loyalty to other members and the organization as a whole.

Organizational culture derives in part from formal organizational structure. The division of labor necessarily brings some people into close contact with each other and keeps others apart. Different groups develop different habits and routines, which come to be accepted as "the way we do things around here" (Berger and Luckmann 1967), thereby creating divergent subcultures. Physical systems, such as the layout of work spaces, also separate people selectively: for example, open work areas versus offices with closed doors; heterogeneous spaces where people from different subunits work near each other versus distinct homogeneous spaces for people in each subunit (Pfeffer 1982; Kabo et al. 2014). Physical systems can also communicate core values: for example, better parking areas and fancy dining rooms for executives communicate a strongly unequal culture, while undifferentiated parking lots and common dining areas communicate an egalitarian culture. In addition, selection procedures match the values of newcomers to those of the organization, socialization and training procedures communicate culture to newcomers, and evaluation and reward systems demonstrate what is and is not valuable (Chatman 1991). And standard operating procedures convey, by their very existence, what is normal. They make clear how things are usually done.

Culture is also derived from the *people* in organizations. Founders and other leaders demonstrate what is approved and why through their language, dress, stories, and everyday behavior, all of which are affected by leaders' backgrounds— their family, education, previous employment experience, political leaning, and religious affiliation. More broadly, the backgrounds of all organizational members shape the norms, values, and expectations that people bring with them into an organization, and thus collectively shape organizational cultures. Cultures develop because leaders and employees bring into organizations their hearts as well as their hands and minds.

Organizational cultures have three effects on people and organizations. First, cultures motivate certain behaviors and discourage others (Vaisey 2009). For example, collectivist values, formally instantiated in rewards for group rather than individual performance, promote information sharing and joint problem-solving (although they can also promote shirking). Second, cultures justify behaviors by helping people make sense of what they do (and do not do) and frame it to others as acceptable (Swidler 1986; Weick 1995). For example, funeral-home directors value "naturalness," which they enact by posing corpses to look as if they are sleeping peacefully, thus cushioning the shock of death for grieving family and friends (Barley 1983). Third, cultures determine the available range of strategies of action, making some things conceivable and others inconceivable, thus enabling some actions and disabling others (Swidler 1986). For example, people in the leveraged buyout industry find it difficult to accept women because their image of the ideal worker is highly masculine (aggressive, competitive, and work-obsessed), which conflicts with their beliefs about femininity and motherhood (Turco 2010).

Environments

As Figure 1.1 indicates, no organization is self-sufficient. Instead, all organizations depend on external elements in their environments. For any organization, its environment is the set of all elements that affect the organization by exchanging with it information, materials, people, or money, or by authorizing, facilitating, impeding, or forbidding its activities. The elements of organizational environments are quite varied:

- individuals and families;
- informal groups, such as unorganized social movements, ethnic groups, and neighborhoods;
- other organizations, including competitors, suppliers, customers, government agencies, unions, social movement organizations, and scientific, occupational, and trade associations;
- laws and regulations, including those promulgated by non-state authorities such as unions, occupational associations, and religious institutions;
- information, both explicit (it can be articulated—put into words, numbers, and/or pictures—and so learned easily) and tacit (it cannot be articulated and must instead be learned by doing);
- societal cultures, which consist of widely shared assumptions (existential statements about how things work), norms (ideas about what is normal and abnormal), and values (ideas about what is good and what is bad);
- material resources such as raw materials, equipment, and partly finished goods;
- intangible resources such as corporation reputation and brand identities; and
- money.

Because organizations are dependent on their environments (to adapt John Donne, "no organization is an island, entire unto itself"), any change in any attribute of an organization's environment will affect it, and any change in that organization will affect its environment.

The most numerous and powerful elements of the environments of organizations are other organizations (including government agencies). Therefore, to understand organizations in their natural habitats, we must be able to distinguish between different kinds of organizations in any focal organization's environment. To do so, we need to be able to determine what form each organization has, based on its goals, structure, power, culture, and identity. Then we must figure out how to group organizations together for analysis. There are two main ways to do this: industry and field. An *industry*[3] is a set of organizations operating in some time and place that shares a common form; that is, they produce similar goods and services, draw on similar inputs and technologies, and serve similar clients or customers. Depending on the research question at hand, industry boundaries may rest on coarse- or fine-grained distinctions. For instance, when analyzing the organizations that generate electricity, we might construe each organizational form and industry narrowly, based on (i) distinctions between entities that generate electricity as their main output (large electric utilities and small-power producers) and those that produce it in the course of other activities (cogenerators) or (ii) distinctions among the many possible fuels and power-generating technologies (coal, natural gas, nuclear, biomass, wind, geothermal, solar, etc.) (Sine, Haveman, and Tolbert 2005). Or, we might define organizational forms and industries more coarsely, distinguishing simply between electricity producers that use "green" (renewable) or "brown" (non-renewable) fuels.

A *field* is the set of actors that, in the aggregate, constitutes a recognized area of institutional life (DiMaggio and Powell 1983; Fligstein and McAdam 2012), as depicted in Figure 1.1. For the analysis of organizations, this means organizations that offer similar products, suppliers, customers, state agencies, social movement organizations, and professional, scientific, and trade associations (DiMaggio and Powell 1983). Fields are social "things" because the members of fields orient their actions toward one another as they jockey for position, define the rules of the game, and accrue the power needed to achieve their goals (Fligstein and McAdam 2012).

Consider a concrete example: the field of higher education in California. Figure 1.4 is from *A Master Plan for Higher Education in California, 1960–1975* (Coons et al. 1960). This plan was developed to handle the huge increase in undergraduate enrollments from members of the post–World War II baby boom. Panel 1.4a shows flows of students from high schools into three forms of public higher education institution—the University of California campuses

---

3. Organizational ecologists, whose research takes what I call the macro-demographic perspective (see chapter 4), prefer the term "population," because much of their work is grounded in human demography and evolutionary biology (Carroll and Hannan 2000). Yet their empirical definitions of organizational populations have typically been particular industries in particular locations.

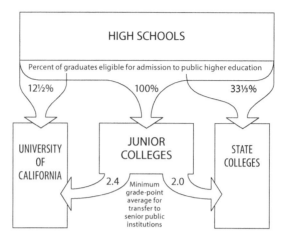

FIGURE 1.4A. The field of higher education in California
Source: Coons et al. (1960: 73).

University of California	California State Universities	Community Colleges
• Undergraduate, graduate, and professional education	• Undergraduate, graduate, and professional education —up to master's degrees	• Vocational instruction and lower-division (years 1–2) academic instruction
• Primary academic agency for research	• Research is secondary— only as much as needed to be consistent with the teaching mission	• No research is expected
• Sole authority for doctoral degrees	• Doctoral degrees only if joint with UCs or private educational institutions	• No advanced degrees
• Sole authority for instruction in law, medicine, dentistry, and veterinary medicine	• Teacher education	• Remedial instruction, English as a second language, adult noncredit instruction

FIGURE 1.4B. Differentiation of function in California's public higher education institutions

(UCs), the California State Universities (CSUs), and the Community Colleges (CCs)—and flows of students among them. The UCs were expected to have the highest standards for admission, accepting only the top eighth of high-school graduates; the CSUs second-highest, accepting the top third of graduates; and the CCs the lowest, accepting all graduates. Panel 1.4b shows how the three forms' functions were distinguished. The UCs were to focus on research, the training of graduate students, and educating professionals (except teachers); the CSUs on undergraduate education and training teachers, and a smattering of other professional degrees; and the CCs on the first two years of undergraduate education, plus remedial and adult education programs. Finally, Panel 1.4a shows that CC students could transfer to UCs or CSUs if they had sufficiently good grades. UCs and CSUs were to enroll at least one student from CCs for every two students who entered straight from high school. Relations between the three organizational forms were managed by a coordinating council, which also included representatives of private colleges and universities in California.[4]

The Path Forward

As an introduction to the study of organizations, this book draws primarily but not exclusively upon research by sociologists and management scholars.[5] It will familiarize you with the main theoretical orientations and show you how they are used to investigate important phenomena. To that end, I will describe the long tradition of research on organizations, but only briefly and with an eye to understanding how early studies of organizations continue to reverberate in contemporary research. The bulk of the book will be devoted to considering current ideas. Although I cite many, many studies, I cannot offer an exhaustive survey of the literature on organizations. Instead, the studies I cite were chosen to offer examples of particular concepts and perspectives on organizations or illustrate larger points about organizational theory. I also reflect critically on existing research and suggest ways to improve it.

Chapter 2 puts organizations in context to explain how they developed and why they are the fundamental building blocks of modern society. Chapter 3 chronicles research on organizations, starting with the influential ideas of the founding fathers of sociology—Marx, Weber, and Durkheim. To add some "flesh" to the bare bones of sociological theory, I explain what motivated these

---

4. This plan was phenomenally successful, greatly enlarging the scale of higher education at a low cost to the public. Over the next forty years, enrollment increased tenfold while the state's population trebled. Access increased for both women and men, and for every ethno-racial group. Because of its success, the California Master Plan was copied by multiple states and by foreign countries like Japan and Norway, as they too sought to handle influxes of children born during the baby boom.

5. There is an unfortunate tendency for researchers in business schools to ignore much research conducted in sociology departments, especially when it is published in sociology journals. And there is an equally unfortunate tendency for researchers in sociology departments to ignore much research conducted in business schools, especially when it is published in management journals. As a faculty member with appointments in both sociology and business, I will try to be more balanced in my review of research by both groups of scholars.

men to develop their ideas—what changes they saw in the world around them. After that, the chapter reviews research traditions that appeared up to the mid-twentieth century—again, with an explanation of why associated scholars studied what they did. The chapter ends by arguing that almost all contemporary research on organizations can be understood as fitting into three perspectives—demographic, relational, and cultural—each of which includes several related lines of thinking. The next three chapters dive deeply into those perspectives, explaining why they came to be developed and discussing research at several nested levels of analysis: individual and group (micro); organization, industry, and field (macro). They are followed by chapter 7, which briefly discusses some examples of how and why scholars have combined perspectives.

The final two chapters set out programs for future research. Chapter 8 considers how organizations have been transformed in the digital age, and how the "big data" revolution—moving from a paucity of information to a (sometimes overwhelming) torrent of information that is complex, richly detailed, and up-to-the-minute—requires rethinking our approach to studying organizations. Chapter 9 lays out an agenda for organizational research that will reconnect it to the mainstream of the social sciences and to critical issues in public policy: a shift toward studying the multifaceted impacts of organizations on society, rather than the impacts of society (i.e., organizational environments) on organizations. Several such topics have already proven fruitful and could be taken much further. I focus on three: economic inequality, politics, and environmental degradation.

Finally, there are two appendices. Appendix A offers advice for young scholars. It lays out my views on the nature of science and scientific theory, as well as suggestions about how to build arguments and convince readers, so that scholarly work is better accepted and has greater impact. Appendix B offers a brief introduction to formal social network analysis, which undergirds much research taking the relational perspective that I discuss in chapter 5.

2

Organizations in Historical Context

ALTHOUGH ORGANIZATIONS are now ubiquitous and immensely powerful, that was not always the case. For most of human history, there were very few organizations. Hunter-gatherers, as far as we can tell, had no organizations at all, just small extended-family groups. In many agrarian societies, there were scattered, small organizations involved in government, warfare, religion, and economic life. Here I put organizations in historical context by describing when and where different kinds first appeared, and explaining why they flourished or failed. Knowing what happened in the past helps us avoid the naïve assumption that what exists today has always been around, and makes us instead appreciate how and why what exists now came to be. Historical knowledge also helps us think about what might change in the future. I first describe a time when organizations were rare and generally unimportant: the traditional societies of several centuries ago. I then discuss how organizations came to be more common and more important: traditional societies gave way to modern ones, which gradually became "societies of organizations" (Perrow 1991). My historical analysis covers a millennium,[6] but to be brief, it glosses over a great deal of heterogeneity and ignores many retrograde moves.

I focus on western Europe because that is where most of the earliest organizations appeared, so understanding it gives us the deepest insights into the origins of organizations. Although some kinds of organizations appeared elsewhere early on, developments in most regions of the world were complicated by the rise of Europe as hegemonic in the world system. Where European powers created colonies (the Americas, Africa, parts of Asia, and Oceania), European organizational models were imported wholesale (Lange 2009).

---

6. In this, I differ from other scholars who date the expansion of organizations to the eighteenth century (Zucker 1983) or even the second half of the twentieth century (Bromley and Meyer 2015). As I show below, many organizations existed before then.

Where colonization did not take hold (the Middle East and parts of Asia), European organizational models were adapted to fit local conditions (see, e.g., Westney 1987).

Traditional Society

To understand the rise of organizations, we need to go back to traditional feudal societies, where the roots of the modern organizational society were first planted. In those societies, which were largely agrarian, people belonged to various *communal institutions* by right or custom (MacIver 1917; Weber [1968] 1978). The five most important were the family, the feudal or liege system, the church, urban areas, and guilds. As I explain below, the church was usually an organization, while urban areas and guilds were quasi-organizations.

The family. This is the first and most basic communal institution: a set of people descended from the same (usually male) ancestors. Families often included extended kinship networks, such as clans. And families sometimes included kithship networks, based on people living in the same household, such as esquires—the sons of the European nobility who were sent to other noble families for training, which created strong bonds between households.

The feudal or liege system. This political-economic system consisted of lords or (rarely) ladies and everyone who swore fealty to them. Feudal systems formed in Europe starting in the eighth century and became widespread in the tenth century (Bloch 1961, 1964; Jacoby 1973; Poggi 1978).[7] They were based on military defense: in return for protection of their land and lives, peasants and artisans swore to provide their liege lords with labor, foodstuffs, manufactured objects like rope and barrels, or (rarely) monetary payments. Feudal systems were often nested, with small fiefdoms under the control of local vassals (knights) who swore allegiance to regional nobles (princes or barons). In addition to serfs (peasants and artisans), many feudal systems included slaves who were owned outright and whose services to their lords had no legal limitation. Starting in the eleventh century, power became increasingly centralized, with princes and barons becoming vassals of kings (Weber [1927] 1981; Bloch 1964; Wallerstein 1974).

The church. Everyone was a member of the monopolistic church in their region (usually Catholic) or else branded as heretics and subject to punishment.

---

7. Although feudal systems varied greatly from location to location and changed over time, and although the concept of feudalism has come under criticism (Brown 1974; Reynolds 1994), it remains useful for describing the vertical ties that characterized many parts of Europe in the Middle Ages.

Priests and monks were the central members. Priests led prayers and other holy rituals, while monks devoted themselves to good works or scholarship. For these men, the church was a total institution (Goffman 1961): their entire lives were circumscribed by their roles in the church. The system of clerics was hierarchical, with rural priests at the bottom; urban priests, cathedral canons, and clerics in episcopal courts in the middle; and abbots, bishops, and archbishops at the top (Bloch 1964).

Urban areas. From the seventh to the fourteenth centuries, towns and cities became politically autonomous quasi-organizations as they won charters granting them particular privileges and the authority to enforce those privileges (Weber 1958; Bloch 1964; Poggi 1978). Therefore, the inhabitants of towns and cities were free from feudal obligations. This freedom was the result of the development of many small improvements in agriculture and the rise (albeit uneven) of long-distance trade from a slow trickle after the fifth-century barbarian invasions to a gushing river in the twelfth century (Pirenne [1925] 2014; Hodges 1982, 2012). Agricultural improvements produced an increasing surplus of foodstuffs and inputs to manufacturing that could be sold in urban markets and traded throughout Europe. Agricultural improvements also freed an increasing (although always small) fraction of people to do something other than farm full-time; instead, they could specialize in making and trading goods or delivering services. In turn, the development of urban markets provided pathways to wealth through goods, services, and money, rather than through land alone, giving urban dwellers leverage to negotiate freedom from feudal obligations (Pirenne [1925] 2014; Weber 1958; Bloch 1964; Poggi 1978; Hodges 1982, 2012).

Urban dwellers—traders, artisans, service providers, and dependent workers alike—could call on legal institutions, such as councils and tribunals, to defend their personal liberties and property rights (Weber 1958; Black 1984). Moreover, as corporate entities (derived from the Latin word for body, *corpus*), towns and cities themselves came to be conceived of as legal persons capable of owning property, such as water supplies, marketplaces, wharves, bridges, fortifications, and communal mills and ovens. Still, urban areas were highly interdependent with rural areas and so had to manage ongoing relations with feudal lords.

Although towns and cities were partly communal institutions—most of their inhabitants were born there—they were also open to newcomers and therefore also partly associative institutions of the type I describe below. Vassals or serfs who moved from rural to urban areas and resided there for a year and one day became citizens or burghers (Pirenne [1925] 2014; Weber 1958). Because medieval urban areas escaped feudal obligations, had increasingly complex social and political divisions of labor, and depended economically on long-distance exchange networks, they were "outposts of modernity" (Braudel [1981] 1992, [1982] 1992; see also Poggi 1978; Anderson [1979] 2013). The manufacturing and trading activities centered in urban areas helped drive modernization (Weber [1927] 1981, 1958; Braudel [1984] 1992). As I explain below, urban areas' charters made them one of the earliest forms of organization: they held property in common, had representative bodies that made decisions, and hired staff to carry out those decisions and maintain records.

Guilds. Merchant guilds first appeared in the ninth century and craft guilds in the eleventh century (Brentano 1890; Weber [1927] 1981; Black 1984).[8] By the fifteenth century, most craft guilds had a clear structure, with three orders of members: masters at the top, journeymen in the middle, and apprentices at the bottom (Weber [1927] 1981). Members moved from apprentice to journeyman to master status on a schedule that depended on time in station and demonstration of skill. Similar to chartered towns and cities, guilds were granted rights for their members and the authority to enforce those rights (Weber [1927] 1981; Levy 1950; Sewell 1980; Black 1984). Craft guilds in particular sought to control quality and maintain prices so masters could earn good incomes.

Guilds were total institutions in two regards (Black 1984). First, they included the whole person of their members, as well as members' families. Second, membership was a lifetime affair: men[9] usually became guild members through inheritance (their fathers were members) and left only when they died or (very rarely) were ostracized. Guilds were religious brotherhoods, centrally concerned with morality. Each transition—from apprentice to journeyman to master—was marked by a ceremony with strong religious overtones to underscore how the guild's body of knowledge and practice transcended any individual member (Brentano 1890).

---

8. They had several precursors. In India as early as 800 BCE, *shreni* (or *sreni*) had hereditary membership and specialized codes, working arrangements, and member obligations (Thaplyal 2001; Khanna 2005). *Shreni* trained artisans, controlled quality, and facilitated the sale of goods. They disappeared after the Muslim invasions of 1000 CE. In Rome starting in the seventh century BCE, trade guilds (*collegia opificum*) were associated with religious cults, most commonly the cult of Minerva (Weber [1927] 1981; Black 1984). In Imperial Rome, craft guilds (*collegia*) emerged; they disappeared after the empire collapsed (Weber 1958).

9. The wives, daughters, and widows of guild members sometimes held positions in guilds, and female outsiders could apply to become apprentices, but women's activities and status were often restricted (Davis 1982). There were only a few mixed and female guilds, like British alewives' guilds, in which women could rise up the ranks (Wensky 1982; Coffin 1994; [S. D.] Smith 2005).

The Transition to Modern Society

From Communal to Associative Institutions

People in modern societies belong to associative rather than communal institutions. *Associative institutions* bring together individuals who may have no communal connection (no connection by birth or custom), but who seek to achieve common goals. Organizations are the most common and important kind of associative institution. Other kinds of associative institutions exist, such as some social movements (like the militantly un-organized Critical Mass, which nevertheless manages to create large crowds of bicyclists swarming over cities across the world on the last Friday of every month) and social clubs (such as the book and gardening clubs that meet in homes or cafes across the Western world). But most are organizations; for example, Greenpeace, soccer clubs, and masonic lodges.

The transition from traditional to modern society, and the accompanying replacement of communal institutions with associative institutions, was slow and occurred in a piecemeal fashion. Therefore, it is impossible to point to an exact date or event for this transition. Because different aspects of society (political-economic, scientific-technological, religious, and cultural) were transformed on different timetables, there was "a series of overlapping histories, developing simultaneously" (Braudel [1973] 1995: 892). If pushed to point to a single (even approximate) date, most scholars would accept that in political-economic terms, most western European societies became modern between the fourteenth and eighteenth centuries, while the U.S. and Japan became modern by the nineteenth century (Wallerstein 1974, 1980; Braudel [1981] 1992, [1982] 1992, [1984] 1992; Jansen and Rozman 1986).

Multiple factors drove modernization. Most basically, the Black Death killed between one-third and two-thirds of the European population between 1347 and 1351 (Herlihy 1997) and recurred frequently over the next three centuries. In western Europe, the resulting scarcity of workers gave them bargaining power against feudal lords and guild masters, weakening feudal bonds (Brenner 1985). Advances in transportation made it easier for monarchs to rule over far larger territories and establish colonial outposts, which in turn drove the growth of state bureaucracies to administer those areas (Weber [1927] 1981; Jacoby 1973). The rise of long-distance trading, made possible by technological innovations such as the full-rigged ship, spurred the development of new kinds of organizations to oversee increasingly large-scale production and trading concerns (Pirenne [1925] 2014; Weber [1927] 1981; Wallerstein 1980; Braudel [1982] 1992; Rosenberg and Birdzell 1986; Appleby 2010). Widely held conceptions of what was acceptable, even possible, changed dramatically, due to the rise of the "Protestant ethic" and its sanctification of work (Weber [1904–5] 1958). Finally, there were legal changes: laws guaranteeing property rights and allowing new forms of organization (Weber [1927] 1981; North and Thomas 1973; Braudel [1982] 1992; Rosenberg and Birdzell 1986), which I describe below. Property-rights law supported the market exchanges on which modern economies depend, while laws authorizing forms of organization delegated state authority to organizations, making them autonomous entities. These biological, technological, cultural, and legal factors reinforced each other, making the transition from traditional to modern society a complex, many-layered process—one that advanced in fits and starts, and sometimes retreated.

The Feudal System Gives Way to the Bureaucratic State

During the early modern era, states evolved from scattered collections of officials into bureaucratic organizations (Weber [1927] 1981; Rosenberg 1958; Strayer [1970] 2005; Jacoby 1973; Wallerstein 1974; Poggi 1978; Anderson [1979] 2013; Braudel [1982] 1992; Tilly 1990).[10] Modern states needed bureaucracies because their goals were both more ambitious and more complex than those of feudal states: they had to coordinate the efforts of an increasing number and variety of officials to handle taxation, fees, fines, and spending; train and lead the growing military forces; oversee judicial affairs; and manage public works. In these bureaucracies, operations were based on rules and routines that were formally documented, with officials arranged in a hierarchy of formal authority (Weber [1968] 1978). The transition to the bureaucratic state began at different points in time in different locations: in the twelfth century in Italy (Sicily), the fourteenth century in France and England, the fifteenth century in Spain, the seventeenth century in the Netherlands, and the eighteenth century in Prussia (Jacoby 1973; Braudel [1982] 1992). State bureaucracies became more elaborate as they continued to acquire more central authority (Tocqueville [1848] 2000; Marx [1852] 2005; Skowroneck 1982).

This organizational development was made possible by the revival of Roman law, which started in Bologna in the twelfth century and spread throughout western Europe by the fourteenth century (Anderson [1979] 2013). This revival provided a rational (rather than mystical) basis for state

---

10. Bureaucratic states existed elsewhere before and during the time they spread through Europe: ancient Egypt and Babylonia had hierarchically organized castes of priestly scribes, China had a highly organized scholarly-bureaucratic government starting with the Han dynasty ca. 200 BCE, South America had a decimal-based Incan bureaucracy starting in the fourteenth century (Jacoby 1973), and the Ottoman empire had a bureaucratic state in the seventeenth century (Barkey 1994).

authority, meaning that state bureaucrats strove to achieve explicit goals (Weber [1927] 1981). The development of bureaucratic states was necessitated by the use of gunpowder in warfare, which was extremely effective but which required large capital expenditures: gunpowder had to be made, weapons manufactured, forts built, and armies and navies trained and equipped.

In some places (France, Prussia, Spain), *absolutist states* emerged as political power became concentrated in the hands of monarchs, bolstered by the power of standing armies, and centralized bureaucracies developed to carry out monarchs' will throughout their territories. In other places (England, the Netherlands), *constitutional states* emerged as political power was shared between monarchs and nobles. Monarchs guaranteed the rights and liberties of citizens through constitutions, the highest legal authority; this guarantee was reinforced by representative assemblies. As time passed and trade expanded, absolutist states felt increasing pressure from the rising bourgeoisie on whom monarchs depended for commercial activities they could tax, so most became constitutional states, either through revolution (e.g., France) or evolution (e.g., Prussia) (Poggi 1978).

One final note: all organizations were—and still are—political creations. For-profit and non-profit organizations require state authorization because they are legal entities whose existence and scope of action are defined by state authorities. Even ostensibly private forms of organization, partnerships and sole proprietorships, have long been legally defined by state authorities.

The One Church Becomes Many

In the modern era, churches became larger, more complex organizations, driven in part by the proliferation of faiths. In western Europe, the Catholic Church's monopoly was toppled by the Protestant Reformation of the early sixteenth century, creating a host of new faiths that competed vigorously for adherents. The Peace of Westphalia in 1648 ended the Eighty and Thirty Years' Wars of religion, with most Protestant and Catholic states agreeing to accept each other's existence and allow their subjects to profess any Christian faith. Although later events revealed continued inter-faith antagonism, religious toleration slowly came to be practiced throughout most of Europe, in part because of the rise of a new code of "civility" among economic and political elites (Elias [1939] 1982; Kaplan 2007).

State-sanctioned religious toleration forced churches to become associative rather than communal institutions. Churches now had to entice people to join them because they could no longer command membership (Finke and Stark 1992). This spurred intense efforts to proselytize. Church officials founded *missionary societies* to "spread the good word" of Christianity at home and abroad. They also launched publishing societies to support missionary efforts by producing devotional literature en masse and distributing it widely. To co-ordinate the efforts of missionary and publishing societies, as well as the activities of individual congregations and schools for training clergy, churches had to develop large and complex bureaucracies, often with local groups nested within regional associations, and regional associations nested within a national or international church authority.

Beyond their own bureaucratization, churches were wellsprings of *non-profit organizations* to help the less fortunate: caring for and confining paupers, people with injuries and non-contagious illnesses, elderly people, and orphans; and providing shelter to travelers and pilgrims (Jones 1989; Orme and Webster 1995; Hickey 1997; Risse 1999). Many had their origins in the Middle Ages, but they grew in number and size during the slow march of modernization, as church authorities sought to solve problems created by urbanization and as clerics grappled with new views of the poor in Protestant and counter-Reformation (Catholic) theology (Mollat 1986; Risse 1999; Brodman 2009). Starting in the seventeenth century, people and their problems were sorted into several specialized organizations and control shifted from religious orders to laypeople. By the nineteenth century, *hospitals* were devoted to the sick and were highly medicalized (i.e., lay physicians and surgeons routinely practiced medicine), *almshouses* served the poor and the elderly, *orphanages* housed children who had no family support, and *schools and colleges* educated children and clerical novitiates.

Reform societies had deep religious roots, as they were buttressed by theological principles celebrating morality and community, but were often founded and managed by laypeople. They sought to provide material aid and moral guidance to the downtrodden, whose numbers were growing rapidly due to industrialization and urbanization (Morris 1983; Mintz 1995; Roberts 2004). They advocated a wide array of social causes: the abolition of slavery; nonviolence and an end to war; strict observance of the Sabbath; temperance in the consumption of alcohol; the reform of prostitutes and seamen; the education of children; protection for widows and orphans; relief for debtors and paupers; care of the insane, blind, deaf, and dumb; political and economic rights for women and workers; and reform of the penal system and elimination of capital punishment. Many were organized into federated structures, with nested national, regional, and local units (Morris 1983; Roberts 2004).

Many of the non-profit organizations spawned by churches secured formal charters, following in the wake of towns and cities. Charters, which came with rights to own property and enter into contracts, were granted by state authorities in exchange for the public services that non-profit organizations offered.

The Family Is Diminished

Starting in the sixteenth century, the family became increasingly regulated or supplanted by organizations. Although the family obviously did not disappear, ties to extended kinship groups weakened (Goode 1963; Cherlin 2012). Churches and states set legal limits on family formation, structure, and functioning, first through canon law concerning marriage (e.g., at the Council of Trent in 1563) and later through state laws defining marriage and proscribing or regulating divorce (e.g., the British Marriage Act of 1753). Educational institutions slowly replaced home schooling, starting with elites in the seventeenth century and extending to the masses in the eighteenth and nineteenth centuries. Around the same time, political parties and social movement organizations began to bring people into formal and informal politics, respectively.

Families increasingly purchased goods and services produced by business organizations (Thirsk 1978; McKendrick, Brewer, and Plumb 1982) and family members became increasingly likely to work for business organizations or state bureaucracies. For example, Figure 2.1 shows trends in self-employment and working for others for the U.S. from 1800 to the present. Data on the nineteenth century are scarce, but we have estimates for 1800 and 1860, which are shown as the large dots (employment in non-farm enterprises) or squares (self-employment). In 1800, only 12 percent of the labor force (defined as persons of ten years or older) worked in employing organizations, compared to 57 percent who were self-employed. By 1860, those numbers had nearly reversed: 40 percent worked in organizations and 27 percent were self-employed. Data for 1900 onward come from various government sources and do not perfectly mesh with earlier data, but they show that the percentage of the labor force that was self-employed fell continuously, while the percentage that worked in organizations generally rose. By the middle of the twentieth century, the shift to working in organizations would be recognized as the rise of "the organization man" (Whyte 1956) or "the company man" (Sampson 1995). This change made family members economically dependent on organizations.

Displacement of the family also occurred in the pursuit of leisure and sociality, through the rise of *clubs, societies, and voluntary associations*, which first appeared in England and Germany in the sixteenth century and which spread to many other countries during the seventeenth and eighteenth centuries (Habermas [1962] 1991; Clark 2000; Morton, de Vries, and Morris 2006; Mackie 2021).[11] Members sought pleasure and relaxation, but they also found community. These organizations were highly diverse: alumni associations;

---

11. Clubs and societies had antecedents in classical Athens and ancient Rome (Kloppenborg and Wilson 1996) and medieval Europe (Clark 2000).

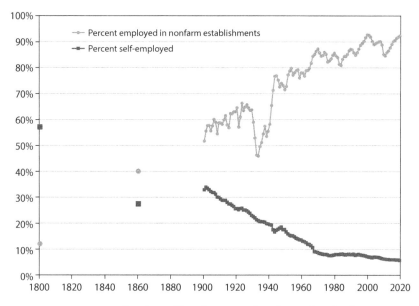

FIGURE 2.1. Trends in self-employment and working in (nonfarm)
employing organizations, United States, 1800–2019
Data from Bureau of Labor Statistics, Bureau of the Census and published
within Lebergott, Stanley (1964) *Manpower in Economic Growth: The American
Record Since 1800*, New York: McGraw-Hill.
Source for data on 1929–2019: Statistical Abstract of the US, various years.

agricultural, artistic, scientific, and learned societies; circulating libraries; debat-
ing, horticulture, literary, and music clubs; ethnic and regional associations;
gambling and sporting clubs; reform, charitable, and mutual-aid associations;
and political and professional bodies. Membership was voluntary and often
paid: pooled funds supported group activities that were managed by committees. While some were purely local, others were branches of regional or national
organizations. Overall, they altered the way people (mostly men) in the mid-
dling and upper classes interacted socially, pulling them away from the family
circle and toward organizations. Over time, membership in these organizations
broadened to include women, subordinated religious and ethnic groups, and the
less affluent.

These organizations were quite common, especially in Britain, the German
states, and the U.S. For example, in the eighteenth century, there were an esti-
mated twenty-five thousand clubs and societies in the English-speaking world
(Clark 2000). In the second half of the nineteenth century, the number of
clubs, societies, and voluntary associations exploded in Continental Europe
(Hoffman 2003) and the U.S. (Tocqueville [1848] 2000; Schlesinger 1944;

Skocpol 1997; Skocpol, Ganz, and Munson 2000). These voluntary organizations had a quasi-private status that generally freed them from state regulation—except in France, where until 1901, the Napoleonic Code required state approval of associations with more than twenty members. Over time, they became more formally organized, with written rules, a hierarchy of officers, standing committees, and regularly scheduled meetings that made them important foci for social and cultural life (Mackie 2021). Some were incorporated, having secured formal state charters to obtain legal protections such as the right to own property (e.g., clubhouses) and enter into contracts.

The growth of clubs and societies was driven by urbanization. As people were uprooted from rural communities, their traditional bonds to family and parish eroded, and they sought new forms of sociability.

Changes in Urban Areas

As government bureaucracies developed in the early modern era, the political autonomy of towns and cities was eroded, replaced by the centralized rule of law (Poggi 1978; Anderson [1979] 2013). Laws concerning property rights supported the economic activities that were important to urban dwellers. Therefore, town and city councils ceded their political powers to monarchs to further their own economic ends, becoming corporations under the authority of central state officials.

Guilds Are Transformed into Unions and Professional Associations

Starting in the fifteenth century, relationships between masters and their journeymen and apprentices evolved into work contracts (Weber [1927] 1981; Kieser 1989; Belfanti 1993). Some who left guilds created artisanal workshops that were not restricted by guild rules and so not burdened with guilds' welfare functions. These renegade organizations drove guilds toward collapse.[12] In some countries, such as France, the Netherlands, and Sweden, craft guilds were abolished by state decree (Sewell 1980; van der Linden 1996). The decline of guilds, and their welfare functions, led to the rise of two kinds of worker organizations:

12. But guilds have not completely vanished. Traces persist in the rules governing many skilled trades, such as electricians and carpenters, who must apprentice and accumulate work experience to be certified and qualify for state-issued licenses (Crowston and LeMercier 2019; Schalk 2019). And academia retains many guild-like features: a long apprenticeship that ends with the production of a "masterpiece" proving expertise and, in some fields, a series of temporary appointments (post-doctoral fellowships) that require moving between posts like medieval journeymen.

unions and professional associations. These were part of the double movement described by Karl Polanyi (1944): the expansion of capitalism and market exchange was met by a counter-movement checking that expansion.

Unions bring workers together to push for better wages and working conditions. They were long opposed by state bureaucrats who feared that worker power would destabilize the established social and political orders, and by the owners and managers of employing organizations, who feared that acceding to workers' demands would reduce their power and eat into their profits.

Unions descended from early modern journeymen's associations, which appeared as the feudal system broke down, loosening guild restrictions and eliminating guild protections (Brentano 1890; Webb and Webb 1920; Sewell 1980; Black 1984; Lis and Soly 1994; Krause 1996). Rather than being a temporary career stage, journeyman became a permanent second-class position, impelling journeymen to join together to gain bargaining power. As guilds lost their monopolies over specialized knowledge and practice, and as artisanal workshops and market stalls evolved into employing organizations, journeymen's associations evolved into craft and trade unions, and they organized an increasingly wide array of skilled workers. Industrial unions to organize less skilled workers appeared much later (Brentano 1890; Sewell 1980).

Britain led the way. In the late fourteenth century, small collections of artisans formed to resolve labor disputes, dissolving after their goals were met (Webb and Webb 1920; Laybourn 1991). Despite masters' opposition, journeymen's associations continued to be formed as guilds lost power. The earliest organizations that could be labeled as unions appeared in the late seventeenth century (Webb and Webb 1920). Because they were illegal until 1824, many took on the guise of mutual-aid societies (Brentano 1890; Cordery 2003). After 1824, some local unions came together to form federated structures with regional and national organizations linking locals, and unions slowly became accepted by the public. They were fully legalized in the 1870s, assuring their continued growth.

In the German states, there were scattered worker combinations (*Brüderschaften*) as early as the fourteenth century (Brentano 1890; Neufeld 1986). By the eighteenth century, they were thriving, connected through regional networks. But they were suppressed in the early nineteenth century under French rule, and labor unions (*Gewerkschaften*) did not begin to develop until after the 1848 revolution. Unions were outlawed from 1878 to 1890. After that, they become grudgingly accepted. During the Nazi era, unions were again suppressed, but after World War II, they rebuilt.

In France in the fifteenth century, journeymen's associations began to be formed clandestinely because they were illegal (Lorwin 1954; Sewell 1980). After the Revolution, all corporate bodies, including journeymen's associations, were banned, and journeymen's associations masqueraded as mutual-aid societies. In 1848, a new right to labor was proclaimed and freedom of association was guaranteed, so workers' organizations began to flourish. But after the coup d'état of 1851, they were outlawed and had to operate clandestinely again. Not until the 1860s were unions legalized, although they were repressed temporarily after the fall of the Commune in 1871.

In the U.S., worker combinations first appeared in the colonial era (Bloch and Lamoreaux 2017). Despite opposition from governing authorities, they continued to be formed as factories appeared (Wilentz 1984). As in Britain, they justified themselves to suspicious state authorities as vehicles for charitable work. They faced hostile employers: some used private armies to deter unionization efforts and break up strikes, sometimes assisted by local and federal police. Not until the New Deal reforms of the 1930s were union formation and activism accepted (Levi et al. 2017).

Although unions helped reduce inequality by raising their members' wages, and by improving working conditions and hours (as the bumper sticker says, the labor movement gave us the forty-hour work week), they also had pernicious effects. In the nineteenth and early twentieth centuries, unions in many countries were often hostile to women, fearing that they would depress men's wages. And American unions were routinely hostile toward Blacks. More benignly, unions influenced politics, either by founding left-wing political parties or supporting parties that protected workers with votes and funding. Most recently, however, American police unions have shielded their members accused of violence, frustrating efforts to hold them accountable and reduce violence against people of color.

Professional associations are the white-collar counterpart to unions. They regulate the technical content of work, create and enforce rules concerning entry, oversee education to prepare new members, and surveil existing members (Larson 1977). They originated in medieval cathedral schools to educate priests, administrators, lawyers, and physicians. Starting in the twelfth century, students and masters detached themselves and chartered scholars' guilds (*universitates*), as masters of law and medicine sought to protect their monopolies, oversee training, and regulate standards of practice (Larson 1977; Krause 1996; Scott 2006).[13]

Professional associations appeared in different places on different timetables. The first British medical guild, the Guild of Saint Mary Magdalene in Dublin, was chartered in 1446, but no effective professional association for doctors formed until the late nineteenth century (Berman 2006; Johnson

13. The oldest university in Europe is the University of Bologna, founded 1088 CE. It was preceded by the Alexandrian Museum of Egypt, which was founded in the third century BCE and renowned in its time for scientific and literary scholarship.

2010). For solicitors, the Law Society in Britain was not granted full regulatory power until 1888 (Johnson 2010). The U.S. generally followed the British model, with doctors and lawyers establishing first local then national professional associations (Haber 1991). In France and Germany, professional associations were usually created from above by state authorities rather than from below by practitioners (Larson 1977; Abbott 1988; Gispen 1988; Jarausch 1990; McClelland 1991; Krause 1996). In France, a revolutionary-era law banning corporations impeded the formation of professional associations. After that law was repealed in 1892, doctors created a national medical association to oversee health insurance, but it had little power. In the law, regional bar associations (*ordres*) appeared in the nineteenth century. Across the German states, standards for and supervisory power over professions varied, but professional associations had little power. Regional professional associations (*Kammern*) were first organized in the early nineteenth century, but suppressed after the failed revolution of 1848. National associations were not formed until the late nineteenth century.

The Rise of Business Organizations

Because so much of organizational theory has focused on business organizations and because the rising numbers, size, and power of business organizations were of central concern for early scholars, I treat them separately in this section. I trace the development of different forms of business organization in approximately the order in which they appeared. I focus primarily but not exclusively on four countries—Britain, France, Germany, and the U.S.—because we have good data on them and because what happened there influenced what happened in many other countries.

Partnerships

Some trade guilds began to evolve into *trading partnerships* as early as the ninth century, when Italian cities renewed trade with the East. Copying Arabian traders' partnerships (*mudaraba*s), Italian traders created maritime partnerships (*commende*) between two classes of ship owners: those who remained in Italy to buy and sell goods transported on jointly owned ships, and those who sailed with those ships to gather goods from distant shores and sell Italian goods there (Weber [1889] 2003, Weber [1927] 1981; Levy 1950; Braudel [1982] 1992; Harris 2000, 2008). The partner on land was liable for losses only up to his (rarely her) investment, while the partner on the ship was liable for all losses (Weber [1889] 2003; Levy 1950). At first, these were family affairs and so communal institutions; later, they included people unrelated by birth and so became fully associative institutions. They spread throughout Europe and Middle East—even to the Far East (Harris 2008). *Commende* had short lives: each lasted a single voyage. But they were long-lived as an organizational form, operating until the end of the sixteenth century.

As ships became larger, it became infeasible for two partners to own all of the goods transported, in part because of the increasing magnitude of the risks involved. Therefore, starting in the fourteenth century, ships and goods were divided into shares owned by multiple partners. Profits, if any, were paid at the end of a series of voyages. The partnership organizational form was later applied to other industries: first milling and mining, then professional services, commerce, and banking (Weber [1889] 2003, [1927] 1981; Levy 1950; Braudel [1982] 1992).

Starting in the thirteenth century, a few merchant families developed large international trading networks that evolved into vertically integrated trading partnerships (*compagnie*) that owned or at least partly controlled manufacturing facilities, ships, and warehouses. Household members' resources and expenses were in separate accounts, and members were collectively and individually liable for losses (Weber [1889] 2003; Levy 1950; Braudel [1982] 1992; Harris 2000). These began as family-owned concerns, but later welcomed members from outside the family (Weber [1889] 2003; Braudel [1982] 1992).

Although general partnerships had many benefits for conducting business on a large scale, they risked not just the funds partners invested in their business, but partners' entire wealth. To remedy this problem, *limited partnerships* were created, starting in the sixteenth century (Braudel [1982] 1992). The Italian states had manufacturing *accomanditi*, France *sociétés en commandite simple*, and the German states *Kommanditgesellschaften*. All had two classes of investors: directors, who still had unlimited liability for the firm's losses and who directed the firm's operations, and investors, whose liability was limited to the amount of money they invested in the venture.

Through a series of legal shifts, shares in partnerships became transferrable between owners. In France, such organizations were called *sociétés en commandite par actions*; in the German states, *Kommanditgesellschaften auf Aktien* (Braudel [1982] 1992; Kindleberger 1993; Freedeman 1979, 1993). After the liberalization of incorporation law in the late nineteenth century, described below, this form of partnership declined, largely replaced by corporations with tradable shares. This form of organization did not exist until 1907 in Britain, and later in the U.S.; it never became common in either country (Guinnane et al. 2008).

In the early modern era, partnerships, as private agreements, did not have to gain state approval to be created. But starting in the eighteenth century, as states expanded their authority, they began to require registration of partnerships.

Business Corporations

Starting in the late sixteenth century, business *corporations* were formed to overcome two legal limitations of partnerships (Braudel [1982] 1992; Harris 2000). Partnerships have no legal personhood separate from their partners; therefore, only partners can enter into contracts. If one partner dies or leaves the business, partnerships dissolve and must be renegotiated to continue operations. Business corporations were modeled on the medieval corporation, which had long been used to organize towns and cities, religious orders, colleges, and hospitals. Such corporations were granted monopolies over some public asset, natural resource, or activity in exchange for benefiting the public. For business corporations, the meant things like promoting economic growth through undertaking foreign trade, or building canals.

Legally, corporations are collective entities with legal personhood independent of their owners (Coleman 1974, 1982; Harris 2000). As legal persons, they need not dissolve when their principals die; instead, they can be dissolved only through strictly defined legal means. And as legal persons, they can enter into contracts in their own names, rather than in the names of their principals (Weber [1927] 1981; Levy 1950; Harris 2000). Moreover, ownership can be divided, dramatically expanding the pool of capital and spreading risk across owners.

The first business corporations, joint-stock merchant companies like the English Muscovy Company (founded 1551), lacked any solid legal framework, but many grew huge because they held monopolies over large trading zones, and some became immensely profitable.[14] From the late eighteenth century, the industrial revolution made it possible to produce machine-made goods, starting in textiles. These enterprises were increasingly likely to be incorporated because they required increasingly large investments in plant and equipment. In the nineteenth century, they were followed by railroad corporations, then by retailers, distributors, and other manufacturers, and finally by banks and utility companies (Chandler 1990; Freedeman 1993; Johnson 2010).

The number of business corporations in Europe was initially tiny, due to a series of eighteenth-century frauds and scandals that impelled state authorities to restrict corporate formation (Tilly 1966; Freedeman 1979; Cottrell 1980; Kindleberger 1993; Harris 2000; Murphy 2005). European governments did not loosen restrictions on corporate formation until the middle of the nineteenth century, when memories of the eighteenth-century scandals had faded and when railroad companies, which needed large capital bases, began to form. Strict chartering requirements were slowly replaced by laws that made it progressively easier to

---

14. One incorporated trading company, the British East India Company, became a quasi-state, seizing control of most of the Indian subcontinent in the late eighteenth century (Bowen 2006).

establish corporations (Henderson 1975; Freedeman 1979, 1993; Taylor 2006; Guinnane et al. 2008; Johnson 2010). In America, in contrast, business corporations proliferated in the eighteenth century because they were preceded by incorporated non-profits whose social benefits were clear (Baldwin 1901; Seavoy 1982; Creighton 1996; Kaufman 2008). Over time, American state governments became swamped by requests for charters, so they enacted general chartering statutes and general incorporation laws, which eased the creation of corporations.

Starting in the 1830s, governments made business corporations even freer by granting them *limited liability*, meaning that if corporations lost money, their shareholders were liable only for the amounts they had invested, not their entire wealth. For the earliest corporations in Europe and the U.S., which were established to administer not-for-profit entities and where the threat of losses was minimal, limited liability was not important. But for business corporations, it was. Thus, from the sixteenth to the nineteenth century, the corporation in some countries (Britain, France, and the U.S.) evolved from a quasi-public entity chartered by a government to accomplish a task for the public good into a private entity routinely created to undertake for-profit enterprise (Levy 1950; Roy 1997; Harris 2000; Perrow 2002; Winkler 2018). This transformation limited the rights of governments in those countries to oversee and regulate corporations as private entities. But in other countries (in particular Germany and Austria), the demand for public benefit remained (Leixnering, Meyer, and Doralt 2022) and governments there could hold business corporations accountable.

Corporations encountered opposition because their ownership and governance differed greatly from those of partnerships. Partners needed good character to get others to join and trust them. In contrast, corporate founders were often speculators and frauds, especially after corporations were granted limited liability, shifting some risk from owners to suppliers and customers (Taylor 2006; Johnson 2010). Some observers aired concerns about principal-agency problems. Adam Smith, no less ([1776] 1981), complained that hired managers would not be as vigilant as owners, so corporations would be inefficient compared to partnerships. And many feared corporations' growing monopoly power. The general pattern is clear: When and where corporations unequivocally served public functions (e.g., providing cities and colleges), opposition to them was sporadic and ad hoc. But when and where corporations were created for private business purposes, people decried their power and privileges.

Recently, two new kinds of business corporation have appeared: benefit corporations and Certified B Corporations.[15] The aim of those who promote

---

15. These new corporate forms were preceded by several corporations that sought to do good in the world, as well as earn profits: Patagonia (outdoor sports apparel and equipment, founded

these new forms is to use the legal system to create new laws and rules undergirding forms of business that seek not just earn to profits for their owners, but actively to solve social and economic problems. These new forms can be seen, therefore, as returning the business corporation to its roots in a legally sanctioned form of organization that was responsible for contributing to the public good. There are currently few instances of these novel organizational forms, but their numbers are increasing at a rapid pace.

Benefit corporations have legally defined goals that include not just profit, but also having positive impacts on society at large, their employees, the communities in which they operate, and the natural environment. These organizations are creatures of law, based on statutes passed in thirty-seven U.S. states (as of March 2022) and laws in several other countries, including the U.K. ("community interest companies"), France (*sociétés à mission*), and Italy (*società benefit*) (Levillain and Segrestin 2019). Note that benefit corporations cannot be formed without a statute explicitly authorizing them. Examples of benefit corporations include the yoghurt maker Danone, the outdoor clothing firm Patagonia, and the funding site Kickstarter.

B Corporations are the creations of a global non-profit organization, B Lab, that evaluates and approves for-profit companies on the basis of their social and environmental performance (Gehman, Grimes, and Cao 2019). To become certified, firms must integrate commitments to society at large and to environmental sustainability into their governing documents, and pay an annual fee to cover assessment costs. They must be recertified every three years. Note that this certification is a private arrangement—it has no legal status, unlike state authorization of benefit corporations. The power of B Lab certification is cultural: it visibly marks corporations as part of a vibrant global social movement (they can incorporate the "Certified B Corporation" logo into company communications), which legitimates their self-image as operating in socially beneficial ways. Examples of B Corporations include Danone (both a benefit corporation and a B Corporation), the ice cream company Ben and Jerry's, and chocolate maker Valrhona.

Private Limited Liability Companies

Over the past century, the publicly traded corporation has been partly eclipsed by the *private limited liability company* (PLLC in Britain and the U.S.; *Gesellschaft mit beschränkter Haftung* or *GmbH* in Germany; *société anonyme à responsabilité*

1973), Ben and Jerry's ice cream (founded 1978), AND1 (basketball shoes and apparel, founded 1993), and Numi Organic Tea (founded 1999). Indeed, the founders of AND1 went on to launch the Certified B Corporation movement in 2006.

limitée or *SARL* in France). In this form of organization, shareholders have limited liability and shares are not tradable on stock exchanges; shares can be traded privately, subject to restrictions (Lamoreaux and Rosenthal 2005; Guinnane et al. 2008). In France and Germany, these organizations are corporations and thus legal persons, separate from their owners. And in Germany, they are among the largest business organizations.

In the U.S., this form did not become available until the late 1970s, when states first began to authorize them (Lamoreaux and Rosenthal 2005; Guinnane et al. 2008). By 1996, all fifty states had authorized PLLCs, and their numbers exploded (Soener and Nau 2019). American PLLCs are more private than corporations and so disclose fewer details. This is different from the situation in Europe (Carney 1995). American PLLCs also have more flexible governance rules than corporations. Moreover, because American PLLCs' profits are taxed once (they "pass through" to owners), while corporate profits are taxed twice (once for the corporation, a second time for the shareholder), PLLC shareholders benefit financially. Recently, hybrids of the corporate and PLLC form have appeared, with American PLLCs being created as subsidiaries of corporations (Soener and Nau 2019).

In the past twenty years, a new form of LLC has begun to appear in the U.K. and the U.S.: the community interest company (CIC, U.K.) or low-profit limited liability company (L^3C, U.S.) (Lang and Minnaugh 2010; Lloyd 2010; Markham and Blair 2019). Formed under law, these organizations are hybrids between for-profit and non-profit companies. Their goals are charity or education, rather than primarily profit; any profits they do earn are usually reinvested or distributed to the communities they serve. The CIC/L^3C form has spread to several other countries. Similar to CICs and L^3Cs are LLCs certified by B Lab—the organization behind the B Corporation movement described above. Like Certified B Corporations, certified B LLCs do not have any legal status, because B Lab certification is a private agreement; but both benefit from being publicly identified with the B Lab movement.

Business Combinations

The development of capitalism was rocky, with booms followed by busts followed by booms. As industrialization proceeded, with mechanical and electrical innovations enabling mass production, and as urban growth increased demand for mass-produced goods, business organizations became more capital-intensive. That put them at greater risk during economic downturns, because letting workers go did not cut costs enough to ensure survival. To stabilize operations and reduce ruinous competition, which often spurred overproduction during booms and thus exacerbated busts, business organizations

experimented with combinations—cartels, trusts, and holding companies—
to coordinate action and stabilize operations. Their ability to form combinations hinged on acceptance of business organizations as "natural" elements of
the economic system.

Cartels are agreements among firms to set prices and limit production. Business owners either send products to central organizations that manage sales
and distribution, or pay fees to agencies (like trade associations) that surveil
cartel members. Such agreements began to appear in the fifteenth century
in the German states (Maschke 1969) and spread widely in the nineteenth
century. They require trust, so they work well when the geographic scope of
business is limited and business owners have informal social relations (Freyer
1992; Roy 1997).

In the U.S. toward the end of the nineteenth century, the "market" became
valorized and any system that "restrained" market competition, like cartels, was
met with suspicion by state authorities (Roy 1997). That made it impossible
for cartels to obtain legal sanctioning, making their agreements unenforce-
able. Despite this, American business organizations continued to write cartel
agreements. In France and Germany, cartels (*comptoirs* or *ententes* in France;
Kartellen in Germany) became common starting in the 1870s, prompted by
falling prices for agricultural and industrial products, which pushed business
owners to restrict competition and stabilize prices (Maschke 1969; Freedeman 1988, 1993; Chandler 1990). In both countries, few legal restrictions
were placed on cartels; indeed, in Germany in 1897, the Supreme Court up-
held cartel agreements as legally binding (Maschke 1969). In Britain, the law
favored self-regulation of business, because state authorities and business
leaders were members of the same small economic elite, so cartels were common (Freyer 1992); but since cartel agreements were not enforceable until
the twentieth century, they were seldom effective (Hannah 1976). The better
solution was control through merger (Mercer 1995; Hannah 1976; Freyer
1992).

Trusts occupy a position between cartels and holding companies. They are
collections of owners of competing companies who give voting power to a
group of trustees. Owners issued tradeable certificates that entitle them to
shares of profits.[16] Trusts, like cartels, require that members trust each other,
so they succeed when business owners are socially connected (Roy 1997). In
the U.S., trusts were used to coordinate corporate action throughout most of the
nineteenth century (Roy 1997). But in response to concerns raised by farmers
and small-business owners about trusts' enormous power to restrain trade,

16. In civil-law countries like France and Germany, trusts do not exist.

anti-trust lawsuits were filed in in several states starting in 1887. In 1890, the federal government passed the Sherman Anti-Trust Act, but it was seldom used to counter trusts until the twentieth century, after the passage of the Clayton Act and the founding of the Federal Trade Commission. In Britain, trusts were outlawed in the early eighteenth century, but resurged early in the nineteenth, despite lacking legal standing (Cottrell 1980; Harris 2000).

Holding companies consist of small central administrative units that control subsidiaries through share ownership. When shareholding is dispersed, control can be secured with less than 50 percent ownership. By sanctioning holding companies, state authorities explicitly offered business organizations a new right: the right to own shares in other corporations (Roy 1997; Prechel 2000). Holding companies can grow very large, operate geographically dispersed businesses, coordinate production within an industry, and control prices. In short, they have the potential to create monopolies.

Holding companies emerged in the late nineteenth century in the U.S. The initial impetus was the development of capital-intensive infrastructure: railroads, natural-gas distribution systems, electrical equipment manufacturing, and electricity distribution systems. The first holding companies required special permission from state authorities, so they were rare. Then, in New Jersey, an 1888 statute authorized all corporations to hold shares in other corporations, including those operating outside the state, and other states followed (Berle and Means [1932] 2001; Chandler 1977, 1990; Roy 1997; Prechel 2000). The number of holding companies grew rapidly at first, declined in the wake of New Deal era laws, and grew again in the 1980s. Contemporary American holding companies often differ from their predecessors in an important way: they contain multiple layers of subsidiaries, which are legally independent of the parent company; this structure camouflages ownership and insulates parent companies from lawsuits against their subsidiaries (Prechel 2000).

In Britain, holding companies became common during a wave of mergers from 1895 to 1902 (Payne 1967; Scott 1987; Chandler 1990). In France, holding companies (*sociétés holding*), which began to appear in the late nineteenth century, were generally focal points for groups of industrial or commercial firms; occasionally firms allied with banks (Scott 1987). Either way, parent companies had little control of subsidiaries. In Germany, the holding company (*Stammhauskonzern* or *Holding-Struktur*) developed in the late nineteenth century, as large universal banks took shares in industrial and commercial firms (Scott 1987). Banks controlled holding companies through voting rights in subsidiaries and through personal relations between bankers and industrialists. But since subsidiary directors also served as bank directors, control flowed both directions. In the twentieth century, the holding company became a dominant organizational form across Europe, used in large industrial and commercial groups.

Holding companies have also been common in Asian countries. For example, in Japan, organizations similar to holding companies (*zaibatsu*), like Mitsubishi and Sumitomo, were founded starting in the late nineteenth century, although they had roots in the seventeenth-century feudal era (Shibagaki 1966). They were transformed into holding companies and their subsidiaries into corporations by the 1920s (Lincoln, Gerlach, and Ahmadjian 1998; Okazaki 2001). Parent companies were often controlled by the members of a single family. Similarly, in Korea, family-controlled holding companies (*chaebol*) were formed with state support starting after World War II (Kim 1996).

The Shifting Demography of Business Organizations

The relative numbers of the different forms of business organization have varied greatly across societies, due to differences in law, culture, and politics. Table 2.1 compares the features of the five main forms of for-profit business organization and explains when each form first appeared in four countries.

For many years, limited partnerships were the most common way to organize large-scale business concerns in many European countries (Cameron 1961; Freedeman 1979; Guinnane et al. 2008; Fohlen 2008). For example, in France, before 1867 when corporate chartering ended and simple registration began, limited partnerships greatly outnumbered corporations, as Figure 2.2 shows.[17] Then, after 1925, when PLLCs were reauthorized (they were first authorized in 1863 but were superseded by publicly traded corporations after 1867), they soon outnumbered all other forms of business organization. The number of general partnerships fell dramatically and limited partnerships nearly disappeared. In Germany before World War I, the vast majority of multi-owner businesses founded were general partnerships, as Figure 2.3 shows. Limited partnerships never constituted more than 10 percent of new businesses. Publicly traded corporations were even rarer than limited partnerships. Finally, PLLCs became increasingly numerous; they outnumbered even general partnerships by 1932.

The situation in Britain was very different for a long time—and then it was not. Figure 2.4 shows the number of business incorporations from 1845, the year after general incorporation began, to 1913, the year before the outbreak of

---

17. For ease of scanning, Figure 2.2b zooms in on relatively rare organizational forms up to 1913.

TABLE 2.1. The principal forms of business organization in France, Germany, the U.K., and the U.S.

Type of form	Definition of form	Availability?
Ordinary partnership	Two or more partners, all unlimitedly liable	Yes in all four countries
Limited partnership	One or more general partners with unlimited liability, and one or more special partners who cannot participate in management but who have limited liability	France: yes Germany: yes U.K.: only after 1907 U.S.: yes, but in an unattractive form
Limited partnership with tradable shares	Same as limited partnership, except special partners' shares can be bought and sold on the market	France: yes Germany: yes U.K.: no U.S.: no
Corporation	All members have limited liability and their shares are tradable	Required special permission until: France: 1867 Germany: 1860s–1870, varying by state U.K.: 1844 without limited liability and 1855–1856 with limited liability U.S.: mostly middle third of nineteenth century, varying by state
Private limited liability company	All members have limited liability but their shares are not tradable	France: 1925 Germany: 1892 U.K.: 1907 U.S.: 1870s–1880s for a few states, but unattractive; laws in 1950s–1970s allowed close corporations to mimic; 1980s–1990s

Source: Guinnane et al. (2007: Table 1)

World War I. Starting in 1856, when all corporations were granted limited liability, foundings accelerated. Figure 2.5 compares the number of new publicly traded corporations to the number of new PLLCs from 1900 to 1938. It shows that new publicly traded corporations were quickly outnumbered by PLLCs after 1907. The U.S. trend is similar to Britain's: over the past thirty years, publicly traded corporations became scarcer and PLLCs more numerous (Davis 2016; Soener and Nau 2019).

Although the predominant form of business organization changed over the twentieth century, as PLLCs replaced publicly traded corporations, large and powerful business organizations are not "vanishing" (cf. Davis 2009, 2016). The largest business organizations have become more private (as the "P" in PLLC suggests), and in the U.S. are less visible to public scrutiny. But large business organizations remain powerful forces in all societies.

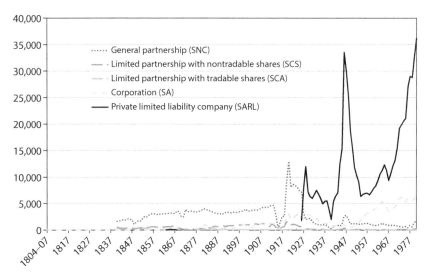

FIGURE 2.2A. Multi-owner businesses founded in France 1804–1980, by form
Source: Freedeman (1979, 1993) and Guinnane et al. (2008: 84, Figure 3).
Data replotted with the authors' permission.
Note: Data on general and limited partnerships are not available until 1840.

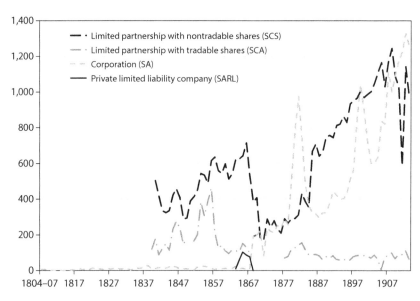

FIGURE 2.2B. Zooming in on rare multi-owner business forms in France before 1914

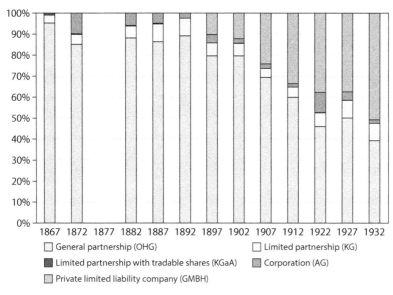

FIGURE 2.3. Percentage of multi-owner businesses founded
in Germany, 1867–1932, by form
Source: Guinnane et al. (2008: 86, Figure 4). Data replotted
with the authors' permission.

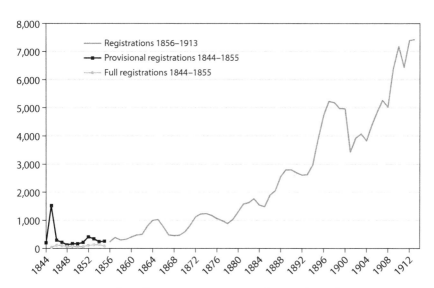

FIGURE 2.4. Number of business incorporations in the United Kingdom, 1844–1913
Source: Johnson (2010: 124, Figure 4.1). Data replotted with the author's permission.

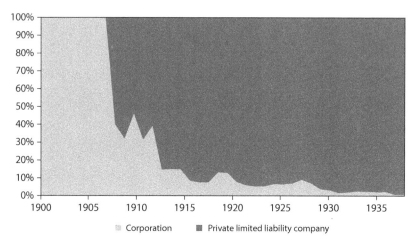

FIGURE 2.5. Percentage of multi-owner businesses founded in the
United Kingdom, 1900–1932, by form
Source: Guinnane et al. (2008, p. 92, Figure 5). Data replotted with
the authors' permission.
Note: Data are not available on general partnerships.

Non-Profit Business Organizations

As for-profit business organizations grew in size, number, and power, they
created many social and economic problems. Agrarian communities were torn
apart when people went to work in mines and industrial factories. The paternalistic bond between lords and peasants, and between guild master and journeyman or apprentice, was broken, and no comparable bond between capitalist
and worker ever developed to take its place.[18] As Marx put it, "natural relationships" dissolved "into money relationships" (Marx and Engels [1932] 1947: 57).
Workers flocked to factories located in towns and cities, and new towns sprang
up near mines. Urban workers often resided in squalid housing, laboring in
harsh conditions for little pay. Women and children joined adult men at work,
for even worse pay. To solve these social and economic problems, three kinds
of non-profit business organizations developed: cooperatives, mutual-aid
societies, and credit cooperatives. All of these combined three previously disparate ideas—community, enterprise, and self-help—to allow farmers, workers,
and small producers to remain independent while reaping the economic benefits

18. By calling these bonds paternalistic, I do not mean to imply that they were mutually
beneficial. Instead, the vast majority of benefits flowed to those at the top of the feudal or guild
hierarchy. But each party had responsibilities toward the other, even if those responsibilities
were not always fulfilled.

of association, notably economies of scale, market power, and risk pooling. They also helped create and maintain social bonds between members, substituting for lost communal institutions.

Cooperatives. These took several forms: agricultural, consumer, and producer. All were member-owned and member-operated businesses that sought to benefit their members through economies of scale and market power. Consumers joined together to purchase goods in volume at low prices and eliminate profit-seeking merchants. Farmers and artisans came together to sell goods and services at higher prices. Their governance was (and remains) democratic, with each member having a vote. In cooperatives, as in all for-profit businesses, earnings in excess of expenses accrued to owners. But in cooperatives, unlike in for-profit businesses, those owners were the customers who purchased goods and services, or the producers who created goods and services.

Cooperatives had two roots. Consumer cooperatives grew out of the consumer revolution of the early modern era, when people in expanding urban areas began to purchase more of their daily needs in markets, rather than making them themselves (Thirsk 1978; McKendrick, Brewer, and Plumb 1982; Auslander 1996; de Vries 2008). Producer and agricultural cooperatives developed to counter economic exploitation by industrial monopolists large and small, ranging from local mills to shops owned by mining and manufacturing companies (Birchall 1997). Cooperatives first appeared in Britain and Switzerland in the late eighteenth century (van der Linden 1996; Birchall 1997). In Britain, they gained legal protection in 1834. Perhaps the most famous is the Rochdale Society, a consumer cooperative founded in 1844 whose underlying principles and organizational structure became global role models (Furlough and Strikwerda 1999). In France, they began to form in the 1830s (Moody and Fite 1984). In Prussia, they began to appear in the middle of the nineteenth century, influenced by the example of Rochdale (Moody and Fite 1984; Fairbairn 1994). In the U.S., they began to form after the Civil War.

Mutual-aid societies were cooperative in nature, but they offered financial services and benefited their members primarily by pooling risk rather than by generating economies of scale and gaining market power. Members paid dues on a regular basis. These dues were combined and used to help needy members and their dependents deal with illness, disability, and death (van der Linden 1996; Clark 2000; Börner 2013).

These societies were first created by early modern guilds as charitable brotherhoods.[19] From the mid-sixteenth to the late nineteenth century,

---

19. Mutual-aid societies had predecessors. In the mesolithic era, Pacific coast tribes established mutual support groups in the form of secret societies (Lowie 1948; Driver 1961). Secret

mutual-aid societies expanded across Europe as guilds declined or were banned, then spread to the Americas and Asia (Gosden 1961; van der Linden 1996; Clark 2000; Cordery 2003; Börner 2013). In most countries, they declined in the twentieth century due the rise of commercial insurance, state pensions, and state health insurance plans, which reduced demand for mutual-aid societies' services.

Credit cooperatives, also called credit unions and cooperative banks, were similar to mutual-aid societies in that they offered financial services. But credit cooperatives' services involved loans and savings accounts rather than insurance. Members combined their savings and borrowed from the collective fund. Thus, like mutual-aid societies but unlike other cooperatives, credit cooperatives pooled risk. Savers earned interest and, in return, faced the hazard of default by borrowers. To reduce this risk, membership was based on common bonds derived from belonging to the same organization (e.g., labor union or fraternal association) or occupation (e.g., teachers or tailors), or living in the same location. Credit cooperatives were generally managed democratically, with each member having one vote, and with earnings above expenses returned to members.

Such cooperatives first appeared in Germany in the mid-nineteenth century (Moody and Fite 1984). They flourished because urban banks made it difficult and expensive for farmers, shopkeepers, and artisans to acquire credit (Guinnane 2001). By 1913, over nineteen thousand credit cooperatives had over two million members, touching the lives of over 15 percent of Germans (Fairbairn 1994; Guinnane 2001). They spread throughout Europe during the nineteenth century, and came to North America in the early twentieth century.

In Britain, a variant called building societies first appeared in the mid-eighteenth century (Price 1958; Cleary 1965; Rex 2017).[20] Because they focused on financing expensive housing, their earliest members were well-paid artisans, masters, shopkeepers, and professionals. As they spread across Britain in the nineteenth century, they admitted less affluent members saving for purposes other than to build or buy a home.

---

societies also flourished in many neolithic settlements, along with mutual-aid societies among stonecutters in ancient Egypt and bricklayers in the Roman Empire (Lowie 1948), and confraternity communities in medieval villages (Hughes 1973). And in China during the Tang dynasty (618–905 CE), there were burial societies (van der Linden 1996).

20. Related was the land association, whose members paid subscriptions to purchase a plot of land, subdivide it, and sell the plots at a profit, which flourished throughout the nineteenth century (Price 1958; Cleary 1965).

1st century	Christian Church (Council of Jerusalem, ca. 50 CE)
4th century	Hospitals (Rome: *xenodocheion* or *xenon*, 373 CE)
5th century	Orphanages (Rome, ca. 400 CE)
9th century	Merchant guilds (Italian states) Trading partnerships (Italian states: *commende*)
10th century	Almshouses (England: bede-houses)
11th century	Universities (Italian states: Università di Bologna, 1088) Bureaucratic states (Sicily) Craft guilds (Italian states)
13th century	Vertically integrated trading partnerships (Italian states: *compagnie*)
14th century	Journeymen's associations (England and the German states: *Brüderschaften*)
15th century	Manufacturing partnerships (England and the German states)
16th century	Clubs (England and the German states) Limited partnerships (Italian states: *accomanditi*) Business corporations (joint-stock companies) (England: Muscovy Company, 1555)
17th century	Friendly societies (England, 1687) Reform societies (England: Society for the Reformation of Manners, 1691) Mutual-aid societies (England and the German states) Limited partnerships with tradeable shares (France and the German states) Craft unions (England)
18th century	Missionary societies (England: Society for Propagating the Gospel among the Heathen, 1701) Constitutional states (France, 1789) Cooperatives (Switzerland and England) Building societies (England)
19th century	Limited-liability business corporations (Prussia, 1843) Credit cooperatives (German states) Cartels (U.S. and western Europe) Trusts (England) Holding companies (U.S.) Industrial unions (Britain) Private limited-liability companies (Germany: *GmbH*, 1892)
20th century	Community-interest company (U.K., 2005, known in the U.S. as a low-profit limited-liability company) Certified B corporation (England, 2006) Benefit corporation (Maryland, 2010)

FIGURE 2.6. Timeline for the first appearance of different forms
of organization in Europe and the U.S.

Conclusion

During the long, uneven process of modernization, communal institutions slowly gave way to associative institutions. The most important and numerous of these were organizations. They appeared at different times in different societies, depending on law, culture, politics, and accidents of history. Figure 2.6 is a timeline showing the first appearance of many forms of organization. In the early modern era, corporations were chartered by state authorities for social benefit, in the form of towns and cities, colleges and schools, missionary societies, hospitals, and other charitable organizations. Then for-profit business corporations appeared; they slowly became less required to benefit society and more allowed to focus on private gain. In reaction to the growing power of for-profit businesses, non-profit businesses appeared, along with unions and professional associations. Most recently, for-profit business forms that seek to balance profits with social and environmental benefits have begun to flourish. Finally, in private life, people came together in an increasing number of clubs, societies, and voluntary associations. The upshot is that modern life is replete with organizations. But although much has changed, the nature of organizations—indeed, their very existence—has always depended on approval from state authorities.

3

The Evolution of Research on Organizations

ORGANIZATIONAL THEORY DEVELOPED as a means of understanding the many kinds of organizations chronicled in chapter 2. Many thinkers recognized that the world around them was changing fundamentally. Before this change was tradition: rural life, agricultural labor, family, and small-scale community. After this change came modernity: urban life, long-distance communication and transportation, industrial labor, and globe-spanning empires. This fundamental change was most visible in the rise of large organizations: government bureaucracies, mines and factories, and all kinds of business and civil society organizations. Because this transformation was so sweeping, touching all aspects of social life, it is not surprising that the study of organizations grew from a disparate set of roots in sociology, economics, engineering, management, political science, and psychology, and that it incorporated insights from anthropology, education, geography, history, industrial relations, law, public health, and public policy.

In this chapter, I touch on three different starting points for organizational theory, which lie in the work of three of the founders of sociology: Karl Marx, Max Weber, and Émile Durkheim. After that, I discuss theories of organizations proposed by other scholars up to the early 1970s. Next, I argue that most contemporary research on organizations can be divided into three dominant perspectives—demographic, relational, and cultural—which differ in terms of their understandings of social structure and agency. But note that the temporal boundary between what I label early and contemporary perspectives on organizations is fuzzy. I place it in the late 1970s, because that is when many of the foundational statements of the three contemporary perspectives were published. But some foundational statements were published earlier (e.g., Pfeffer 1972; Granovetter 1973) and some early perspectives remained influential beyond the 1970s.

This chapter is based on my reading of key works by the authors discussed here, but also on the writings of those who have surveyed and criticized this field of study: Howard Aldrich (1979), Jeffrey Pfeffer (1982, 1997), Charles Perrow (1986), W. Richard Scott (Scott 2003; Scott and Davis 2007), Mauro Guillén (1994), Yehouda Shenhav (1999), Paul Adler and the contributors to his edited volume (2009), and Bob Hinings and Renate Meyer (2018). I am grateful for their insights, even if I do not always agree with their interpretations. And, to be clear, what I lay out in this and the following four chapters is my own understanding of organizational theories. I take the role of impartial rapporteur, seeking to be complete but not partisan, despite my own participation in this intellectual journey.

Classical Sociology and the Study of Organizations

Three pioneering scholars have had a huge impact on the study of organizations. Karl Marx proposed a theory about the legal and material contexts within which business organizations operated and their effects on owners and workers alike; Max Weber developed an explicit theory of organizations themselves; and Émile Durkheim laid out a theory about the impact of organizations, with their fine-grained division of labor, on social relations.

Karl Marx

When Marx was born in 1818, steam power was beginning to be used in manufacturing and transportation. During his lifetime, he saw the emergence of new technologies dominated by chemicals and electricity: electric light bulbs, telegraphy, machine tools, synthetic dyes, and artificial flavors. Using these technologies required huge bases of capital, as they involved large, expensive, and complicated machinery, hordes of workers to operate and maintain machinery, and costly inputs like steel and cotton. In this dramatically changing environment, Marx studied law and philosophy in university, where he became increasingly radicalized. After obtaining his PhD, he was barred from academic posts due to state opposition to leftist views like his own, so he turned to journalism. While working as a journalist, he studied political economy and history, and began to write about the horrific conditions of the working class under industrial capitalism. He observed the rise of huge factories and mines that took in streams of workers, raw materials, and money, and emitted foul clouds of smoke,[21] fetid streams of waste, and industrial goods—along with fat profits for their owners and meager wages for their workers. Marx was appalled by the immiseration of workers and railed against

21. These were the "dark satanic mills" of William Blake's poem *Jerusalem*, published in 1811.

the "bourgeoisie," meaning the capitalists who owned and ran mines and factories. He held that the fundamental division in society is class (characterized in relation to the means of production) and that the lower class (workers) are in perpetual struggle with those above them in the class hierarchy, meaning landowners and, increasingly, owners of industrial enterprises (Marx [1867] 1992). He also argued that capitalism's corollary—the industrial division of labor—alienates people from the fruits of their labor and from themselves and their fellows. Under capitalism, workers cannot control their actions or their relationships with fellow workers and their bosses, and they do not own what they help produce. Thus industrial capitalism dehumanized workers, reducing them to mere cogs in the wheels of production. His own words convey the depths of his anger:

> [We] have shown that the worker sinks to the level of a commodity, and moreover the most wretched commodity of all; that the misery of the worker is in inverse proportion to the power and volume of his production; that the necessary consequence of competition is the accumulation of capital in a few hands and hence the restoration of monopoly in a more terrible form; and that, finally, the distinction between capitalist and landlord, between agricultural worker and industrial worker, disappears and the whole of society must split into the two classes of *property owners* and propertyless *workers*. (Marx [1844] 1993; emphasis in the original)

Marx viewed the development of capitalism as a consequence of technology (changes in production systems, particularly the shift from home-based to factory-based manufacturing) and economics (power struggles between capitalists and workers, and competition among capitalists for profit). Indeed, he put economics in the driving seat, arguing that technological innovation is made necessary by the economic system that the bourgeoisie constructed to dominate workers. Consider this quotation from *The Communist Manifesto*:

> The bourgeoisie cannot exist without constantly revolutionizing the instruments of production, and thereby the relations of production, and with them the whole relations of society. All fixed, fast-frozen relations, with their train of ancient and venerable prejudices and opinions, are swept away, all new-formed ones become antiquated before they can ossify. (Marx and Engels [1848] 1964: 62–63)

In Marx's view, capitalism necessitates the ceaseless creation of novel technologies and work processes, which requires altering the ideologies that justify relationships of production and exploitation. If capitalists did not find new ways to extract ever more profit from workers, market pressures would force their enterprises to fail.

Marxist theory undergirds research on power differences among workers, managers, and owners.[22] Well-known early Marxist analysts of organizations include Robert Blauner (1964), Harry Braverman (1974), Michael Burawoy (1979), Richard Edwards (1979), and Dan Clawson (1980). These scholars viewed firms as tools of exploitation, domination, and control of workers by capitalists and managers who set wages far below the value that workers added to products. More optimistic early Marxist scholars took inspiration from Marx's claim that the cooperative nature of work could create solidarity and resistance among workers, and thus a revolutionary class consciousness (Hyman 1975). More recent work in this tradition extended a Marxist understanding of workplaces as sites of class domination and exploitation to examine how gender, race, and nationality shape the labor process (Salzinger 2001) or how firms build trust relations to exploit highly educated service workers, in contrast to the less educated production workers studied by earlier scholars (Adler 2001).

Other Marxist analysis focused on the organization of the capitalist class and its relationship to corporations (Useem 1984). This work led to an interest in the constraints and opportunities afforded by relationships between corporations through their boards of directors (Mizruchi 1982; Mintz and Schwartz 1985). Related work examined how, when, and why state officials craft public policy in the interest of the capitalist class (Domhoff 1983; Block 1987). A final line of Marxist analysis examined the growth of multinational corporations as capital accumulation, thus linking organizational structures to the developmental trajectories of nation-states (Hymer 1972).

In contrast to the flourishing of Marxist analysis of organizations in many sociology departments and labor-relations schools, it is not entirely surprising that Marx's impact on the research conducted in business schools has been slight. Even though most management professors are politically left-leaning, they swim in a culture that glorifies management, money, and power, and the students they teach are being trained to become the business owners and managers whom Marx deplored. It is impossible to envision anyone who cares about their teaching ratings declaiming to a classroom of MBA students the Marxist slogan, "Workers of the world unite! You have nothing to lose but your chains!"

Max Weber

Weber was born in 1864. During his lifetime, he experienced the unification of the German states under Emperor Wilhelm (formerly Prince of Prussia) and the consolidation of power under Chancellor Otto von Bismarck. He also

---

22. For a review, see Adler (2009).

experienced the continued development of industries based on coal and steel, and the rise of industries based on chemistry and electricity. Like Marx, Weber studied law in university, as well as history and economics. While his early research was in economic history, in the 1900s he began work on the texts that have had the biggest impact on the study of organizations: *The Protestant Ethic*, *General Economic History*, and *Economy and Society*. This work was motivated in part by German state-building. His knowledge of Roman law, in particular, drove Weber's ethical and philosophical ambivalence about the changes wrought by the rise of bureaucratic states and industrial capitalism. One the one hand, he realized that bureaucratic rationalization of government produced a reliable, dependable system of decision-making for the public good, while capitalism made possible many beneficial economic advances. But on the other hand, he feared that bureaucratic rationalization and industrial capitalism locked people into an "iron cage" that eliminated their individual humanity. I expand on both themes below.

In contrast to Marx, whose explanations of social life emphasized economics, Weber emphasized *ideologies*. The most prominent instantiation of this emphasis is *The Protestant Ethic and the Spirit of Capitalism* ([1904–5] [1958). In this essay, Weber argued that the ascetic ideals of Calvinism, a religious movement that began in sixteenth-century Switzerland and spread across northern Europe, facilitated the rise of capitalism. Two features of Calvinism— asceticism and the doctrine of predestination—were at the core of Weber's explanation. Asceticism demands self-denial: Calvinists were supposed to lead austere lives, without luxuries. Predestination is the idea that nothing you do, good or bad, affects your ultimate fate, your salvation: before you were born, God had decided whether or not you were one of the "elect" who would ascend to heaven. To stave off "salvation panic," Calvinists looked for earthly signs of God's blessing, notably economic success. To secure economic success, they threw themselves into work, holding that people had an ethical obligation to work and earn money. Because of their asceticism, Calvinists did not spend money on themselves or their families; instead, they accumulated their earnings and (re)invested it in businesses. Slowly, over centuries, this religious ideology helped create a new way of thinking: capital accumulation was rationalized through the adaptation of religious tenets to everyday life.

In this way, Weber recognized the importance of the subjective meanings, intentions, and interpretations that people bring to any social situation. He wrote about how these cognitive-emotional factors translated into action. He distinguished between four kinds of meanings, intentions, and interpretations ("rationalities" was the term he used) that could drive action: tradition or ingrained habit, emotions and feelings, values and ethical beliefs (*Wertrationalität*), and instrumentality and means–end relationships (*Zweckrationalität*)

(Weber [1968] 1978: 24–26). Note that these four kinds of rationality were ideal types that were neither exhaustive (just the most relevant) nor mutually exclusive. In the real world, we would often see that two or more were combined. For example, the Calvinist ideals of work and wealth discussed above combined value rationality and instrumental rationality. Weber further argued that behavior results from a combination of these cognitive-emotional factors and external factors like state policy and technology. In sum, the Weberian mode of empathetic understanding—*verstehen*—requires us to decipher the meanings, intentions, and interpretations that people import into society, which guide their reactions to that society and thus their actions in that society.

Weber's training in law and history made him keenly aware that political power had been centralized in national governments. Bureaucratic states reached into more and more corners of life, authorizing some actions and punishing others. They made laws authorizing large and powerful business organizations. Weber's interest in political power is seen is his analysis of rational-legal bureaucratic structure and functioning ([1968] 1978)—specifically, of the German military and government administrative apparatuses (see also work by Weber's colleague Hans Rosenberg [1958]). Weber compared state bureaucracies to collegiate, honorific, and avocational forms of administration—that is, to administration by notables who were appointed to their offices because of who they were, not because of their skills, training, or experience. Ideally, notables were aristocrats who had a sense of social responsibility, but in reality they usually used their positions for power or personal enrichment. Bureaucratic state organizations were developed to open positions to the talented. To do that, they developed ways to gauge people's skills, such as standardized testing (e.g., British civil service exams) and established formal routes of education. Observing these developments, Weber concluded that without an efficient and impersonal state bureaucracy, the work of the nation-state and capitalist economic development would both be hindered.

Weber believed that bureaucratic coordination was the hallmark of modern society, the result of the increasing rationalization of human activities. He talked about bureaucracy as an ideal type—an abstraction helpful in theorizing because it represents the purest understanding of a theoretical construct—rather than a form of organization observable in the real world. Weber's ([1968] 1978) ideal-typical bureaucracy consists of the following elements:

- official jurisdictional areas whose regular activities, patterns of formal authority, and employment are ordered by rules (i.e., by laws or administrative regulations);
- a hierarchical structure in which authority flows from top to bottom and information flows from bottom to top;

- formal, written documents that allow organizational memory, accountability, and continuity;
- separation of bureaucrats' official capacities from their personal lives
(e.g., managerial decisions are based on written rules rather than personal
bias, and personnel are functionally rather than personally involved in
their duties);
- specialization in training and a clear division of labor;
- official activity that requires the full working capacity of bureaucrats; and
- management that follows general, written rules, which are more or less
exhaustive.

In combination, these features make the ideal-typical bureaucracy effective, as
it gets the right job done the right way, and efficient, as it gets the job done with
the fewest inputs per unit output. In Weber's ([1968] 1978: 973) own words:

> The decisive reason for the advancement of bureaucratic organization has
> always been its purely technical superiority over any other form of organ-
> ization. The fully developed bureaucratic apparatus compares with other
> organizations exactly as does the machine with the non-mechanical modes
> of production. Precision, speed, unambiguity, knowledge of the files, con-
> tinuity, discretion, unity, strict subordination, reduction of friction and of
> material and personal costs—these are raised to the optimum point in the
> strictly bureaucratic administration.

No real organization exactly mirrors the features of Weber's bureaucracy,
for three reasons (Perrow 1986). First, no organization can eliminate outside
influences on its operations, because its members have lives outside that
organization and because every organization depends on suppliers, customers,
and government authorities, and so must often bow to their demands. Second,
the features of the ideal-typical bureaucracy function perfectly in a world
where nothing is changing and everything can be predicted. But no organization operates in a static environment, so organizations must experiment to
adjust to change, and change upends bureaucratic systems. Third, people's
thinking is only limitedly rational (Simon [1947] 1976, 1955), so they cannot
design the formal structures of organizations to handle all possible situations;
instead, organizational members must often improvise to deal with the unexpected (Blau [1955] 1963).

Despite his praise for the efficiency of bureaucracy, Weber saw grave dan-
gers in it. First, the bureaucratization of administration centralizes power and
concentrates resources in the hands of a few officials. This undercuts representative democracy, especially when elected officials defer to unelected
bureaucrats—the mandarinate. Second, echoing Marx, Weber recognized that

the bureaucratization of administration reduces workers to just another piece of a large system that they could not control: "Rational calculation . . . reduces every worker to a cog in this bureaucratic machine and, seeing himself in this light, he will merely ask how to transform himself into a somewhat bigger cog. . . . The passion for bureaucratization drives us to despair" (Weber [1968] 1978: lix). By limiting workers to their defined tasks, bureaucratization threatens individual freedom.

Weber's ideas, notably his concerns about the power and limitations of rational-legal bureaucracy, inspired research by Robert Merton and his students at Columbia, including Phillip Selznick (1949), Seymour Martin Lipset (1950; Lipset, Trow, and Coleman 1956), Alvin Gouldner (1954), Peter Blau ([1955] 1963), and David Sills (1957), as well as a myriad of other organizational sociologists across North America and Europe (e.g., Crozier 1964; Hirsch 1975). I discuss their work below, in the section on post-war organizational sociology. Weber's ideas continue to be fundamental to studies on organizations that emphasize the importance of history (sensitivity to the peculiarities of time and place) and that are centrally concerned with understanding what people in that time and place think and feel, and how they react to external forces (e.g., Dobbin and Dowd 1997; Scott et al. 2000; Haveman, Habinek, and Goodman 2012). Weber's ideas also reverberate in the study of power and relationships within and between organizations, even although that work seldom cites Weber; for example, actors who inhabit different positions in structures of exchange develop different understandings of the social world (Keltner, Gruenfeld, and Anderson 2003; Magee and Galinsky 2008).[23]

Émile Durkheim

Durkheim was a contemporary of Weber's, born in 1858. He studied at a prestigious Parisian educational institution (the *École normale supérieure*) that trained academics. There, he came to disdain humanistic and literary inquiry, and value instead philosophy, morality, and sociology—a discipline that was not yet established in France. After graduation, he taught for a couple of years, then continued his study of sociology at German universities, where the new discipline was better developed. Armed with knowledge of French, German, and British sociology, economics, and philosophy, he was appointed to the first French professorship in social science at the University of Bordeaux.

Durkheim, like Marx and Weber, studied the emerging modern social order. But he generally shied away from politics and social policy, focusing on

23. For a review of Weber's influence on organizational theory, see Clegg and Lounsbury (2009).

the consequences of modernization for everyday life, rather than its consequences for workers (Marx) or democracy (Weber), or its appearance in bureaucratic organizations (Weber). Durkheim was interested in social relations in part because he had witnessed France being literally torn apart, with Alsace and some parts of Lorraine (where he was raised) ceded to Germany at the end of the Franco-Prussian War. He was also motivated by the history of the French Revolution and its tumultuous aftermath, as well as the Revolution of 1848 and the coup d'état of 1851. These events demonstrated that seemingly stable societies could change quickly. Durkheim wanted to understand why.

He traced the move from a traditional, undifferentiated, and holistic social order to a modern, highly differentiated, and interdependent one, and explained how modernization altered social bonds. He asked how individuals could retain any autonomy if modern (complex, interdependent) societies required a centralized authority to maintain order. In *Suicide* ([1897] 1951: 209), which empirically investigates an extreme instance of lack of social control and social solidarity, Durkheim proclaimed, "When society is strongly integrated, it holds individuals under its control." Although he did not analyze organizations as such, two of his works have important ramifications for organizational sociology.[24]

In his doctoral dissertation, which was published as *The Division of Labor in Society* ([1893] 1984), Durkheim proposed that as societies moved from traditional (small, rural, and agricultural) to modern (large, urban, and industrial), people's social connections shifted from being holistic and undifferentiated, based on similarity of role (mechanical solidarity) to being based on differentiated roles and interdependence between them (organic solidarity).[25] Because industrial modes of production seek efficiency by dividing up tasks finely (see also Smith [1776] 1981), people in different kinds of organizations hold different jobs. As a result, people in modern societies have less in common than people in traditional societies, who (almost) all did the same work (primarily farming) in similar settings. But, paradoxically, people in modern societies depend on each other more than did people in traditional societies. People in traditional societies were largely self-sufficient (growing and making almost everything they needed), while people in modern societies are highly interdependent, exchanging the goods and services they produce for money to buy goods and services produced by others. In sum, then, Durkheim's research explains how people's attachment to others changed as societies modernized.

24. For reviews of Durkheim's influence on organizational theory, see Starkey (1992) and Dobbin (2009).

25. This pair of concepts is similar to Ferdinand Tönnies's ([1887] 1988) concepts of *Gemeinschaft* (community) and *Gesellschaft* (society).

In *The Elementary Forms of Religious Life,* Durkheim ([1912] 1996) laid out a cultural theory of symbolic classification: people collectively make sense of the world by classifying social actors and objects, assigning meaning and value to them, and developing causal models to explain their power. In contrast to Marx, who saw culture as largely epiphenomenal and reducible to the economic bases of social structure, Durkheim argued that ideas "follow their own laws once they are born" (p. 426) and can act on the material world, shaping the structures from which they arose.

Durkheim's concern with solidarity and the social dislocations spawned by the industrial division of labor influenced the human-relations school (discussed below) to attend to how the work process fulfilled (or failed to fulfill) workers' social and emotional needs (Mayo [1933] 1960, 1945). In addition, Durkheim's concern with symbols, rituals, and shared meanings reverberates in research on organizational culture (Pettigrew 1979; Van Maanen and Schein 1979; Kunda 1992). These "social facts," as Durkheim called them, are exterior to individual organizational members. When organizational cultures are strong and accepted by all (or most) organizational members, they bind members together. But when organizational cultures are weak and subcultures develop, integration into a coordinated whole is problematic. Finally, Durkheim's emphasis on how external ideational constraints shape behavior resonates with the insights of the institutionalist theory that I survey in chapter 5, specifically the ideas that organizational legitimacy and survival depend in part on conformity with normative practices and "institutionalized rules" (Meyer and Rowan 1977). Thus, Durkheim's work emphasizing the importance of shared beliefs has influenced scholars of organizations to attend to normative, social, and emotional elements of exchange and organizing that tend to be neglected in more purely economic approaches.

Other Early Theories of Organizations

Georg Simmel

Simmel, like Durkheim, was born in 1858. He studied philosophy and history at Humboldt University of Berlin and wrote a dissertation in philosophy. Descended from Jews, he was baptized as a Protestant, yet his academic career was hampered by growing German anti-Semitism. Despite being a renowned (unsalaried) teacher (*Privatdozent*) at the University of Berlin, and despite support from Max Weber and other prominent German intellectuals, he was unable to secure a professorial position until three decades after he earned his PhD. Still, he devoted himself to writing on a wide array of topics—not just philosophy and ethics (his main areas), but also sociological methods, psychology, economics, religion, and literary and fine-art criticism.

The part of Simmel's intellectual territory that lies within sociology is the study of urban life and of social interaction and affiliation. Most germane to the study of organizations, he analyzed affiliation in small groups, which we would call social ties, explicating how the twin processes of subordination and superordination, which we would call hierarchy (bosses over workers), generated conflict (Simmel 1955). While agreeing with Marx that conflict is endemic to social life, Simmel departed from Marx in arguing that conflict may not produce social change; instead, conflict may sharpen or crystallize existing social divisions.

In addition to his well-recognized attention to affiliation, Simmel understood the importance of numbers (Simmel 1950). Thus Simmel's definition of social structure encompasses both patterns of interactions among people (which today we would call relational structure) and patterns defined by peoples' distribution across social positions (which we would call demographic structure). The idea that social structure consists of social relations and demographic distributions remains influential in contemporary research on organizations, most strongly in research on power and resource dependence between individuals and organizations (Burt 1992; Obstfeld 2005), which I explain in chapter 5, and research on internal organizational demography (Blau 1977; Kanter 1977; Pfeffer 1983), which I explain in chapter 4. Relational work takes from Simmel a recognition that a dyad (a pair of actors) is fundamentally different from a triad (a triplet), a triad from a tetrad (a set of four), and so on. Demographic work takes from Simmel the idea that numbers matter: majority groups are very different from minority groups. Finally, contemporary research on organizational identity, which often takes an interactionist stance, is also indebted to Simmel (Whetten and Godfrey 1998; Gioia et al. 2010; Anteby and Molnár 2012).[26]

In conclusion, Simmel's eclectic output and his lack of standard academic appointment help explain why there is no large school of Simmelians in contemporary sociology—although Peter Blau (Blau 1970, 1977, 1994; Blau and Schoenherr 1971) self-identified as a disciple of Simmel.

Scientific Management

During the industrial revolution, the machines that mass-produced goods in factories and extracted ore from mines were expensive, complicated, and prone to breakdown, so they required expert attention. Trial and error by machinists slowly led to the development systematic ideas based on mathematics (especially calculus) and physics to guide equipment design and maintenance.

---

26. For a thoughtful consideration of why Simmel's ideas matter to organizational theory, see Kanter and Khurana (2009).

By the middle of the nineteenth century, the men[27] who did this work had organized themselves into a new profession—mechanical engineering—but had to struggle to get capitalists to accept their claims of expertise (Krause 1996; Shenhav 1999). In the late nineteenth century, mechanical engineers expanded their reach from tending industrial equipment to fixing the social systems in which that equipment operated, responding to capitalists' discovery that running such complex organizations well was exceedingly difficult. The result was scientific management and the creation of a new profession, industrial engineering.

Scientific management aimed to increase worker productivity and organizational efficiency—indeed, the proponents of scientific management legitimated efficiency as a management goal (Shenhav 1999). Industrial engineers offered a tempting solution to the problem of industrial inefficiency. Many were in the U.S., in part because their emphasis on logic, rationality, and system was congruent with the ideals of the Progressive movement (Shenhav 1999), which swept across America in the first two decades of the twentieth century and which sought to promote "continuity and regularity, functionality and rationality, administration and management" as solutions to the problem of social order (Wiebe 1967: 295). You could think of scientific-management scholars as precursors to the denizens of Silicon Valley who today believe that technology can fix anything. But scientific-management scholars did more than that—they acted as intermediaries between owners and workers, applying scientific ideals to resolve industrial strife, which had grown more common in the late nineteenth and early twentieth centuries.

The most prominent proponent of scientific management was Frederick Taylor (1911).[28] He sought to increase industrial efficiency by redesigning industrial work through six simple steps (Shenhav 1999):

1. Find the most productive worker.
2. Break this worker's job into its simplest components and formalize them into a set of rules and procedures that all other workers can follow.
3. Analyze human capacities to perform this formalized job.

27. As far as I can tell from reading histories, these were all men.

28. Taylor's book was one of the most influential in management (Bedeian and Wren 2001). But unlike the research traditions described above, scientific-management research was not led by any single individual. Although Frederick Taylor's writing is (and was) the best known, he was far from being this theory's sole source of inspiration. The shift from individual scholar to collection of scholars has continued: all research traditions I discuss from this point on involve multiple scholars.

4. Hire and train unskilled workers.
5. Set goals for them consistent with their human capacities.
6. Link financial and career rewards to task performance.

Taylor proposed "conception by superiors, execution by subordinates" to discover "the one best way" to organize and manage. He believed that manual laborers were not capable of carrying out the design of work. The side benefit of this belief was a secure position for Taylor and other industrial engineers, because it suggested that they should be given control over work practices. Taylor also emphasized economies of specialization: tasks should be highly fragmented and grouped into narrow jobs, which in turn should be grouped within limited functions. Finally, Taylor held that workers are best motivated with money, promotions (to jobs that pay more), or threats of dismissal, and that they must be controlled directly with rules and oversight. Taylorism found its apotheosis in the huge Rouge River plant of the Ford Motor Company—although neither Henry Ford nor his engineers had read Taylor's work.

One consequence of such fine specialization in job design is that it dehumanizes work, thereby degrading and deskilling workers (Braverman 1974). This was revealed most powerfully in *Working*, an oral history of working life by journalist Studs Terkel (1972). He interviewed dozens of people in all kinds of occupations—including a grocery-store bagger, a gas-station attendant, a bartender, a teacher, a professional athlete, and an actor—to find out how they felt about their jobs. Thus, although Taylor was a devout Quaker who held a utopian view of how technology could improve the world (Hinings and Meyer 2018: 21–23), he was Marx's ideal villain, disempowering workers and empowering their supervisors. Paradoxically, his ideas dovetail nicely with Marxist analysis of corporations and employment arrangements: Taylor's assumption that workers respond to incentives is consistent with both Marx's theory of industrial capitalism and Weber's theory of bureaucracy.[29]

Taylor's fellow-travelers included Henry Gantt, the inventor of the Gantt chart (Gantt 1916) and the husband-and-wife team Frank and Lillian Gilbreth, who pioneered time-and-motion studies (Gilbreth and Gilbreth 1917). In France, the mining engineer Henri Fayol ([1916] 1930) developed fourteen "principles of management" that paralleled Taylor's. Fayol's focus was broader than Taylor's, as he considered the role of management in general, which he divided into four responsibilities: forecasting and planning, organizing (i.e., designing formal organizational structures), commanding and controlling,

---

29. For a thoughtful review of Taylor and other engineering-based approaches to organizations, see Shenhav (1999). For engaging diatribes on the non-scientific nature of scientific management, see Stewart (2006) and Lepore (2009).

and coordinating workers with interdependent tasks. His conception of organizations was less mechanistic than Taylor's. Those differences may explain why Fayol's ideas had more lasting influence on management scholars than those of Taylor and most other proponents of scientific management. What remains of scientific management is, however, critical: the unquestioned assumption in management practice that efficiency is a fundamental goal, which is a basis of organizational design. Consider, for instance, the strict attention to efficiency in assembly lines in fast-food restaurants and factories.

Human Relations

Given its draconian nature, firms that applied the principles of scientific management often faced resistance from their workers. In response, some management scholars in the 1920s and 1930s sought an alternative approach, which came to be labeled "human relations." It was sympathetic to workers and sought to understand their needs and the informal social norms and processes prevailing in the workplace. And it was fundamentally pragmatic in that it sought to improve worker productivity, similarly to scientific management. But human-relations scholars strove to ameliorate the problems created in organizations that were designed according to the rigid, mechanistic principles of scientific management: staff boredom, low morale, absenteeism, conflict, and turnover (Follett [1927] 1941; Mayo [1933] 1960).

The first scholar working in this tradition was Mary Parker Follett.[30] Most observers describe her work was a preface to, rather than part of, the human-relations school, perhaps because she never held an academic position, due to prejudice against women in academia; instead, she became a social worker. That said, her work had the same goals and focused on many of the same phenomena as later human-relations work. Her thinking was influenced by her undergraduate studies in philosophy and politics. As a social worker, she observed the problems that the urban poor had with employment, leading her to do industrial research. Her focus was on how workers come together to coordinate their tasks through informal peer relations and how managers can ethically lead them and exert power over them (Follett [1927] 1941). In democratic societies, she argued, managers should try to enable the cooperation of employees—participation that is willing rather than coerced through compensation or threats of dismissal. Her emphasis on informal processes in work groups stands in sharp contrast to scientific management's concern for formal supervisor organization and control of front-line workers. Follett's impact has

---

30. For a review of Follett's work, see Ansell (2009).

ebbed and flowed. British human-relations scholars continued to be influenced by her. And Chester Barnard's reflections on his leadership of AT&T, which inspired the Carnegie School that I discuss below, were influenced by Follett's thinking about communication and informal exchanges in organizations (Barnard [1938] 1968). But after Barnard, Americans scholars did not pay much attention to her ideas.

Most scholars point to three men as the pioneers of the human-relations school: Elton Mayo, Fritz Roethlisberger, and William J. Dickson.[31] Guided by Mayo, Roethlisberger and Dickson conducted an experiment concerning the physical conditions of work at Western Electric's Hawthorne plant (Roethlisberger and Dickson 1939). Rather than pinpoint the physical factors that improved worker productivity, they discovered puzzles. When they turned up the lights in a "test" group's workroom, productivity rose. But when they did nothing to the lights in a "control" group's workroom, productivity also rose. And when they turned the lights in the "test" group's workroom down again, productivity again rose. They interpreted these results as being due to common social factors—in particular, the extra attention the researchers were paying to workers. This became known as the "Hawthorne effect": managerial attention improves worker morale, which in turn improves productivity. They conducted a dozen other experiments to determine what other changes might improve worker morale and thus productivity.

Their studies were immensely influential in psychology, sociology, and management. They also inspired the founding of a journal, *Human Relations* (http://journals.sagepub.com/loi/hum) that is still published today. Human-relations studies are laudable in that they seek to balance the technical efficiency needs of the employing organization with the human needs of the organization's workforce. But they were criticized for their core concern for management interests and their conception of workers as mere tools to achieve management goals, even as they recognized that workers had social and emotional needs. In particular, Roethlisberger and Dickson's studies were beset by myriad flaws, including lack of adequate controls, confounds (slow workers were replaced by fast workers and incentives were changed), and dismissal of contrary evidence (Perrow 1986). A later reanalysis revealed that 90 percent

31. Other influential human-relations scholars included Luther H. Gulick and Lyndall F. Urwick (1937), who focused on improving government bureaucracies by blending principles of scientific management with those of human relations; Rensis Likert (1967), who pioneered his eponymous scales in surveys of managers measuring organizational climate and decision-making styles; Kurt Lewin (1947), who pioneered field theory and whose organizational work focused on leadership styles; and Abraham Maslow (1943), who developed a theory of human motivation. For an insightful critique of this research tradition, see Perrow (1986).

of the findings were due to things like incentives, quality of inputs, and layoffs elsewhere in the plant (Franke and Kaul 1978). This history should give all scholars of organizations pause, as it clearly demonstrates that we should not limit ourselves to considering the arguments proposed, but also carefully and objectively weigh how research is designed and the empirical evidence that supports or counters our arguments.

Post-War Organizational Sociology

After World War II, sociologists began to study organizations in earnest again. Their work is sometimes labeled "institutional," because they focused on the distinctive character of organizations, which often transcends the mere technical production of goods or services (Selznick 1957).[32] It was spurred by the translation of Weber's writings into English—*From Max Weber: Essays in Sociology* appeared in 1946, and *The Theory of Social and Economic Organization* in 1947—which prompted new ways of thinking about organizations.[33] American sociologists began to assess how bureaucratic real organizations were, and when they diverged from Weber's ideal type, why they did so. Following Weber, they adopted a cultural perspective to investigate the values that permeate organizations and the subjective meanings and interpretations shared by people in organizations.

This line of work began at Columbia with Robert Merton and his students. Merton analyzed many things that Weber ignored, such as the dysfunctions of bureaucracies—the things that they did poorly (Merton 1940), which Merton

32. Indeed, this work is often labelled "old institutionalism," to distinguish it from "new institutionalism," which I discuss in chapter 6. But that label was not applied until decades after the post-war research was done. I discuss post-war organizational sociologists as a group because many today conceive of them as such, although I am uncomfortable with reading history backward. Because this research tradition has fuzzy boundaries—it includes virtually all North American and French sociologists who studied organizations qua organizations between the 1940s and 1960s—my discussion undoubtedly omits several scholars. Moreover, there are sociologists who seldom, if ever, studied organizations, but whose ideas are related to those of post-war organizational sociologists, including George Herbert Mead, Charles Horton Cooley, Robert Park, W. I. Thomas, and Everett Hughes. And there is related research in economics that influenced some post-war organizational sociologists, including work by Thorstein Veblen, John Commons, and Westley Mitchell, as well as in political science, by Woodrow Wilson and L. A. Willoughby. To keep this section short, I do not discuss those scholars here. Scott (2003) provides an overview of this broader body of work.

33. Of course, some sociologists such as Robert Merton, Philip Selznick, and Robert Park read Weber in the original German—as did Peter Blau, a refugee from Austria. But translating Weber's work into English made it more widely accessible to American sociologists.

argued led to "unanticipated consequences," meaning outcomes that are not anticipated when planning action (Merton 1936). Unanticipated consequences occur because decision makers do not know everything that affects organizations, or because they apply ideas that worked in the past to deal with new circumstances where the ideas do not apply. For example, David Sills's (1957) study of the National Foundation for Infant Paralysis (now the March of Dimes) revealed how that charity's volunteers shifted from their original goal of alleviating polio—the value of which became moot after the polio vaccine was developed—to eradicating childhood diseases in general. In their work, Merton's students questioned Weber's theory and in doing so, extended it to consider informal aspects of organizations—power, conflict, culture, and informal social groups—and their impact on formal goals, rules, and procedures (Selznick 1949; Lipset 1950; Gouldner 1954; Blau [1955] 1963; Lipset, Trow, and Coleman 1956; Sills 1957). Their studies also showed how cultural, economic, and political factors shape organizational goals, structures, and operations. Finally, these studies were phenomenon-focused, concerned with the problems that individual organizations grappled with, as well as society-wide issues (Selznick 1996).[34]

For example, consider Selznick's (1949) study of the Tennessee Valley Authority (TVA), a federal agency that was part of Franklin Roosevelt's New Deal charged with damming rivers to generate electricity, control flooding and improve navigability, preserve forests, and economically develop this poor rural region. Selznick revealed that the TVA was constrained by external actors—that is, state colleges (except Black-serving colleges) and wealthy (White) farmers. When the TVA co-opted local elites by bringing them into leadership positions, its own goals were fundamentally altered because they had to take these new leaders' goals and interests into account. In the same vein, Gouldner's (1954) study of a gypsum mine and factory demonstrated that bureaucratic rules have histories: who initiates them (bosses or workers), why (due to external or internal issues), and how (through authoritarian, consultative, or participative decision-making) determines how they are understood and how well they are accepted. Blau's ([1955] 1963) analysis of a state employment bureau and a federal law-enforcement agency revealed how people in organizations responded to changes in formal rules and procedures, and in the process developed parallel, informal social relations and cultures that subtly reshaped their formal structures. The emphasis was on how informal organizational elements became institutionalized—that is, became accepted and enduring parts of organizational goals, activities, and structures.

One of the most influential pieces in this line of work was Selznick's (1957) *Leadership in Administration*. This essay distinguished between organizations

---

34. For reviews of this work, see Haveman (2009) and Reed (2009).

and institutions—that is, organizations that are and are not institutionalized. Institutionalization involves creating order, stability, and deeper meaning out of what had been unstable, disorganized, and narrowly technical activities. Concern for institutions can also be found in work by a wide array of American sociologists outside the Columbia group, notably Arthur Stinchcombe (1959), Charles Perrow (1961), Joseph Gusfield (1963), Mayer Zald (Zald and Denton 1963), Burton Clark (1970), and Paul Hirsch (1975).

Much post-war research was concerned with the communities in which organizations operated. For example, the beginning of Gouldner's *Patterns of Industrial Bureaucracy* (1954) described in detail the city where the organization was headquartered, the town where the local plant and mine operated, and the surrounding villages and farmland. It also described the ethnic and occupational backgrounds of the plant and mine workers, and put them and their employer in historical perspective.

In Europe, French sociologist Michel Crozier (1964) studied uncertainty, power, and conflict through a comparative ethnography of the French postal bank and the French national manufacturer of cigarettes and matches. Inspired by American organizational sociology, he argued that bureaucratic rules grant workers, even lower-level ones, considerable discretion, because rules can never be complete enough to handle non-routine situations; on this point, see also Blau ([1955] 1963). When faced with uncertainty that they can control, even lower-level workers acquire considerable informal power and prestige. In the cigarette factory Crozier studied, maintenance mechanics had power because they were the only ones who could keep the cranky machinery, which was central to the production process, working.

Crozier's work inspired generations of scholars, especially in France (e.g., Friedberg 1997; Musselin 2001; Borraz 2011) because of his insistence that national culture constrains both formal and informal organizational features, and how people maneuver within organizations. In North America, these ideas had scant impact on research (Anteby 2017), which is surprising, because Crozier's focus on power and conflict as sources of change and inertia in organizations has clear implications for all three contemporary perspectives on organizations. For example, the idea that workers benefit when they monopolize knowledge about how to do specific tasks (what Wilmers [2020] called "job turf") is central to Crozier's analysis.

The Carnegie School: A Decision-Making Theory of Organizations

Around the same time, three professors at Carnegie Tech (now Carnegie-Mellon University)—Herbert Simon, James March, and Richard Cyert—developed a new approach to the study of organizations that viewed organizations as decision-making systems.[35] Their backgrounds in economics, political science, and statistics, and the iconoclastic culture of the institution in which they worked, led them to take a decidedly interdisciplinary approach. They combined insights from political science, economics, and psychology, as well as from early management scholars, and conducted both statistical and formal mathematical analyses.

Simon's key insight, for which he won the Nobel Memorial Prize in economics in 1978, first appeared in the first major work in this tradition, *Administrative Behavior* ([1946] 1976). In this book, he recognized that human beings are not the perfect calculators and decision makers that economics had assumed. People lack perfect information and cannot consider all possible options when making choices, especially when the issues at hand are not clearly formulated and time is limited. Moreover, people's preferences are not fully fleshed out, which helps explain why issues are not clearly formulated. As a result of these real-world limits on rationality, people are boundedly, if intendedly, rational.[36]

Extending Simon's ideas on bounded rationality, the second major work in this tradition, March and Simon's *Organizations* ([1958] 1993) defined rationality in terms of "administrative man," and assumed that his choices are always exercised with respect to a simplified model of the real situation. Organizations overcome bounded rationality by having managers give subordinates clear goals, define standard operating procedures, monitor subordinates' performance, and adjust goals and procedures as necessary. Organizations also seek to balance the incentives they provide to workers with the contributions they seek from them. In sum, decision-making in organizations involves satisficing (getting a satisfactory outcome, one that is good enough, given goals)— rather than optimizing (getting the best possible outcome). Alternative courses of action and consequences of action are discovered sequentially through search processes; search stops when decision makers find an alternative that satisfies their objectives. Over time, organizations develop repertoires of action that provide alternatives for choices in recurrent situations. Each repertoire of action deals with a restricted range of consequences and is only loosely connected to other repertoires. Thus formal organizational structure improves human decision-making—although it cannot optimize it.

35. For a review of their research program and a projection for future research, see Gavetti, Levinthal, and Ocasio (2007).

36. Simon's work was heavily influenced by Chester Barnard, an executive at AT&T whose *The Functions of the Executive* ([1938] 1968) reflected his experience, and which was, in turn, influenced by Mary Parker Follett ([1927] 1941). Perrow (1986) reviewed Barnard's ideas in depth.

The third major work in this tradition, Cyert and March's *Behavioral Theory of the Firm* ([1963] 1992), focused on how organizations set and manage goals, through a process they labeled "problemistic search." They identified five types of goals: production, inventory, sales, market share, and profit. For each, they proposed that goals are set based on an organization's past goals, its past performance, and the past performance of comparable organizations. Problems are identified when performance does not meet goals or does not match the performance of comparable organizations. Moreover, goal formation is a process of continuous learning over time. In addition, they recognized that organizations are not unitary actors; instead, different units have different goals, knowledge, and preferences. Therefore, goal formation is a bargain struck between groups with different information and interests, and decision-making requires negotiation and, often, the use of formal power.

Later work by March (Cohen, March, and Olsen 1972; March and Olsen 1976; Levitt and March 1988) focused on ambiguity in decision-making, memorably claiming that decision-making in organizations is similar to sorting through the contents of garbage cans:

> Organizations can be viewed for some purposes as collections of choices looking for problems, issues and feelings looking for decision situations in which they might be aired, solutions looking for issues to which they might be an answer, and decision makers looking for work. . . . One can view a choice opportunity as a garbage can into which various kinds of problems and solutions are dumped by participants as they are generated. The mix of garbage in a single can depends on the mix of cans available, on the labels attached to the alternative cans, on what garbage is currently being produced, and on the speed with which garbage is collected and removed from the scene. (Cohen, March, and Olsen 1972: 1–2)

This work is more pessimistic about organizational rationality and thus about organizational effectiveness than earlier Carnegie-school work. It holds that goals are ambiguous (they may not even be clear until after decisions are made), people in organizations have conflicting and inconsistent goals and information, and experience can be misleading because the past can differ in important ways from the present. As a result, learning from experience can be "superstitious," meaning that decision makers respond to what they perceive as happening, rather than to what really happened. Or learning can be ambiguous, if it is not clear what happened. Or different people can learn different things, based on different goals and information, in which case conflict ensues and is settled through rhetoric and power plays. Decisions can also be shaped by emotion, intuition, tradition, and faith, rather than by coldly rational calculation. Finally, organizations can fall into "competency traps" (Levitt and

March 1988) when they stick to the routines they know, even though alternatives (which often seem radical and risky) would yield better performance.

This school of thought is most evident today in analyses of individual and organizational learning (e.g., Miner and Haunschild 1996; Baum, Li, and Usher 2000). It also underpins much contemporary research on organizational innovation and change (e.g., Cohen and Levinthal 1990; Greve 1998).[37] And its spirit of theoretical creative destruction, which undermines rationalistic accounts of decision-making and learning, inspired institutionalist research about legitimacy, conformity with institutionalized rules, and the decoupling of formal structure from actual behavior.

Contingency Theory

From Weber to the human-relations school, much early organizational research sought to figure out what combination of structures and practices would optimize performance. Other work—in post-war organizational sociology and the Carnegie school of decision-making—conducted in-depth studies of organizations, documenting how unlikely—if not impossible—it was for researchers to discover any "one best way" to organize, and explaining why. Spurred by these accumulated findings, many scholars in North America and Britain in the 1960s developed new lines of inquiry that harnessed the increasing power of computers to compare multiple organizations. These scholars directed their attention to something that scientific-management and human-relations scholars had ignored: organizational environments. They characterized organizational environments along three dimensions: complexity, meaning the number of environmental elements dealt with simultaneously by any organization; uncertainty, meaning the variability over time of those elements; and interdependence, meaning the extent to which those elements are related to one another. But they did not neglect the importance of internal human factors; instead, they developed a combined socio-technical approach that balanced technological imperatives with human concerns. This research tradition came to be labeled "contingency theory," because of the idea that organizational design choices are contingent on environmental conditions.[38] The basic precepts can be summarized in three sentences: *There is no one best way to organize. All ways of organizing are not equally effective. The best way to organize depends on the environment in which the organization operates.*

---

37. These ideas also influenced transaction-costs economics (Williamson 1975), which is prominent in strategy research.

38. Hinings and Meyer (2018) provide a detailed overview of these lines of research.

There were three variants.[39] The first, *structural contingency theory*, emphasized differences in the essential designs and operations of organizations in
placid versus rapidly changing environments (Burns and Stalker [1961] 1994;
Woodward [1965] 1994; Thompson 1967; Lawrence and Lorsch 1967; Pugh
et al. 1968; Pugh, Hickson, and Hinings 1969; Blau and Schoenherr 1971).
Structural contingency theorists surveyed large numbers of organizations and
assessed the interplay among many features of organizations, most notably
production technology, organizational size, and environmental uncertainty.
They viewed environmental conditions as exogenous to organizations and
argued that to perform well, decision makers had to adapt their organizations
to environments. More recent work dug deeper into organizations, using direct observation, interviews, and/or archival data to discover how workplace
interactions, reward systems, and external (state) policies and (societal) values
fit together (e.g., Perlow, Gittell, and Katz 2004). This variant had strong roots
in Weberian analysis of bureaucracies, as it followed Weber's path of searching
for ideal combinations of organizational features.

The second variant, *strategic contingency theory* (Hickson et al. 1971; Child
1972), held that organizational structure and performance are not fully environmentally determined. Rather, power-holders within organizations (usually
managers) decide on strategic actions. Not only do managers choose organizational structures, but they also choose relevant performance standards and
manipulate environmental features by deciding which markets to target.

The third variant stressed the *information-processing requirements* of navigating
environments (Galbraith 1973). As environmental complexity and uncertainty
increase, and as interdependencies among organizational tasks increase, so
does the amount of information needed to perform those tasks. This, in turn,
requires organizations to do one of two things: (1) reduce the need for information processing (e.g., by changing structures, specifically by grouping together people whose tasks require them to mutually adjust their actions, or by
creating slack resources such as inventories of spare parts) or (2) improve the
capacity to process information (e.g., by strengthening formal hierarchies and
forging horizontal relations to improve communication).

All three variants of contingency theory were broadly and ambiguously
formulated. The precise form of contingencies was never specified, which
made it impossible to empirically test (i.e., falsify) them (Schoonhoven 1981;
Perrow 1986). Eventually, contingency theory evolved into an orienting

---

39. Others who surveyed this research perspective divided up contingency theories in ways
that differ in some details but are generally congruent with my own categorization scheme. See
Perrow (1986) on "technology" and Guillén (1994) on "structural analysis."

strategy for organizational sociology—a meta-theory. All contemporary research on organizations recognizes explicitly that organizational structure is contingent on external forces and that organizational performance is jointly contingent on structure and environment.

From the 1970s Onward:
Contemporary Perspectives on Organizations

By the mid 1970s, organizational theory was dominated by three lines of research: the human-relations school, the original Carnegie School, and contingency theory. All three were rationalist and adaptationist: they assumed organizations sought efficient and effective performance, those in charge could survey what was happening on the ground and determine what to do to improve performance, and organizations could easily change strategies and structures to improve performance.[40] Moreover, the original Carnegie School and contingency theorists viewed organizations as atomistic actors, where those in charge could make decisions and take action based on internal preferences, constrained only by the availability of resources. These theories also ignored societal inequality, social solidarity and division, and the concentration of corporate power—issues that had come to the forefront of public consciousness by the 1970s and forced many scholars inside the field of organizations and outside to rethink their research objectives.

In reaction to these assumptions, and to address broader social concerns, organizational scholars developed a seemingly bewildering array of new theories and proto-theories. Almost all can be fit into three categories—demographic, relational, and cultural—that reflect underlying conceptions of social structure and agency. *Social structure* is the "thingness" of societies that makes them powerful forces in our lives. Structure consists of recurring patterns and resources that create opportunities for and constraints on individual and collective action (Giddens 1984; Sewell 1992; Emirbayer and Mische 1998). *Agency* is the willingness and capacity of social actors (individuals, groups, and organizations) to alter their situations (sometimes even entire societies) by acting. Willingness involves actors' understanding of what can and should be done and their own interests in doing something; capacity involves access to the resources required to do something. Thus, social actors' positions in social structures determine how they maneuver and thus whether they maintain existing

---

40. This summary excludes later work by James March (e.g., Cohen, March, and Olsen 1972; March and Olsen 1976) that was critical of rationalist thinking and proposed instead that due to ambiguity and conflict, decision-making is often shaped by emotion, intuition, tradition, and faith.

structures, alter them, or create new entirely ones. Another way to put it is that social life evolves recursively: social structure shapes what agents can and want to do *and* agents' actions either maintain or change social structure.

Sociologists have conceived of social structure in three main ways: in terms of demographic characteristics (Blau 1977, 1994), social relations (White, Boorman, and Breiger 1976; Emirbayer 1997), and cultural schemas (Berger and Luckmann 1967; Sewell 1992; Mohr 1998). These conceptions of structure logically imply three different conceptions of agency. If social structure is demographic, consisting of cross-cutting distributions of actors across salient positions in social space, then actors' motivations and capacity to act derive from those positions, absolute or relative. If social structure is relational, consisting of connections and exchanges among actors, then actors' motivations and capacity to act are constituted by connections and exchanges. If social structure is cultural, consisting of actors' shared, patterned understandings of reality and possibility, then actors' motivations and capacity to act are shaped by these shared understandings. These three perspectives are shared by many management scholars, although they seldom use the terminology of social structure and agency.

The distinction between these three conceptions of social structure and agency is seen in most sociological research, including the study of organizations. A central concern for *demography*—the distribution of individuals, groups, and organizations along salient dimensions of social life like individual age or organizational form—characterizes internal organizational demography (Blau 1977; Kanter 1977; Baron and Bielby 1980; Pfeffer 1983) and organizational ecology (Hannan and Freeman 1989). A focus on webs of *relationships* among individuals, groups, and organizations drives research on social capital (Granovetter 1973; Bourdieu 1980; Coleman 1988; Burt 1992), power within organizations (Emerson 1962; Pfeffer 1981), and resource dependence (Pfeffer and Salancik 1978; Burt 1983). A focus on *culture*, meaning shared beliefs, norms, and values, is reflected in institutional approaches, both micro (Scully and Creed 1997) and macro (Meyer and Rowan 1977; DiMaggio and Powell 1983; Scott 2014), and in research on organizational culture (Pettigrew 1979; Smircich 1983; Schein 1996).

On the macro level, the demographic and cultural perspectives developed as corrections to rationalist and adaptationist theories that were in use in the 1960s and early 1970s. Both perspectives broke with the assumption that organizations could be adapted to external conditions. For the demographic perspective, inertial pressures prevent adaptation, while for the cultural perspective, conforming to institutional rules can prevent efficient operation. On the micro level, the development of the demographic and cultural perspectives was driven by a combination of concerns about social inequality and pragmatic concerns about the performance of individuals, groups, and organizations, and the inadequacy of existing theories to explain puzzles researchers observed in real organizations. As a result, both micro demographic and cultural research broke with the assumption that behavior in organizations is geared toward efficiency and effectiveness. Instead, the micro demographic perspective holds that behavior is driven by differences between people along salient positions in social space, which generate inequality in access to many outcomes controlled by organizations, as well as conflict and barriers to communication. For its part, the micro cultural perspective emphasizes how routines, implicit logics, and meaning-making processes drive individual and collective behavior in ways that are often at odds with efficiency.

The relatiosnal perspective developed at the same time in response to a different concern: that focusing on the atomistic characteristics of social actors (attitudes and attributes) is too limited, because atomistic characteristics are secondary and relationships between individuals and collectives involving exchanges of value (goods, services, information, deference, symbols) are primary. Therefore, we must put relationships—between people, work groups, and organizations—front and center, and recognize that the emergent properties of organizations and their constituent elements are based on their patterns of relationships. Relationships determine what people can and cannot do, as well as what they are motivated to do because individuals, groups, and organizations are interdependent. As I explain in chapter 5, the notion that relationships are central to social structure was revolutionary when it began to really take hold, in the 1960s and 1970s, because the most prestigious sociology research involved either abstract or functionalist theory that was difficult, if not impossible, to test empirically.

These three perspectives have been applied to the study of both formal and informal organizational features. As explained in chapter 1, formal features include the configuration of jobs and work units, and the designed linkages between them (the "organization chart"), as well as written rules and documented programs and procedures. Informal features include the actual (as opposed to formally designed) communication channels (who really talks to whom, not just who is supposed to talk to whom), the actual behaviors of workers (what they really do every day), and informal norms and practices (what is expected and valued). The formal and the informal are often only loosely coupled, as informal practices and norms often deviate from formal procedures and rules (Weick 1976). Moreover, these three perspectives have been used to explain behavior at five nested levels of analysis: the individual, the small group or organizational subunit, the entire organization, the industry, and the interorganizational field. Table 3.1 summarizes the three perspectives and explains how they are used at different levels of analysis.

TABLE 3.1. Three contemporary perspectives on organizations

	Demographic perspective	Relational perspective	Cultural perspective
Basic principle	Social actors' positions in social space determine patterns of action by defining opportunities for action and constraints on action.	Social actors' relationships determine patterns of action by defining opportunities for action and constraints on action.	Social actors' shared understandings/schemas determine patterns of action by defining opportunities for action and constraints on action.
Social structure consists of . . .	. . . cross-cutting distributions of individuals and collectives (e.g., organizations, subgroups) along salient dimensions of social position (e.g., individual gender or education level, family income, organizational age or size).	. . . relationships between individuals and collectives (e.g., organizations, families) involving exchanges of value (goods, services, information, deference, symbols).	. . . shared cognitive representations (cultural schemas)—shared understandings of reality and possibility—beliefs, norms, values, and expectations of what is (not) done/possible/good.
Individual social, psychological, and economic experiences as an organizational member depend on . . .	. . . internal organizational demography: (a) individuals' demographic characteristics (e.g., gender, race or ethnicity, age, tenure, education area and level) and (b) their demographic characteristics relative to other people in the organization.	. . . egocentric and dyadic relations, and ego's position in the larger network: (a) individuals' relationships with other people and (b) the number and structure of relationships they have with people inside and outside their organization.	. . . individual sense-making and learning; symbolic interactions: individuals' beliefs, norms, values, and expectations, which they develop through interactions with others.
Group/subunit behavior and effectiveness (conflict, innovativeness, creativity, ability to make good or timely decisions, turnover, etc.) depend on . . .	. . . internal organizational demography: group or subunit size and demographic composition (eg, gender, race or ethnicity, age, tenure, education level, income)	. . . aggregated networks of interpersonal relations: the number and structure of relationships among group or subunit members—egocentric and dyadic relations aggregated to the group level.	. . . social cognition and symbolic interaction: shared understandings—the beliefs, norms, values, and expectations that group or subunit members develop through interaction; a group's underlying logic(s).

Organization functioning, behavior, and performance (structural change, growth/shrinkage, economic performance) depend on . . .	. . . organizational ecology: an organization's own characteristics (e.g., age, size, technology, target markets, identity) and the characteristics of other organizations (e.g., their numbers, their absolute and relative sizes)	. . . interorganizational networks: (a) relationships between an organization and other organizations and (b) the number and structure of relationships among organizations in the organization's industry or field.	. . . the social construction of reality: shared understandings—the beliefs, norms, values, and expectations organizational members have developed through interaction; underlying logic(s).
Industry structure and vital rates depend on	. . . organizational ecology: the number of organizations in an industry; their aggregate size, their distribution along salient dimensions (e.g., age, size, technology, target markets); and their identities (social codes).	. . . interorganizational networks: the structure of relationships among organizations within an industry.	. . . the social construction of reality: shared understandings—the beliefs, norms, values, and expectations that industry members have developed through interaction with each other and with external actors; the industry's underlying logic(s).
Field emergence, structure, and stability depend on . . .	. . . community ecology: the number of organizations in different industries within a field; field member organizations' aggregate sizes, distributions along salient dimensions, and identities.	. . . interorganizational networks: the structure of relationships among field member organizations, both within and across industries.	. . . the social construction of reality: shared understandings—the beliefs, norms, values, and expectations that field member organizations have developed; the field's underlying logic(s).

Conclusion

The study of organizations has deep roots in sociology. Three of its founding fathers—Marx, Weber, and Durkheim—developed theoretical frameworks to understand the transition to modernity. For Marx, who emphasized class struggle, workplaces were arenas for the alienation, exploitation, and domination of workers, but also places where workers could forge a revolutionary class consciousness. For Weber, the rationalization of human activities that was the hallmark of modernity found its ideal-typical embodiment in rational-legal bureaucratic organization. For Durkheim, increasing specialization in the context of differentiated organizations necessitated forms of solidarity characterized by interdependence. Their ideas continue to exert broad influence on the study of organizations today.

Later theorists from sociology, management, political science, economics, engineering, and psychology focused less on placing organizations within sweeping narratives of history and attended more closely to meso- and micro-level processes that occur within and between organizations. Simmel called attention to processes of affiliation and hierarchy that resonate with contemporary relational research on organizations, and to the importance of numbers that is at the core of contemporary demographic research on organizations. Scientific-management and human-relations theories took a pragmatic approach, prioritizing managers' goals and asking how worker productivity and workplace efficiency might be optimized. Scholars in two other traditions reacted against this effort to find the "one best way" to organize and against the premise that organizational decision-making could be perfectly rational. Members of the Carnegie School highlighted constraints on information and decision-making, drawing attention to the bounded rationality of decision makers and thus limitations on rationality in the organizations they design and manage. Finally, contingency theorists stressed the role that complexities, uncertainties, and interdependence with elements of organizational environments play in shaping organizing processes and outcomes. Departing from the concerns of early scholars (Marx, Weber, and Durkheim), these later theories of organizations had little, if anything, to say about how organizations shaped social structure and contributed to or reduced inequality or other social ills.

The next three chapters trace the development of the three perspectives—demographic, relational, and cultural—that have dominated the study of organizations over the past four decades, and that developed out of frustrations with the assumptions of existing theories and concerns about social ills. The development of these perspectives made it possible to ask—and answer—new questions about organizations, such as "Why are women still paid less than men for the same work?", "Which is harder to change: younger or older organizations?", "Why do front-line staff at Disneyland act the way they do?", "Which group has the most influence on company policies, finance or marketing, and under what conditions?", "Why does the curriculum in third-grade classrooms differ from school to school in the same district?", and "Why do corporations move their headquarters to new locations, and what determines the locations they choose?"

4

The Demographic Perspective

THE MOST OBVIOUS or basic way to study organizations and the people in them is to study their attributes: such as how old or large organizations are, what goods and services they produce, and where they operate; then whether the people in them are male or female, their age, race or ethnicity, education, work experience, and so forth. This is precisely what scholars taking the demographic perspective have done. This perspective encompasses several streams of work about the attributes of organizations and the people in them that were motivated in different ways, ranging from desires to ameliorate social inequality along racial and gender lines, to solving puzzles in real organizations, to understanding whether change in social systems was driven by internal or external factors. To understand the motivations of demographic scholars requires an understanding of their research programs; so let me sketch those programs now. On the micro level, *internal organizational demography* analyzes individuals and small groups within organizations. This work studies the distribution of people in organizations along salient dimensions of social position such as gender and tenure (e.g., Kanter 1977; Baron and Bielby 1980; Pfeffer 1983). As I explain below, it has multiple roots in sociology, management, and social psychology. On the macro level, *organizational ecology* (sometimes called "population ecology," after the title of the first paper in that stream of work) analyzes entire organizations and industries. This work studies the distribution of organizations themselves along strategically or sociologically important dimensions, such as size and technology (e.g., Hannan and Freeman 1989; Carroll 1985). This work also has multiple roots, this time in sociology, demography, and evolutionary biology, which I detail below. A few demographic studies of organizations investigate connections between micro and macro, linking what happens to individuals in organizations, such as job mobility or status attainment, to what happens to organizations themselves, such as organizational founding, failure, or growth (Haveman and Cohen 1994; Stovel and Savage 2006; Sørensen and Sorenson 2007; Huffman, Cohen, and Pearlman 2010; Ferguson and Koning 2018). But micro and macro demographic research on organizations developed separately, and connections between the two levels did not appear for two decades.

I begin by describing why research on internal organizational demography began and how it evolved, and then do the same for organizational ecology.

Micro Research: Internal Organizational Demography

The 1960s and 1970s saw great social upheaval in the U.S. The civil rights movement began in the 1950s with a long series of protests against Jim Crow laws that enforced racial segregation in the South. These protests and related efforts to regain voting rights for blacks were often met with horrifying brutality. In reaction to press coverage of this brutality, the movement gained visibility and increasingly widespread support in the 1960s, culminating in passage of the Civil Rights Act of 1964. The women's movement also began in the 1950s, starting with the translation of *The Second Sex* ([1949] 1952) by the French philosopher Simone de Beauvoir, which chronicled the oppression of women throughout history and ridiculed contemporary gender relations. This movement gathered steam with the publication of *The Feminine Mystique* (1962) by the American journalist and activist Betty Friedan, which revealed the unhappiness of middle-class women and offered a scathing critique of the masculine-dominated social order. The Indigenous people's rights movement in Canada and the U.S., led by tribal councils in British Columbia and Québec, pushed to reclaim Indigenous sovereignty and force national governments to offer legal redress, including recognition of land claims, for over two centuries of broken promises. Organized opposition to the Vietnam War attracted a wide array of adherents ranging from high-school students to elderly nuns, all protesting a war that cost over a million lives, mostly those of Vietnamese, Cambodian, and Laotian civilians, and injured millions more. Finally, the leftist student movement erupted in the 1960s. Motivated by Southern (mostly Black) students' involvement in the civil rights movement (through the Student Nonviolent Coordinating Committee), protestors at Berkeley, Columbia, and other universities demanded freedom of speech on campus, an end to the Vietnam War, and equal civil and political rights for Black Americans. Together, these social movements revealed tremendous economic and political inequalities along multiple axes, striking at the core of social stratification systems that put White (usually Protestant) men at the apex—although these movements varied in their success at effecting lasting change.

In this time of social, cultural, and political turmoil, it is not surprising that many social scientists sought to investigate and ameliorate social inequalities. To this end, several groups of scholars contributed theoretical and empirical innovations that I place under the umbrella term "internal organizational demography." I trace their motivations and contributions in approximately chronological order.

First, the work of sociologist Rosabeth Moss Kanter was grounded in post-war organizational sociology and structural contingency theory (Kanter 1977). She was inspired by the women's movement and feminist critiques of organizations (e.g., Epstein 1971; Acker and Van Houten 1974) to place differences between the experiences of men and women at the center of her analysis.[41] Her thinking was also informed by Simmel's theory of numbers. Her methods— a combination of direct observation, interviews, surveys, and document analysis—yielded richly detailed data on organizational structure, power relations, and culture. Her goal was to understand the structural determinants of gender inequality, in contrast to current individual-based explanations, which often seemed to "blame the victim." As I explain below in some detail, she argued that numbers matter: when women are tiny minorities in organizations, they are highly visible and taken to represent their entire sex (as "tokens"), so their male coworkers have great difficulty communicating with them and fail to support them, which lessens women's social integration and commitment. She also argued that jobs are designed to reflect social stereotypes about what men and women should be and do, and so reinforce those stereotypes and the masculine-dominated social order.

A closely related theory of demographic similarity and difference was developed by Peter Blau (1977, 1994; Blau and Schwartz 1984), building on both his earlier contributions to post-war organizational sociology and structural contingency theory (Blau and Schoenherr 1971) and his research on social exchange (Blau [1964] 1992). Like Kanter, Blau's thinking was informed by Simmel's theory of numbers. Unlike Kanter, he did not characterize differences based on nominal variables like sex or gender and race or ethnicity as involving inequality per se, but organizational scholars who adopted his theory usually did so (e.g., Lincoln and Miller 1979). As I explain below, his arguments often paralleled those of Kanter: the more unequal the size of demographic subgroups, the more salient is subgroup membership, which hampers

---

41. Cynthia Epstein's book *A Woman's Place: Options and Limits in Professional Careers* (1971), cited by Kanter, is a neglected gem that carefully documented how the scant opportunities offered by employing organizations limited women's ambitions, recognition of and rewards for their work, and career advancement. Epstein argued that societal-level gender stereotypes influenced organizational decision-making. Yet a search of the Web of Science revealed no citations by organizational scholars, perhaps because of its focus on professions. This book merits more consideration by scholars interested in how organizations sustain gender inequality. Epstein's second book, *Women in Law* (1981), delves into how that profession disadvantaged women, and also merits more consideration.

communication and reduces trust. Similarly, the more varied group members are in terms of graded variables like age and education level, the more social interaction is inhibited.

Second, sociological social psychologists began to study inequality in terms of people's status in small groups (for a summary, see Berger, Rosenholtz, and Zelditch [1980]). Their development of status-expectations theory was motivated by concerns about how status hierarchies developed in group interactions—even among White men—and informed by Simmel's work on social interaction. This work recognized that nominal social categories like gender or race are often used to mark statuses with different social ranks (Ridgeway 1991). Their ideas complemented those of psychological social psychologists, who were developing a theory of social identity and social categorization (Tajfel and Turner 1979, 1986; Tajfel 1982). Neither group of social psychologists explicitly studied organizations, although the first group did focus on teams carrying out collective tasks, which translated quite naturally into organizational settings. Yet, as I explain below, their ideas guided many demographic studies of organizations.

Third, led by James Baron and William Bielby, many young scholars of social stratification and mobility found their interests in social inequality to be too broad to fit into the prevailing theoretical framework, which focused on relationships between people's status (education, occupation, and income) and their parents' status (Blau and Duncan 1967; Featherman and Hauser 1976, 1978). These young scholars were also frustrated that the framework offered no insights into how policy makers could ameliorate inequality. Inspired by contemporary social movements, Marxist critiques of capitalist systems (e.g., Braverman 1974; Blauner 1964; Burawoy 1977), and economic analysis of labor markets and job mobility (e.g., Doeringer and Piore 1971), these young scholars began to examine how organizations created pathways for or obstacles to social mobility, thus sustaining inequality. They focused on labor-market sectors (an oligopolistic core dominated by large firms vs. a competitive periphery of small firms) and, most germane for our purposes, the features of employing organizations (e.g., Bibb and Form 1975; Stolzenberg 1975, 1978; Kluegel 1978; Baron and Bielby 1980).[42] Yet a paucity of data limited the scope of their analysis to such simple features of employing organizations as size.

Fourth, management scholars also began to study internal organizational demography to solve puzzles they observed in real organizations. Why did old-timers think so differently from newcomers? Why was it so difficult to

42. Around the same time, management scholars also began to study the impact of organizations on inequality (e.g., Pfeffer 1977).

communicate, trust, and work with some organizational members, but so easy to communicate, trust, and work with others? Why did some groups within organizations, like R&D or sales teams, perform better than others? These pragmatic concerns led them to consider the social positions of organization members—starting with achieved characteristics like tenure, rank, or functional background—and to investigate both the causes and consequences of demographic distributions. Most prominently, Jeffrey Pfeffer built on Kanter's work and on work in human demography (Ryder 1965) to propose a new theory focusing on tenure (Pfeffer 1983). He argued that cohort size (the number of people with the same tenure) was correlated with the power that cohorts had, especially in organizations that espoused democratic ideals. And tenure distributions—such as whether or not there were big gaps between when cohorts arrived—were associated with factors ranging from conflict between cohorts, to turnover, to organizational performance. His work later expanded to study gender inequality (e.g., Pfeffer and Davis-Blake 1987) and his ideas had considerable impact on later management and sociology studies of other demographic variables.

In sum then, the study of internal organizational demography has several related theoretical foundations. Sociological *group interaction theory* holds that people prefer to interact with similar others (Simmel 1955; Blau 1977; Kanter 1977)—a phenomenon known as homophily (McPherson, Smith-Lovin, and Cook 2001). The *structural theory of stratification* holds that organizations are the meso-level structures that put people from different demographic groups in different positions—different in terms of power and potential for advancement—thus creating inequality (Pfeffer 1977; Baron and Bielby 1980). Sociological *expectation-states theory* holds that different levels of esteem and competence are attributed to people in different social positions, creating interactions in which these expectations become self-fulfilling prophecies (Berger, Rosenholtz, and Zelditch 1980; Ridgeway 1991; Ridgeway et al. 1998). Social-psychological *social identity and categorization theory* holds that we classify people to understand their behavior, and that our identity and self-worth derive in part from the groups we belong to (Tajfel and Turner 1979, 1986; Tajfel 1982). Both group interaction and social-identity processes result in sharp lines between in-groups and out-groups, generate stereotypes about groups (especially out-groups), and promote in-group biases. Finally, *demographic theory* explains rates of employee entry into and exit from organizations, as well as rates of social interaction as a function of the number of people in different social positions (Ryder 1965; Pfeffer 1983).

No matter their theoretical origins, all studies of internal organizational demography attend to "any categorical difference that has a significant impact on group interaction and outcomes" (DiTomaso, Post, and Parks-Yancy 2007:

474). Early work focused on gender (Kanter 1977; Wolf and Fligstein 1979) and tenure in the organization (Pfeffer 1983; McCain, O'Reilly, and Pfeffer 1983). Later research widened the focus to include age (Zenger and Lawrence 1989), race and ethnicity (Tomaskovic-Devey 1993; DiBenigno and Kellogg 2014), functional background and occupation (Smith et al. 1994; DiBenigno and Kellogg 2014), sexual orientation (Tilcsik 2011), social class (Rivera 2012; Laurison and Friedman 2016; Thomas 2018), and intersecting identities (Pager 2003; Correll, Benard, and Paik 2007; Pedulla 2014). Some of this work shows how nominal parameters (unordered categories) are transformed into graded parameters (hierarchical rankings) (Ridgeway et al. 1998): nominal attributes like gender, race or ethnicity, and functional background become axes of inequality, determining who gets authority, status, and material resources. For organizational scholars, this means that employing organizations are key sites for the production of group-based inequality (Pfeffer 1977; Baron and Bielby 1980).

Although these theories have very different origins, their implications are intertwined. Therefore, internal organizational demography is most easily classified and reviewed by level of analysis—by whether the outcomes under study occur to individuals or groups. Below, I consider research on both levels in turn, paying attention to how the underlying theoretical principles are invoked, often in combination.

Consequences of Demography for Individuals

The theories introduced above reveal that people—coworkers and supervisors—perceive people with different demographic characteristics (men vs. women, Blacks vs. Whites vs. Asians vs. Hispanics, engineers vs. English majors, old-timers vs. newcomers) differently, and treat them differently. These theories led to new research questions: Why do women and Blacks earn less than men and Whites? Is it better to have a boss who is the same race as you? Are women better off in work groups with mostly male members or those with a fairly even mix of male and female members? These and related questions led to three lines of research that I survey below: demographic (dis)similarities between focal individuals and others in their workplaces, demographic (im)balances in work groups, and the segregation of people with different demographic characteristics into different jobs and work units.

Demographic differences. The main issues are whether (or, for continuous variables like age, how much) focal individuals are similar to or different from others in their workplaces, and whether they are members of higher-status or lower-status groups. Membership in demographic groups matters because of *stereotyping*, generalizations from groups to individuals, which generate expectations of behavior (Allport 1954). For example, men are stereotyped as agentic (rational, achievement-oriented, autonomous, and inclined to take charge), while women are stereotyped as communal (concerned for others, collaborative, emotionally sensitive, and deferential) (Heilman 2012). Stereotyping harms lower-status group members by devaluing them and reducing their influence.

Although stereotypes can be moderately accurate about groups (Eagly and Diekman 1997; Jussim, Crawford, and Rubinstein 2015), they are far less likely to be accurate about individuals, because there is often greater variation in terms of personality, attitudes, and behavior within demographic groups than between them (see, e.g., Hyde 2014). Moreover, stereotype accuracy may not be due to innate differences between groups, but rather to differences in context. For example, gender inequality in the labor market and the overall status of men versus women varies greatly across countries, and these factors are strongly associated with the scores of boys versus girls in different countries on international mathematics tests (Penner 2008). Differences in achievement in mathematics, in turn, help drive gender differences in the representation of women in mathematics-heavy occupations: women constitute 57 percent of scientists in Lithuania and 54 percent in Norway, but only 25 percent in Luxembourg and Hungary (Thornton 2019). Finally, even favorable stereotypes about groups can have harmful effects because they are perceived as depersonalizing—the affected people are seen only as members of their group, not as individuals (Czopp, Kay, and Cheryan 2015).

Demographic differences generate inequality between members of demographic groups due to a combination of social categorization and stereotyping, homophily preferences, and status expectations, as summarized in Figure 4.1. Demographic differences hamper communication between people in organizations (Zenger and Lawrence 1989), reduce trust and liking (Dumas, Phillips, and Rothbard 2013), increase conflict (Lau and Murnighan 1998), and reduce cooperation (Chatman and Flynn 2001). These interactional difficulties reduce job satisfaction for workers and lower their commitment to their work groups and employing organizations (South et al. 1982; Zenger and Lawrence 1989; Smith et al. 1994). Demographic differences may reinforce each other; for example, racial or gender differences reinforce the interactional difficulties faced by workers in different occupational groups (DiBenigno and Kellogg 2014). As a result of these interactional difficulties, workers in lower-status demographic groups are devalued relative to coworkers.

The problem starts with hiring: devalued workers are less likely to be interviewed for jobs and hired into them. For instance, compared to otherwise similar men, women are less likely to be hired into organizations with higher fractions of men (Cohen, Broschak, and Haveman 1998; Gorman 2005). These differences may be due, at least in part, to human-capital differences (educational level and field of study). For example, women and men (and Blacks and Whites) in the U.S.

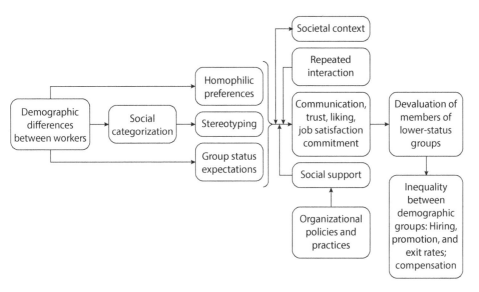

FIGURE 4.1. The impact of demographic differences in the workplace

tend to study different subjects, so women (and Black people) remain under-represented in science, technology, engineering, and mathematics fields, which lead to higher-paid jobs (Charles and Bradley 2009; Cech 2014). The educational attainment of women and some people of color has improved dramatically in recent decades, relative to that of White men (Gamoran 2001; Buchmann, DiPrete, and McDaniel 2008), but we do not know whether or how much the leveling of educational attainment has reduced inequality at work.[43]

When researchers use experimental or quasi-experimental methods to clearly identify causation and discount human-capital explanations, they find that bias, homophily preferences, status expectations, and stereotyping explain these patterns. For example, when symphony orchestras switched to "blind" auditions (job applicants performed behind a screen), female musicians' relative likelihood of advancing from preliminary auditions rose by 10 percent, while their relative likelihood of being hired more than doubled

43. Human-capital arguments ignore the fact that some differences in educational attainment between demographic groups are involuntary. For example, in the past, Jews were less likely than Christians to be admitted to Ivy League schools (Karabel 2005), which are recruitment sites for high-status and high-income jobs. Most egregious is that in the U.S., Black children have consistently been segregated in public schools with fewer resources than public schools catering to Whites, limiting Blacks' educational attainment—even though the Supreme Court declared racially segregated school systems unconstitutional in 1954.

(Goldin and Rouse 2000). Black men are less likely than otherwise identical White men to be selected for interviews, because Blacks are stereotyped as more dangerous—indeed, Blacks without a criminal record are less likely than Whites with a criminal record to be interviewed (Pager 2003). Similarly, Black job candidates with BAs are less likely to be interviewed than otherwise similar White candidates; moreover, Black job candidates from elite universities do no better than White candidates from less selective universities (Gaddis 2015). In the Netherlands, job candidates with Arabic names are less likely than those with Dutch names to interviewed (Blommaert, Coenders, and van Tubigen 2014).

Devalued workers are less likely to be promoted (Cohen et al. 1998; McGinn and Milkman 2013) and are compensated less. For example, male workers are paid and promoted more than female workers (Cohen and Huffman 2007; Gorman and Kmec 2009) because most organizations value stereotypically masculine attributes and behaviors over stereotypically female attributes and behaviors (Acker 1990; Budig 2002).[44] Stereotypes can even lead to inequality within disadvantaged groups. For instance, women with children suffer a "motherhood penalty": they are perceived as less qualified and promotable, are less likely to be interviewed, and are offered lower starting salaries than otherwise comparable women without children, because mothers are considered less competent and less committed to work (Correll, Benard, and Paik 2007). In contrast, men with children receive a "fatherhood bonus" relative to otherwise comparable men without children. Some of the demographic compensation gap may be due to demographic differences between workers and supervisors, which generate lower performance evaluations for workers (Tsui, Egan, and O'Reilly 1992; Roth 2004; Pearce and Xu 2012). Finally, devalued workers are more likely to exit organizations (McCain, O'Reilly, and Pfeffer 1983; McGinn and Milkman 2013), which can harm work-group and organizational performance, especially when labor markets are tight.

Despite these unfair patterns, there is hope: organizational procedures that increase accountability and transparency in personnel evaluation systems can reduce inequalities across demographic groups (Castilla 2015). Accountability makes decision-making more analytical and careful, while transparency reduces ambiguity about evaluation criteria. Inequalities across demographic groups can also be reduced by practices and policies that bolster social support from superiors and peers for members of lower-status groups. For example,

---

44. Economic theorists (e.g., Becker 1957) argue that demographic differences are proxies for quality when decision makers lack evidence about individual workers. But that argument is not borne out in research, which shows that demographic differences in decision-making persist even when decision makers have data on individual quality (Yang and Aldrich 2014; Botelho and Abraham 2017).

the use of cross-functional teams creates opportunities for members of lower-status groups to work with a wider range of people and demonstrate their capabilities, which reduces stereotyping and segregation (Kalev 2009), as well as wage differences between higher- and lower-status workers (Shin 2009). Organizations that support women, in particular by accommodating work–family balance, reduce the salience of gender at work and so reduce gender discrimination (Stainback, Ratliff, and Roscigno 2011). Findings from survey studies are in line with a randomized controlled experiment in one large firm: implementing a policy promoting employee control over work and increasing supervisor support for workers' personal lives reduced stress and increased job satisfaction for female employees (Moen et al. 2016).

The effects of demographic differences may decline with repeated interaction, which facilitates treating people as individuals, rather than members of a demographic group. Repeated interaction brings to the surface invisible (deep-level) similarities, such as personality, attitude, and values (Harrison et al. 2002), reducing the power of stereotypes. For example, basketball players get more playing time, net of past performance, from same-race coaches than from different-race coaches, but that gap decreases as coach–player relationships become longer (Zhang 2017).

Demographic effects on individuals may also depend on societal context, which can affect or reflect the strength of the underlying theoretical mechanisms. For example, "Black = danger" stereotypes are more salient when and where violent crime is rampant, which widens the Black–White hiring gap (Mobasseri 2019). Similarly, gay men were less likely to be interviewed for jobs in states where no laws guaranteed the right of gays to work and where the public was supportive of gay rights (Tilcsik 2011), and the gender gap in entrepreneurs' access to funding widened during the Great Recession (Thébaud and Sharkey 2016) because investors sought "safe bets," which they perceived as being male entrepreneurs. And, as noted above, changing organizational context, such as by making evaluations transparent and evaluators accountable, can reduce demographic pay gaps (Castilla 2015).

Tokens. Through social categorization and stereotyping, homophily preferences, and group status expectations, people who are numerical minorities become tokens who are perceived as representatives of their demographic subgroup rather than as unique individuals (Kanter 1977).[45] The presence of

45. Kanter divided organizations' demographic distributions into skewed (0–20% from the minority group), tilted (20–40%), and balanced (40–60%). The managerial ranks of most corporations in the 1970s, when Kanter was studying this issue, had skewed gender distributions, which is where she predicted tokenism would be most pronounced.

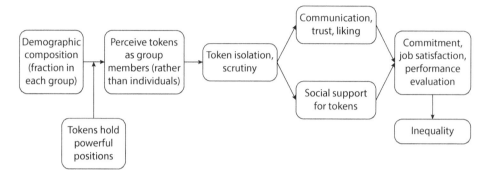

FIGURE 4.2. Tokens

tokens polarizes work groups, heightening boundaries between tokens and majority-group members. Tokens are perceived as different from coworkers and supervisors, and tokens perceive themselves as not fitting in ("not my kind of organization") (Tsui, Egan, and O'Reilly 1992: 554). As a result, tokens become isolated and more visible, more scrutinized. Tokenism hampers trust and communication between tokens and majority-group members (Zenger and Lawrence 1989), reduces majority-group support for tokens (Wallace and Kay 2012), lessens tokens' social integration into work groups and commitment to organizations (Mueller et al. 1999; Chattopadhyay 1999), and reduces their job satisfaction (Mueller et al. 1999; Wharton, Bird, and Rotolo 2000).

Tokenism has important implications for inequality, as Figure 4.2 shows. Tokens are evaluated in a biased way, which reduces their perceived performance, lessens their compensation, limits their chances of upward mobility, and increases their chances of leaving. Evidence from observational data support this argument. For example, female marines are rated lower than their male counterparts on combat readiness and forcefulness (Williams 1989), while Black and female managers are less likely than their White male colleagues to be promoted early in their careers (Thomas and Gabarro 1999; Bell and Nkomo 2001; Merluzzi and Sterling 2017). And barriers to upward mobility for minority groups generate pay gaps within jobs between minority-group and dominant-group members (Cohen and Huffman 2007). But to demonstrate that observed associations between tokenization and inequality are indeed due to bias, and not to some other mechanism, we need evidence from experiments or observational studies that use statistical techniques like fixed effects, matching, and regression discontinuity to better identify causal relations.

The effects of tokenism diminish when members of minority groups occupy powerful positions (due to homophily) and when the number of people in the

minority group increases (because minorities become more likely to be perceived as unique individuals, rather than as representatives of their group)
(Kanter 1977; Ely 1995; Cohen and Huffman 2007). For example, women and
people of color are more likely to be promoted to positions of authority when
there are more of them in their job (Wolf and Fligstein 1979; James 2000; Stainback and Tomaskovic-Devey 2009; Huffman, Cohen, and Pearlman 2010). And
when there are more workers of color in a job, they are better paid relative to
White workers (Joshi, Liao, and Jackson 2006) and less likely to leave their
organization (Zatzick, Elvira, and Cohen 2003; Sørensen 2004); both results
are due to homophily—when there are more workers of color in a job, they
have better ties to other workers, especially mentoring relationships.[46] But again,
identifying causation requires experiments or applying statistical techniques
like matching.

The effects of tokenism are different for members of socially dominant
groups (e.g., men, Whites) than for members of socially subordinate groups
(e.g., women, people of color): positive for the former and negative for the
latter because the former benefit from positive stereotypes and status expectations. For example, male nurses are treated differently from female nurses:
called on more frequently to lift patients, discouraged from specializing in
pediatrics, and perceived more favorably by patients and their families (Floge
and Merrill 1986; Williams 1989). This differential treatment generally accords
male nurses greater respect, autonomy, and prestige. As a result, token men, such
as male nurses, elementary-school teachers, librarians, and social workers, earn
more than their female peers; they also land on "glass escalators" (Williams
1995) that accelerate their promotion rates (Hultin 2003).

Segregation. People in different demographic groups are often segregated
into jobs that vary in quality. Specifically, lower-status groups like women and
workers of color tend to hold jobs with less status and power, and shorter
career ladders (Kluegel 1978; Baron, Davis-Blake, and Bielby 1986; Elliott and
Smith 2004; Huffman, Cohen, and Pearlman 2010), for reasons I discuss
below. Segregation is most apparent when researchers study fine-grained data;
for example, when studying physician specializations, such as surgery versus

---

46. Yet the opposite may occur: as the fractions of people in minority groups increases, their
turnover rates may increase and their promotion rates decrease. Such a pattern can be explained
by sociological theories of *group competition and group threat* (Blalock 1967). The combination
of homophilic tendencies and social-categorization processes, on the one hand, and group
competition and group threat, on the other, may generate non-linear effects: the former processes may dominate when minority groups are smaller; the latter when minority groups are
larger (Cohen et al. 1998; Zatzick, Elvira, and Cohen 2003; Yu 2013).

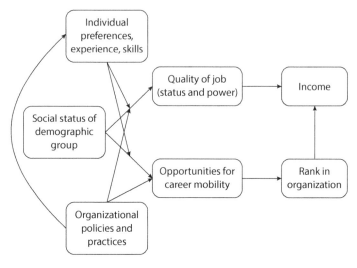

FIGURE 4.3. Segregation of members of demographic groups into different jobs

primary care, rather than physicians overall, or when studying human-resources versus sales managers, rather than managers overall.

Figure 4.3 charts arguments about segregation. Let me start with its consequences. Segregation increases inequality across demographic groups in terms of status and power, and therefore income. Holding jobs with lower career ceilings reduces the chance that women will reach the higher ranks of organizational hierarchies, relative to men (Baron, Davis-Blake, and Bielby 1986). Almost all of the pay gap between male and female workers in the U.S., net of human-capital controls, is due to gender segregation (Tomaskovic-Devey 1993; Petersen and Morgan 1995). A smaller, but still substantial, fraction of the pay gap between Black and White workers, net of human-capital controls, is due to racial segregation (Tomaskovic-Devey 1993).

Segregation is caused by both individual preferences, experience, and skills (supply-side factors) and organizational policies and practices that determine who is hired and promoted, and into what jobs with what compensation level (demand-side factors). On the supply side, women in the U.S. tend to study in different academic fields from men (Charles and Bradley 2009; Cech 2014) and therefore qualify for different kinds of jobs. Some of this difference is due to cultural factors, such as socialization into gender roles. For example, in the U.S., young women perceive themselves to be less proficient in mathematics than do young men, which makes women less likely to study mathematics, precluding them from majoring in science, engineering, and mathematics (Correll 2001), where jobs pay well. Even when men and women earn the same degrees and so are comparably qualified, socialization into gender roles leads women (more than men) to shy away from jobs that they perceive as offering a worse work–family balance (Barbulescu and Bidwell 2013). Some of the difference in job application preferences is due to stereotypes about the ideal worker: women are less likely than men to apply to jobs in areas that are stereotypically male, like finance. And because women expect to do more domestic work than men, they are more willing to trade money for work flexibility (Wiswall and Zafir 2018).

On the demand side, stereotypes and homophilic preferences push women into jobs where other women work and keep them out of jobs where men work (Roth 2004). But having more female managers can reduce sex segregation by increasing the fraction of women hired and promoted (Baron, Mittman, and Newman 1991). Using open rather than network recruiting strategies and having formalized personnel policies to guide hiring and promotion increase women's (versus men's) likelihood of holding managerial jobs, because decision makers have less opportunity to use stereotypes and act on homophily preferences (Reskin and McBrier 2000; Elvira and Graham 2002). Segregation also affects the way jobs are conceived, with female-dominated jobs being conceived as needing less specialized training than men's jobs; in turn, less training yields lower earnings for female-typed jobs than for male-typed jobs (Tomaskovic-Devey and Skaggs 2002).

Supply- and demand-side factors are interdependent. Gender differences in job preferences may be partly due to structural barriers, such as actual or perceived experiences with or expectations of discrimination. For example, when women expect they will not be offered jobs, which is more likely in stereotypically masculine jobs, they are less likely to apply for them (Barbulescu and Bidwell 2013). Similarly, women who have been rejected for top management jobs are less likely than similar men to apply to the same firms in the future, because they are more likely to interpret rejection as employer beliefs that they do not belong (Brands and Fernandez-Mateo 2017). People's job preferences and their concerns for balancing work and family are formed in response to gendered norms, with women more likely than men to favor jobs that facilitate that balance (Pedulla and Thébaud 2015). Educational aspirations, which affect who is qualified for well-paying jobs, are also patterned by concerns for balancing work and family; for example, women who have children are less likely than otherwise similar men to aspire to a professional or doctoral degree (Allison and Ralston 2018). Finally, changes in the demographic composition of people in jobs are associated with the status and rewards that accrue to those jobs (Pfeffer and Davis-Blake 1987; Bird 1990), but which is the cause and which is the outcome remains unclear.

Consequences of Demography for Groups
(and Entire Organizations)

Internal organizational demography has important consequences for groups, where "group" can mean a small team, an administrative unit, or an entire organization. Demography's impact on groups can be negative or positive. On the one hand, as demographic variation among group members increases, social categorization and homophilic tendencies reduce overall cohesion, because people are less likely to form social ties to demographically dissimilar others (Smith et al. 1994). As explained above, this leads to worse communication, more conflict, and less cooperation among group members. The causal mechanism is less social integration (less liking and respect among group members), which determines how much and how well they work together to achieve group objectives (Chatman and Flynn 2001; Dumas, Phillips, Rothbard 2013). On the other hand, as demographic variation among group members increases, their range of social relations and information sources expands, which can foster creativity (Ancona and Caldwell 1992; Reagans, Zuckerman, and McEvily 2004; Gibson and Gibbs 2006; Page 2007). This improves groups' ability to innovate and adapt to changing environments (Dezső and Ross 2012), which in turn improves performance. Increasing demographic variation among group members can also increase sales by reaching more diverse customers, thus improving group performance (Herring 2009). Figure 4.4 charts these causal mechanisms. But little research empirically tests these causal mechanisms (Lawrence 1997; for exceptions see O'Reilly, Caldwell, and Barnett 1989; Smith et al. 1994; Chatman and Flynn 2001).

On balance, the negative effects of demographic variation on group outcomes tend to be seen with highly visible ascriptive characteristics like race and gender; the positive effects with less visible achieved characteristics like education, tenure, and functional background. This may happen because variation in ascriptive characteristics involves more salient differences and so is more likely to trigger social categorization processes and homophilic tendencies. In contrast, variation in achieved characteristics involves fuzzier and more diffuse differences. Moreover, variation in achieved characteristics may be more likely to represent variation in information sources and ways of thinking, which enhance creativity and innovation. Yet ascriptive diversity is sometimes associated with task-relevant differences in information sources, while achieved diversity sometimes leads to the formation of subgroups that trigger social categorization and homophily (van Dijk, van Engen, and van Knippenberg 2011).

Meta-analysis of studies of workplace diversity shows that only when performance measures are subjective does ascriptive diversity have negative effects and achieved diversity positive effects (van Dijk, van Engen, and van

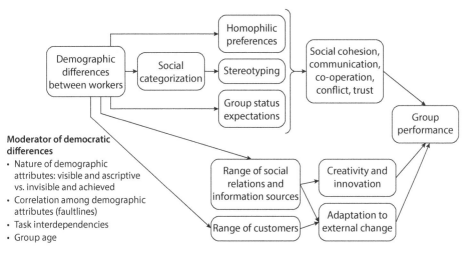

FIGURE 4.4. The impact of group demographic composition on
within-group interactions and performance

Knippenberg 2011). When performance measures are objective, there are virtually no significant effects of either type of diversity. Moreover, organizational
practices that actively engage managers in leading change efforts, such as recruitment outreach and management training programs, as well as transparency
programs that ease access for disadvantaged groups and increase managerial
accountability, can reduce any negative effects of ascriptive diversity (Kochan
et al. 2003; Castilla 2008, 2015; Dobbin, Schrage, and Kalev 2015).

Because discordant results about the consequences of demographic diversity were piling up in the late 1990s, research shifted in two new directions.[47]
First, scholars began to investigate relationships among multiple demographic
attributes. When correlations between demographic attributes are high, fault
lines cleave groups into relatively homogeneous subgroups: for example,
younger Blacks versus older Whites (Lau and Murnighan 1998). The stronger
the correlations, the worse demographic diversity is for group functioning and
performance (Reagans, Zuckerman, and McEvily 2004). Second, scholars
began to examine moderators—variables that might accentuate or attenuate
theorized relationships. Demographic diversity is more likely to have positive
effects when task interdependence is high, because group members must communicate more (Jehn, Northcraft, and Neale 1999). And the longer groups
work together, the more they know about each other, which may lead them to

47. For reviews, see van Knippenberg and Schippers (2007); Guillaume et al. (2017).

discount stereotype-based impressions and reduce frictions due to social categorization (Chatman and Flynn 2001; Harrison et al. 2002). In sum, all demographic factors can have positive or negative effects, depending on how they are correlated, what the context is, and what task is at hand.

In addition to its impact on social relations, internal organizational demography affects how groups and organizations are perceived by others. For example, when corporations have more gender-diverse boards of directors, investors tend to perceive that they value diversity more and stock price less, especially for firms with higher ratings for gender-equality efforts (Solal and Snellman 2019). In turn, this shift in perception reduces the market value of firms with more gender-diverse boards. That is not to say that all aspects of diversity are perceived negatively—consider for instance awards given to firms that are perceived as the best places to work for women or people of color. To paint a full picture, we need more research on external perceptions of organizations' demographic diversity.

Macro Research: Organizational Ecology

Organizational ecologists conduct demographic analyses where the objects of study are organizations rather than individuals (Carroll and Hannan 2000). As in other demographic analyses, the focus is on numbers of organizations and rates of founding and failure. Ecological work began in the early 1970s with Michael Hannan and John Freeman, two young scholars steeped in rigorous statistical analysis, evolutionary theory, and the theory of human ecology, all of which I describe below. Rather than studying the internal structures, processes, power dynamics, and cultures of individual organizations, as most organizational scholars did, they conceived of organizations as existing within ecologies of other organizations. And they focused on the dynamics of those ecologies—how they evolved through organizational founding, failure, change, and growth or contraction. In keeping with the upheavals of the 1960s and 1970s, which sought social change driven by factors internal to societies, they sought to understand whether change in organizational systems was endogenous or exogenous. And they were uneasy with existing theories that assumed organizations could easily and quickly adapt to performance shortfalls or to changes in their environments.

Although I label this theory demographic, it had multiple progenitors beyond demography alone. First it applied ideas from biological evolution (Levins 1968; May 1973) to explain organizational dynamics in terms of population numbers and environmental characteristics (Aldrich 1979; Aldrich and Ruef 2006). Second, and more sociologically, it applied concepts from human ecology, which began as studies of the dynamics of people in urban communities (some strands built on bioecology) before expanding its focus to human dynamics in many social, economic, political, and biological environments (McKenzie 1926; Park 1936; Hawley 1950, 1968; for a recent example, see Liu and Wu 2016). From both theories, organizational ecologists adopted the concept of the "niche," meaning the resources on which organizations rely and the customers or clients they serve, which ecologists translated to positions in social and geographic space. Variation in resources and customers drives competition and mutualism (i.e., mutually beneficial interactions), and thus organizational dynamics. Third, this perspective applied models and methods from human demography (Shryock and Siegel 1971; Keyfitz 1977) to explain how organizational features (e.g., age and size) affect rates of growth, change, and failure. This was relatively easy to do, because human demography is congruent with evolutionary models. But to apply human demographic models, ecologists had to recognize how organizations differ from humans: unlike people, organizations can experience many different kinds of "birth" and "death" processes, and can change their structures, goals, and demographic attributes in many different ways.

One key assumption of this perspective is the importance of "population thinking" (Hannan and Freeman 1989: 15). *Populations* are aggregates of organizations that produce similar goods or services, use similar resources, and have similar identities, so they occupy similar niches; empirically, populations are the same as industries. Examples include newspapers (Carroll 1985), labor unions (Hannan and Freeman 1989), breweries and soda manufacturers (Carroll and Swaminathan 2000; Hiatt, Sine, and Tolbert 2009), savings and loan associations (Haveman 1992), radio stations (Greve 1998), social movement organizations (Minkoff 1999), film producers (Mezias and Mezias 2000), and intergovernmental organizations (Ingram and Torafson 2010).

Ecology has four theoretical foci: structural inertia, organizational attributes such as age and size, density dependence, and resource partitioning. I discuss each in turn.

Structural Inertia

A central assumption of this perspective is that organizations change slowly, if at all, because of strong pressures against change—that is, inertia (Hannan and Freeman 1989). Past investments (sunk costs) in plant, equipment, personnel, and operating procedures; vested interests; limits on information; entry and exit barriers; and legitimacy considerations: all favor organizations that perform reliably and account for their actions, which requires highly reproducible (unchanging) organizational structures. If inert organizations are favored over changeable ones, inert organizations will be less likely to fail.

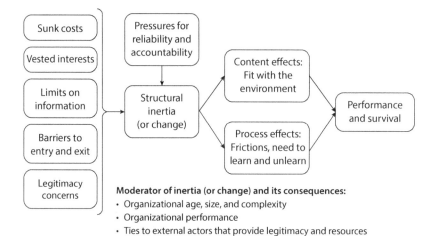

FIGURE 4.5. Structural inertia

When organizations do change, resources are diverted from operating to reorganizing, reducing organizations' effectiveness and increasing their chances of failure. Ecologists distinguish between the *process effects* of change, which stem from the inevitable frictions generated by undertaking change (e.g., the effort needed to dismantle old systems and built new ones) and which are inherently deleterious, and the *content effects*, which derive from how change alters fit with the environment and which may be good if fit is improved or bad if fit is worsened (Barnett and Carroll 1995). Figure 4.5 summarizes this argument in a causal model.

There is strong evidence to support the claim that it is quite difficult for organizations to change, whether in terms of entering new market segments and leaving old ones (Greve 1999; de Figueiredo, Rawley, and Rider 2015), developing new products and production processes (Henderson and Clark 1990; Tripsas 2009), or undertaking radical strategic and structural change (Huy, Corley, and Kraatz 2014). But evidence concerning the consequences of change is more mixed. Most research shows that organizational change harms performance, but some research shows that change can benefit organizations if they are performing poorly (Haveman 1992; Greve 1999). Organizations that change their strategies regularly (rather than irregularly) perform better (Klarner and Raisch 2013). Incremental change benefits larger firms more than smaller ones, because the latter have less capacity to absorb the harmful process effects of change (McKendrick and Wade 2010). Ties to external institutions that provide resources and confer legitimacy can buffer the harmful process effects of change (Baum and Oliver 1991; Minkoff 1999). Finally, although attempts to change can generate momentum, increasing the likelihood of subsequent change attempts

(Kelly and Amburgey 1991), those results are likely due to heterogeneity in organizations' propensity to undertake change, and they are reversed (yielding the finding that prior change reduces the likelihood of subsequent change) when researchers control for between-firm heterogeneity (Beck, Brüderl, and Woywode 2008).

When organizations seek to alter their formal features, change does not occur all at once; instead, a series of cascading changes unfolds because organizations' structural elements are interconnected (Hannan, Pólos, and Carroll 2007). For example, when General Motors adopted the multi-divisional form and pushed decision-making from central headquarters down to the division level, it had to adjust how different divisions (and units within divisions) coordinated their activities and how funding decisions were made (Sloan 1963). The more complex the organizational structure, the longer change takes, and the more time is spent directing resources away from operations and toward reorganization. Despite the risks, organizations undertake structural changes, because decision makers cannot foresee the costs of change relative to the benefits (Hannan, Pólos, and Carroll 2007).

The main implication of the inertia thesis is that organizational populations evolve through selection rather than adaptation. For example, from the 1870s to the 1920s, California savings and loans evolved from club-like associations that valued community and mutual aid to impartial bureaucracies that celebrated efficiency and individual rationality (Haveman and Rao 1997). But most change (72 percent) occurred through the differential founding and failure of different organizational forms, and only a little (28 percent) occurred through existing organizations adopting new forms.

If organizations are inert and if prevailing conditions (norms and values; production, distribution, and administrative technologies; political-legal systems; and so on) are "imprinted" on them when they are founded (Stinchcombe 1965), then they will reflect those conditions throughout their lives. There is considerable support for this thesis (Marquis and Tilcsik 2013). For example, in the seventeenth century, the Paris Opera was conceived as a royal academy, a high-status organizational form devoted to discussion of elite topics such as literature, fine art, dance, and science among academy members (Johnson 2007). But, pushed by the king, Louis XIV, whose permission was required to found any organization in the France of that era, it was launched as a hybrid of the royal academy and the commercial theater, a much lower-status organizational form. Not only did it incorporate elements of two organizational forms, but those elements persisted for centuries. Similarly, the organizational "blueprints" of high-tech firms reflect founders' imprints many years after founding (Baron, Burton, and Hannan 1999), while the functional backgrounds of the first people to occupy positions in startups influence successors many years later (Beckman and Burton 2007). And law firms whose founders come from firms with many women in leadership positions are more likely to promote women into leadership (Phillips 2005).

Imprinting can extend beyond individual organizations to interorganizational networks and geographic communities. For example, in American cities established before the airplane age, corporations developed board interlocks (the same director sitting on both boards) with firms near them; in these cities, board interlock networks remained highly localized even after air travel became common (Marquis 2003). And Norwegian towns and cities where mutual fire-insurance companies and savings banks were founded early in their history were, decades later, more likely to have cooperative stores founded (Greve and Rao 2012).

The theory of inertia has been challenged by two related lines of research. The first focuses on *routines*: patterns of interdependent actions that organizations develop to handle frequent tasks. Routines are viewed by ecologists as sources of inertia because they channel efforts along well-known pathways and away from novel pathways (Hannan and Freeman 1989). But routines can instead drive change and foster innovation (Nelson and Winter 1982). Change can result because each routine provides a repertoire of possible actions, rather than a single fixed or automatic action, which leaves room for agentic choices by organizational members (Pentland and Rueter 1994). Moreover, organizational members can refine routines in response to previous failures of routines or to new opportunities revealed by previous implementations of routines (Feldman 2000).

Second, research on *organizational learning* builds on the idea of problemistic search (Cyert and March [1963] 1992), which occurs when organizations perform below aspiration levels, search for solutions, implement them, and continue to monitor performance relative to aspiration levels (Greve 1998; Posen et al. 2018). Organizations learn from both their own experience and the experience of other (nearby or similar) organizations (Miner and Haunschild 1996; Baum, Li, and Usher 2000). But not all learning benefits organizations. Sometimes, experience can lead organizations into "competency traps": they learn to do what they are already good at, not what is best given the environment (Levitt and March 1988; Lawrence 2018). Moreover, learning can be "superstitious" when connections between causes and consequences are unclear; if so, subsequent change will fail to maximize performance (Levitt and March 1988). For example, U.S. investment banks "learn" that they should offer underwriting services for a new type of security (collateralized debt obligations) when they observe that share prices for other banks offering this service increase, even though such increases can be due to many other factors (Pernell-Gallagher

2015). Superstitious learning may be especially likely when the type of change undertaken is rare (Zollo 2009).

Organizational Attributes and Vital Rates

Much ecological analysis focuses on how attributes such as age, size, and product portfolios, affect organizations' performance and life chances. Because organizational ecology is an inherently dynamic theory, concern for the impact of age is most basic. There are three different arguments about the relationship between age and performance or survival. First, there may be a negative relationship, a "liability of newness" (Stinchcombe 1965). New organizations have more limited resources than established ones: few skilled employees and poorly developed management systems; constrained funding; no reputations because they have no track records; shaky relationships with suppliers, distributors, and customers; and often no finished products to sell (Stinchcombe 1965; Hannan 1998). Over time, organizations develop the capabilities they lacked at founding: they hire employees with specialized skills; design better management systems; develop reputations and solidify relationships with buyers, suppliers, and oversight agencies; and produce better goods and services. Therefore, older organizations perform more efficiently and effectively than younger firms, so older organizations are less likely to fail than younger ones.

Second, there may be a ∩-shaped relationship due to a "liability of adolescence" (Brüderl and Schüssler 1990; Levinthal 1991). Most newly founded organizations have stocks of resources, even if small, to buffer them from failure. Over time, two things happen. First, during the early years of their lives, new organizations deplete their stocks of resources as they invest in production and marketing and as they (inevitably) make mistakes; this increases their chance of failure. Second, however, they gradually develop—by learning from their mistakes, amongst other things—the capabilities they lacked at founding; thus, at some point they add to their stocks of resources and become more legitimate, and the chance of failure begins to decline. In combination, these dynamics yield a ∩-shaped relationship between age and failure.

Third, there may be a positive relationship, due to a "liability of obsolescence" (Barron, West, and Hannan 1994). Obsolescence hinges on whether organizations can adjust to changes in their environments, such as shifts in customer needs, technological innovations and the rise of competitors deploying those innovations, or changes in government or professional regulations that open up new lines of business and alter or close down existing lines. At founding, organizations may be aligned with environmental demands. But if they become more inert with age, and if external conditions change, then organizations' alignment with their environments will deteriorate, harming performance and raising the risk of failure.

Some empirical studies have confounded the effects of age with those of size. Findings that failure rates decline with age may be spurious, because there is a positive correlation between size and age, and a negative effect of size on failure (Hannan and Freeman 1989; Barron, West and Hannan 1994; Hannan 1998). Thus, although age on its own may have a negative effect on failure, after including size in the analysis, the effect of age could become positive, while the effect of size should be negative. The situation is complicated by variation between organizations of any age or size, not just in terms of their stocks of resources, but also in terms of how well they perform (and so add to those stocks of resources, net of expenditure) and how well they learn to keep up with innovations in their industry and improve their positioning vis-à-vis competitors (Le Mens, Hannan, and Pólos 2011). As a result, there are no universal relationships between age and size, on the one hand, and performance and survival, on the other. Instead, the relationships are contingent on learning, other organizations' attributes, and the environment.

Density Dependence

This theory holds that organizational founding and failure depend on population density, meaning the number of organizations in a population (in a given environment—usually conceptualized as a geographic region) (Hannan and Freeman 1989). As density increases, both the legitimacy of the focal population and competition within that population increase, as Figure 4.6 shows. The X-axis plots density; the Y-axis, the level of legitimacy (dotted line) and competition (solid line). The horizontal arrows show equal-sized changes in density at different levels of density. The vertical brackets show how much these changes affect legitimacy and competition.

As the figure shows, legitimacy increases at a decreasing rate, while competition increases at an increasing rate. So when density is low, increasing density produces a large increase in legitimacy and a small increase in competition, but when density is high, increasing density produces a small increase in legitimacy and a large increase in competition. Legitimacy makes it easier to found new organizations and reduces the chance of failure for existing organizations. Competition, for its part, makes it harder to found new organizations and increases the chance of failure for existing organizations. Therefore, density has a ∩-shaped relationship with founding (first increasing when the effect of legitimacy dominates, then decreasing when the effect of competition dominates) and a ∪-shaped relationship with failure (first decreasing when the effect of legitimacy dominates, then increasing when the effect of

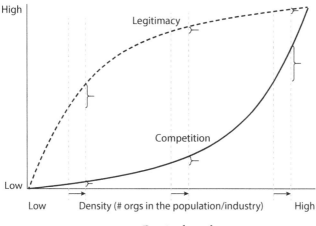

FIGURE 4.6. Density dependence

competition dominates). This theory has considerable empirical support (for a review see Carroll and Hannan [2000]).

The theory was refined to analyze subpopulations of organizations, based on characteristics such as size, market niche (specialist or generalist), technology, or location, and to consider interactions within and between organizational forms (Barnett and Carroll 1987; Carroll and Swaminathan 2000; Barnett and Woywode 2004). For example, a study of competitive interactions (those that harm one or both parties) and mutualistic interactions (those that benefit one or both parties) between commercial (for-profit) and mutual (non-profit) telephone companies in Iowa disaggregated population density according to technology and location relative to the focal organization (Barnett and Carroll 1987). This analysis revealed that the non-local density of both commercial and mutual telephone companies raised failure rates, as did the local density of commercial companies. These results indicate purely competitive interactions. Only the local density of mutual companies contributed to mutualistic interactions.[48]

Another approach to disaggregating density is to allow for the fact that organizations in a population often differ in degree rather than kind, so their niches overlap. For example, different voluntary social service agencies attract different kinds of members, in terms of age, gender, and education level, so

48. This finding is consistent with the finding in relational research, discussed below, that organizations that are structurally equivalent—they rely on the same or similar suppliers and target the same or similar customers—compete, while organizations that are in different network positions find it easier to coexist.

agencies whose niches overlap compete (McPherson 1983). Similarly, competition and mutualism among day-care centers varies with overlap in the ages of children enrolled: greater overlap raises failure rates, while greater nonoverlap lowers them (Baum and Singh 1994). And newspapers espousing adjacent ideologies experience more competition (e.g., right-wing vs. centrist) than do papers espousing ideologies at opposite ends of the political spectrum (right-wing vs. left-wing) (Barnett and Woyvode 2004).

Resource Partitioning

Resource partitioning theory also involves organizational subpopulations—in this case, organizations that serve a wide range of clients with a diverse array of products ("generalists") and those that focus on a more limited clientele, offering a narrower set of products ("specialists") (Carroll 1985). This theory developed out of Glenn Carroll's interest in urban sociology and his desire to understand organizations in their local environments, where it was feasible to assume that organizations interacted directly. His basic insight was that when organizations benefit from economies of scale and/or scope in production, marketing, or distribution, *and* they depend on resources (inputs and output) that have a single rich central region and poor peripheral regions, their resource "space" can become partitioned, with generalists occupying the center and specialists the periphery (Carroll 1985; for a review and summary, see Carroll, Dobrev, and Swaminathan [2002]). The resource space is most often conceptualized in terms of the attributes of the goods and services produced or the attributes of the customers who buy those goods and services, less often in terms of the resources required to produce goods and services, and rarely in terms of geographic location.

Resource partitioning happens because generalists compete with one another to control the rich center of the resource space by offering products with broad appeal or by offering many different products that appeal to many different customer segments. Specialists avoid competing with generalists in the center, instead exploiting peripheral regions by serving small customer segments with idiosyncratic tastes or needs. Because economies of scale and scope favor large organizations, the generalist subpopulation concentrates in the center and competition among them intensifies. Larger generalists outcompete smaller ones, reducing the number of generalists and increasing their average size. As generalists concentrate (that is, they become fewer in number but larger), they focus more tightly on the center of the resource space, so more of the periphery becomes available to specialists. Resource partitioning benefits specialists by sharpening the contrast between generalists and specialists, reducing competition between the subpopulations (Liu and Wezel 2014;

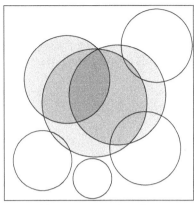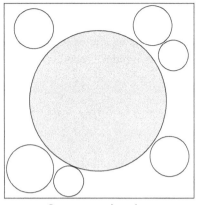

Uncosncentrated market   Concentrated market

FIGURE 4.7. Resource partitioning

Negro, Visentin, and Swaminathan 2014), so specialist failure rates decline and founding rates rise.

Figure 4.7 illustrates this theory, showing a two-dimensional resource space occupied by organizations that vary in size and location. The shaded organizations are generalists; the unshaded ones are specialists. The panel on the left shows an unconcentrated resource space with overlap between organizations' niches. The panel on the right shows a concentrated resource space dominated by a single large generalist at the center with smaller specialists on the periphery. Specialists' niches do not overlap with generalists'—the resource space is effectively partitioned between them.

Resource partitioning operates through three causal mechanisms: location relative to the center of the resource space, product customization, and demand for crafted (rather than mass-produced) goods and services (Carroll, Dobrev, and Swaminathan 2002). First and most basically, location relative to the center determines how large organizations will be: larger closer to the resource-rich center, smaller closer to the resource-poor periphery. Economies of scale and scope benefit larger firms, so organizations near the center become large generalists, while organizations near the periphery remain small specialists. Second, specialists can avoid competing with generalists by tapping into demand for specialized customer products and hand-crafted (rather than mass-produced) products (Carroll and Swaminathan 2000). The latter is possible when craft production is perceived by customers as yielding more authentic, higher-quality, or higher-status products than mass production.

Note the difference between this theory and standard industrial-organization economic theory, which predicts that the increasing concentration of firms in an industry will increase competition for all firms. Resource-partitioning theory assumes differences in the niches of specialists and generalists; such that while increasing concentration of generalists increases competition among generalists, it reduces competition between specialists and generalists.

Conclusion

Micro research

The demographic distribution of individuals in a group or organization is important because it shapes social interactions, who has power, and how (well) people work together. Moreover, the effects of demography are nested, with differences between organizational members affecting interactions in supervisor–subordinate dyads and work groups, and these interactions affecting individual, group, and organizational functioning. Finally, the uneven distribution of economic and status rewards conferred by schools, government agencies, and workplaces contributes to inequality among demographic groups. The triumph of this line of inquiry is its ability to explain the behavior of individuals and groups by reference to social structures rather than psychological states, which are often very hard to measure.

Notwithstanding its successes, the micro demographic perspective has three limitations. First, it has focused primarily on individual- and group-level outcomes, and has seldom sought to explain the behavior of organizations or external reactions to them. More internal demographic research that examines organization-level outcomes would develop a keener understandings of human agency in organizations. A few such studies exist, showing that internal organizational demography shapes power distributions (Shenhav and Haberfeld 1992), innovation (Wiersema and Bantel 1992), and performance (Smith et al. 1994; Herring 2009). We should extend this line of work and determine which demographic features influence which organizational outcomes, under which circumstances. Two factors that might condition such effects are organizational age and size. Because young organizations and organizations in emerging industries are relatively more plastic, they should be relatively susceptible to variations in the demographic profiles of their members. Their structures have not yet ossified, so they are more likely to be influenced by the idiosyncratic features of their workforces. Similarly, small organizations may be more affected than large ones by variations in demographic profile, because any individual in a small organization is likely to have a bigger overall effect on demography and thus organizational capabilities than is the same individual in a large organization.

Second, this work often fails to capture causal mechanisms, specifically access to information and social (dis)integration, which are consequences of demographic diversity and influence group performance (Lawrence 1997; Reagans, Zuckerman, and McEvily 2004). Instead, this work often assumes that demographic similarity or difference affects processes like communication, cohesion, and conflict without measuring these mediating factors. The solution is obvious: measure individuals' and groups' demographic profiles, their access to and use of information, and their social interactions. There is some work that does just this (Jehn, Northcraft, and Neale 1999; Reagans, Zuckerman, and McEvily 2004; Dahlin, Weingart, and Hinds 2005), but more could be done. Most of the work that captures proposed causal mechanisms is quantitative. It could usefully be augmented by research using ethnographic or in-depth interview techniques, or by process-tracing analysis of administrative data such as chains of memoranda or emails.

Third, much of this work is static and therefore ignores questions of how demographic homogeneity or heterogeneity is created and maintained (Lawrence 1997). Existing dynamic analyses have focused on tenure distribution; far less has been done on the dynamics of organizational gender and ethno-racial composition, even though gender and race are the main dividing lines in many societies (for an exception, see Ferguson and Koning 2018). Focusing more on how (and how much) gender and ethno-racial composition change over time would help explain important sources and consequences of inequality. It would also reveal to what extent organizations' demographic profiles are resistant to endogenous change (Davis-Blake 1992) and to how much we must rely on exogenous pressures, including the law, to equalize opportunity.

The dearth of dynamic research on organizational gender and ethno-racial composition is not due to any inherent theoretical limitation; instead, it is due to an almost complete lack of longitudinal data on demographic features other than tenure. It may be that we will remedy this situation only by launching a serious longitudinal survey of organizations' demographic profiles, one that could eventually be as widely used as the National Longitudinal Survey of Youth or the Panel Study of Income Dynamics. Alternatively, we could shed our parochial focus on North America and search for data on organizations and employees in state archives in countries that collect and store economic and social data centrally, such as France, Sweden, and Norway.

Macro Research

The distribution of organizations across salient demographic dimensions generates immense variation in organizational behavior and performance. Organizational ecologists study organizations' vital rates—of founding, failure, growth, and change—and explain these rates in terms of organizational characteristics and the material and cultural features of their environments. They have examined several related phenomena: the extent, causes, and consequences of organizational change or inertia, the impact on vital rates of organizational attributes such as age and size, and population characteristics such as density. In doing so, they have pushed much macro organizational research, including research taking the relational and cultural perspectives, to become dynamic.

A great strength of macro demographic research on organizations is its high level of paradigmatic consensus (Pfeffer 1993). Organizational ecologists know what outcomes to study (founding, failure, growth, performance, and change), what explanatory factors to consider (density, size, age, strategy, location, and technology), and what analytical strategies to employ (quantitative analysis of longitudinal data covering entire industries). Because scholars in this tradition have always built on and refined each other's work, they have produced solidly cumulative knowledge about organizational dynamics.

But this strength reveals a weakness: precisely because organizational ecology is such a "normal science" activity, some find it too narrow to interest anyone except ecologists themselves (Hedström 1992). Narrowness may overtake this paradigm because much work clarifies and refines the basic theory without extending it in truly novel directions.[49] To avoid this, ecological research could move beyond its reliance on quantitative data toward more qualitative research, which would help ecologists develop more nuanced insights into organizational *processes*, in contrast to the current focus on events and structures. We have little knowledge of how major organizational events—founding, change, and death—unfold: for example, how entrepreneurs gather the resources and confidence to found new ventures, or how firms' structures and processes are altered in the wake of merger. We would benefit greatly from seeing on-the-ground variation within and between organizations in these processes.

Ecological research should also be more deeply situated in time and place by incorporating contextual effects. This would allow scholars to assess whether ecological models are time-stationary: that is, whether parameters vary across historical periods. More historically sensitive ecological theory can also be developed by applying statistical techniques to demarcate historical periods using shifts in parameter estimates (Isaac and Griffin 1989) or macroscopic changes, such as fluctuations in political regimes and economic cycles (Dobbin and Dowd 1997). More historically sensitive research would have to attend to early contingencies and subsequent path dependence, meaning that

---

49. Despite my criticism, I applaud the evolution of organizational ecology research into studying organizational forms as socially coded identities, which combines the demographic and cultural perspectives to generate a rich and vibrant new line of work. I discuss this work in chapter 7.

the route taken determines the outcome, so that past actions affect future actions (Mahoney 2000; Pierson 2004).

Resource-partitioning theory is one of the most intriguing components of organizational ecology. But one thing is missing: recognition that specialist organizations are heterogeneous, while generalists are quite (if not completely) homogeneous. In Figure 4.7, the locations of specialists in resource space vary tremendously. That suggests that factors beyond those included in current resource-partitioning analysis—for example, temporal variation in level of demand or availability of inputs—might moderate relationships between market concentration among generalist organizations, on the one hand, and the vital rates of differently located specialist organizations, on the other. One way to investigate this would be to adapt Blau's measures of heterogeneity (when niches are measured using categorical variables) and inequality (when niches are measured using continuous variables). The more varied specialists are, the better their survival chances may be, especially when concentration among generalists is high. Ecologists could also distinguish between specialist organizations based on their niche categories or overlaps between their niches, similar (but not identical) to research on subpopulations (e.g., McPherson 1983). The impact of how proximate a focal specialist's niche is to those of other specialists is unclear, but that impact is likely to be greater when concentration among generalists is higher.

5

The Relational Perspective

THE PIONEERS of the relational perspective were dissatisfied with explanations of social life that ignored social context, meaning interaction, communication, and the resulting expectations of what people (should) do. As one early relational scholar put it, "[T]he survey is a sociological meat grinder, tearing the individual from his social context and guaranteeing that nobody in the study interacts with anyone else in it" (Barton 1968: 1).[50] Relational scholars insist that to explain behavior, we need to consider social context. As a result of this concern, they look at the social world in a way that is radically different from most other social scientists. Relational scholars hold that *social relations* are primary and the *attributes* of social actors (individuals, groups, organizations) are secondary. In other words, it's not about you, it's about who you know: who you know determines who you are, what you want to do, and what you can do (Granovetter 1985; Podolny 2001).

Relational scholarship is radical in a second way. It has always been deeply *empirical*. Measures of theoretical constructs and methods of gathering and analyzing data in statistically valid ways have developed simultaneously with theories. Concern for statistical validity has been essential, because analyzing social relations violates the assumption underlying the general linear model that observations are independent, which complicates statistical analysis. The close connection between the development of relational theory and advances in network-analysis methods stands in contrast to most demographic and cultural research, where theory has often been developed in advance of efforts to gather, measure, and analyze data. It stands in even starker contrast to a long tradition in sociology—one that was dominant in the U.S. before the 1970s—of grand theory, such as Marxism or structural-functionalism, and which is often only distantly related to data and methods, and so does not provide a

---

50. The same complaint could be made of interview-based and archival data studies that do not take broader social relations into consideration.

useful guide for empirical research.[51] Thus, early relational scholars in sociology were driven to connect their thinking about social context tightly with measures and methods in order to avoid the pitfalls they saw in much existing social science research.

Despite its double radicalism, thinking relationally has deep roots in the social sciences. Some scholars trace it back to Auguste Comte's efforts in the mid-nineteenth century to develop sociology as a systematic science (Freeman 2004), but most credit Georg Simmel as the first relational analyst. The quantitative analysis of interpersonal relations ("sociometry") began to appear in the 1930s, with seminal work by psychotherapist Jacob Levy Moreno and social psychologist Helen Hall Jennings, who sought to understand the therapeutic impact of relationships between patients and people in their social circles (Moreno 1932, 1934). Moreno's fame helped spread the study of interpersonal relations to the fields of sociology, anthropology, social psychology, and business, as diverse scholars tried to understand a wide array of phenomena they perceived as relational: kinship networks, stratified relationships among members of urban communities, and influence patterns among students, professionals, researchers, and factory workers (e.g., Bavelas 1948; Homans 1950; Festinger, Schachter, and Back 1950; Coleman, Katz, and Menzel 1957).

This approach became more systematic starting in the 1960s, with fundamental advances in graph theory—the formal (mathematical) analysis of networks (e.g., Harary, Norman, and Cartwright 1965; Lorrain and White 1971). At that time, Harrison White and his students at Harvard innovated theoretically and methodologically to counter grand theory and much existing statistical research, arguing that both neglected concrete social relations (Schwartz 2008; Breiger 2021 personal communication). Empirical work on social relations using network-analysis methods was made much easier by the development of ever faster, ever cheaper computing power. Communities of relational sociologists began to develop at several other schools, notably Michigan, Chicago, SUNY-Stony Brook, the University of California Irvine, and the University of Amsterdam (Freeman 2004). Many young scholars, motivated by the upheavals of the 1960s (like the young demographic scholars discussed above), seized on the relational perspective as a fresh approach to studying pressing social issues like social mobility, class relations, the power of the corporate elite, and cohesion and division in urban life.

In the 1970s, sociologists began to apply relational ideas and social network techniques to the study of organizations, both relations among individuals

51. For critiques of grand theory, see Mills (1959) and Merton (1968: 39–72).

and small groups inside organizations and relations among organizations (e.g., White 1970; Lincoln and Miller 1979; Burt 1983; Laumann and Knoke 1987). As meso-level social orders, larger than small groups but smaller than entire societies, organizations proved to be very fruitful topics for studying the nature, origins, and consequences of social relations. One particularly rich line of inquiry began as an attempt to understand social inequality based on access to good jobs (Granovetter 1973, [1974] 1995); it burgeoned into a rich stream of research that I discuss below under "social capital."

At the same time, management scholars Jeffrey Pfeffer and Gerald Salancik (Pfeffer and Salancik 1978; Pfeffer 1981) found that existing theories of organizations were problematic in two different ways. One line of organizations research was rooted in psychology and emphasized the power of leadership (e.g., Stogdill 1948; House 1977), which did not accord with empirical observations that leaders' actions were often constrained. A second line of organizations research, which was then just being formulated, viewed organizations as inert and unable to adapt to changes in their environments (Hannan and Freeman 1989), which did not fit with empirical observations that managers and other organizational members could be agentic and change organizations in fundamental ways. To overcome these limitations of existing theories, Pfeffer and Salancik drew on exchange theory (Homans 1950; Emerson 1962; Blau [1964] 1992) to develop resource-dependence theory, which I detail below. And, as I explain, this theory was soon enhanced by the application of formal social network ideas and techniques (Galaskiewicz and Wasserman 1981; Burt 1983).

Because understanding the relational perspective on organizations requires understanding formal social network analysis, appendix B introduces key topics in that field: graph theory, node characteristics, network structure, and roles and positions. Ideas central to this perspective have been applied to multiple levels of analysis, from individual to field. Therefore, I survey relational research topic by topic, starting with resource dependence and continuing through social capital, network structure, and roles and positions in social networks.

Power and Dependence: Resource-Dependence Theory

Based on exchange theory, much relational research assumes that *power is an attribute of a relationship*, not of an atomistic actor, and that *power is the inverse of dependence* (Emerson 1962; see also Homans 1950; Dahl 1957; Blau [1964] 1992). Consider the power-dependence relationship between two people, Pat and Chris. Pat's power over Chris—the pressure Pat can exert on Chris to do

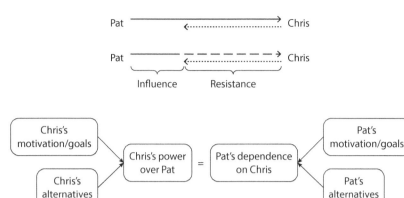

FIGURE 5.1. Power is the inverse of dependence

what Pat wants—is a function of Chris's dependence on Pat. The power Pat can exert is a function of Chris's motivation and alternatives: the more Chris wants what Pat can provide, the more Chris depends on Pat, and the more power Pat has over Chris. In addition, the more alternatives Chris has, the less Chris depends on Pat, and the less power Pat has over Chris. Figure 5.1 illustrates these ideas. At the top, it shows the pressure Pat can exert on Chris (solid arrow) and the pressure Chris can exert on Pat (dotted arrow). The two arrows are not equal, so Pat has more power over Chris than vice versa. The influence Pat can exert on Chris, net of Chris's power to resist, is shown at the bottom as the difference between the solid and dotted arrow.

The application of these ideas to the study of organizations is generally labelled *resource dependence* (Pfeffer and Salancik 1978) in recognition of the fact that individuals, groups, and entire organizations depend on exchange partners, whose goals and expectations may conflict with their own.[52] Internally, the division of labor creates task interdependencies; therefore, individual organizational members and work groups must rely on each other to accomplish their assigned tasks (Thompson 1967; Pfeffer 1981). Externally, organizations rely on financial institutions and government agencies for funding; on educational institutions, recruiting firms, and temporary agencies for people; on suppliers for raw materials and components; on distribution channels to get products to customers; on customers for sales; and on local communities, government agencies, and professional, trade, and business associations for approval (Pfeffer and Salancik 1978; Burt 1983).

52. For reviews, see Davis and Cobb (2010); Wry, Cobb, and Aldrich (2013).

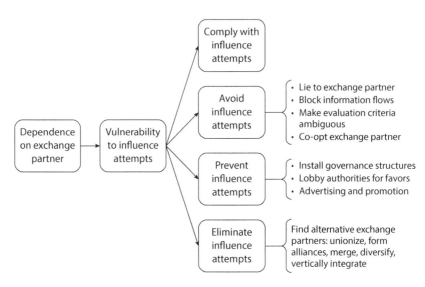

FIGURE 5.2. Responses to resource dependence

Dependence on exchange partners makes all social actors (individuals, groups, and entire organizations) vulnerable to influence attempts. For example, the French state cigarette manufacturer relied on equipment that often broke down; the resultant uncertainty empowered lowly maintenance mechanics (Crozier 1964). In a very different context—post-reform China—the willingness of state bureaucrats to exert control over firms they owned was determined, in part, by bureaucrats' dependence on firm financial performance (Walder 1995). Bureaucrats closer to the bottom of the administrative hierarchy (in rural townships and villages) were more dependent and more willing to push firms than those closer to the top of the administrative hierarchy (in central state ministries).

To reduce their vulnerability, social actors can do many different things (Pfeffer and Salancik 1978), as summarized in Figure 5.2. First, they can *comply* by following rules, acquiescing to norms, and imitating role models. But doing so leaves them vulnerable to future demands to comply. Second, they can *avoid influence attempts*, by lying (creating the illusion that they are satisfying demands), restricting information flows to and from exchange partners (creating bottlenecks), or manipulating evaluation criteria (making them ambiguous). For example, to court prospective students by inflating their graduates' employment figures, unscrupulous law schools counted as employed graduates with low-level jobs that did not require law degrees. But such means of avoiding influence pressures may backfire, as it did for law schools: one year after *The New York Times* exposed these practices (Segal 2011), the American Bar Association, on which law schools depend for accreditation, tightened its rules for counting employed graduates (Espeland and Sauder 2016).

Sometimes, avoiding influence attempts involves *co-opting* exchange partners; this was central to Selznick's (1949) pioneering analysis of the TVA. In the same vein, farmers in a Uruguayan non-profit co-opted the exchange partners of their exchange partners, and used the resulting two-step leverage to avoid their exchange partners' demands (Gargiulo 1993). And in China, after private firms began to flourish in the wake of economic reforms, the Communist Party admitted entrepreneurs and other businesspeople into its ranks in order to gain their support for the persistence of the single-party state (Dickson 2003).

Avoiding influence may also involve *preventing* exchange partners from making demands in the first place or, if that fails, preventing them from formalizing demands. One common approach is to lobby exchange partners for favors that benefit the lobbying organization over others. Another is to devise governance structures to manage demands. One example of governance structures involves open-source software pioneers, who devised "copyleft" licenses to safeguard ownership of all improvements, thus preventing derivative software from becoming proprietary (O'Mahony 2003). This was necessary because employees of commercial firms volunteered to improve open-source software and those firms might have claimed the improved software as their own property. The foundations that were assigned ownership of open-source software enforced licenses through discussion, cease-and-desist letters, and lawsuits.

Avoiding influence attempts is easier when actors have more power vis-à-vis their exchange partners. For example, American corporations' reactions to pressures to downsize has varied, depending on the relative influence of investors, top managers, and workers (Jung 2016). When investors had more power, they found it easier to accomplish both overall and managerial downsizing; when unions had more power, they could resist overall downsizing but push for managerial downsizing; and when top managers had more power, they could resist managerial downsizing—unless corporate governance mechanisms aligned top managers' interests with those of investors.

Third, actors can *eliminate influence attempts* by expanding their webs of social relations. This involves forming coalitions with others who can act in concert during interactions with their powerful shared exchange partner. The most common example is workers forming a union to act for them as a single voice in their negotiations with management, which can make employees' power more nearly equal to that of management, raising wages and improving workplace conditions (Freeman and Medoff 1984; Farber et al. 2018). Unions can also raise wages for non-unionized workers, either through the "union threat effect" (Freeman and Medoff 1984; Leicht 1989) or through spreading norms concerning fair pay (Western and Rosenfeld 2011). For organizations, expanding social relations can involve integrating vertically (taking over suppliers or distribution channels), expanding horizontally (diversifying into new product lines or customer segments and therefore reducing reliance on any set of exchange partners), or entering into partnerships (creating strategic alliances, joint ventures, or director interlocks),[53] or joining business groups or professional, industry, or regional associations.

Many studies of resource dependence focus on American corporations, a convenient sample due to the plethora of easily available data on publicly traded firms. American corporations are more likely to merge when they are mutually dependent with potential merger partners, but they are less likely to do so when they have less power over those partners than those partners have over them (Burt 1983; Casciaro and Piskorski 2005).[54] They are more likely to bring banking executives onto their boards of directors when they have more need for funding (Mizruchi and Stearns 1988). And they are less dependent on their main investment banks when they have more power, in terms of the overall number and dollar value of the deals they do, and the number of deals they do relative to the number their main investment banks do (Baker 1990). Director interlocks facilitate corporations' cooperating to influence politicians and shape public policy (Mizruchi 1992; Burris 2005). The impact of director interlocks can be augmented by social ties between corporate leaders based on their co-membership in organizations like the Business Roundtable and the Chamber of Commerce (Vogel 1989).

It is important to differentiate between horizontal and vertical dimensions of power-dependence relationships. Within organizations, at every level in the hierarchy, people are formally invested in power to surveil and direct people at lower levels; this power is formal in that it resides in the position held, not in the person holding the position (Weber [1968] 1978). Vertical (i.e., hierarchical) power is formally conferred on supervisors by organizational decision makers, and workers formally agree to work under the authority of supervisors. In contrast, horizontal power derives from task interdependencies (e.g., between work groups at the micro level or between partner firms

---

53. The differences between two of the forms of business partnership are subtle. Strategic alliances are agreements between two or more companies to undertake a project together. Joint ventures are partnerships owned by two or more companies, in which profits and losses are shared by those companies. Director interlocks exist when one company's director serves on a second company's board, or when two companies' directors serve on the same (third) board.

54. Although a merger may initially be touted as a marriage of equals, one firm inevitably comes to dominate the other. As a result, all mergers are really acquisitions.

in joint ventures at the macro level). Vertical and horizontal power-dependence relations are not independent, as leadership roles emerge even in informal task groups (Carnabuci, Emery, and Brinberg 2018). Both vertical and horizontal power-dependence relations influence who gets power and what happens when they wield power (Pfeffer and Salancik 1978; Pfeffer 1981). With regard to vertical relations, changes in American antitrust laws and in American corporations' strategies and structures led to the successive rise of executives from different backgrounds: first entrepreneurs and manufacturing executives, then those from sales and marketing, and later those from finance (Fligstein 1990). With regard to horizontal relations, the strategies of Chinese listed corporations depend on their boards of directors, whose decisions are shaped by their own career experience. Firms whose boards are dominated by people with experience in the market (rather than government) sector are more likely to engage in mergers and acquisitions (Greve and Zhang 2017).

Between organizations, vertical ties are seen in flows of goods, services, and information through chains of organizations in buyer–supplier networks and flows of money in the opposite direction. Horizontal ties are seen in direct ties such as joint ventures and strategic alliances, and in indirect ties such as those mediated by corporate boards and business associations. For example, American automobile manufacturers benefit economically from exchanges with suppliers (vertical ties) when they and their suppliers are mutually dependent, because mutual dependence improves the quality of their information exchanges (Gulati and Sytch 2007). And startup firms with ties to more prominent alliance partners and equity investors (horizontal and vertical ties, respectively) undergo initial public offerings of stock faster and at higher market valuations (Stuart, Hoang, and Hybels 1999). Vertical and horizontal ties between organizations are interrelated. When executives of American corporations sit on the same boards as executives of their suppliers (horizontal ties), information flow between corporations and their suppliers (vertical ties) improves, which reduces uncertainty (Burt 1983).

Finally, on a societal scale, some scholars have argued that the dense corporate networks created by board interlocks have helped maintain a powerful economic elite by socializing newcomers, fostering solidarity, coordinating political action, and facilitating control over public policy (Mills 1956; Zeitlin 1974; Domhoff 1983; Useem 1984). Scholars have also argued that the same pattern develops from board interlocks in other countries (see Berkowitz et al. [1979] on Canada; Stokman, Ziegler, and Scott [1985] on western Europe) and international interlocks (Murray 2017). In this view, corporations are tools of elite control (Clawson 1980; Domhoff 1983). Yet the evidence to support this argument is mixed (Mizruchi 1996).

Actors in Organizational Research: Social Capital

Social capital is generally defined as the *resources and identities actors derive from social relations* (Bourdieu 1980; Coleman 1988; [Nan] Lin 2001; Podolny 2001).[55] It is important to recognize that this analysis encompasses both existing and potential social relations—that is, both exchange relations and the empty spaces among an actor's exchange partners (Burt 2005; Phillips 2013). On the micro level, social capital is generally defined in terms of individuals' ties to kin and schoolmates, to current and former coworkers, or to powerful or prestigious actors; it can also be defined in terms of work groups' ties to other groups or to powerful or prestigious individuals. On the macro level, social capital is generally defined in terms of organizations' ties to other organizations: suppliers, customers, government agencies, or professional, trade, industry, or regional associations. Between-organization ties may be rooted in individuals (e.g., directors in board interlocks) or organizations themselves (e.g., buyer–supplier exchanges of goods or services, ideas, and money).[56]

The pattern of social actors' relations affects their access to information and material resources; it also affects how social actors are perceived by others (Podolny 2001). In turn, both resources and perceptions can shape status, increase or reduce uncertainty, and thus drive many social, psychological, and economic outcomes. For example, people who get new jobs through social ties have a head start over people who come in "cold," as the former are better prepared and can more easily "time" their applications (Fernandez, Castilla, and Moore 2000). For this reason, job applicants who are referred by employee contacts are ten times more likely to be offered jobs than applicants without referrals (Fernandez and Galperin 2014). However, it can be difficult to mobilize social capital, especially if job seekers' contacts fear their own reputations would suffer if those whom they vouch for do not perform well ([Sandra S.] Smith 2005).

Within organizations, professionals and managers who have horizontal ties to people in otherwise disconnected groups have wider sources of information, perform better, are more likely to be promoted early, and earn higher

---

55. I dislike the term "social capital," because it invites naïve comparisons to economic capital. As my colleague Claude Fischer noted, using this term leads us to ask nonsense questions: "Where can I borrow social capital? What is the going interest rate? Can I move some of my social capital off-shore?" (Fischer 2005: 19). Despite my distaste for the term, I use it here because it has become popular as a metaphor for the resources and constraints that derive from positions in webs of relations.

56. For a review of research on social capital and organizations, see Sorenson and Rogan (2014).

salaries (Burt 1992, 2005). And bank officers with sparser and more hierarchical loan-approval networks (i.e., more ties to higher-ups) are more likely to
close deals than those with denser and flatter loan-approval networks, because
the former are better able to "sell" their deals to gatekeepers (Mizruchi and
Stearns 2001). Strong ties between people promoting organizational changes
and powerful others who are neutral to proposed changes allow change pro-
moters to co-opt fence-sitters and get changes approved, but strong ties to
powerful others who disapprove of proposed changes reduce the chance of
getting changes approved (Battilana and Casciaro 2013). At the top of corporate hierarchies, CEOs have higher compensation levels when they have degrees from more prestigious educational institutions and when they have more
seats on corporate boards (Belliveau, O'Reilly, and Wade 1996).

Social networks can affect the performance of individuals, groups, and entire organizations. For example, the British East India Company, one of the
first commercial organizations to operate globally, developed a dense, complex
network of exchange in the seventeenth century (Erikson 2014). Ships' captains traded at multiple ports, both for the company and (piggybacking on
company resources) for their own private gain. The ship's-captain trade network helped the East India Company monopolize trade with India and enriched many captains.

On the macro level, new firms have no track records on which to base evaluations, so observers use the reputations of exchange-partner organizations like
venture capital and law firms as proxies for quality. Biotechnology startups with
more prominent investors undergo initial public offerings of stock sooner and
at higher stock prices because they can "borrow" the prestige of their investors
(Stuart, Hoang, and Hybels 1999). The greater the uncertainty (proxied by
startup age and size), the bigger the benefit biotechnology startups get from
prominent funders. But organizations can also imperil their status through
interorganizational ties, if their partners' quality is questioned (Jensen 2006).
Such status concerns can prompt the dissolution of interorganizational ties.

It is important to remember that social capital involves not only resources,
but also *obligations*, which channel action along particular paths and preclude
action along other paths (Giddens 1984; Portes 1998; Lin 1999). For example,
coethnic ties can facilitate access to the resources immigrant entrepreneurs
need to launch their businesses, but those same ties can stifle entrepreneurs by
opening them up to requests for favors (Portes and Sensenbrenner 1993). The
impact of obligations derived from social capital can be surprising. For example,
among Kenyan stock-market investors, coethnic ties, which engender trust, can
leave investors open to fraud; in contrast, non-coethnic ties require monitor-
ing, which protects investors from fraud (Yenkey 2018). Finally, firms' ties to
powerful partners create the potential for coercion by those partners, even

TABLE 5.1. Strengths and weaknesses of strong and weak ties

Strong ties		Weak ties	
Strengths	Weaknesses	Strengths	Weaknesses
• Increase trust and mutual appreciation	• Can trap actors in "echo chambers"	• Provide access to novel sources of information	• Easy to manipulate alters and behave opportunistically
• Facilitate norm enforcement	• Foster collusion	• Constrain action less than strong ties	• Alters may have inconsistent role expectations
• Improve cooperation and information transfer	• Require considerable effort to develop and maintain	• Can spark creativity	

misappropriation of firms' resources, because powerful partners can wield outsize influence on firms (Katila, Rosenberger, and Eisenhardt 2008).

Tie strength. Different types of social ties—strong versus weak—generate different opportunities and constraints (Granovetter 1973). *Strong ties* are based on multiple currencies of exchange (information, advice, and/or money) or are very intense (in terms of time, intimacy, and/or trust). *Weak ties* are based on a single currency of exchange or limited in intensity. Strong and weak ties have different strengths and weaknesses, which Table 5.1 summarizes.

Strong ties, which bond actors tightly, improve knowledge transfer and facilitate norm enforcement, increasing trust and improving group functioning (Coleman 1988). At the micro level, strong ties between people facilitate innovation (Hansen 1999; Obstfeld 2005). For example, bioscience researchers who have stronger ties to other researchers generate more knowledge (based on citations to published articles), especially when the ties among their exchange partners are sparse (McFayden, Semadeni, and Cannella 2009). These researchers benefit from the trust and commitment of their strong ties and from the novel sources of information from others to whom they were not directly connected. In the same vein, when American bankers have stronger ties—involving social relations, not just business exchanges—with managers in client firms, they offer client firms lower interest rates on loans because strong ties promote sharing of private information, increasing trust (Uzzi 1999). The expectation of increased trust is borne out in research in a different setting—microfinance in Latin America—where borrowers miss fewer payment when they have personal ties to lenders (Doering 2018). In the same vein, temporary-staffing agencies with longer-term relationships to workers have better access to private information about workers' skills and abilities, which they can leverage to capture higher fees from client firms (Bidwell and Fernandez-Mateo 2010).

At the macro level, there are similar findings. Garment manufacturers that maintain strong (ongoing and exclusive) relations with subcontractors have better survival chances than manufacturers that maintain weak (arms'-length) relations, because strong relationships make it easier to forecast supply and demand using price data, improving manufacturers' and subcontractors' matching of production schedules, and reducing costs (Uzzi 1996). Stronger ties also benefit suppliers by making manufacturers more willing to pay higher prices (Elfenbein and Zenger 2014). Finally, strong (multiplex) ties between Japanese firms generate mutual trust and appreciation, which benefits economically weak firms, even when it harms economically strong ones (Lincoln, Gerlach, and Ahmadjian 1996).

Notwithstanding the many benefits of strong ties, they have their weaknesses. Most obvious is that when networks are replete with strong ties, they can trap actors in "echo chambers." For example, garment manufacturers with mostly strong ties to suppliers perform more poorly when demand changes, because they are insulated from external information (Uzzi 1996). Similarly, investment firms' staff tend to be hired out of a narrow set of schools (where their current employees went) and they tend to do deals with other firms whose staff went to those same schools (their staff know those firms' staff), which boxes investment firms into specific positions in their industry (Rider 2012). Moreover, networks replete with strong ties can also promote collusion and unethical behavior (Baker and Faulkner 1993).

Weak ties tend to greatly outnumber strong ties because strong ties require far more effort to maintain. Therefore, people tend to have only a few close colleagues, but may have dozens of colleagues with whom they have a passing acquaintance. Because weak ties outnumber strong ties, people have far more potential information sources through weak ties than through strong ties. Because people to whom you are tied tend strongly to move in the same circles you do, the information they receive overlaps considerably with your own. People to whom you are tied weakly, by contrast, know people you do not and so they receive more novel information—they can offer insights into social worlds that you don't connect to in any other way, and so bridge social worlds. For this reason, acquaintances may be better sources of new information than friends—for instance, about finding a job or obtaining a scarce service (Granovetter 1973, [1974] 1995).[57] This is the mechanism underlying the "strength" of weak ties. This mechanism holds even though people to whom you are strongly tied may be more motivated to help you than people to whom you are weakly tied.

---

57. But this is not universally true. For instance, in socialist China, strong ties characterized by trust and obligation were needed to persuade state officials to assign jobs as favors (Bian 1997).

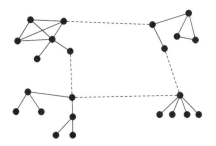

FIGURE 5.3. Bridging and bonding ties
Note: The solid lines indicate bonding ties within groups.
The dashed lines indicate bridging ties between
groups—i.e., ties that bridge structural holes.

Weak ties can *bridge structural holes* in networks, linking otherwise uncon-
nected groups (Burt 1992), as shown in Figure 5.3. The solid lines (within the
four groups) are bonding ties, which tend to be strong, while the dashed lines
(between groups) are bridging ties, which tend to be weak. When actors' networks include more such "bridging" or "brokering" ties, they are more likely to
be gatekeepers. Because the bridged groups have access to different sources of
information, bridging ties can provide novel, non-redundant information
(Granovetter 1973, [1974] 1995; Burt 1992, 2005; Yakubovich 2005). At the micro
level, people whose networks include many brokering ties have less constraint
on their actions: greater autonomy, more fluid identities, and greater control
over information flows; as a result, people with more brokering ties perform
better and are better compensated (Burt 1992, 2005; Padgett and Ansell
1993)—although those findings may be limited to high-level professional and
managerial positions, because those jobs require their incumbents to combine
knowledge and skills from multiple sources. Moreover, bridging structural holes
can spark creativity and innovation (Burt 2005; Perry-Smith 2006; Fleming,
Mingo, and Chen 2007). At the macro level, inter-governmental agencies (IGOs)
that link nations with weak or non-existent trade ties are more likely to thrive
than IGOs that link nations with strong trade ties (Ingram and Torafson 2010),
because the former benefit more from the connective function of IGOs than the
latter, who can use trade ties instead of IGO ties to connect with each other.

It is important to recognize that brokers can engage not only in socially
beneficial acts like innovation and conflict mediation, but also in socially undesirable acts like manipulation and corruption. As a result, researchers need
to consider carefully where they draw the system boundaries when analyzing
the costs and benefits of bridging ties (Stovel and Shaw 2012). For example,
interorganizational bridging ties hamper innovation because they make it
easier for firms to behave opportunistically (Ahuja 2000).

Being a broker comes with psychological costs. First, brokers may have to adapt to incompatible expectations from the groups they bridge (Podolny and Baron 1997). Second, they may feel morally inadequate ("dirty") if they use their positions for instrumental purposes (Casciaro, Gino, and Kouchaki 2014). As a result, the broker role is a fragile one that may not last long (Stovel and Shaw 2012).

Because their costs and benefits differ, bonding (usually strong) and bridging (usually weak) ties are complements (Burt 2005; Adler and Kwon 2002). At the micro level, for example, professional and managerial employees' career mobility is enhanced by bridging ties in their strategic-information networks and by bonding ties in their social support networks (Podolny and Baron 1997). Work groups are most creative when members have diverse weak ties to people outside the group *and* strong ties within their groups (Hansen 1999; Reagans, Zuckerman, and McEvily 2004; Fleming, Mingo, and Chen 2007). And such groups often find it easier to implement creative ideas. At the macro level, strong (multi-deal, high-value deal) ties between firms and investment banks provide superior service due to investment banks' deep knowledge of client firms, while weak (single-deal, low-value deal) ties with multiple investment banks reduce client firms' dependence on their main banker (Baker 1990). In a very different context, civic associations benefit from both dense clusters with strong ties ("social bonds") and bridging ties that are more instrumental in nature ("transactions") (Baldassarri and Diani 2007). Finally, the value of both bonding and bridging ties is contingent on social context—specifically, on local values and norms (Adler and Kwon 2002). For example, while bridging ties improve professional and managerial employees' careers in American firms (Burt 1992), they harm careers in Chinese firms, where the collectivistic culture clashes with brokers' agency (Xiao and Tsui 2007).

Centrality

In addition to tie strength, link network centrality affects *power* and *status* (sometimes labeled *prestige* or *prominence*).[58] Network analysts have identified four types of centrality: degree, closeness, betweenness, and eigenvector. Figure 5.4 illustrates these four and allows us to compare them. In this network, actor D has the highest degree of centrality—the highest number of ties. Actors F

---

58. Much relational research on organizations uses measures of status that mix information derived from network analysis with information derived from other sources, such as third-party rankings of firms or individuals. Examples include studies of grand-cru classifications in Bordeaux wines (Malter 2014) and law-firm rankings (Rider and Tan 2014).

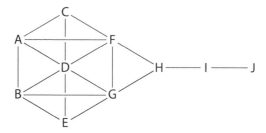

FIGURE 5.4. Comparing forms of centrality
Notes: Actor D has the highest degree centrality (6, 0.67 when normalized),
meaning the number of ties (or, when normalized, the number relative to all possible ties).
Actors F and G have the highest closeness centrality (1.56), meaning the lowest average
path distance between the focal node and all other nodes in the network.
Actor H has the highest betweenness centrality, meaning how many times the node
is present in the shortest path between other nodes.
Actors C and E share the highest eigenvector centrality score, meaning how much
nodes are connected to many nodes that are themselves connected to many other nodes.
Source: Krackhardt (1990: p. 351, Figure 2)

and G share the highest closeness centrality score—the lowest average path distance between them and all other nodes in the network. Actor H has the highest betweenness centrality score—the number of times it is present in the shortest path between other nodes. Finally, actors C and E share the highest eigenvector centrality score—they are the most strongly connected to many actors that are themselves highly connected to other actors (highly degree-central).

Degree centrality captures exposure to information and the influence of others, as well as ego's influence over others. It can also denote freedom from constraint due to having multiple alternatives (Burt 1983; Baker 1990). When we know the direction of a relationship—for example, who asked whom for advice—we can distinguish between in-degree centrality (ties from others to the focal actors) and out-degree centrality (ties from the focal actor to others). In-degree centrality can be interpreted as popularity and influence; out-degree centrality as the likelihood of influencing others. At the micro level, degree centrality is positively associated with perceived influence and with use of influence tactics (Brass and Burkhardt 1993), as well as access to information and thus to innovativeness, especially in organizational subunits that invest a lot in research and development (Tsai 2001). At the macro level, biotech firms with higher degree centrality grew faster than firms with lower degree centrality, because the former had better access to a broad range of knowledge (Powell, Koput, and Smith-Doerr 1996). Finally, studying the degree centrality of relations among elements of organizational structure and practice can reveal what is core to an organization (Siggelkow 2002).

Closeness centrality, the reciprocal of the sum of the distances from the focal actor to all other actors, captures how quickly whatever is being exchanged reaches the focal actor. At the micro level, for example, rapid access to others, especially those in an organization's dominant coalition, is positively associated with perceived influence (Brass 1984). But closeness centrality can be beneficial or harmful, depending on what is exchanged. For example, individuals' proximity to others in an illegal interorganizational price-fixing conspiracy network was associated with longer recommended prison sentences because more direct contacts yielded more potential witnesses (Baker and Faulkner 1993). Closeness centrality can beget centrality: biotech firms with higher closeness centrality are more likely to form research and development ties with others (Powell, Koput, and Smith-Doerr 1996).

Betweenness centrality, meaning how many times an actor is present in the shortest path between other actors, indicates control over flows—gatekeeping power or brokerage. At the micro level, it is associated with perceived influence (Brass 1984; Krackhardt 1990), creativity (Mehra, Kilduff, and Brass 2001), and job performance, promotion, and compensation (Cross and Cummings 2004; Burt 2005). The same effect is found at the macro level, where control over information in networks of biotech firms and public research organizations generates more patents (Owen-Smith and Powell 2004). But note that betweenness centrality provides gatekeeping power only when ties are difficult to form, as in the case of trust ties. If ties are easy to form, then actors can bypass actors with high betweenness centrality by forging direct connections.

Finally, eigenvector centrality is the extent to which the focal actor is connected to many actors that are themselves connected to many others. It thus captures the centrality of those tied to the focal actor. It indicates popularity or status when ties are asymmetric (unidirectional), and membership in the network core when ties are symmetric (bidirectional) (Podolny 1993). At the micro level, people with ties to those who are central to an advertising and public-relations agency's informal social network have more impact on administrative innovations, such as creating new departments and systems (Ibarra 1995). At the macro level, the more that central commercial banks are in director interlock networks, the more easily they can influence corporate strategic decisions (Mizruchi 1982; Mintz and Schwartz 1985).

Network Structure

While we can learn much from ties between actors (resource dependence) and from actors' positions in webs of relationships (social capital), those things don't give us the entire picture, because webs of relationships vary greatly in their overall structures, their configurations. For example, some work groups are highly centralized, revolving around a single central actor (usually a manager), while others are highly decentralized, with group members connected to many others in the group. The opportunities and constraints that individuals, groups, and organizations face are shaped by network structure. For example, information transfer is slower in highly centralized work groups than in decentralized ones. And centralized work groups are more fragile: if the central actors leave, the groups fall apart. Despite its evident importance, there is much less research on network structure than on resource dependence or social capital, because the data collection and data analysis requirements are greater. Here, I discuss the ideas behind four aspects of network structure—network density, centralization, clustering, and small worlds—and offer a few examples of existing research.

Density and centralization. These two aspects of network structure are linked, so I discuss each separately and then consider them in combination. The greater the *density* of a social network, the more actors in the network are tied to each other. This means network members interact more. As a result, density captures how cohesive a network is. Because mutual interaction increases trust, cooperation, and information sharing, networks with greater density have stronger norms concerning members' behavior, and members learn more easily from each other. Most empirical research on social network density has been at the micro level, studying individuals interacting in laboratory experiments or in real organizations. The primary hypothesis is that denser work groups perform better, which is generally supported: a meta-analysis of thirty-seven studies found that work groups with greater density tended to perform better and to be more committed to staying together (Balkundi and Harrison 2006).[59] Yet network density may instead have negative effects on group performance: for example, it may lead to "groupthink" (Janis 1982), meaning excessive conformity in attitudes and beliefs because group members overlook information that does not fit the group's thinking (Moody and White 2003). Therefore, groupthink can reduce creativity. At its worst, groupthink can lead groups into what outsiders would label deviant behavior, because group members are insulated from broader norms and values, focus on one or a few goals, ignore collateral consequences, and suppress their own views in deference to the group consensus. Finally, the effects of groups' network density depend on ties to others outside the group; such external ties can provide access to novel sources of information that can

59. This finding resonates with micro-level research on the demographic composition of work groups that I discussed in chapter 4, which shows that demographic diversity can hamper communication and other interactions (making groups less densely connected), thereby harming performance.

benefit group performance—even when groups are highly cohesive (Reagans, Zuckerman, and McEvily 2004).

The more *centralized* a social network is, the more a few actors dominate interaction and exchange. There are multiple ways to measure centralization, based on degree, closeness, betweenness, and eigenvector centrality. Because it is manifested in multiple ways, centralization can affect both entire networks and individual network members through multiple causal mechanisms, yielding both beneficial and harmful effects. For example, work groups that are more centralized tend to share less knowledge with other groups, because leaders are torn between competing and cooperating (Tsai 2002). And members of an illegal interorganizational price-fixing conspiracy were less likely to be sentenced to prison when their conspiracy network was more centralized (Baker and Faulkner 1993).

Density and centralization are inversely related, so their effects are often offsetting. For example, experimental work shows that maximally dense task networks (everyone is connected to everyone else) allow for more effective sharing of member expertise than maximally centralized task networks (one member is a hub and all others are connected through that hub); therefore maximally dense network configurations yield excellent performance on interdependent tasks (Argote, Aven, and Kush 2018). But that relationship holds only when network membership is stable. In the face of member turnover, new members of maximally dense networks develop expertise more slowly than new members of maximally centralized networks and are less well integrated into groups, hampering group performance.

Clustering. Clusters are groups of actors that are more closely tied to each other than they are to actors outside the cluster: for example, *dyads* (pairs), *triads* (triplets), and *cliques* (three or more actors all tied to each other). Figure 5.3 shows one cluster of four members in the top-right group and one cluster of three members in the top-left group. Members of such clusters are more similar in terms of perceptions, attitudes, and behavior (individuals), or logics, strategies, and behaviors (organizations) than are disconnected actors. Cluster members are more strongly "glued" together through increasing surveillance capacity and flows of information, opinions, and resources; this generates trust and social solidarity. Depending on the task, such social "glue" can result in superior performance by cluster members. For example, at the micro level, greater clustering among members of task-oriented groups eases groups' search for information, but it also hampers groups' ability to generate novel solutions (Shore, Bernstein, and Lazer 2015). At the macro level, more extensive connections between mental health provider organizations, through a combination of ongoing referrals and case coordination, are associated with improved patient outcomes (Provan and Sebastian 1998).

Much research on clustering takes as the unit of analysis the actor (usually the individual or the organization) rather than the cluster, and measures differences between actors based on the characteristics of the clusters within which they are embedded. At the micro level, a study of corporate R&D teams demonstrates that having one's alters more strongly connected to each other facilitates knowledge transfer among employees, by engendering norms of cooperation (Reagans and McEvily 2003). In the same vein, high-school students who are more deeply embedded in clusters of friendships are more emotionally attached to their schools (Moody and White 2003). At the macro level, manufacturing firms that are more deeply embedded in clusters of director interlocks have more similar patterns of political donations (Mizruchi 1992). Corporations that are more deeply embedded in clusters of director interlocks are more likely to resist adopting the shareholder-value orientation to corporate governance, which places priority on maximizing stock prices to benefit shareholders. Instead, such corporations maintain a managerialist orientation and resist calls to focus exclusively on stock prices, because their top managers have more power vis-à-vis shareholders (Benton 2016). Moreover, variation in embeddedness in clusters is driven by top-manager preferences, with corporations that have stronger managerialist orientations toward corporate governance more likely to appoint new directors from other firms with stronger managerialist orientations.

Small worlds. Small worlds are networks with many small cohesive clusters connected by a few bridging ties, so the average path between any two network members is short. Hence these social "worlds" seem small. Many organizational systems resemble small worlds. At the micro level, the structure of relations between managers in many large firms has small-world properties (Burt 2005). And at the macro level, so do a wide array of interorganizational networks: institutional investor ties among large German companies in the 1990s (Kogut and Walker 2001); interlocking directorates among large U.S. companies in the 1990s (Davis, Yoo, and Baker 2003); strategic alliances among American firms in high-tech industries (Schilling and Phelps 2007); and collaborations among the teams who mount Broadway shows (Uzzi and Spiro 2005).

Despite being common, small worlds are not ubiquitous. For example, the collaboration network of social scientists does not have a small-world structure (Moody 2004). And small worlds are not necessarily permanent fixtures of social life. Perhaps the clearest example comes from studies of American corporate interlocks. For much of the twentieth century, the bridges between clusters of corporations constituted an "inner circle" (Useem 1984) or "power elite" (Mills 1956). But in the twenty-first century, this small world fell apart: the number of directors with many board appointments plummeted, so the average path between corporations grew longer (Mizruchi 2013; Chu and Davis 2016).

In short, the power elite in the U.S. fractured, although many tightly connected sub-networks of corporate directors remain (Benton 2016). If a power elite persists, it is a largely transnational group, forged by the globalization of trade and the rise of massive multinational enterprises (Murray 2017).

Information, trust, and norms flow efficiently through small-world networks because they have great "reach," meaning that exchanges can flow across clusters in a few steps. As a result, novel information can be easily combined, facilitating creativity and innovation. For example, firms in small-world-like strategic alliance networks generate more innovations than firms not in such networks (Schilling and Phelps 2007). But there is a downside to small-world structures. At the extreme, they can result in actors sharing the same information and developing extremely strong norms that hamper creativity and innovation, and instead promote conventional thinking that yields copycat behavior and outputs. For example, Broadway shows mounted by teams with intermediate small-world characteristics (moderately short average path length and intermediate clustering) receive better reviews from professional critics and perform better at the box office than shows from teams with strong or weak small-world characteristics, because the former are more creative (Uzzi and Spiro 2005). But for the vast majority of teams, the relationship between small-worldliness and performance is positive; a negative relationship is seen in only 10 to 15 percent of teams, indicating that "too strong" small-world structures are rare. That is why most studies find increasing benefits to stronger small-world characteristics.

Positions and Roles in Organizational Networks

Positions are sets of actors that have similar ties. Roles are patterns of relations between actors that are based on similar network positions.[60] Position and role constitute a duality: each defines the other. For example, teachers in different elementary school classrooms have similar patterns of ties to their students, which are very different from the patterns of ties among students themselves. And school principals in a district have similar patterns of ties to teachers, which are very different from patterns of ties among teachers. Figure 5.5 illustrates this, showing people as letters and the groups they participate in as numbers, along with the ties between each set of actors, plus a matrix summarizing role-position links between people and organizations. The positions individuals hold shape

---

60. For a discussion of non-relational roles which do not involve social ties, but rather sets of activities, such as jobs, see Nadel (1957). For an application of this theory to organizations, see Barley (1990).

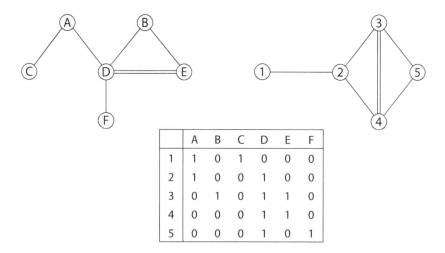

	A	B	C	D	E	F
1	1	0	1	0	0	0
2	1	0	0	1	0	0
3	0	1	0	1	1	0
4	0	0	0	1	1	0
5	0	0	0	1	0	1

FIGURE 5.5. The duality of positions and roles
Note: The letters refer to people; the numbers to groups they belong to.
The top left graph shows ties between individuals based on their co-membership in groups. The top right graph shows ties between groups based on their shared members. The matrix on the bottom summarizes the relationship between individuals and groups; each cell is coded '1' when the focal individual is a member of the focal group, and '0' otherwise. This figure was adapted from Breiger (1974).

their roles, meaning the expectations of those who are (and are not) tied to them, as well as providing access to material and cultural resources. As Figure 5.5 shows, it makes no difference whether you define individuals' positions (and thus the roles, like bridges, they play in the ecology of groups), or you define groups' positions (and thus the roles they play in individual behavior). Starting with individuals or with groups yields the same pattern.

That positions and roles constitute a duality, however, does not imply that positions determine roles, that positions are set first and roles evolve later. Instead, actors can first claim roles and then create webs of relations that correspond with those roles (Baker and Faulkner 1991). There is little organizational research on this topic, but here I describe examples of two related conceptions of roles and positions: equivalence classes and core–periphery distinctions.

In *equivalence classes*, actors have social relations with the same others (*structural equivalence*) or similarly positioned others (*automorphic or role equivalence*), as I explain in appendix B (see especially figure B.5). Similarity in roles and positions is consistently associated with similarity in behavior. At the micro level, role-equivalent restaurant workers tend to influence each other's turnover: turnover snowballs among workers in advice and help-seeking communication networks (Krackhardt and Porter 1986). The equivalence of individuals is related to the equivalence of organizations: not only do the managers of structurally equivalent firms tend to hold the same attitudes, but their firms also tend to donate to the same charities and the same congressional candidates' political action committees (Burt 1983; Galaskiewicz and Burt 1991; Mizruchi 1992; Murray 2017). But because they are connected to the same actors, structurally equivalent actors also compete more with each other (Burt 1983).

Because roles provide access to resources, roles affect behavior and thus performance. For example, in the Hollywood film industry, after the success of *The Godfather* ushered in the blockbuster era, the screenwriter and director roles became increasingly integrated, with one person playing both roles (Baker and Faulkner 1991). Films created by teams with such integrated role structures performed better at the box office than films created by teams with different people in those roles.

Core–periphery distinctions. Core actors are members of densely connected clusters within networks, while peripheral actors are more sparsely connected to each other and to actors in the core, as I explain in appendix B (see especially figure B.6). For example, the Hollywood film industry in the 1970s contained a small core of composers who wrote the majority of film scores, ringed by a medium-sized semi-periphery of composers who wrote two or three each, and a very large periphery of composers who wrote one each (Faulkner 1983). Position in the core versus the periphery matters: core film composers garner a disproportionate share of awards and work on films that greatly out-earn films that semi-peripheral and peripheral composers work on. But core–periphery structures may not benefit the entire network. For example, when work groups charged with solving complex problems have stronger distinctions between core and peripheral members, they perform worse (Cummings and Cross 2003). And core–periphery structures can make networks unreceptive to newcomers and innovators: industry insiders (members of the Hollywood movie industry) favor movies made by core industry members, while outside observers (critics) favor movies made by peripheral members (Cattani, Ferriani, and Allison 2014).

Conclusion

Relational research on organizations is conducted at multiple levels of network structure (the egocentric network, the subnetwork component, and the entire network) and at multiple levels of organizational analysis. This range of application facilitates integrating micro and macro phenomena (Coleman 1986). Moreover, relational analysis can reveal patterns of opportunity and constraint that research subjects are unaware of. And relational research can consider organizations' formal and informal structures simultaneously.

But relational analysis also has several limitations. First of all, network methods have sometimes been applied reflexively, leading scholars to reify networks—to treat all social relations as the same no matter the form or content of the exchange, and apply the same principles to all social relations. With regard to *form*, much relational analysis ignores the fact that some ties are unidirectional, others are bidirectional. The direction of social relations matters, because it can tell us who initiated the relationship (critical if we are to understand social network dynamics) and the extent to which both exchange partners are involved (important for understanding how social relations operate and what their impact is). With regard to *content*, what is exchanged varies widely: advice, emotional support, deference, influence, information or baseless rumors, goods or services, money, praise or criticism, and trust or suspicion. And ties can carry positive, negative, or neutral emotional valence. Content matters because content determines why social relations are formed, maintained, and dissolved, as well as their impact. Because both relational form and content vary greatly; there can be no single relational theory. Instead, there must be multiple, albeit related, theories.

Relational scholars also often ignore the *nature* of the actors they are treating as nodes in graphs, even though they could be individuals, small groups, or large organizations, and scholars tend to apply the same theory to all actors. But actors' behavior can differ greatly, based on factors beyond their social network roles and positions. For example, higher-level employees tend to be more senior—and more male and White—than lower-level ones, so higher-level employees face less discrimination when they try to cultivate social ties; hence, higher-level employees may perceive discrimination as a less important barrier to social exchange than do lower-level employees. Moreover, actor attributes play critical roles in generating and maintaining social ties (Brint 1992; Ibarra 1995), so actors' roles and positions and their atomistic attributes may jointly affect behavior. As I explain in chapter 7, substantial insights can be gained by attending to social actors' characteristics as well as their relationships.

Furthermore, although relational scholars are increasingly likely to have panel data, they seldom clearly *identify causality*. Until recently, most work has been cross-sectional, with "snapshots" of data taken at a single point in time, making it impossible to determine whether social ties are causes, consequences, or correlates of demographics, cultural elements, and performance. For example, the finding that job applicants who are referred by employee contacts are more likely to be offered jobs than applicants without referrals (Fernandez, Castilla, and Moore 2000) may be spurious, because people tend to have ties to similar others. Therefore, any observed effect of social capital may be due to unobserved individual-level attributes that are correlated with both the outcome of interest and tie formation, rather than to the information and influence that social ties can provide (Mouw 2003). With observational data, there are three solutions: conduct fixed-effects analyses that eliminate between-person comparisons to focus on within-person comparisons (Yakubovich 2005; Fernandez and Galperin 2014); use statistical methods like instrumental variables to substitute for endogenous network ties (Sterling 2015); or use matching procedures to reduce the effects of observable confounds (Liu and Srivastava 2015; Azoulay, Liu, and Stuart 2017). Although none of these approaches is perfect, they all improve greatly on standard practice. A very different alternative involves conducting experiments—the gold standard for identifying causality.

Relatedly, relational analysis too seldom examines *network dynamics*: how and why social relations are formed, maintained, and dissolved, with the notable exception of research on resource dependence. Because most empirical studies take snapshots of social relations, they assume implicitly that social relations are stable—thus implying that stable relations are what matters. The general neglect of network dynamics is puzzling, given long-standing arguments that webs of social relations are always evolving, and so networks are inherently dynamic (e.g., Simmel 1950; Emirbayer 1997), so I elaborate on this issue more than the first three. Individuals routinely enter and exit organizations, move between jobs and subunits (e.g., White 1970), and connect and disconnect with others in their workplace and beyond. For their part, organizations routinely enter into new exchanges with suppliers, peers, and customers (e.g., Gulati and Gargiulo 1999), and they exit or alter old exchanges (e.g., Palmer 1983). Moreover, exogenous factors, such as changes in legal regimes, broad cultural shifts, technological breakthroughs, and unexpected events such as earthquakes and terrorist attacks, often disrupt existing social relations and impel their transformation and the formation of entirely new relations (e.g., Dobbin and Dowd 1997; Corbo, Corrado, and Ferriani 2016). In response, both individuals and organizations add and drop social ties wholesale. On a related note, too seldom does relational analysis recognize that social relations have different *histories*: some are long-standing, others newly formed (for an example, see Baum, McEvily, and Rowley [2010]). The histories of social relations will affect not only their strength, but also their likelihood of spawning other social relations.

There are several theories about the antecedents of social relations based on factors such as homophily (McPherson, Smith-Lovin, and Cook 2001), physical proximity (Festinger, Schachter, and Back 1950; Sailer and McCulloh 2012), organizational structure (Lincoln and Miller 1979), prestige (Podolny 1993; Han 1994), and strategic complementarity (Gulati and Gargiulo 1999). Yet little has been done to assess the impact of these factors in dynamic models that would predict the persistence or dissolution of social relations. A notable early exception is a longitudinal comparative ethnography of how introducing new technology changed both roles and relationships in hospital radiology departments (Barley 1990).

To deal with concerns about changes in networks and causal identification, there has been a laudable surge in studies of network dynamics recently, using both observational and experimental data. These studies are quite varied. On the micro side, they reveal how leaders emerge in peer groups (Carnabuci, Emery, and Brinberg 2018), how concerns about organizational versus occupational status drive career moves within and between restaurants by chefs in the field of American fine cuisine (Borkenhagen and Martin 2018), and how preexisting social ties shape the development of new employees' work-related social networks (Sterling 2015). On the macro side, they trace the rise and fall of interorganizational ties in the global computer industry as a function of both homogenization and fragmentation (Gulati, Sytch, and Tatarynowicz 2012) and show how past network structure constrains network evolution in the wake of large-scale events such as acquisitions and mergers (Briscoe and Tsai 2011).

We now have statistical models for analyzing network dynamics, including the coevolution of ties and actor characteristics (e.g., individual attitudes or emotions; group or organizational size or performance) as a function of the choices made by actors (Snijders 2001, 2017). So far, only a few organizational scholars have used these techniques. One such study traced how the September 11, 2001 terrorist attacks altered the logic of attachment between global airlines (reducing their preference for high-status exchange partners), which in turn altered their patterns of interorganizational ties (Corbo, Corrado, and Ferriani 2016). Another study examined how the Sarbanes-Oxley Act of 2002, which imposed new requirements upon and engendered new norms about corporate governance, made firms' choices of board members more dependent on their existing interorganizational ties (Withers, Kim, and Howard 2018).

A final point bears mention. Digital sources of data on organizations, such as the web portal LinkedIn and AI-driven management software, which I discuss in chapter 8, can provide access to richly detailed data about networks within and between organizations. These new data sources generate many new opportunities for studying the dynamics of social networks in organizational contexts.

6

The Cultural Perspective

Although interactions and demographic attributes shape behavior, they miss one critical factor: how we understand and evaluate interactions and attributes, and how these understandings and evaluations affect behavior. Research taking the cultural perspective is centrally concerned with shared and patterned understandings and evaluations. Cultural scholars focus on how social actors figure out what is and should be, and how things are and should be done, and how social actors come to agree on shared interpretive schemas that guide the thoughts and actions of people, groups, and organizations. It is the fact that these understandings and evaluations are shared that make this research cultural. And it is the fact that they are patterned that makes comparison across cases possible.

Different lines of cultural research on organizations focus on different topics and operate at different levels of analysis. And different lines of cultural research were motivated by different social concerns and empirical puzzles. Below, I define and discuss each line of cultural research in approximately chronological order of development: organizational culture, organizational institutionalism (legitimacy and institutionalization, isomorphism, strategic action, institutional logics), and institutions on the ground. For each, I pay special attention to what motivated the pioneers in each line of work.

Micro to Macro: Organizational Culture

As I explained in chapter 1, organizational culture consists of underlying assumptions (existential statements about how things work, cognitive schemas), espoused values (understandings of what is good and bad), shared norms (understandings of what is normal and abnormal, of what we do and how we do it), and symbols (tangible artifacts like clothing, logos, and office décor; intangible elements like stories, jargon, and ceremonies) (Selznick 1957; Geertz 1973; Pettigrew 1979; Schein 1996). The first studies of organizational culture were conducted by members of the human-relations school (Mayo [1933]

1960; Roethlisberger and Dickson 1939). In the 1950s, sociologists at Columbia (Gouldner 1954; Lipset, Trow, and Coleman 1956; Selznick 1957) and other American sociologists (Stinchcombe 1959; Hirsch 1975) shifted the focus from the pragmatics of what organizational members believed and did to the symbolic nature of their actions and beliefs—although they didn't frame their work in terms of organizational culture. They were joined in France by Michel Crozier (1964) and his students, who emphasized power and uncertainty. But the study of culture qua culture by scholars in the U.S. was limited to studies of occupational cultures (Becker et al. 1961) and college cultures (Clark 1970).

Starting in the late 1970s, interest in organizational culture resurged in the U.S. when scholars returned to ideas first developed by symbolic interactionist research (e.g., Goffman 1961; Becker et al. 1961; Blumer 1969), a micro-sociological tradition that focuses on how people develop meanings for the situations they face through interaction, and how these meanings guide their decisions and actions. This line of work was motivated in part by current events; indeed, one pioneering study of how police officers were socialized into their jobs (Van Maanen 1973) was driven by the author's personal experience with brutal police responses to the protests of the 1960s and his knowledge of the urban riots of the same period. Scholars of organizational culture (e.g., Pettigrew 1979; Barley 1983; Trice and Beyer 1984), whose reading bridged management, sociology, anthropology, linguistics, and pragmatic philosophy, viewed culture as complicated and messy, analogous to life in biology and force in physics. Getting empirical purchase on such a phenomenon required taking deep dives inside organizations and observing culture on the ground. Only through this method did these scholars believe they could develop a rich understanding of how individuals and groups in organizations create and maintain values, norms, and beliefs.

This work revealed that organizational cultures arise from efforts by owners, managers, and workers to create shared goals, identities, and meanings for their actions through specific practices (Pettigrew 1979; Smircich 1983; Van Maanen and Schein 1979; Kunda 1992). Building and maintaining organizational cultures, they found, was inherently pragmatic—people develop particular behavioral patterns and ways of thinking in response to the problems they face. For example, to ensure that visitors experienced Disney theme parks as "happy" places, employees go through an elaborate socialization process to inculcate strict rules about appearance, countenance, and style of interaction with "guests"; this socialization engenders a culture of orderly and friendly, yet impersonal, service that suppresses employees' natural emotions and creates instead a gloss of cheerfulness (Van Maanen 1991). Similarly, high-tech firms engineer a culture of hard work, long hours, technical accomplishments, and risk-taking through workshops, manuals, executive speeches, newsletters, and banners introducing new employees to company values and reminding established employees of those values (Kunda 1992). Finally, everyday manifestations of culture, such as the language organizational members use (Barley 1983), the clothes they wear (Van Maanen 1991; Rafaeli and Pratt 1993), and the rituals and rites of passage they go through (Trice and Beyer 1984) convey organizational values to both insiders and outsiders.

This work was later complemented by research conducted by management scholars trained in industrial-organization and social psychology who conceive of organizational culture as a mechanism of social control (Chatman and O'Reilly 2016). This work was initially prompted by recognition of how much the U.S. military depended on socializing values into recruits, and how those values were reinforced by recruits' interactions with leaders and their peers. Another early influence was observations of cults and religious sects like the Hare Krishna, Synanon, and the Unification Church (popularly known as the Moonies), which thrived from the 1960s to the 1980s and, in some cases, beyond. These fringe groups—some not formally organized—could firmly regulate and restrict their members' thoughts and actions despite having few economic resources and despite being subject to widespread skepticism. As a social control mechanism, organizational culture is subtler than formal structural elements like incentives and procedures, although culture is created and maintained by formal selection, training, and reward systems. In contrast to the ethnographic scholars described above, management scholars used surveys and experiments to investigate culture.

Organizational culture influences behavior at multiple levels. At the individual level, employees' "fit" with their organization's values and those of their colleagues improves commitment to the organization and job performance (Chatman 1991; Goldberg et al. 2016). Strongly held and widely shared organizational cultures promote behavioral consistency and thus can improve organizational performance (Gordon and DiTomaso 1992; Chatman and O'Reilly 2016). For example, tech firms' cultures emphasize innovation and collaboration; in the 1970s and 1980s, this helped them rebound from Japanese competition (Saxenian 1994). But strong organizational cultures can also hinder experimentation and learning, impairing performance in changing environments (Sørensen 2002; Van den Steen 2010).

A notable recent shift on cultural research is toward computational text analysis, a set of techniques that blend ideas from linguistics with iterative computer algorithms.[61] One of the earliest examples is an analysis of poverty relief

---

61. These techniques are also called "natural language processing." For a primer on these methods, see Jurafsky and Martin (2021).

agencies, which traced their changing goals over three decades, based on self-descriptions (Mohr and Duquenne 1997). More recently, analysis of employee emails shows that how well employees fit their organization's culture predicts their career success (Goldberg et al. 2016). Similarly, analysis of Federal Reserve Board meeting minutes before the 2008 financial crisis reveals that board members filtered data through a macroeconomic frame, which blinded them to meso-level (that is, organizational) connections between mortgage foreclosures and mortgage-backed securities, and prevented them from predicting the collapse of the financial system (Fligstein, Stuart Brundage, and Shultz 2016).

Organizations and their cultures are shaped by external factors, most prominently societal cultures. For example, a shift in broad business norms (the legitimation of hostile corporate takeovers in the 1980s) engendered a "culture of honor" among the executives of a manufacturing firm, supplanting a culture of genteel disagreement (Morrill 1991). The new culture was highly aggressive, with public feuds between departments and across levels; it was manifested in a vocabulary of warfare: virtuous "white knights" dueled with villainous "outlaws" wearing "black hats." Studying organizations in different countries can shed light on the external forces impinging on organizational cultures. Perhaps the most prominent example is a study of IBM's corporate culture, which revealed six dimensions of culture that vary across countries—power distance (high/low), uncertainty avoidance (high/low), individualism/collectivism, masculinity/femininity, long-/short-term orientation, and indulgence/restraint—and that shaped the cultures of local facilities (Hofstede 1980).

A closely related stream of research focuses on *organizational identities*: shared beliefs organizational members hold about what makes their organizations distinctive (Whetten and Godfrey 1998). Organizational identities act as subliminal guides for organizational responses to unanticipated operational or strategic issues, shaping how people in organizations interpret issues and influencing their motivations for acting on them (Dutton and Dukerich 1991). Organizational identities arise through multiple intertwined meaning-making processes: a leader must articulate a distinctive vision for the organization, contrast that vision with the visions of other organizations, shepherd organizational members toward consensus on their organization's identity, and figure out the optimal level of distinctiveness for that identity based on feedback from internal and external observers (Gioia et al. 2010). Organizational identities were originally conceived of as resistant to change, but they may change when pushed by external factors, such as regulatory shifts or the emergence of strong competitors (Fiol 2002), or by internal factors, such as acquisitions or changes in legal status (Biggart 1977).

Macro: Legitimacy and Institutionalization

Perhaps the most substantial line of cultural research on organizations is labeled *institutional theory*,[62] because institutions are central to it. Institutions are social facts: phenomena perceived by people to be both external to themselves, meaning understood by others, and coercive, meaning backed by sanctions (Durkheim [1982] 1995). Institutions both constrain and enable action, by driving it in certain directions and away from others. Institutions persist because they develop routines for reproducing themselves over time, so they endure even without people collectively mobilizing to support them and without authorities like the state or the professions intervening to approve them (Jepperson 1991; Clemens and Cook 1999). Yet institutions can be disrupted—altered or undermined (Oliver 1992; Clemens and Cook 1999)—in several ways, which I discuss below. Institutions take many forms besides organizations and organizational structures, policies, and practices: rituals like shaking hands, roles like mother and child, and physical tokens like paper currency and wedding rings. Here, I limit my assessment to institutions related to organizations.[63]

The cultural analysis of organizations as institutions is a direct descendent of work by post-war American sociologists (Merton 1940, 1968; Selznick 1949, 1957; Gouldner 1954; Blau [1955] 1963). In the late 1970s, the analytical focus shifted to cognition and the phenomenological focus to unreflective ritualized activity and conformity (Meyer and Rowan 1977; Scott 2014). For example, John Meyer's pioneering work on educational organizations as institutions (e.g., Meyer 1977; Meyer and Rowan 1977) was a reaction to functionalist research on the minutiae of organizational structures, which focused on such things as the ratio of administrative to production workers or on how production technologies determine structure and work process (e.g., Woodward [1965] 1994; Lawrence and Lorsch 1967; Blau and Schoenherr 1971). His thinking was inspired by the immensely creative work of his Stanford colleague James March (e.g., Cohen, March, and Olsen 1972; March and Olsen 1976), who proposed such subversive ideas

---

62. Although it is commonly labeled a theory, this work is more of a loose perspective than a tightly coherent theory in the Mertonian sense (for more on what constitutes theory, see appendix A). And as I explain in chapter 3, this line of work is sometimes labelled "new institutionalism" to distinguish it from "old institutional theory," which I label post-war organizational sociology.

63. Borrowing from economics, some sociological institutionalists emphasize rationality, rules, and risk (Brinton and Nee 1998). Ingram and Clay (2000) review this work. Another group of sociological institutionalists analyzes the entire globe (Meyer et al. 1997). Clemens and Cook (1999) and Schneiberg and Clemens (2006) review this work, as well as the organizational institutionalism I discuss here.

as the technology of foolishness, organized anarchies, and garbage-can decision-making. As a result, Meyer and his students were highly skeptical of organizations, especially with regard to goal-oriented rationality. Their stance stood in sharp contrast to that of most organizational scholars in the 1970s and challenged the conventional thinking, which, as I explained in chapter 3, was highly rationalist.

The work of Meyer and his followers emphasizes *social construction*: organizations and the roles people play in them are created through social interaction, generating shared knowledge and belief systems (Berger and Luckmann 1967). People institutionalize recipes for understanding and action in stages. First is *habituation*: we recognize patterns in our own actions and interactions. Next is *typification*: we make sense of other actors, their actions, and the situations in which we and they operate as types by recognizing their repetitive patterns. Then comes *institutionalization*: we share typifications widely and come to view them as natural, normal—even necessary. The resulting institutions stabilize social relations by establishing expectations for behavior in the form of norms, values, and roles. Like research on organizational culture, this line of work also has roots in symbolic interactionism (e.g., Becker et al. 1961; Blumer 1969). It has several related foci, which I divide into three sections. This section covers legitimacy and institutionalization; later sections cover isomorphism and strategic action.

Institutionalist research is centrally concerned with legitimacy and institutionalization. These two concepts are interdependent. Organizations are *legitimate* when they are *institutionalized*, when their structures, policies, and practices become "infused with value beyond the technical requirements of the task at hand" (Selznick 1957: 17). More concretely, organizations are legitimate when they are comprehensible and taken for granted as the natural way to achieve some collective goal, when they are justified and explained on the basis of prevailing cultural models and accounts (Meyer and Rowan 1977; Douglas 1986), when they are sanctioned or mandated by authorized actors (DiMaggio and Powell 1983), or when those involved cannot even conceive of alternatives (Zucker 1983). Highly institutionalized organizations are perceived as objective and exterior facets of social life (Berger and Luckmann 1967; Tolbert and Zucker 1996).

Organizations are confronted with *institutionalized rules* maintained by social interaction, which are by-products of modernization; specifically, the rise of legal rationality and increasingly dense webs of relations between organizations. Institutionalized rules are taken for granted or supported by public opinion or the force of law, and so are not subject to conscious or unconscious evaluation. They are ceremonial, in that acting in accordance with them is judged in relation to categorical rules, not outcomes; that is, they are rules people must follow because they are accepted by society (or some relevant subset of society), rather than rules that refer to some desired goal. Demonstrating conformity to institutionalized rules is essential for organizations' legitimacy, and ultimately their survival—even though such conformity may be inefficient (Meyer and Rowan 1977).

There are three bases for legitimacy: *regulatory*, which includes the statutes, regulations, and judicial decisions that constitute the rules governing organizations; *normative*, meaning expert (i.e., professional and scientific) sources of information and value judgments about organizations; and *cognitive*, meaning widely shared perceptions of organizations (Scott 2014). Although these three bases for legitimacy are analytically distinct, empirical research often spans two or all three of them (Hirsch 1997). No matter the basis, the greater the legitimacy attributed to a form of organization, the less likely any organization with that form will require active justification and the more likely it will be accepted or taken for granted. Legitimacy improves organizations' access to resources, including funding, skilled personnel, raw materials, and distribution channels. Legitimacy also improves acceptance in the eyes of customers, thus fueling demand for products. In sum, legitimacy contributes to organizations' ability to expand and persist (Meyer and Rowan 1977).

To maintain legitimacy, organizations often decouple what they claim they are and do (formal structures) from what they actually are and do (everyday practices) (Meyer and Rowan 1977), or only loosely couple them (Weick 1976). In either case, the goal is to get core tasks done, whether or not the work or the means to perform it conforms to prevailing institutional rules, while achieving legitimacy by presenting an image of socially constructed rationality to evaluators, both internally and externally. Decoupling and loose coupling allow organizations to maintain a logic of confidence or good faith (March and Olsen 1976) through discretion, avoidance of inspection, overlooking anomalies, and buffering core internal activities from outside influence. For example, in schools, reforms are announced and reports are written to signal compliance with external demands, but what happens in classrooms does not change, and teachers' practices are not standardized. School administrators may have authority on paper, but they seldom influence everyday teaching practice. Figure 6.1 illustrates arguments about institutionalized rules, legitimacy, and decoupling or loose coupling.

Empirical research has largely supported these ideas in studies of many different kinds of organizations. Non-profit day-care centers with ties to "good" schools (in the form of site-sharing arrangements) are more legitimate and have better survival chances (Baum and Oliver 1991). Smaller and younger day-care centers benefit most from these relationships. Conforming to industry norms about strategy improves regulatory endorsement of commercial banks (Deephouse 1996). New advertising agencies become more legitimate

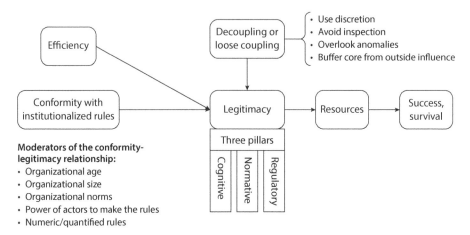

FIGURE 6.1. Institutionalized rules and legitimacy

when they imitate established agencies' structures and participate in award competitions, which in turn facilitate agency growth (Khaire 2010). Legitimacy (and its lack) can spill over from one organization to another (Zucker 1988). For example, a mutual-fund provider that was a subsidiary of an insurance firm beset by scandal lost legitimacy—but so did mutual-fund providers that were subsidiaries of other similar organizations not involved in the scandal (Jonsson, Greve, and Fujiwara-Greve 2009).

Decoupling and loose coupling are common. For example, in many Christian denominations, women occupy leadership positions even though they are formally forbidden to do so (Chaves 1997). Similarly, hospitals often deploy social workers to buffer their technical core (care by doctors and nurses) from uncertainty and risk stemming from concerns raised by patients and their families (Heimer and Mitchell 1997). Decoupling and loose coupling are not limited to the non-profit world. Corporations adopt incentive programs for executives but seldom use them (Westphal and Zajac 1994). And corporations sometimes claim to adopt policies promoting environmental sustainability without actually following through because it is difficult for most stakeholders to disentangle what corporations say from how they say it (Crilly, Hansen, and Zollo 2016).

But organizations cannot always manage to shield their practices from external scrutiny; instead, they may yield to institutional pressures and tightly couple them. Tight coupling can be driven by either external or internal factors. Externally, organizations are more likely to yield to external demands when they are more visible and more proximate to the organizations that are making those demands (Edelman 1992), or when the organizations making demands are more powerful and their targets are more dependent (Basu,

Dirsmith, and Gupta 1999). For example, the U.S. Government Accountability Office (GAO) was more susceptible to the expectations of Congress, which provides the GAO's budget, than to those of the news media (Basu, Dirsmith, and Gupta 1999). Internally, organizations are more likely to yield to external demands when they are congruent with organizational norms (Binder 2007). Moreover, the nature of the pressure on organizations matters: they are more likely to yield to institutional pressures when they are well publicized and involve numeric scores, making adherence commensurable across the organizations facing those pressures (Espeland and Sauder 2016). For example, when law-school rankings began to appear in the *US News and World Report* (*USNWR*) in the 1980s and 1990s, they forced law schools to change many of the things they did, including tightening admission standards and spending more on marketing and career services; some law schools also "gamed" the rankings by falsifying data used as input to the *USNWR* ranking algorithm, shifting students with lower test scores to part-time or evening programs, and hiring unemployed graduates to boost graduates' employment statistics (Espeland and Sauder 2016).

The degree of coupling depends upon why organizations adopt a structure, policy, or practice—looser if motivated by legitimacy; tighter if motivated by the technical demands of core tasks—and whether or not internal forces reinforce external pressures. For instance, universities' recycling programs are less ceremonial and more tightly coupled with everyday practices when students (rather than administrators) push for these programs, in part because then universities are more likely to hire full-time (rather than part-time) recycling managers (Lounsbury 2001). And nation-states' adoption of stock exchanges is more symbolic (smaller exchanges, with fewer listed firms, and those that were listed being economically less important) when they are coerced by international funding agencies (Weber, Davis, and Lounsbury 2009).

Several different factors can drive *recoupling*, such as increased scrutiny by external evaluators. In American elementary schools, the recent push for accountability has recoupled teaching practices to district and state standards, reducing teacher autonomy in the classroom (Hallett 2010). In law schools, rankings have recoupled the career success of law-school graduates to school evaluation (Espeland and Sauder 2016). The entrenchment of professional staff can transform ceremonial actions into substantive ones; for example, human resources staff who are committed to preventing racial and gender discrimination (Kelly and Dobbin 1998). Scandals can also prompt recoupling. For example, outcry about biased judging in Olympic figure skating led to reforms in judging that resulted in more precise and nuanced criteria (Lom 2016).

The flip side of institutionalization is *deinstitutionalization*: the erosion or discontinuation of what was formerly an institutionalized organization, practice, or activity (Oliver 1992). And the flip side of legitimation is *delegitimation*: the reduction or complete elimination of acceptance or taken-for-grantedness of an organizational form, activity, or practice. The persistence of organizational elements may be inherently problematic because of social systems' natural tendency toward disorder—toward "social entropy" (Zucker 1988). The less tightly connected an organizational element is to other elements, the more likely it is to be deinstitutionalized through social entropy. For example, performance evaluations in work settings are affected somewhat by the backgrounds and preferences of evaluators. If the performance evaluation process is not well connected to other organizational processes, evaluations can vary greatly and become contentious and thus delegitimated; in turn, contestation may lead decision makers to replace them with new processes that fit better with other organizational elements.

Deinstitutionalization can be precipitated by technological, political, economic, and cultural forces (Oliver 1992), as Figure 6.2 shows. For example, the decline of the conglomerate form of organization (corporations composed of many, often unrelated, businesses) in the 1980s was precipitated by a shift in beliefs rooted in economic research (Davis, Diekmann, and Tinsley 1994). The idea of the firm as a bounded social entity, analogous to a sovereign body that could not be divided, lost legitimacy in the face of evidence that conglomerates were inefficient; as a result, many were broken up. Similarly, several forms of savings-and-loan associations, each embodying a different set of opinions, beliefs, and judgments, were extinguished by a combination of technical pressures (changes in human population and employment patterns) and cultural pressures (changes in attitudes toward saving and borrowing) (Haveman and Rao 1997). Most recently, selective American universities, especially public institutions and those with lower status, responded to political attacks on race-conscious admissions policies by dismantling them (Hirschman and Berrey 2017). In contrast, more elite schools retained those policies. In the same vein, a Chinese manufacturing firm had to respond to shifts in norms and values during the transition from state socialism to market capitalism. It succeeded by framing changes as inevitable because they were mandated by the central state and by grounding new values in old values, such as grounding pay for performance in the old value of absolute equity by limiting pay inequality (Raynard, Lu, and Jing 2019).

Deinstitutionalization can be driven by contagion and display momentum. For example, faced with uncertainty, radio stations are more likely to abandon a practice if others in their reference group have already done so (Greve 1995). Although poor performance triggered the abandonment of permanent-employment practices in Japan, leading to spates of downsizing, abandonment accelerated with the number of firms that had downsized (Ahmadjian and

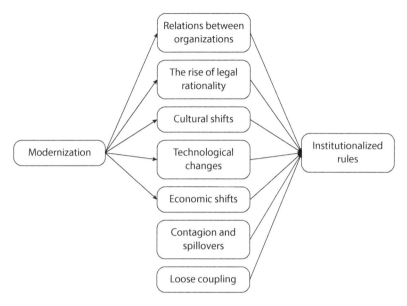

FIGURE 6.2. The antecedents of institutionalized rules (and their deinstitutionalization)

Robinson 2001). Deinstitutionalization can also spill over from one domain (e.g., education) to another (e.g., business). For example, agency theory, developed by business-school faculty and taught to MBAs, delegitimated diversification as a corporate strategy in the 1990s: after climbing to the top of the corporate ladder post-MBA, CEOs trained when agency theory became prominent shunned diversification and instead followed focused strategies (Jung and Shin 2019).

Macro: Isomorphism

One of the central research questions in macro cultural analysis of organizations is, "[W]hy is there such startling homogeneity in organizational structures and practices?" (DiMaggio and Powell 1983: 148). Accordingly, one of the most important concepts used in this perspective is that of *isomorphism* (literally, "same shape-ism"). Paul DiMaggio and Walter Powell both started their careers doing research with a cultural focus, paying attention to the processes of meaning-making and power plays inside organizations (Coser, Kadushin, and Powell 1982; DiMaggio 1982a, 1982b; Powell 1985). When they wrote their 1983 paper, they were disenchanted with most organizational theory at that time (i.e., contingency theory) and inspired instead by the playful work of James March and his colleagues (e.g., March and Olsen 1976), and the cultural-institutional work of Meyer and his students (e.g., Meyer 1977; Meyer and Rowan 1977), as well as by management theorists who took a more cultural perspective (e.g., Hirsch 1975; Weick 1976). Finally, they wanted to bring into the explanatory focus large social structures beyond organizations' environments.

In their pioneering paper on isomorphism, DiMaggio and Powell argued that as communities of organizations evolve, interorganizational power relations—the state and professions—and competition promote similarity within sets of organizations that either play comparable roles or are tied directly to other (DiMaggio and Powell 1983).[64] The idea of isomorphism was based on their observations of how organizations like consulting firms could influence very different client organizations (e.g., art museums and news broadcasters) to do the same thing (e.g., adopt a multi-divisional structure). They differentiated between competitive isomorphism, which stems from pressures for effective and efficient operation, and institutional isomorphism, which they argued operates through three processes: coercive, normative, and mimetic. *Coercive isomorphism* stems from pressures imposed by states and others who authorize particular organizational structures and activities, and prohibit others; it can also stem from pressures imposed by resource dependencies with suppliers and customers. *Normative isomorphism* involves pressures imposed by collective actors such as professional and trade associations, which create informal expectations, if not formal rules, about what organizations ought to look like and how they ought to behave. *Mimetic isomorphism* is the achievement of conformity through imitation. It can result from responses to uncertainty ("when in doubt, do what other organizations do") or from bandwagon effects ("if many organizations adopt, follow their lead"). Note that the three processes driving isomorphism—coercive, normative, and mimetic— map onto the three bases of legitimacy—regulative, normative, and cognitive, respectively. Figure 6.3 illustrates these arguments.

Coercive pressures accelerate the spread of organizational structures and practices. For example, structures mandated by the state diffuse more rapidly than structures encouraged, but not mandated, by the state (Tolbert and Zucker 1983). But over time, coercive pressures can shade into normative pressures. Many studies have shown that in the early stages, diffusion tends to be "rational," driven by coercion or technical need, while later on, it tends to be

---

64. Note the connections between the cultural and relational perspectives. Isomorphic pressures develop as interorganizational fields become structured as webs of relations between organizations in different positions stabilize. Moreover, organizations that are in the same position (structurally equivalent) are prone to the same cultural influences.

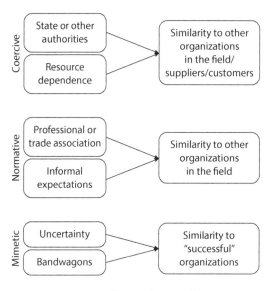

FIGURE 6.3. Forms of isomorphism

symbolic, driven by imitation or norms (Tolbert and Zucker 1983; Baron, Dobbin, and Jennings 1986; Edelman 1992; Westphal, Gulati, and Shortell 1997). For example, hospitals that are early adopters of quality-management programs are less likely to conform to prior adopters' programs, because they customize programs to meet their own idiosyncratic needs and capabilities, while late adopters are more likely to conform, because they are driven by normative (symbolic) isomorphism (Westphal, Gulati, and Shortell 1997). As a result of innovation driven by normative pressures, structures, products, and policies that spread widely may be ineffective. For example, although legally acceptable human resources policies have become widespread, they often fail to reduce inequality (Dobbin, Schrage and Kalev 2015).

Although statutes, regulations, and judicial decisions appear to be coercive forces, the reality is often more complex, as state authorities often allow discretion in their interpretation (Edelman 1990, 1992; Dobbin and Sutton 1998; Gualtieri 2020). For instance, in the wake of the civil rights movement of the 1960s, legal mandates to avoid employment discrimination did not provide a clear roadmap to compliance. In response, firms experimented to demonstrate compliance, implementing several different equal-employment policies and affirmative-action structures. Over time, organizations trying to comply with these laws observed what others were doing. Thus, organizational experimentation socially constructed the meaning of compliance by inducing a combination of normative and mimetic pressures. Eventually, court rulings showed one structure to be sufficient, after which the sanctioned approach diffused widely (Edelman 1992; Dobbin et al. 1993).

Normative pressures can sometimes dominate coercive ones. As explained above, the spread of human resources practices among U.S. employers was not driven by clear legal mandates. Instead, human resources professionals and labor lawyers used the ambiguity inherent in employment law to promote particular solutions—those that would solidify their power—and discourage others (Edelman 1992; Dobbin et al. 1993). Taking a broader perspective on the issue, the civil rights mandates of the 1960s created a normative environment that led employers to adopt human resources procedures even in the absence of formal legal sanctions (Edelman 1990). Organizations that were most visible—large organizations and those close to the public sector—were most likely to adopt the procedures, suggesting that a concern for legitimacy promoted adoption. Yet others might view their actions as responses to anticipated coercion.

Mimetic pressures are ubiquitous. Large corporations are more likely to adopt the multidivisional form when other firms in their industry have done so (Fligstein 1990). Financial services firms are more likely to expand into new service areas when large and profitable firms are active there (Haveman 1993; Strang and Still 2004). Hospitals are more likely to adopt standardized (as opposed to customized) total quality management programs when many other hospitals (and other firms) have done so (Westphal, Gulati, and Shortell 1997). Newspapers have become more similar in the age of the internet than they were before, because they imitate competitors' websites as they update news stories (Boczkowski 2010; Caplan and boyd 2018).

The three isomorphic processes can be difficult to disentangle because they shade into each other conceptually (DiMaggio and Powell 1983: 150; Mizruchi and Fein 1999). For example, in the 1990s, Chinese firms adopted rationalized (bureaucratic) structures common to Western firms (e.g., grievance procedures and promotion tests)—not because they believed bureaucracies are efficient, but because leading Chinese firms had done so (Guthrie 1999). The likelihood of adopting bureaucratic structures depended on their industry (mimesis more than coercion or norms), whether they had joint ventures with Western firms (coercion from Western partners), whether their general managers had backgrounds in economics or business (professional norms), and whether they were under the jurisdiction of municipal companies (coercion more than mimesis). Similarly, after World War II, French and German firms selectively adopted aspects of "the American model," with coercive, normative, and mimetic forces combining in complex ways (Djelic 1998).

Over the past three decades, there has been an increase in formal evaluators of organizations that generate rankings of organizations, and thus create a combination of coercive and normative pressures.[65] Prominent examples include evaluations of corporations by financial analysts (Zuckerman 1999); ratings of movies by Rotten Tomatoes (Hsu 2006); rankings of colleges, universities, and professional schools by *U.S. News and World Report* (Espeland and Sauder 2016); ratings of firms as "best employers" by several sources (Hannon and Milkovich 1996; Arthur and Cook 2009); and reviews of restaurants and other retail outlets by Yelp (Kovács, Carroll, and Lehman 2017). Increasingly ubiquitous evaluations make it easier to compare organizations by making them commensurable (Espeland and Stevens 1998). They also push organizations to be more accountable and transparent.

Macro: Strategic Action

Organizations do not just react to environmental demands; instead, they can be proactive and try to control their environments. Recognizing this, cultural scholars have moved beyond assuming that organizations are confronted with institutional rules to which they must conform; instead, they recognize an array of alternative responses, including *compromise, avoidance, defiance*, and *manipulation* (Oliver 1991). For example, American employers reacted to a 1981 law offering tax breaks for family-friendly policies by setting up dependent-care expense accounts rather than, as framers of the law intended, on-site child-care centers (Kelly 2003). Japanese firms responded to a law mandating equal opportunity for women in various ways: some complied substantively by hiring more women, as the law intended; others complied symbolically by creating sex-segregated job ladders, some for female employees tied to particular locations and others for male employees who moved between locations; still others avoided the law by outsourcing the jobs held primarily by women, reducing the number of women employed, counter to the law's intention (Mun 2016). By eliminating "female" jobs, Japanese firms disengaged from the law, moving beyond the its reach. In some circumstances, organizations fail to comply outright; for example, Dutch bars were less likely to comply with a new E.U. smoking ban when their local communities were more socially cohesive (Simons, Vermeulen, and Knoben 2016). In sum, organizations have many different tactics for

65. Such evaluations have historical precedents, the most notable and far-reaching being the International Organization for Standardization (formed 1947) and its predecessor, the International Standards Association (formed 1926). These organizations developed common standards, first for physical products (screw threads and bolts), then for work processes, pollution, human rights, and quality management (Yates and Murphy 2019). Even earlier examples exist, such as nineteenth-century credit ratings that assessed the risks inherent in trade with and lending to American firms (Carruthers 2013).

gaining legitimacy (conform to the environment, select the environment, or manipulate it), maintaining legitimacy (police internal activity, eschew obvious appeals for legitimacy, and stockpile goodwill), and repairing legitimacy (offer normalizing accounts and restructure) (Suchman 1995).

Empirical work on strategic action often focuses on how *rhetoric* is used to legitimate it. After a public-relations crisis involving concerns about food safety, human health, and environmental degradation, the California cattle industry repaired its legitimacy through verbal accounts (Elsbach 1994). When industry participants acknowledged the concerns (e.g., "we recognize [something bad] happened, but we had good reasons for what we did" or "yes, there were harms, but there were also benefits"), they appeared more legitimate than when they denied those concerns (e.g., "it didn't happen"). Industry responses to criticism, particularly acknowledgments, that referred to the industry's institutional features (e.g., by reference to external evaluators like the U.S. Department of Agriculture) were more effective than those that referred to its technical features (e.g., by reference to efficiency and reduced costs for consumers). In the same vein, the Canadian accounting profession was "framed" as being under threat, so broadening accounting's professional scope was portrayed as a natural solution (Greenwood, Suddaby, and Hinings 2002). And HIV/AIDS activists framed consultation and information exchange between community organizations and pharmaceutical companies as consistent with existing routines and as being in many stakeholders' interests (Maguire, Hardy, and Lawrence 2004).

Strategic action is especially obvious when people are trying to create new kinds of organizations. Such *institutional entrepreneurship* (DiMaggio 1988) requires the skillful use of social resources to overcome skepticism and persuade others to believe entrepreneurs' representations of social reality and support their new kinds of organizations (Fligstein 1997). For example, art historians and their wealthy patrons cooperated in the late nineteenth century to develop art museums as a distinct form of organization by creating a framework that distinguished vulgar art from high art and by establishing them as non-profit enterprises, which distanced them from "dirty" commerce (DiMaggio 1991). Similarly, product-testing organizations and consumer leagues promoted non-profit consumer watchdog associations by tapping into the growing customer service and truth-in-advertising movement, and by linking their activities to the already legitimate home economics academic field (Rao 1998). Such actions conferred normative appropriateness on consumer watchdog associations and shielded them from opposition. And the earliest management consultants forged relationships with recognized authorities and social elites, and emphasized the benefits of their ventures for society at large (David, Sine, and Haveman 2013). Even groups that are marginalized and have little power—like women in the nineteenth and early twentieth centuries—have been able to take strategic action and launch organizations that have become powerful (Clemens 1997).

Macro to Micro: Institutional Logics

The study of institutional logics emerged in the 1990s and is now a booming line of research. The pioneers of this research tradition, Roger Friedland and Robert Alford, were always interested in power, guided by the zeitgeist of the social upheavals of the 1960s and 1970s. They rejected both rationalist theories of organizations (notably contingency theory and organizational ecology) as ignoring power. They also rejected Marxist theory as a totalizing system that left no room for institutional variation. Inspired by Max Weber's ([1904–5] 1958) writings on value systems, they sought to reconcile instrumental rationality and value rationality by recognizing their coexistence in the logics that guided behavior, set the rules of the game, and determined what practices can (indeed must) be used. They were also influenced by Bendix's (1956) theory of managerial ideologies in capitalist enterprises. Finally, they wanted to bring back larger social structures that operated beyond the immediate (industry) environments of firms—institutional orders—into the study of organizations.

They initially defined institutional logics as "sets of material practices and symbolic constructions [that] constitute [the] organizing principles" of institutional orders (Friedland and Alford 1991: 248–49). This definition means that institutional logics are societal-level phenomena, as each of the institutional orders—in modern Western societies, these are the capitalist market, the bureaucratic state, democratic politics, the nuclear family, and Christian religion—has a different central logic. In highlighting the power of institutional orders, Friedland and Alford reoriented organizational theory toward societal-level explanations. They argued that institutional logics are historically specific because they exist in particular times and places, and so organizations' responses to them differ across time and space. And institutional logics determine both what should be done in order to achieve desired outcomes and what is good to do—both instrumental and value rationality. Thus, logics are both frames for action and products of action (Holm 1995). In any society, multiple logics exist, sometimes competing, at other times coexisting (more or less) peacefully. Note that this theory privileges structure over agency: societies create constraints and opportunities for organizational action, while organizations create constraints and opportunities for individual action. This argument leaves little room for maneuvering around or challenging societal logics.

Starting in the 2000s, institutional logics increasingly came to be seen as existing at multiple levels of analysis: in individual organizations, industries, or interorganizational fields (Dunn and Jones 2010; Thornton, Ocasio, and Lounsbury 2012). This representation separates institutional logics from societal-level institutional orders. In this view, institutional logics *both* constrain the choice sets available to individuals, groups, and organizations *and* provide opportunities for them to socially construct and reconstruct logics in ways that reflect their interests. Individuals, groups, and organizations can use the cultural elements of higher-level logics to create, transform, bolster, or undermine lower-level logics. This implies that while actors are embedded in institutional logics, they are at least partly autonomous from them. This theoretical shift places greater emphasis on power and agency, and less on cognition and structural constraints, than did earlier theorizing.[66]

My preferred definition of institutional logics is purely cognitive: "systems of cultural elements (values, beliefs, and normative expectations) by which people, groups, and organizations make sense of and evaluate their everyday activities, and organize those activities in time and space" (Haveman and Gualtieri 2017: 1). Material phenomena, such as organizational structures, practices, policies, rituals, and roles, are the *consequences* of action guided by institutional logics: *manifestations* of logics.[67] And material phenomena shape institutional logics, as the very existence (and prevalence) of material phenomena can support, transform, or challenge logics. Thus, there is a duality of logics and their material manifestations: they are co-constitutive (Haveman and Rao 1997). Keeping the two parts of the duality conceptually distinct prevents conflating them and facilitates the development of empirically testable theory.

An example will clarify the co-constitution of logics and their material manifestations. Early thrifts, financial institutions that brought people together to save money and build or buy houses, were guided by a series of institutional logics involving beliefs about how to organize saving and home ownership (Haveman and Rao 1997). The first logic celebrated mutual cooperation and rigidly structured action, predicated on the idea of community as the source of interpersonal trust. It was instantiated in collections of people who came together at regular intervals to save money, borrowed from the growing communal fund to build homes, and dissolved their associations when their joint task was completed. A half-century later, the dominant logic celebrated bureaucracy (division of labor by role and time) and voluntary,

---

66. As I explain below, this reconceptualization is sometimes explicitly informed by symbolic interactionism (McPherson and Sauder 2013; Binder, Davis, and Bloom 2016), which is used in micro-cultural research studying institutions on the ground.

67. Note that since organizational cultures involve shared ideologies that are revealed in language, rites, and rituals (Pettigrew 1979; Trice and Beyer 1984; Van Maanen 1991), organizational cultures are everyday manifestations of institutional logics.

instrumentally rational action, predicated on the notion of bureaucracy as the source of interpersonal trust. It was instantiated in permanent organizations run by professional managers. It distinguished between owners of installment shares (which could be withdrawn at any time, or augmented at any time in any amount) and guarantee shares (capital investment that was non-withdrawable and used to guarantee earnings on installment shares). It also distinguished between savers (owners of installment shares) and borrowers, as not all savers had to borrow to build or buy homes. Thus, different institutional logics were associated with different goals, authority structures, financial intermediation technologies, roles for members, and services. Changes in thrifts' institutional logics were driven by two external factors: the rise of a transient and hetero-geneous population, which undermined the community pillar of the first thrift logic, and the Progressive movement, which undermined the structured or forced action of the first thrift logic and paved the way for acceptance of the impersonal bureaucratic pillar of the logic that came to dominate the thrift industry.

As this example illustrates, institutional logics can vary over time and across space, depending on external events like legal changes and social movements, the composition of field actors, and actors' preferences and knowledge about or skill with practices. For example, in book publishing, the editorial logic, which viewed editors as professionals and emphasized their relationships with authors as the key to success, was replaced by the market logic, which viewed editors as corporate executives and emphasized competition as the main de-terminant of success (Thornton and Ocasio 1999). The shift in logics, driven and reinforced by rising competition from firms outside the industry that ac-quired incumbents and focused on profits and growth, dramatically altered the ways publishing companies grew (by nurturing new authors versus by acquiring other firms) and the determinants of editorial succession. Similarly, American hospitals changed their policies and procedures as the prevailing logic of health care shifted from professional dominance (doctors rule) to managed care (insurance companies rule) (Scott et al. 2000). These changes were driven by legal changes—the passage of laws authorizing the Medicare and Medicaid programs in 1965 and two bills in 1981 and 1982—that altered the rules governing health care providers and their incentive structures. Fig-ure 6.4 depicts the causes and consequences of institutional logics.

Although the strength of institutional logics varies over time, they may not die out completely. For example, in American medical schools, the strength of two logics—care and science—fluctuated in response to contestation among physicians, competition with rival health care practitioners, funding changes (the rise of managed care), and the increasing representation of women (Dunn and Jones 2010). In a more extreme case, the craft brewing

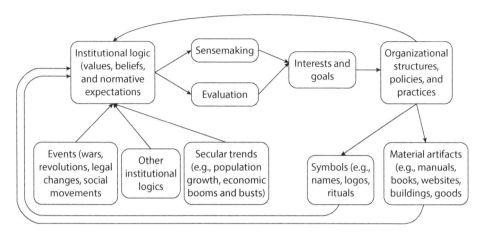

FIGURE 6.4. Causes and consequences of institutional logics

logic almost disappeared from the Netherlands, but it regained strength as craft brewing resurged in other countries (Kroezen and Heugens 2019). Its re-emergence was facilitated by the "institutional remnants" of the craft logic: artifacts such as writings about beer, brewery names, and buildings.

Many scholars have studied how *multiple logics* interact. For example, Spanish firms' actions depend on the location of their branch establishments: those with operations more concentrated in regions with higher levels of government spending on economic development are less likely to downsize, emphasizing an equity logic over an efficiency logic (Greenwood et al. 2010). Similarly, local Spanish banks whose founders are motivated by a finance logic are more likely to finance growth using risky deposit instruments than are banks whose founders are motivated by a community logic (Almandoz 2014).

Logics can vary in their compatibility with and centrality to organizational functioning (Besharov and Smith 2014). Considering both dimensions yields a four-cell typology of situations where two or more logics coexist. (1) Low compatibility and high centrality of both (or all) logics yields contestation and extensive conflict. For instance, a wave of bank acquisitions in the U.S. in the 1990s and 2000s, driven by the logic of efficient geographic diversification, led those who supported the logic of community banking (local bankers) actively to oppose such acquisitions by launching new local, community-focused banks (Marquis and Lounsbury 2007). (2) High compatibility and high centrality yields alignment (or blending/hybridization) and minimal conflict. For example, in public–private energy industry alliances, people grapple with very different logics of success: they are forced to synthesize the logics into a new one as they confront outcomes that are successes when viewed through the logic of public service, but failures when viewed through the logic of client service (Jay 2013). (3) High compatibility and low centrality (meaning one logic is core to organizational functioning) yield a single dominant logic and no conflict. For example, the shareholder-value logic, which posits that corporations' primary goal is to maximize share price by cutting costs to ensure short-term profits, has dominated business corporations since the 1980s (Fligstein 2001; Fligstein and Shin 2004). This logic is so overpowering that it was not imperiled even by the 2008 financial crisis. (4) Low compatibility and low centrality yields one dominant logic and moderate conflict, as people adjudicate between logics. For instance, in one cultural organization, the cultural-preservation and professional logics coexisted peacefully, but then they were confronted with a market logic espoused by senior managers and funding agencies; however, the market logic was peripheral to the organization's goals, so conflict was moderate for a long time (Townley 2002).

Institutional logics affect individuals, entire organizations, and society at large. For example, the shareholder-value logic has pushed many corporations to downsize (Jung 2016)—although managers have been less affected than line workers and support staff (Goldstein 2012). Most of the low-level employees who remain are paid less and offered fewer benefits, while managers, professionals, and skilled technical workers receive better pay and benefits (although they are expected to work longer hours); the result is increasing earnings inequality (Fligstein and Shin 2004). The shareholder-value logic promotes financialization, meaning increasing reliance on financial instruments like bonds, stocks, and derivatives (Krippner 2005), because it resonates with the finance backgrounds of corporate executives. The impact ranges far beyond for-profit corporations. For example, this logic led U.S. higher education institutions to increase their dependence on debt capital (among non-profit institutions) or equity capital (among for-profit institutions) (Eaton et al. 2016). Reliance on debt increased operating costs, which were passed along to students and their families in the form of tuition fee increases, saddling them with often unmanageable debt and further increasing economic inequality.

Micro: Institutions on the Ground

Starting in the 1990s, some scholars became concerned that institutionalist research on organizations had become too macroscopic—concerned with entire industries or fields—and so neglected the interests, ideas, and actions of the people who inhabited (gave life to) organizations. These scholars reacted by developing a new approach to the cultural analysis of organizations, using ideas from early micro sociology (Cooley 1902, 1909; Mead 1934) and symbolic interactionism (Goffman 1959, 1974; Blumer 1969). As explained above, these earlier literatures analyzed the meanings that people develop through interaction—symbolic systems that guide evaluation and action—and how people (re)interpret these meanings as they continue to interact, and thus create and maintain them. Although these ideas had been used in sociological research outside the field of organizations, little attention was paid to the larger structures within which people are embedded, so only a few studies of organizations were built on them, and those were focused on occupations, not organizations per se. For example, the "emotional labor" (creating desirable emotional displays) that is central to flight attendants' training inculcates "feeling rules" that guide interactions with customers (Hochschild [1983] 2003). And cooks and chefs in a wide array of restaurants negotiate the balance between economic necessity and aesthetics (Fine 1996).

The result of this inward turn is research on *inhabited institutions* (Scully and Creed 1997; Hallett 2010), which focuses on the meanings (I would call them logics) that organizational members (e.g., workers or students) attach to their roles (e.g., for workers, jobs; for students, academic careers), the conflict and consensus that these meanings drive when they are enacted, and the resulting organizational structures, cultures, and behaviors. For example, in drug courts, probation officers, defense and prosecuting attorneys, and clinicians use different logics (criminal punishment, rehabilitation, accountability, and efficiency) to negotiate decisions (McPherson and Sauder 2013). In elite universities, undergraduates' beliefs about "good" careers are shaped by interactions (with other students, faculty, staff, and corporate recruiters) and organizational structures (e.g., housing, faculty–student ratios, class registration procedures), which funnel almost half of graduates into jobs in finance, consulting, and tech (Ho 2009; Binder, Davis, and Bloom 2016). Logics can be developed and maintained by people in multiple organizations to handle conflicting logics within and between organizations (DeJordy et al. 2020). Finally, while institutional pressures may force changes in organizational members' logics, those pressures may not alter their practices. For example, staff at a rape crisis center originally interpreted their work through a feminist lens, but when increased demand forced them to open their doors to non-feminist volunteers, the lens changed to a therapeutic one, even though volunteer training and patient practices remained the same (Zilber 2002).

A related line of inquiry examines *institutional work*: what people do to create, maintain, transform, or disrupt institutions. This institutional work in turn affects the logics associated with institutions (Lawrence and Suddaby 2006). *Creating* new or alternative institutions involves reconstructing rules or regulations through advocacy and reconfiguring belief systems by constructing new identities and educating others (Lawrence and Suddaby 2006). For example, in the 1970s, a group of young but celebrated French chefs banded together to change the norms of restaurants, such as menu length and flavor, to create the "nouvelle cuisine" logic, which dictated shorter menus and more natural flavors than the classical cuisine logic (Rao, Monin, and Durand 2003). Creating institutions can require serious negotiation. For example, establishing international labor standards was facilitated by union negotiators creating joint initiatives to solve problems, such as issuing reports to both management and the union, which generated integrative (win–win) solutions (Helfen and Sydow 2013).

Maintaining existing institutions involves enabling, policing, deterring, celebrating and critiquing, and embedding and routinizing (Lawrence and Suddaby 2006). For example, consulting and law firms engage in "cultural matching" during hiring: they identify good job candidates based on shared cultural experiences: school prestige, extracurricular activities, and academic majors (Rivera 2012). This requires valorizing and accepting traits and tastes that match those of current employees. Similarly, elaborate dining rituals at the University of Cambridge—formal attire, multiple courses, fine wine, and servants—inculcate in students the norms, values, and behaviors of the top tier of the British class system, transforming students' identities (Dacin, Munir, and Tracey 2010). The effects of these transformative rituals last long after graduation, helping to maintain a rigid class hierarchy. In contrast, *disrupting* or *transforming* institutions involves undermining or deinstitutionalizing them by disconnecting the associated sanctions and rewards, dissociating their moral foundations, or undermining their assumptions and beliefs (Oliver 1992). For example, the logic of conventional medicine was disrupted by the introduction of the new logic of integrative medicine, which led to much questioning of the assumptions and beliefs of conventional medicine (Heinze and Weber 2016).

Together, studies of institutions on the ground provide a much-needed micro perspective, given that the majority of cultural research on organizations has been meso- or macro-level (focusing on organizations, industries, or fields). Micro-level studies reveal the subtle complexities of institutional change and stability, legitimation and delegitimation—heterogeneity that is necessarily masked by much meso- and macro-level research (Bitekine and Haack 2015).

Conclusion

The cultural perspective has a sweeping reach. Consider the core concepts *institution* and *institutionalization*. Scholars working in this tradition have identified the carriers of institutions at multiple levels of analysis: the routines, rules, scripts, and schemas that guide the perceptions and actions of individuals, groups, organizations, occupations, and fields; societal norms and codified patterns of meaning and interpretation. They have claimed that institutionalization is both an outcome, which suggests attention to stability, and a process, which suggests attention to change (Tolbert and Zucker 1996). They have identified a wide array of mechanisms through which institutionalization occurs: typification and habituation, blind or limitedly rational imitation, normative conformity, accreditation, social obligation, and outright coercion. In building theory, they have drawn not only on sociology, but also on anthropology, cognitive psychology, philosophy, and linguistics. Finally, they have employed a wide array of methodologies, ranging from ethnographies and qualitative historical studies, to laboratory experiments, to statistical analyses of survey, administrative, and archival data.

But the strength provided by this broad reach also generates a critical weakness. If the terms "institution" and "institutionalization" mean everything and explain everything—change and stability; individual routines, organizational structures, and societal cultures; cognitive, regulatory, and normative processes—then they mean nothing and explain nothing. The cultural analysis of organizations currently encompasses a loose collection of propositions and proto-theories, some seemingly incompatible and others only tenuously connected. For example, it is unclear when cognitive, normative, or coercive pressures predominates (Mizruchi and Fein 1999). It is also unclear whether there is any meaningful difference between blended and hybrid logics (Haveman and Gualtieri 2017). Given these fundamental uncertainties, debates in this tradition tend to be unproductive feuds about definitions and concepts, rather than substantive arguments about logic or evidence.

To remedy this situation, cultural scholars must develop tighter theory— likely a series of related theories. Paradigm consensus can benefit cultural research, as it has research in the macro demographic perspective, by making studies more comparable, the efforts of scholars better coordinated, and the findings of multiple studies more easily accumulated into a coherent body of knowledge. The path toward developing paradigm consensus has (at least) three steps. The first is to achieve agreement on the meaning of central constructs. What general attributes define an institution? How do these abstractions apply to observable phenomena? How does institutionalization unfold (e.g., are there obvious stages)? The second step is to formulate clear statements about relationships between constructs. This will require bounding claims about causation. Which explanations for isomorphism are most compelling—cognitive, regulatory, or normative—for what kinds of institution, at what levels of analysis? Who has the power to institutionalize? Because causal mechanisms vary across settings, specifying clearly when and where different institutionalization processes operate, when and where various institutional actors are potent, is essential. The third step is to reach agreement on research priorities. What outcomes are central to the theory and so must be accorded highest priority? What kinds of data and what analytical techniques are best suited to test the most compelling explanations of those outcomes? Some institutional work already achieves these objectives, most notably research on firms' responses to changing legal and cultural conceptions of employees' civil rights (Edelman 1990, 1992; Dobbin et al. 1993; Dobbin and Sutton 1998; Guthrie and Roth 1999; Skaggs 2008). This work has been extended to consider the civil rights of students on college and university campuses (Gualtieri 2020). But most lines of institutional research are not cumulative to such an extent.

Concretely, my prescription involves developing and testing multiple related theories, meaning logically interconnected sets of propositions concerning a delimited set of social phenomena, derived from assumptions about essential facts (axioms), that detail causal mechanisms and yield empirically testable (i.e., falsifiable) hypotheses (Merton 1968). This requires being consistent about how concepts are used in theoretical statements. It also requires forbearing from minting new concepts for the sake of "advancing theory" (i.e., getting journal editors to accept papers). A proliferation of concepts that are not logically interconnected retards, rather than advances, the development of theory. Developing systematic theory also compels us to assess the reliability and validity of our empirical measures. This effort would benefit from conducting meta-analyses of the many inductive studies that have been published to develop deductive theory, and compare it with the deductive theory snippets that have already appeared in published work.

There are likely to be philosophical differences, both ontological (concerning the nature of reality) and epistemological (concerning what researchers can know), between scholars working with this perspective, making their arguments incommensurable. For example, positivists tend to focus on objective, external social facts. In contrast, phenomenologists tend to reject the possibility of objective facts; they focus instead on social construction and subjective interpretation. As a result of such fundamental differences, any paradigm-building effort is likely to incite theoretical schisms. The result would be multiple internally coherent theories-in-progress, each of which would undoubtedly have a more limited scope of application than today's undifferentiated mass of cultural research, but also multiple explanatory voices, each more focused and more powerful than current work.

One final point bears mention. Almost all work on organizational identities has been qualitative, but there is room for engagement by scholars using quantitative methods. Since organizational identities are created, transformed, and maintained through language (Fiol 2002; Anteby and Molnár 2012), such work could follow the lead of recent research on organizational culture and use computational text analysis.

7

Hybrid Research

COMBINING PERSPECTIVES

AS THE PRECEDING CHAPTERS make clear, each of the three contemporary perspectives on organizations has upsides and downsides. To overcome some of the downsides, many organizational theorists have found it fruitful to combine insights from multiple perspectives in a single study. Here, I review some of the liveliest intersections of perspectives. But to keep it brief, this review is by no means comprehensive. I also suggest fruitful avenues for future research.

Demographic and Relational Perspectives

Originally, relational scholars, both micro and macro, often assumed that social relations are primary and atomistic attributes are secondary (epiphenomenal), even though atomistic attributes often determine whether ties are created and maintained, as well as the nature of ties (Blau 1977, 1994). For their part, some early demographic scholars did not make explicit the role that social relations play in determining the origin of achieved attributes or the impact of ascribed and achieved attributes (Reagans, Zuckerman, and McEvily 2004). But more and more scholars are recognizing the interdependence of demography and social relations.

Demographic characteristics, social networks, and work. On the micro level, managerial *information-processing and communication theory* focuses on how the access to information and information-processing styles of people in different social positions affect trust, commitment, and creativity (Ancona and Caldwell 1992). This work was motivated by observations of the problems facing many organizations: what makes some teams work well and others not? Researchers observed that internal factors like clear goals could not explain many differences between teams. Instead, they induced that ties between the focal team and other teams mattered greatly. And they observed that what affects team members' likelihood of forming ties is demography.

Prompted by these observations, scholars began to investigate how people communicate and process the information they receive from those with whom they interact when interaction partners are from similar versus different demographic groups (e.g., Ancona and Caldwell 1992; Reagans 2005). People are more likely to form strong social relations with others who are in similar demographic groups—that is, who have similar tenure or who are of a similar age—due to interpersonal attraction and similarities in identity and interests (Reagans 2005, 2011). And spatial proximity amplifies the positive effect of some demographic similarities (Reagans 2011). This line of thought cascaded to a wide array of investigations of how demography and social relations jointly affected team (and organizational) innovation and creativity (e.g., Reagans, Zuckerman, and McEvily 2004; Gibson and Gibbs 2006; Page 2007).

Along the same lines, but examining different dimensions of demography, persistent concerns about inequality motivated an upsurge of research on how social networks differ between members of ethno-racial groups and between the sexes, and how these differences explain differences in job opportunities and workplace outcomes. At the point of hiring, Blacks and women are less likely than White men to use social ties (specifically, referrals from current employees) to find a job, so they are less likely to get interviews and job offers (Petersen, Saporta, and Seidel 2000; Mouw 2003; Fernandez and Sosa 2005; Fernandez and Fernandez-Mateo 2006). Their relative lack of referrals means that when Blacks and women do get job offers, they are paid less than White men. Black job-seekers' contacts are less likely to refer them to prospective employers than are those of White job-seekers (cf. Granovetter 1973 vs. [Sandra S.] Smith 2005). And female and minority job-seekers are less likely than White male job-seekers to have high-status social ties ([Nan] Lin 2001; McDonald 2011), so even when women and people of color obtain referrals to employers, they gain less advantage from referrals than do White men (Fernandez and Fernandez-Mateo 2006; Silva 2018).

After they are hired, women and people of color are less likely to form strong social ties to other work-group members, especially to men and Whites, which in part is due to differences in social status across these demographic groups (Brass 1985). As a result, women and people of color segregate into different social networks from men and Whites. Compared to men and Whites, women and people of color also tend to occupy more peripheral positions in work-related and friendship networks, especially networks that contain powerful alters, which helps explain why women and people of color are less influential (Brass 1985; Lincoln and Miller 1979; Ibarra 1992; McGuire 2000). Women and people of color are less likely than men and Whites to form homophilous (same-sex or same-race) social ties; these results hold even after taking into consideration the differing availability of homophilous alters

(Ibarra 1992, 1995). The relationship between demographic attributes and tie formation tends to be stronger for instrumental networks of mentoring and advice than for social support networks, because women and people of color make greater efforts than men and Whites to find same-sex or same-race friends. But that pattern seems to be due to the nature of the employing organizations studied. In the work cited above, women and people of color were numerical minorities. When Whites are numerical minorities, as is true for teachers in some public schools, the pattern changes: numerical-minority White teachers make great efforts to form same-race social ties to secure professional, political, and emotional resources at work (Nelson 2019). In contrast, numerical-minority Black teachers form same-race ties more to secure emotional resources and less to secure professional and political resources.

Not only do the social networks of women and people of color differ greatly from those of men and Whites, but their returns to their social networks (the benefits derived from them) also differ greatly. For example, in the U.S. film industry, women's career prospects—their likelihood of continuing to work in films—depended on the networks they developed over the course of their careers (Lutter 2015). Women's career prospects were worse than men's when they had been part of more cohesive networks, meaning they had worked in teams whose members knew each other better from past collaborations and therefore had stronger social ties. In contrast, women's career prospects were similar to men's when they had been part of more diverse and open networks, meaning they had worked in teams whose members had a wide range of experiences across genres, so they had weaker social ties. Cohesive networks provide better access to redundant information about future job opportunities, while more diverse and open networks provide better access to diverse information about film-making. In a very different setting, the Champagne industry, female grape growers had less access than their male counterparts to information that influenced the prices they could get for their grapes (Ody-Brasier and Fernandez-Mateo 2017). But female grape growers were able to overcome this informational disadvantage by developing social relations with other female grape growers, which resulted in their obtaining higher prices for their grapes than male grape growers. In contrast, among senior managers in a large firm (who were scattered geographically and across product divisions), women benefited from cohesive rather than diverse and open networks (Burt 1998). The difference between these studies' findings suggests that context may matter—in terms, that is, of the overall cohesiveness of the networks under study and the extent to which the networks involve relations between (rather than within) organizations.

Formal mentoring programs may improve access by women and people of color to organizational and industry elites. Improved access to elites is expected to make them more visible to organizational decision makers, more legitimate, and more valued, which in turn should improve their career outcomes. But little careful research has been conducted on the causal impact of such programs. One study of a Chinese software firm combined interview and experimental methods to reveal that such programs do indeed improve women's access to elites, help them engage with successful others in their organizations, and signal their worth (Srivastava 2015). Obviously, there is room for more such research.

Group-level demography and social relations. Other research examines the impact of group demography on workplace interactions. When group demographic diversity undercuts cohesion and trust (thus reducing the number of bonding ties within a group), group performance declines, but when diversity exposes group members to non-redundant sources of information (through bridging ties to people outside a work group), group performance improves (Reagans, Zuckerman, and McEvily 2004). Group demographic diversity reduces group cohesion but expands the range of ties to people outside the group; both internal cohesion and external range improve group performance. As a result, it is easier to improve group performance by manipulating social networks than by manipulating demographic profiles. Importantly, this work demonstrates that network mechanisms mediate the impact of diversity. The value of considering both demography and social relations is clearest when groups consist of relatively homogeneous subgroups based on two or more correlated demographic attributes (e.g., younger women vs. older men), which cleave groups along fault lines (Lau and Murnighan 1998). When fault lines exist, group performance depends on how much the tendency toward homophily yields social relations that are segregated on either side of fault lines (Ren, Gray, and Harrison 2015). When people in subgroups across demographic fault lines are friends, those social ties help bridge multiple demographic divides, enhancing communication and reducing conflict between subgroups. But the nature (content) of the ties also matters: not surprisingly, negative ties (animosity) across fault lines hamper communication and increase conflict, while positive ties (friendship) do the opposite.

Some research on work-group demography and social relations is explicitly dynamic, examining how demographic processes such as hiring and turnover affect the formation and dissolution of social relations between work-group members. For example, exit by middle-level professionals from both advertising agencies and their client firms—the people who manage interorganizational relationships on a daily basis—made agency–client relationships more likely to dissolve (Broschak 2004). But these interorganizational relationships are not often dependent solely on a single pair of people. Instead, they often involve multiple people in each firm. If so, the structure of relations within professional-service firms *and* between those firms and their clients will moderate the effect of turnover on interorganizational relations. For example, when advertising agencies had multiple (rather than single) employees tied to a focal client, executive exit was less likely to result in relationship dissolution (Rogan 2014). Similarly, when the internal networks of law firms were more cohesive, lead partner exit was less likely to result in less work from the affected clients and thus lower billable hours for law firms (Briscoe and Rogan 2016).

Power, networks, and the demography of organizations. On the macro level, theoretical connections were made between the demographic and relational perspectives starting in the 1980s, when researchers called for the use of relational techniques to define organizational niches and forms based on interorganizational networks (McPherson 1983; DiMaggio 1986; Burt and Talmud 1993). The first such study mapped voluntary social service organizations onto the demographics of their members in terms of gender, age, education, and socioeconomic status (McPherson 1983). Organizations that appealed to the same demographic groups occupied the same niche, meaning they competed over members, which affected their rates of growth (and decline) and failure (McPherson 1983; McPherson and Ranger-Moore 1991). Members are an important resource for which many kinds of organizations, not just voluntary social service organizations, compete: supporters of political parties and social movement organizations (Heaney and Rojas 2014), customers and employees of corporations (Sørensen 2004), students and teachers in educational institutions (Baum and Singh 1994), and adherents to religious denominations (Land, Deane, and Blau 1991).

Other macro demographic-relational research focuses on organizational products. For example, in the semiconductor industry, market niches can be defined as sets of firms whose patents are structurally equivalent—meaning they draw on the same literature and cite the same earlier patents (Podolny and Stuart 1995). The presence of higher-status organizations in a technology-based niche increases the probability that other firms will enter that niche by filing patents. In contrast, niche crowding lowers the probability of entry of firms. In addition, firms are more likely to thrive when their niches have higher-status inhabitants, and less likely to thrive when their niches are more crowded. In a very different context, the network positions of inter-governmental organizations (IGOs) like the World Bank and NATO, based on their member countries, had strong effects on both their founding and failure rates (Ingram and Torafson 2010). For instance, IGOs that connected national governments with more similar governance structures, or that were more geographically proximate, were more likely to be founded and less likely to fail. And in the health care sector, a relational analysis of journal articles and conference proceedings revealed three dimensions for organizational forms, based on their service portfolios: degree of financial risk (low for hospitals and ambulatory care facilities; high for health-maintenance organizations and insurance companies), duration of care (short for private practices and teaching hospitals; long for nursing homes and home-care agencies), and degree of patient risk (high for nursing homes; low for private practices and health-maintenance organizations) (Ruef 1999).

A similar logic applies at the micro level. At this level, niches are defined as webs of relationships of employees involved in the same activities. People in more crowded niches are less effective at obtaining the information they need to ensure career success, while those in niches with higher-status alters are more effective (Liu, Srivastava, and Stuart 2016).

Demographic and Cultural Perspectives

The combination of demographic and cultural perspectives has been immensely generative for both micro and macro research. It has enriched demographic research by making explicit causal mechanisms that have often been implicit. And it has enriched cultural research by explicitly recognizing that norms, values, and behavioral expectations of different demographic groups vary widely, and that organizational cultures are lenses that yield very different understandings of different demographic groups.

Cultural schemas and institutional logics shape evaluations of demographic groups. On the micro side, a growing stream of research reveals how the evaluation of workers with different demographic attributes is shaped by cultural schemas. Most of this research focuses on gender. For example, in financial services firms, women face competing cultural expectations—devotion to work and devotion to family—while men face only the former; this harms women's careers by making them seem less well-suited to jobs in this type of firm (Blair-Loy 2003; Turco 2010). This finding is not limited to financial services. In general, job applicants who leave work to care for children are less likely to be hired when they re-enter the labor market, because they violate the gendered ideal-worker stereotype, the cultural lens through which workers are evaluated (Weisshaar 2018). In a similar vein, the cultural schemas law firms deploy when they evaluate recruits vary in terms of how much weight they give to stereotypically masculine traits (ambition, assertiveness, and self-confidence) versus stereotypically feminine traits (cooperation and friendliness) (Gorman 2005). Law firms with cultural schemas that were more stereotypically masculine (feminine) hired more men (women). Gendered cultural schemas about family versus work affect even those who do not (yet) have children. For instance, university hiring committees were concerned with the relationship status of female applicants but not of male applicants, because they assumed women with partners were less moveable than men with partners (Rivera 2017).

Gendered cultural schemas about family versus work can trump other cultural schemas, including racial ones. For example, in the leveraged buyout (LBO) industry, gender is a more relevant criterion for social exclusion than race, because women do not possess key cultural resources and do not fit the ideal-worker profile, while Black men do (Turco 2010). To gain acceptance at work, LBO employees need access to knowledge of and interest in sports, a cultural resource that is more likely to be possessed by Black men than by women of any color. Moreover, the ideal LBO worker is highly aggressive, competitive, and work-obsessed, attributes that fit cultural beliefs about masculinity, including Black masculinity, but conflict with cultural beliefs about femininity and motherhood.

Gendered cultural schemas can vary across jobs. For example, when engineering jobs are primarily technical (e.g., involving research, product development, or coding), women are disadvantaged more, relative to men, than when engineering jobs are primarily social (e.g., involving administration or teaching), because the ideal-worker stereotype for more technical jobs is more masculine and for more social jobs it is more feminine (Cech 2013). Gendered cultural schemas can also vary within a single job over time. For instance, in an emergency medical unit, cultural schemas for doctors are more stereotypically masculine for late-stage residents than for early-stage residents, as evaluation criteria shift from valorizing cautious learners to celebrating confident leaders (Brewer et al. 2020). As a result of changing gendered cultural schemas across stages in physician training, performance evaluations of female residents become less positive in their third year, relative to male residents' evaluations, even after controlling for objective performance.

Beyond gendered cultural schemas, coercive and normative pressures from legal systems that are undergirded by societal-level institutional logics, such as equality and opportunity (Friedland and Alford 1991), influence women's and minorities' access to jobs. Specifically, both state statutes and judicial interpretations of equal opportunity laws create normative pressure for greater representation of women and people of color in high-income, high-status positions. Firms in states with more explicit equal opportunity language in their statutes are more likely to have female CEOs (Guthrie and Roth 1999). Similarly, firms operating in more progressive federal circuit-court jurisdictions are more likely to have female CEOs and more women in other managerial positions (Guthrie and Roth 1999; Skaggs 2008).

As this review shows, the primary focus of research on demographic attributes and cultural schemas has been on gender. Hence, there are opportunities for studying variation in cultural schemas about other demographic features, such as race and ethnicity, age, sexuality, (dis)ability, education, functional background, and work experience. Such work is needed, because the impact of cultural schemas and societal logics is likely to vary across demographic features, as the study of LBO firms (Turco 2010) demonstrates. We cannot simply assume research on gender will be replicated in research on other demographic attributes.

The joint impact of group demography and organizational culture on group behavior. Micro-level research has examined how organizational culture moderates the impact of work-group demography. For instance, the effects of demography on work-group cooperation and productivity are more positive in organizations with collectivistic cultures than in organizations with individualistic cultures (Chatman et al. 1998). In the same vein, work groups where two or more demographic attributes (e.g., gender and work experience) are aligned perform better when their group norms about task performance are the same as their department's norms (Bezrukova et al. 2012). Not surprisingly, when employing organizations' cultures are more supportive of workforce diversity, ethno-racial diversity is associated with less conflict (Ely and Thomas 2001). More surprising is that organizational cultures emphasizing respect for coworkers can make demographic differences more salient; if so, different people may be more likely to perceive a focal coworker differently, which would increase conflict (Randel and Earley 2009).

The joint impact of group demography and many more aspects of culture, beyond collectivism and support for demographic diversity, could be studied, including uncertainty avoidance and long- versus short-term orientation (Hofstede 1980) and the extent to which organizational culture is gendered (Acker 1990; Britton 2000). And since organizational cultures are not usually monolithic, scholars should do more to investigate the differential joint impacts of demography and organizational subcultures. Finally, the joint impact of demography and culture strength (i.e., the extent to which organizational members agreed on what is [un]important and valued or debased) merits investigation.

Organizational form as identity category. At the macro level, insights from the demographic and cultural perspectives are blended in the flourishing stream of work that analyzes organizational forms as socially coded identities: recognizable patterns that take on rule-like standing and are enforced by observers (Hannan, Pólos, and Carroll 2007; Hannan et al. 2019).[68] This work was inspired by the realization that the ecological studies that were most convincing were those in which the population under study was a socially meaningful category, rather than a set of organizations that happened to appear in some

---

68. For reviews, see Negro, Koçak, and Hsu (2010); Durand, Granqvist, and Tyllström (2017).

sort of list. If forms of organizations are socially recognized (and bounded), then theory has to take into consideration the people who are judging which categories organizations fit into—and how well they fit. As a result, this theory builds on ideas from three sources. First is cognitive-psychological theories about category recognition (Rosch 1973, 1975; Smith, Shoben, and Rips 1974; Barsalou 1985; Hampton 1998) and statistical inference about categories (Ashby and Alfonso-Reese 1995; Feldman, Griffiths, and Morgan 2009). Second is sociological ideas about distinctions between social categories (Durkheim and Mauss [1903] 1963; Douglas 1966; Becker 1982; Zerubavel 1991; Lamont and Molnár 2002) and shared cognitive schemas (DiMaggio 1997). Third is computational-linguistics thinking about the geometry of concepts (Widdows 2004; Gärdenfors 2014).

According to this line of research, observers—customers, suppliers, current and potential employees, and oversight agencies—place organizational members, forms, and products in identity categories based on product offerings and visible elements of organizational structures.[69] Categories simplify audience members' perceptions and evaluations by grouping similar organizational members, organizations, and products together. Categories comprise both rules of conduct and signals to observers. Rules of conduct provide guidelines delimiting what members of identity categories should be and do, while signals define what members of identity categories are and do.[70]

The most recent formulation of this theory distinguishes between concepts and categories (Hannan et al. 2019). *Concepts* are mental representations— cognitive schemas—that people use to classify the objects, events, and actors they encounter. *Categories* are sets of objects, events, and actors that fit specific concepts. So concepts are used to identify and give meaning to objects, events, and actors, while categorization is the assigning of objects, events, and actors to concepts. This work formally incorporates social context, which determines which concepts are available to categorize objects, events, and actors, providing "situational knowledge" of what concepts mean and how they are related. Like other cultural research, it recognizes that concepts and associated categories develop through interaction—that they are products of cultural (that is, meaning-making) processes. This line of thinking has been used primarily to guide research on organizations and their products, but it has broad applicability.

---

69. A related line of work conceives of organizational strategies and actions as driven by managerial perceptions of competitors and suppliers (Porac, Thomas, and Baden-Fuller 1989; Ody-Brasier and Vermeulen 2014).

70. In blending description and prescription, categories of organizations are similar to stereotypes.

Conformity with the concept associated with an organizational or product category is rewarded by observers, while violation is punished. To judge conformity, observers focus on features that distinguish one category from another and ignore features that are common across categories. All organizations demonstrate their membership in a particular form by adopting elements that are distinctive of that form. For example, American craft brewers make beer in small quantities using natural ingredients and traditional methods, while mass-market brewers make beer in huge quantities using industrial techniques (Carroll and Swaminathan 2000).

Categories are often conceived of as fuzzy (rather than crisp) sets, with some organizations being more fully category members than others, so that organizations' "grade of membership" in a category (Hampton 1998) or their typicality (Rosch 1973, 1975) varies greatly (Hannan, Pólos, and Carroll 2007; Hannan et al. 2019). For example, corporations may be more, or less, typical of an industry category, depending on their level of activity in that industry and their overall level of diversification (Zuckerman 1999). Graded membership and variance in typicality occurs when boundaries between concepts and categories are only weakly institutionalized; when concepts and categories are not clearly distinct to internal and external audiences; when many small, perhaps unintended, changes in the things being categorized accumulate; or when organizations intentionally combine elements from multiple categories (Hannan and Freeman 1989; Hannan, Pólos, and Carroll 2007). Those with lower grades of membership are more often perceived as not "typical" (Rosch 1973, 1975) and so are more likely to be overlooked. If not overlooked, those with lower grades of membership are evaluated less positively (Zuckerman 1999; Hsu 2006; Bowers 2015). For example, when small breweries contract production out to another firm, rather than controlling it in-house as is expected, they are penalized for violating the features of the craft brewery form (Carroll and Swaminathan 2000). Similarly, feature films that that are perceived as being in more genres (e.g., western, science fiction, romance, and comedy) are less appealing to moviegoers than films that are perceived as being in fewer genres (e.g., western and romance only), so the former sell fewer tickets than the latter (Hsu 2006). More somberly, terrorist organizations whose beliefs span multiple (and more distant) ideologies are more likely to disband and less likely to succeed at killing people (Olzak 2016).

But sometimes low grades of membership benefit organizations. For example, microfinance lenders in developing economies successfully combine the features of non-profit development agencies with those of for-profit lending institutions (Battilana and Dorado 2010). Organizations can more successfully straddle or blend categories when they have higher status (Phillips and Zuckerman 2001; Ody-Brasier and Vermeulen 2014), when categories are emergent or in flux (Battilana and Dorado 2010), or when category combinations are relatively common (Ruef and Patterson 2009). Moreover, organizations and products can be classified based on multiple categorization systems simultaneously, which can attenuate the negative effects of not fully conforming to any single category's code (Kacpercyzk and Younkin 2018).

Identity categories evolve through several channels. New categories of products and producers often emerge from collective action (Carroll and Swaminathan 2000; Rao, Monin, and Durand 2003; Jones et al. 2012; David et al. 2013). And members of an emerging category can strategically link their category to existing, socially accepted categories through discourse ([Mark] Kennedy 2005; Khaire and Wadhwani 2010; David et al. 2013).

As time passes, categories become institutionalized. Institutionalization makes categories more constraining if category boundaries are sharper and more scrutinized (Ruef and Patterson 2009). But institutionalization can instead make categories less constraining, if it means taken-for-grantedness, so observers are less vigilant, giving category members more leeway to deviate from category codes (Hsu and Grodal 2015). And despite segregating mechanisms that create sharp category boundaries, high-status organizations may have leeway to combine elements of two or more categories (Phillips and Zuckerman 2001); such actions can jump-start a cascade of recombination by other, lower-status actors that eventually erodes category boundaries (Rao, Monin, and Durand 2005).

Relational and Cultural Perspectives

Early on, relational scholars generally assumed that social relations (interactions) determined shared meanings and so they did not investigate whether shared meanings affected social relations. For their part, while early cultural scholars (symbolic interactionists) recognized that shared meanings were created through interaction (e.g., Goffman 1961; Blumer 1969), much cultural research on organizations ignored this connection and focused on the nature and impact of shared meanings. The important exception is ethnographic studies of occupational and organizational cultures (e.g., Van Maanen 1973; Barley 1983), which built directly on symbolic interactionism. But over time, more and more lines of research on organizations developed to link these perspectives, recognizing the joint effects of social relations and shared systems of meaning.

Cultural embeddedness. Social theorists have long called for deeper theorization in relational analysis by recognizing that culture is inherently relational because it is created by social interaction, and calling for relational analysis of cultural elements (Brint 1992; Emirbayer 1997; Mohr 1998). In this view, cultural elements are embedded in shared meaning structures because social relations determine actors' perceptions and evaluative schema. As yet, only a few studies of organizations have engaged deeply with these ideas. One investigated transactions between regulators and workers in three industries (trucking, steel, and academic science); these transactions influenced how workers perceived workplace safety, health, and environmental inspections (Gray and Silbey 2014). Intraorganizational differences in workers' positions—specifically, their autonomy and frequency of inspections—accounted for differences in their understandings of inspectors as threats, allies, or obstacles. Another study analyzed the spread of stylistic elements, such as fabric colors or patterns like stripes or spots, among high-fashion houses as a function of the evolving network positions of those elements, which conveyed meaning about their appropriateness (Godart and Galunic 2019). Stylistic elements were the nodes in these networks; two nodes were tied when the same fashion house used both in its designs. Stylistic elements that bridged structural holes were substantially more popular. Although these two studies were very different in terms of methods and context, they both demonstrate how relational structure generates and sustains cultural structure.

Research identifying institutional logics through relational analysis is conceptually similar. This work captures institutional logics empirically by mapping organizations onto cultural categories, such as product types and customer segments, through relational analysis of textual claims about what the organizations under study do. Again, pairs of nodes (in this analysis, product types and customer categories) are tied together, this time when the same organization is associated with both. For example, the institutional logics of late nineteenth-century social relief agencies (who they should serve, how, and why) distinguished between two classes of "the poor" (Mohr and Duquenne 1997). *The destitute* constituted an underclass that often grew up in poverty; relief-agency managers thought they ought to be investigated and labor for pay. In contrast, *the needy* had shorter histories of poverty, having fallen on hard times. They were perceived as worthy of sympathy, so relief-agency managers believed they ought to be offered money without requiring labor, food, job training, advice, or shelter in exchange.

Other work examines how cultural schemas about forms of organization are created by the media. Here, cultural embeddedness in media accounts derives from organizations being mentioned in the same account; the cultural embeddedness of organizational forms solidifies over time as co-mentions accumulate. These media accounts categorize firms as belonging in specific business segments that vary in how well known and therefore how legitimate they are. When organizations (or their products) do not fit into established categories, they can be overlooked or evaluated negatively (Zuckerman 1999;

Hsu 2006).[71] For example, when the computer workstation sector was new (ca. 1980), press releases that mentioned multiple workstation manufacturers garnered those firms more attention from news outlets because such press releases embedded firms in a solid category (Kennedy 2008). But firms got "lost in the crowd" if their press releases mentioned too many other manufacturers.

At the micro level, some scholars have applied network-analysis methods to study organizational cultures, by analyzing what organizational members say to each other. This work builds on research about extracting culture from text by analyzing relationships among concepts (Carley and Palmquist 1992). It assumes that language is central to how people codify and uphold (or transgress) organizational culture. For example, the more similar the language people use when they interact, meaning the more similar their topics, emotional tones, and linguistic styles, the better they fit with each other's norms and values (Goldberg et al. 2016). Cultural fit allows employees to reap the benefits of social ties by improving their performance ratings.

Relational analysis of product evaluation. A different line of work focuses on how cultural products like music, films, books, or art are evaluated. This work is varied: some studies apply formal network methods; others conduct qualitative analysis. In the early jazz industry, success depended on authenticity, which in turn depended on jazz musicians' location in networks of recording artists (Phillips 2013). Like network-based studies of blocks (White et al. 1976) and structural holes (Burt 1992), this study focused on *disconnectedness*, which was a function of both the number of ties to and from a node and the density of ties among other nodes. In this analysis, nodes were recording locations—cities around the world—and ties occurred when the same song was recorded in two cities. Jazz recordings from artists in more strongly disconnected locations appealed more to listeners and were more successful— more likely, that is, to be re-recorded. This was especially true when these recordings did not fit into established categories: when they used uncommon instruments, were recorded by groups whose names did not signal their style, or had titles that did not signal their category. These findings suggest scope conditions for theories of organizational identities as social codes and theories of products as fitting into categories (e.g., Zuckerman 1999; Hsu 2006; Bowers 2015). That work has not yet taken into consideration whether and

---

71. It is difficult to draw a sharp boundary between research on the cultural embeddedness of organizations and research on organizational forms as codes. Although I have listed the first line of work as combining the relational and cultural perspectives and the second as combining the demographic and cultural perspectives, the first also involves categories of organizations and so is related to the second.

how producers' network locations alter the impact of not fitting into established categories.

Another study of music, this time contemporary popular songs, used formal network methods to evaluate song features such as key, tempo, and instrumentation (Askin and Mauskapf 2017). It revealed that the most popular songs were those whose features were optimally distinctive from previous songs—neither so different as to be unappealing nor so similar as to be boring. And in the book trade, publishers must categorize novels to "pitch" them to booksellers and reviewers (Childress 2017). Book categorization is relational in two ways. First, it requires iterative comparisons between the features of the focal novel (e.g., historical, romance, mystery) and those of already published novels, keeping in mind the economic and critical reception of the latter. Second, publishers communicate with potential retailers and reviewers. To be successful, they must anticipate retailers' and reviewers' reactions to how they classified the focal novel.

Social movement power through cultural work. Culture and power are also linked outside of the context of networks, in work that examines how social movement organizations exert pressure on organizations. Social movements' success depends in part on social movement rhetorics, specifically how well their goals and values are framed to resonate with those of their targets (Snow et al. 1986; Benford and Snow 2000). For example, anti-Muslim messages from fringe organizations were picked up by U.S. news outlets in the aftermath of the 9/11 terrorist attacks because they were emotionally charged, which was congruent with that fear-filled time (Bail 2012). Some social movement frames resonate with some audiences but repel others. For instance, the immigrant-rights movement in the U.S. has used three different frames: human rights, economic benefits, and family. A survey experiment revealed that only exposure to the family frame increased public support for the legalization of undocumented immigrants (Bloemraad, Silva, and Voss 2016). The effect of movement frames depended on subjects' political leanings: only moderates were swayed by the human rights frame, and only conservatives were swayed by the family frame. Social movement organizations can use cultural products like films, songs, and novels to frame their goals, generate public interest, and mobilize activists. For example, the documentary film *Gasland*, with its vivid images of setting methane-contaminated tap water on fire, mobilized bans on fracking in the communities where it was screened by increasing public attention to fracking, amplifying mass-media coverage, and stimulating discussions of bans and moratoriums (Vasi et al. 2015).

The frames promulgated by social movement organizations have the power to alter the actions of business organizations. Social movements "theorize" change in businesses by articulating the problems businesses create and offering solutions to those problems (Strang and Meyer 1993). For instance, to motivate American farmers to switch from feeding cattle corn and grain to feeding them grass, activists valorized authenticity, sustainability, and natural-ness (associated with grass), and denigrated manipulation, exploitation, and artificiality (associated with corn and grain) (Weber, Heinsze, and DeSoucey 2008). After the oil crises of the 1970s and 1980s, environmental-movement organizations framed renewable energy as the solution to twin problems—environmental degradation and industrial pollution (Sine and Lee 2009). This framing, in turn, mobilized support for the emergence of the wind-power in-dustry in the U.S. Finally, cannabis activists established a moral and legal foot-hold for their products through framing (Dioun 2018). Initially, they framed cannabis as a palliative for the dying and chronically ill. Later on, the growing legitimacy cannabis gained from the first frame made it possible for activists to extend the frame to "wellness" in general.

The diffusion of innovations. The most compelling theory of diffusion pro-poses that an organization's propensity to adopt an innovative structure, prac-tice, or tactic is a function of its intrinsic susceptibility to adopting the focal innovation, the infectiousness of each prior adopter, the social proximity of the focal organization and each prior adopter, and time since the prior adopter adopted the focal innovation (Strang and Tuma 1993; Strang and Meyer 1993). Thus pathways for diffusion are both relational (through social networks) and cultural (via social similarity). Different kinds of network ties promote diffu-sion of innovations through different mechanisms (Guler, Guillén, and Macpherson 2002). Network ties promote customized adoption of new prac-tices early in the diffusion process but conformity-driven adoption later on (Westphal, Gulati, and Shortell 1997). And diffusion of tactics is more likely among similar organizations (Wang and Soule 2012). Even deviant cultural elements can diffuse: take, for example, hostile takeovers of corporations by corporate raiders (Hirsch 1986).

Innovations diffuse more easily when they are theorized (Strang and Meyer 1993): when problems are identified and the focal innovation is framed as a solution. Theorization accelerates the diffusion of innovations. For example, when human resources professionals took contentious affirmative action pro-grams, which had failed to spread beyond a small fraction of potential adopt-ers, and repackaged them as diversity management programs that could solve management problems, they spread widely (Kelly and Dobbin 1998).

Organizational fields as relational systems of meaning and power. Orga-nizational fields are composed of organizations that engage in common activities, are subject to similar environmental pressures, and have ongoing interactions (DiMaggio and Powell 1983; Fligstein and McAdam 2012). They include competitors, suppliers, customers, regulatory agencies, news media, and

professional, scientific, and trade associations. They are inherently both relational and cultural: organizations and individuals interact, and they have a
shared understanding of what is at stake, how the game is to be played, and
who has (more) power. For example, in the book publishing industry, there
are three linked organizational fields: the creation of a cultural object (by writers who often work in universities to support their art and the literary agencies
that represent writers), the production of that object (by publishing houses),
and the reception of that object (by booksellers, reviewers, and readers) (Childress 2017).

Interorganizational fields are inherently dynamic. External factors, such as
the development of novel technologies, economic booms and busts, changes
in government regulation, or shifts in cultural mores, can upend relations of
power, raising up formerly subordinate actors and lowering formerly dominant ones. For example, the rise of the gay liberation movement of the 1960s
and 1970s altered the nature of gay- and lesbian-movement organizations from
predominantly heterophilic (seeking to educate the public) to emphasizing
gay pride (aiming to build gay culture and community) and working to gain
legal protections (Armstrong 2002). These new organizational forms succeeded because they deployed new institutional logics that resonated with
other social movements, broadening support for gay rights. Similarly, the
higher education field has seen increasing demands for "sustainable" practices:
reducing waste disposal and replacing it with recycling and composting,
adopting "green" building codes, and shifting to renewable energy sources
(Lounsbury 2001; Augustine and King 2019). Analysis of an online forum for
environmental activists revealed that over time, discourse among activists became more coherent (contributors discussed the same topics in similar proportions), but activists seldom reached agreement, instead seeing common
issues as "worthy of debate" (Augustine and King 2019).

Conclusion

More and more scholars, both micro and macro, have come to combine theoretical perspectives on organizations. To combine *the demographic and relational perspectives*, scholars increasingly ask how social networks differ between
members of ethno-racial groups and between the men and women, and how
these differences explain differences in job opportunities and workplace outcomes. They also inquire how demographic similarity or diversity affects
interactions in the workplace, and how demographic processes like hiring,
promotion, and turnover alter workplace social relations. At the macro level,
they apply relational techniques to define organizational niches and forms
based on interorganizational networks (in terms of either shared members or

similar products). To combine *the demographic and cultural perspectives*, scholars increasingly ask how cultural schemas and institutional logics shape evaluations of members of different demographic groups. They also investigate the joint impact of demography and culture on the behavior of individuals, groups, and entire organizations. And they understand organizational forms and niches as being based in cognitive-cultural schemas and socially constructed identities. To combine *the relational and cultural perspectives*, scholars study how cultural elements are embedded in shared meaning structures—webs of ideas and values. They investigate how products are evaluated using relational methods. They also study how social movement organizations gain power through cultural work. And they trace the diffusion of innovations through networks. Finally, they study organizational fields, meso-level relational systems of meaning, interaction, and power. While much has been done, there is still ample room for new projects that combine two or all three perspectives to yield new insights into the nature, dynamics, and performance of organizations and the groups and individuals in them, and the impact of organizations on society at large.

8

Organizations and Organizational Theory in the Digital Age

THE PREVIOUS CHAPTERS generally had a backward orientation because they focused on the past. In addition to explaining what organizations are and why they are important, those chapters described how organizations came to dominate societies as they modernized, and what social scientists have learned from studying organizations over the past 150 years. Now I shift to a forward orientation and focus on the future. In this chapter, I begin by tracing the rise of digital communication since World War II, the development of ever "bigger" data, and the invention of new data-science tools and techniques for analyzing those data. Then, I explain how organizations are being transformed in the digital age. Next, I consider what the torrent of data and the availability of new data-science tools and techniques hold for how we study organizations. Finally, I briefly consider ethical issues raised by these new tools and techniques.

The Digital Age

From the middle of the twentieth century onward, computer processing speeds and storage capacity improved tremendously, while processing and storage costs fell. As Figure 8.1 shows, processing speed (Figure 8.1a) doubled every three years from 1976 to 2016, while processing costs (Figure 8.1b) halved every 1.1 years (Kurzweil 2017). These advances, spurred and supported financially by government agencies such as the Defense Advanced Research Projects Agency in the U.S. and the Conseil Européen pour la Recherche Nucléaire (CERN) in Europe, made possible the development of the internet and the World Wide Web. Figure 8.2 shows the almost-exponential growth of internet traffic from 1990 to 2017. The solid unmarked line includes all internet traffic, including data flowing through national core systems. The solid line with dots captures traffic between residential and commercial subscribers, on one end, and internet service providers, cable companies, and

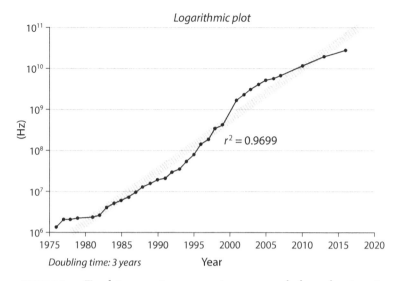

FIGURE 8.1A. Trends in computing power: microprocessor clock speed 1976–2016
Data sources: (1) Data from 1976–1999: E. R. Berndt, E. R. Dulberger, and N. J. Rappaport,
"Price and Quality of Desktop and Mobile Personal Computers: A Quarter Century of
History," July 17, 2000, http://www.nber.org/~confer/2000/si2000/berndt.pdf.
(2) Data from 2001–2016: International Technology Roadmap for Semiconductors, 2002
Update, On-Chip Local Clock in Table 4c: Performance and Package Chips:
Frequency On-Chip Wiring Levels—Near-Term Years, p. 167.
Published by the Semiconductor Industry Association.

other service providers, on the other. The dashed line captures traffic that travels through cellphone towers.

The development of internet-based systems has also been supported by governments in terms of laws and regulations. For example, for more than two decades, the U.S. government used tax law to encourage internet commerce. The Supreme Court (1992) exempted states from compelling internet retailers to collect sales taxes from state residents unless retailers had a physical presence in that state, thus reducing customers' costs relative to shopping in bricks-and-mortar stores. This favorable situation persisted until the Supreme Court (2018) overturned that decision. All but five U.S. states now collect sales tax on internet purchases (World Population Review 2022). Even in those five states, municipalities (e.g., Nome, Alaska) have passed laws to charge sales tax on internet purchases. In contrast, in the E.U., member states have enacted a patchwork of laws and regulations that has discouraged internet commerce, especially across national borders. As of 2018, 60 percent of E.U. citizens surveyed used the internet to purchase goods or services, but only one-third of those transactions involved purchases across national borders (Eurostat 2019).

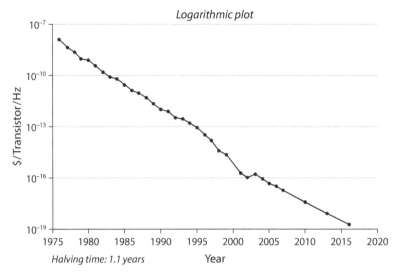

FIGURE 8.1B. Trends in computing power: Microprocessor cost 1976–2016
Data: Average transistor price: Intel and Dataquest reports (December 2002), see Gordon E. Moore, "Our Revolution," http://www.sia-online.org/downloads/Moore.pdf.

Artificial intelligence. As a result of advances in computing, the hope for harnessing artificial intelligence (AI), first espoused in the 1950s, has resurged over the past fifteen years.[72] AI involves computers carrying out tasks in ways that humans would interpret as intelligent, such as by winning games like chess or Go, translating text with good fidelity to the meaning in the original language, or accurately parsing images. An important subset of AI involves machine learning (ML) algorithms, such as k-means clustering, naïve Bayes, random forests, support vector machines, and neural nets. ML algorithms build probabilistic models to uncover clusters of data points in order to classify something in terms of crisp sets (in or out of a category) or fuzzy sets (membership in a category is probabilitistic), or to predict continuous variables like prices or likelihoods.[73] ML algorithms do this without using explicit, human-coded instructions (i.e., rules based on classic "if-then" logic) (Jordan and Mitchell

72. This resurgence is due, in large part, to research by Geoffrey Hinton, Yann LeCun, and Yoshua Bengio into deep neural nets. This work was funded by the Canadian Institute for Advanced Research—another example of government support for digital technologies.

73. For a gentle introduction to ML, see Burkov (2019). While this book is wide-ranging, it does not cover the analysis of text data (also known as natural-language processing). On that topic, see Jurafsky and Martin (2021).

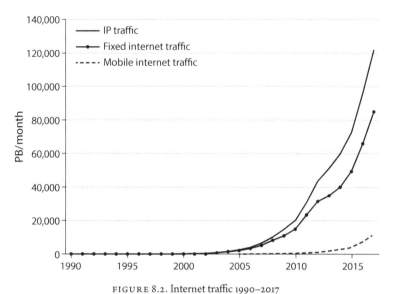

FIGURE 8.2. Internet traffic 1990–2017

Sources: Wikipedia & Cisco, https://en.wikipedia.org/wiki/Internet_traffic

2015), so they are more flexible than traditional rule-based algorithms.[74] Instead, ML algorithms "learn" from existing patterns in data and derive predictions about patterns in other data. Figure 8.3 illustrates the difference between traditional rule-based programming and ML. In traditional rule-based programming, the inputs are data and human-written rules, while the outputs are answers. In ML, the inputs are data and answers, while the outputs are algorithm-derived rules. After testing and validation, which I explain below, those rules are applied to other data to produce new answers. The goal is to build algorithms that are complex enough to incorporate the patterns that exist in large datasets with many variables, but not so complex that they "over-fit" the data by incorporating noise (random errors).

ML algorithms begin with randomly assigned parameters that link input data to output predictions; they then iterate to calculate new values for parameters, gradually optimizing their fit to the input data using probabilistic equations that allow for error. Algorithm developers divide data randomly into three subsets. The first "trains" the algorithm, using comparison to human-coded examples (supervised ML) or using induction (unsupervised ML) to

74. Although many commentators elide the terms AI and ML, some AI algorithms (e.g., those that apply dictionary methods to tag parts of speech in text data) are based on explicitly coded rules.

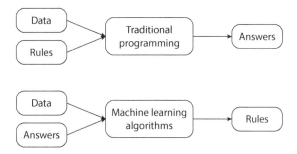

FIGURE 8.3. The difference between traditional computer algorithms and ML algorithms

iteratively improve the fit of model parameters to the data.[75] During training, parameters are adjusted to minimize the error using a loss function to calculate how bad results are. The training subset is the largest of the three, because the accuracy of ML algorithms increases with the size of the training data. The second subset validates the algorithm by having it predict responses for new, hitherto unseen, data, and if necessary tunes the algorithm by adjusting parameters. The third subset tests the final algorithm on new data.

In supervised ML, algorithms calculate the loss function by comparing the predicted output to human-labeled target values. The difference (the error) between each predicted output value (calculated by the algorithm based on its parameters and one input data point) and its corresponding target value (coded by a human being for that input data point) is aggregated across all input data points. For each parameter, this aggregation yields a continuous variable that may be positive or negative. If positive, the parameter should be increased in the next iteration of the algorithm; if negative, it should be decreased. The magnitude of this variable indicates how much the parameter should be changed: the higher the value, the larger the change. In unsupervised ML, there are no human-labeled target data; instead, algorithms look for underlying structure in the training data. For example, clustering tasks involve uncovering latent groups of observations that are similar along many dimensions, such as by minimizing distances between observations in the same cluster and maximizing distances between observations in different clusters. Prediction tasks involve finding combinations of (usually very many) variables that explain a large fraction of the variance in the data.

75. In between is semi-supervised ML, which uses a small set of human-labeled data plus a large set of unlabeled data (Chappelle, Schölkopf, and Zien 2006). This reduces the cost and effort involved in creating human-labeled data while allowing algorithms to uncover patterns that may not be apparent in labeled data.

ML has particularly demanding computational needs, because training ML algorithms improves with the volume of training data: large datasets are essential to ensure sufficient variance in values across the full range of the phenomena of interest and large datasets require great storage capacity and processing speed. Figure 8.4 shows that since 2012, the maximum computing power requirement for ML systems has doubled every 3.4 months, resulting in an astonishing three hundred thousand-times increase by 2018 (Perrault et al. 2019: 65). Applied to ever larger and ever richer databases, and at speeds approaching real time, ML techniques can dramatically lower the cost of data analysis.

What algorithms do. In the past fifteen years, ML algorithms have become able to do what in the past could only be done by humans: namely, uncover new patterns in complex data, such as genetic code, biochemical assays, biomedical images and reports, internet search records, financial transactions, mobile-phone records, employee emails, resumés, and social media posts. As a result, ML algorithms can read and parse texts, recognize images and speech, translate between languages in real time, steer robots and vehicles, design new drugs, diagnose illnesses and injuries, personalize product suggestions based on customer actions and attributes, winnow down pools of job applicants, and trade currencies, bonds, stocks, and derivatives. Of course, whether ML algorithms do these things more effectively and efficiently than humans, as their proponents claim (e.g., Brynjolfsson and Mitchell 2017), requires careful research involving statisticians and computer scientists, as well as social scientists—including organizational scholars, who have the expertise to assess how well technologies actually achieve organizational goals and assess how (and in whose interest) those goals are set.

Concrete examples abound of how AI has changed our lives. Most visibly, AI has enabled the creation of multitudes of digitally connected devices at work and home (e.g., smartphones, TVs, refrigerators, thermostats, air-quality sensors, speakers, and locks) and wearable mechanisms (e.g., fitness monitors, biometric identification badges, smart watches, virtual-reality gear, baby monitors, and pet collars). This has been heralded as the development of the "internet of things." Less visibly, AI has enabled people to interact at great distances in new ways, creating new forms of social relations. Most prominent are social media firms such as Facebook, Twitter, Instagram, and LinkedIn that allow people to share facts, ideas, opinions, and events through "virtual" social networks in textual, pictorial, video, and/or audio form. People can meet fellow enthusiasts on generalist forums like Reddit or 4chan, or more specialized forums like Pinterest (for those interested in lifestyle topics like home décor, food, and fashion), Jalopyjournal (for hot-rod devotees), or Ravelry (for knitting and crochet enthusiasts). More prosaically, people can read news through the web from traditional (print) newspapers' websites; from

Petaflop/s-days

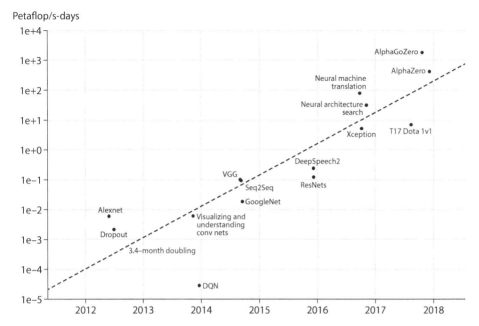

FIGURE 8.4. Computing power consumed by machine learning systems
Source: Open.ai, https://openai.com/blog/ai-and-compute

native online sites such as the Huffington Post, the Drudge Report, or Vice; or from news feeds filtered through social media firms by algorithms that analyze users' web footprints to predict their reading preferences. People can also get more specialized information and advice from sites like Tripadvisor (for travel), Yelp (reviews of movies, stores, and service providers), Glassdoor (employee reviews of firms), and wikiHow (how-to advice). People can communicate relatively easily and cheaply online via voice or voice plus video, as the Covid-19 pandemic has shown. We are beginning to discover how virtual-reality systems can create and strengthen group bonds, and how they can be used in training and socialization. People can come together to build, explore, or destroy worlds—and sometimes each other—in massive multiplayer video games like Minecraft, Assassin's Creed, and the Sims. Through internet platforms, people can easily mobilize large groups of people to push for political, social, or economic change—think #MeToo, #BlackLivesMatter, #ArabSpring, or the original, #OccupyWallSt. And people increasingly find romantic partners online, using dating sites like Match.com, Grindr, and FarmersOnly. With all these ways of interacting online, it is not surprising that the average internet user across the globe spends over six hours per day, on average, online (Kemp 2020), much of that on social media.

The digital age has ushered in a host of novel web-based services. Many of us use Wikipedia, the largest, most-consulted, and most respected encyclopedia in the world (*Economist* 2021), with entries available in hundreds of languages. Our sources of entertainment have expanded as internet downloads have become faster, with a host of for-profit and non-profit organizations offering short video clips, TV shows, movies, concerts, virtual art tours, theatrical performances, and comedy sets. We increasingly shop online; for example, U.S. online sales rose from 5 percent of retail sales (excluding food service, travel, financial brokers and dealers, and ticket sales) at the start of 2012 to 11 percent at the end of 2019—even before the Covid-19 pandemic, during which online sales spiked to 15 percent of retail sales (U.S. Census Bureau 2021). We also increasingly learn online, not just from remote-taught classes during the pandemic, but also from courses mounted by organizations like EdX, Coursera, and the Khan Academy, as well as many universities, including such prestigious institutions as Harvard and University College London.

Although the social connections and information exchanges made possible by AI systems may at first glance seem universally beneficial, they can have serious downsides for individuals, groups, organizations, and entire societies. Social media apps and many other online forums are designed to be addictive, through features like infinite scrolling, nudges, reaction buttons (e.g., like, clap, upvote), push notifications, and game-like elements (e.g., badges, challenges). Interacting with these features releases dopamine in users' brains,[76] stimulating temporary pleasure responses; to maintain these positive feelings, users must continue to engage. As a result, many users have become obsessed to the point of avoiding face-to-face interactions. As Chamath Palihapitya, an early executive at Facebook, said during an interview at Stanford Business School, "The short-term, dopamine-driven feedback loops we created are destroying how society works. No civil discourse, no cooperation, [instead] misinformation, mistruth" (Wong 2017). Heavy use of online interactions can cause loneliness, depression, and many other mental health problems, especially in young people, whose brains are more malleable than those of adults (Karim et al. 2020; Wells, Horwitz, and Seetharaman 2021).

Compounding this problem is that our privacy is at risk. Most social media sites do not charge users subscription fees; instead, they earn profits by selling advertising. To maximize advertising revenues, they use data gleaned by tracking users' digital "footprints" across multiple sites to predict how much

---

76. Dopamine is a neurotransmitter made in the brain. It acts as a chemical messenger between neurons. It is released when the brain is experiencing a reward.

they will be interested in what advertisers are selling. Moreover, platform companies, including but not limited to social media, have created applications that gather data to predict and surveil people in real time, augmenting—and sometimes fundamentally transforming—activities within work organizations such as police forces and newsrooms. Some of these transformations (e.g., providing real-time feedback on organizational actions, offering support to supplement scarce staff) may be socially beneficial, but others (e.g., threatening worker autonomy by replacing it with algorithmic authority) can be harmful (Christin 2020; Brayne 2021). Online sites can also harm the social fabric by spreading misinformation and hatred. We attend more to emotion-filled content, so inflammatory posts generate more engagement than calm ones (Bail 2012). Moreover, because we engage more with novel information, false news spreads online faster and wider than true news (Voshoughi, Roy, and Aral 2018). Most disturbingly, misinformation and hate speech on social media have often incited violence: for example, hate speech on Facebook in 2018 spurred a prolonged campaign of human rights abuses against the Rohingya ethnic minority in Myanmar.

Many of the negative effects of online sites are a direct result of the for-profit model used by most, but not all, sites. Although there are multiple efforts to design algorithms for online sites that will ameliorate, if not eliminate, these negative consequences (Applebaum and Pomerantsev 2021), those efforts are mostly led by technologists. Those efforts might be improved if social scientists got involved, especially organizational scholars, who have insights into individual behavior and small-group interactions; organizational structures, strategies, cultures, and power relations; and relations between organizations in interorganizational fields, and the institutional logics that guide action in organizations and fields. This presents opportunities for organizational scholars to have real beneficial impacts on society, in line with the charge I bring to our field in the next chapter.

Some civil society organizations are ramping up to ameliorate the social damage spawned on the internet. For example, Amnesty International developed Troll Patrol, a platform that lets concerned citizens analyze Twitter messages sent to female politicians and journalists, and tag them when they are sexist. Amnesty is scaling up its efforts using algorithms to learn from human-coded messages and apply those lessons to millions of tweets. Other civil society organizations are probing the ethics of AI and mobilizing members to rein in the use of AI algorithms. For example, the American Electronic Privacy Information Center and the German Algorithm Watch are checking for bias in the criminal justice algorithms that are used in almost every American state and sixteen European countries. Although these algorithms do not use race or ethnicity as an input—instead, they use factors like criminal history, family, work status, and social marginalization—some input factors are highly correlated with race and ethnicity. As a result, algorithms may generate disparate impacts for members of different ethno-racial groups: flag far more Blacks than Whites, for example, as being at high risk of recidivism or failure to appear in court. Indeed, the algorithm used by Florida and many other jurisdictions predicted that Black defendants were twice as likely as Whites to reoffend within two years, although its predictive accuracy was low, especially for Blacks: 55.1 percent for Blacks versus 76.5 percent for Whites (Angwin et al. 2016).

My review here of the rise of computing, the growth of the internet, and the development of AI, including ML, has merely scratched the surface. But it is broad enough to prepare us to assess how the nature of organizations has been transformed as a result of these changes.

Organizations in the Digital Age

Enormous increases in computing power, which led to the development of the internet and the rise of AI, have fundamentally altered what organizations are and how they operate. Here, I focus on the three main types of organizational activities being reshaped by AI applications: automating routine processes, analyzing data to drive decisions, and improving relations with key people and organizations (employees or members, clients or customers, and suppliers).

Automating Processes

This is the simplest way in which AI has changed how organizations operate, leveraging computers' ability to analyze ever larger datasets much faster than people can. In this way, AI enhances—and sometimes takes over—existing tasks. It lowers costs, reduces uncertainty, and increases the accuracy of predictions (Brynjolfsson and McElheran 2016; Brynjolfsson and Mitchell 2017). For example, AI systems can quickly and accurately take input from existing systems to update records on and handle routine communications with employees or other organizational members, customers or clients, and suppliers. AI systems can also update inventory logs and reports prepared for regulators. AI-based records management systems may replace routine work and thus reduce employment, but they may also free scarce bodies for other, more challenging, tasks. For example, legal staff can dramatically reduce the amount of time they spend reviewing documents and focus on analyzing the sections highlighted by AI systems. Such AI interventions can also eliminate (or at least shrink) bottlenecks, by speeding up procedures. For example, the U.S. Census Bureau developed algorithms to predict survey-taking propensities by neighborhood and direct extra staff to low-propensity sites; it also used algo-rithms to speed up procedures for classifying business establishments and tracking residential construction projects.

Analyzing Data and Guiding Decision-Making

ML algorithms can automate tasks and procedures only to the extent that they are routine. When they are non-routine—that is, when the data on which decisions are made differ substantially from the training, validation, and test data that were used to create the algorithms in the first place—ML algorithms perform poorly. Such non-routine situations include rare events and novel situations that arise due to changes in suppliers, customers, technologies, laws, competitors, or macroeconomic, cultural, and political conditions. In non-routine circumstances, we have to augment ML systems with human beings who make careful judgments based on their knowledge and experience. In ad-dition, it may be difficult to determine whether or not (or how much) the data used to create ML algorithms are similar to the data that organizations feed into them. In such circumstances, we need human beings to judge whether or not situations are routine. The increasing volume and complexity of the data available to develop ML systems means that the scope of what is routine continues to expand, but the jury is still out on how much such systems will replace existing tasks, versus how much they will prompt organizations to do new things. Here, I discuss several key ways that ML-driven data analysis is already changing organizations: how organizations recruit and manage employees, how they detect problems with operations, and how they improve existing activities—or even develop the capacity to do entirely new things.

Managing people. Labor costs—compensation and benefits—constitute almost 60 percent of business organizations' expenses (U.S. Bureau of Labor Statistics 2021a), so it is not surprising that firms are quickly adopting ML systems to sort through job applications and identify the most promising can-didates. This is especially likely to be useful in the early stages of the employee-search process (Barach et al. 2019). Even before job applications arrive, firms are harnessing ML algorithms to craft job descriptions to better meet strategic needs, such as diversifying their workforces.

Once people have been hired, firms are increasingly using "people analytics," meaning data-driven decision-making about human resources, to pinpoint best practices. For instance, algorithmic analysis of transcripts of conversations between salespeople and customers makes it possible for firms to assess employee performance, offer feedback, and provide further training in areas highlighted by the algorithm. One study revealed that relative to human coaches, an AI coach proved especially beneficial for middle-ranked salespeople, who are neither overloaded due to poor performance nor resistant to coaching due to excellent performance (Luo et al. 2021). But deploying AI algorithms does not yield unalloyed benefits. For instance, algorithms analyzing data on real-time employee actions (e.g., from web-page traffic logs and radio frequency identification badges) can alter employee motivations in both desirable and undesirable ways (Christin 2020; Ranganathan and Benson 2020).

Some algorithms analyze group, rather than individual, performance, by analyzing workplace exchanges through emails, calendars, corporate social media, "smart" badges, GPS trackers, and file-sharing sites. Network analysis of such data can reveal who is in a position most likely to spur creativity and the development of new innovations, and who is situated best to influence the implementation of those innovations. Such analysis can also reveal communication gaps between groups—otherwise known as structural holes (Burt 1992). But digital traces often cannot capture unscheduled meetings between employees. And digital traces often cannot capture the content of employee interactions—just their existence, membership, and timing. Finally, digital traces can serve as tools of rational employee control, so they may alienate workers in new ways—as input into real-time, fine-grained, and often opaque decisions about task assignments, worker evaluation, and worker rewards or sanctions—that reduce motivation and induce active resistance (Griesbach et al. 2019; Kellogg, Valentino, and Christin 2020; Ranganathan and Benson 2020; Brayne 2021).

Detecting problems with operations. ML systems can read and analyze documents like legal contracts, customer emails, and product development records using natural-language processing (NLP) to extract information as input for human decisions about common problems with everyday operations. For example, ML systems from companies like Ravelin.com and Zendesk.com can analyze customer claims to identify credit-card or loan fraud and improper client claims, and flag suspicious records for human intervention. Moreover, companies can use similar data to predict product defects. And ML systems from companies such as textio.com can adjust corporate communications, such as job postings and announcements, to reduce gender, ethno-racial, and age bias.

Enhancing existing activities and enabling new ones. The most obvious way that AI systems improve operations is by streamlining them. For example, AI algorithms can analyze extremely large databases on customer orders and returns to better predict customer behavior. The German e-commerce firm Otto has used such algorithms to more accurately predict customer demand, more effectively restock its distribution centers, and deliver products faster (*Economist* 2017). Better demand forecasts make it possible to reduce inventories and still meet demand. Faster delivery also increases customer satisfaction and retention, and reduces returns (and delivery charges) by preventing customers from going to bricks-and-mortar stores to find the items they ordered.

More generally, internet-connected devices like fitness monitors and "smart" speakers feed huge amounts of data from customers to the firms that sell these devices. Similar sources of data on customers derive from services offered on internet-connected TVs, smartphones, laptops, and e-readers. Firms can develop new income streams based on the analysis of these data, using predictions about customer activities, locations, and preferences to develop narrowly targeted product promotions. They can also sell targeting data to outside marketing organizations.

The public sector is also harnessing AI to enhance activities. Perhaps best known is the case of criminal justice systems applying ML algorithms to support decisions about where to send police patrols, which individuals and groups to surveil to prevent violent crimes, whether to remand alleged criminals to jail while awaiting trial or let them out on bail or their own recognizance, how to sentence criminals after trial, and whether to offer parole to prison inmates (Brayne 2017, 2021). A more anodyne example is the use of transportation management algorithms to better synchronize the deployment of trains, trams, and buses as demand rises and falls, which can reduce both costs and greenhouse gas emissions, while saving commuters time and effort.

In the health care and pharmaceuticals sectors, AI abounds. A prominent example is IBM's Watson AI system, which was trained on thirty billion Xray, MRI, and CT images, allowing it to read medical image data faster and more accurately than human radiologists, thus streamlining diagnoses. ML output is couched in statistical terms, so radiologists are still needed, but their focus is shifting from reading images to helping other physicians interpret those readings. Firms are accelerating drug discovery by using ML algorithms to predict which small molecules are most likely to be effective drugs, based on how well they bind with disease targets, while minimizing toxic side-effects by not binding with organs and other tissues. Beyond established applications, myriad research studies suggest potential future applications. For example, one AI algorithm was able to detect a wide array of heart arrhythmias in electrocardiogram scans and diagnose underlying heart problems (Elul et al. 2021); another was able to identify colorectal polyps with 90 percent accuracy, while ruling out 80 percent of "false flags" (Trasolini and Byrne 2021).

One of the newest things that AI algorithms allow organizations to do is quickly and cheaply to test their internet-based activities using "A/B testing"— randomized experiments with two or more variants. Although we often think of this as something that for-profit firms do, all kinds of organizations are harnessing this tool. Companies conduct A/B tests to set price points for new digital services, fine-tune advertising campaigns, and improve website appeal.

Political parties and electoral campaign organizations conduct A/B tests to understand how potential voters respond to policy proposals and other messages. Non-profits use A/B testing to increase donation rates. Healthcare organization use A/B testing to improve patient attendance at scheduled appointments. And government agencies use A/B testing to make their websites easier to navigate, thus improving their ability to serve the public.

Managing Relationships

The capacity of AI algorithms to analyze new kinds of data quickly at huge scale has created new ways for organizations to manage relationships with exchange partners and the communities where they operate. Many relationship management algorithms are embedded in novel kinds of organizations, such as two-sided "platform" companies harnessing AI to create new ways of interacting with individuals, groups, and organizations. Here, I consider five types of platforms: online sales, peer production, evaluation, intelligent agents, and contract labor.

Online sales. This is perhaps the most obvious change wrought by the development of the internet. Platform organizations in many sectors sell (and in some cases deliver) products to customers and clients around the world: brokering the sale of new and used goods and the resale of personal goods; renting or selling television shows, films, and other video entertainment; arranging short-term rentals for residential space; and selling "digital" goods and services, including educational courses, photographs, and mobile apps. Business-to-business platforms provide "software as a service" to manage supply chains, human resources, and customer relations management services. Web-based sales systems greatly expand the range of goods and services available; for instance, Amazon advertises far more books than any bricks-and-mortar store can— even Powell's Books in Portland, the world's largest independent bookstore. Because of their "long tail," web-based sales systems can serve an extremely wide array of customers.

Financial-technology ("fintech") firms offer a range of services, including accelerating mortgage approvals with traditional funders, selling insurance, lending money to individuals and businesses, offering credit cards, and managing investments. Related to fintech are crowdfunding sites, which have proliferated to operate in the business, political, and civic sectors. Crowdfunding sites can greatly improve access to capital, but that access can be uneven. For example, among business startups, Black entrepreneurs tend to raise less than Whites (Younkin and Kuppuswamy 2018). And by improving access to capital, these sites can replace dependence on traditional sources of finance like governments for civic projects and banks and angel investors for business startups. For business startups, crowdfunding sites are especially useful in the early stages of the startup life cycle and in locations where venture capitalists are less active (Sorenson et al. 2016).

This shift to online service delivery via platforms is not limited to the business sector. Government bureaus ranging from tax-collection agencies, to motor-vehicle departments, to grants agencies offer services through online platforms. For their part, civil society organizations are increasingly using websites to advertise and deliver goods and services (Powell, Horvath, and Brandtner 2016).

Peer-production networks. These are less visible than online sales, but they are critical to many sectors of the economy, especially software development. Software-focused peer-production networks include large-scale commons-based organizations, open-source software projects, and open-source code repositories. For example, the Project Jupyter group has developed Jupyter Notebooks—interactive computer interfaces combining text, computer code, logs from running code, and results, and which have become standard data-science tools—as well as multi-user Jupyterhubs for teaching and team-based analysis. These new modes of collaborative production are among the most significant internet-mediated organizational innovations (Raymond 2001; von Hippel 2005). Peer production fuses technological, organizational, and institutional advances to enable diverse, geographically dispersed individuals to communicate, coordinate, and integrate otherwise fragmented knowledge. In such communities, ownership and contracts are irrelevant to determining who does what, when, with what resources, and with whom—except for "copyleft" agreements ensuring that no one can transform freely shared intellectual property (e.g., open-source tools) into personal property (O'Mahony 2003). With free access of participants to projects in the absence of centralized control and coordination, peer production is structured by voluntary participation (von Krogh, Spaeth, and Lakhani 2003; Weber 2004).

Although peer production is most prominent in software development, it is also used in other fields. Large internet-mediated communities (within and between organizations) have been created to generate knowledge collectively in fields like architecture, law enforcement, microbiology, and teaching. Many participants seek to share ideas, products, and information with others in the same organization or occupation and help solve common problems. Like peer-production networks in software, these online communities depend on voluntary participation.

Evaluation. As I mentioned in chapter 6, the internet has made possible a rise in platform organizations that evaluate other organizations: sites like Rotten Tomatoes rate movies and TV shows; media outlets, most prominently the *U.S. News and World Report*, rank colleges, universities, and professional schools; and sites like Yelp rate retail establishments and service providers. In these systems, evaluation shifts from a few expert authorities to many, many ordinary people. As a result, evaluation criteria become more informal and vary more across evaluators, increasing uncertainty for the targets of evaluation (Orlikowski and Scott 2014). Organizational theorists studying organizational forms as categories (e.g., Hsu 2006; Kovács, Carroll, and Lehman 2017) and investigating coercive pressures through rankings (e.g., Espeland and Sauder 2016) have begun to tap into these platforms. But there is much more organizational scholars could do with such data: for example, harnessing them to investigate relationships with offline expert evaluation systems, or probing the cultural schemas they contain.

Beyond simple evaluation, many organizations (especially but not only businesses) use intelligent agents to analyze and direct the behavior of employees or other organizational members, and of customers or clients. Chatbots on sales and service platforms answer questions about products and organizational policies to increase sales and improve customer or client satisfaction. Chatbots on hiring sites provide individualized information to attract more high-potential job applicants. For current employees, intelligent agents answer questions about organizational policies and benefits, offer career advice based on resumes, HR records, and open-job lists, and suggest employee-development actions and employee-compensation levels to managers—all to improve employee retention rates and optimize compensation relative to external labor markets. Intelligent recommender systems suggest products to customers in order to increase sales.

Contract labor. Rather than hiring people to perform services for customers, a host of platform companies have sprung up to act as market intermediaries between workers and customers. Some connect workers to firms seeking to fill short-term skilled jobs. Others—the so-called "gig" platforms—connect individuals and organizations in order to perform physical tasks like driving you somewhere, fixing something in your home or office, or delivering purchases, or they connect workers to jobs involving micro (very short-term) online tasks like filling out surveys, transcribing audio files, or proofreading text files. In the performing arts, media, fashion, and design, creative workers do "aspirational labor" (Duffy 2017): they post their work on platforms in the hope that someone will financially reward their effects through advertising or subscriptions. All of these platforms offer new ways for organizations to outsource labor to temporary or contract workers, shifting economic risk from employers to workers. Many scholars have argued that contract labor platforms thereby increase both employer profits and economic inequality (Schor and Attwood-Charles 2017). But contract labor platforms may instead reduce inequality, to the extent that workers on these platforms are seeking income to supplement their normal jobs, rather than attempting to cobble together a living wage from many small labor exchanges. And contract labor platforms may threaten firms' discretion (by channeling their decisions) and hamper learning, prompting firms to strategically limit their use of platforms (Barach et al. 2019).

Conclusion

AI systems have strong effects on existing organizations. Online marketplaces have dramatically reduced demand for traditional "bricks-and-mortar" businesses, which is why many, ranging from family-run stores and independent restaurants to large retail and food-service chains, have created online presences. Civil society organizations, such as social movement organizations, human-rights groups, information agencies, and religious congregations, have also created online presences to publicize their activities, recruit members, and solicit donations—often more easily and cheaply than through the mail, telephone calls, or face-to-face interactions. Contract labor platforms link employing organizations, workers, and customers in ways that can destroy existing businesses (like taxis and hotels) or augment them (like transcription services). And "algorithmic control" tools seek to improve efficiency and effectiveness (Barley 2015). Their proponents claim that AI systems will also promote administrative, process, and product innovation (Brynjolfsson and Mitchell 2017). But it will take much more study for us to discover how valid those claims are.

One general point merits consideration: relying more and more on ML systems is likely more deeply to entrench instrumental rationality (*Zweckrationalität*) (Weber [1968] 1978: 24–26) in organizations, because ML enables data-driven decision-making (Brynjolfsson and McElheran 2016). ML algorithms have explicit goals—to optimize the fit of outputs to inputs. Increasing their use means that more activities are subject to means–ends considerations and fewer to concerns about values and ethical beliefs (*Wertrationalität*) (Lindebaum, Vesa, and den Hond 2020). Because ML algorithms take goals as givens, they cannot adapt to changes in the technical or institutional environment. Indeed, because existing goals become entrenched in ML algorithms, changing goals requires revising or replacing algorithms. And to the extent that ML algorithms (e.g., artificial neural nets) are opaque, it becomes more difficult to hold them, and the organizations that create and use them, accountable for the unanticipated consequences of their predictions.

Implications for Organizational Theory

Advances in information processing and the rise of AI have led to the development of new sources of data as well as new tools and techniques, which can, if used thoughtfully, improve our ability to test and extend existing theories. For example, longitudinal digital data on employee interactions (via email, Slack, etc.) make it easier to conduct causal analysis of how workplace social relations emerge and evolve. Beyond that, changes in our sources of data and scientific tools are likely to drive changes in theories, because new data and tools give us opportunities to investigate new concepts and new relationships between concepts (Merton 1968). For example, granular, large-scale data make it possible to map heterogeneity and trends in organizational features, such as cultures and webs of interorganizational exchange, across entire economic sectors, and to see how the features of pre-internet companies differ from those of internet "native" companies. Large-scale data also make it much easier to study rare actors and activities. Even more novel is that digital devices like sensors attached to vehicles, computers, and employee clothing can trace activities in fine-grained detail (and less obtrusively) than direct observation by managers or interviews with and surveys of employees. Similarly, unsupervised NLP techniques like topic modeling and word embeddings can be used to induce new concepts like novel cultural schemas or to get new purchase on relationships between existing cultural schemas and political opinions. And harnessing digital data sources can make it possible for organizations to conduct field experiments on employees or customers and clients.

Yet studying organizations in the digital age is still contingent on organizational theory's past. Like all scientific fields, the evolution of this field is path-dependent: past research affects future research (Augier, March, and Sullivan 2005), as the previous chapters have shown. This means that we are unlikely to abandon the three theoretical perspectives (demographic, relational, and cultural) that have served us well for four decades. Instead, we will apply these perspectives to twenty-first-century models of organizations— and update them if necessary in the light of new forms of data analyzed using new tools and techniques. The reason to expect substantial theoretical continuity is simple. Both the novel forms of organization that have emerged in the digital age and the forms of organization that emerged earlier face similar fundamental problems, such as how to divide up tasks among members; how to attract, evaluate, and reward members; how to manage flows of information; how to nurture and sustain cultures that fit organizational goals and reinforce organizational policies; and how to maximize organizational autonomy in relations with exchange partners. These problems can be understood through existing theories, even if the technologies involved in solving them have changed. Organizational theories have already been applied successfully to organizations in the railroad, telephone, and airplane ages. Why wouldn't they apply to organizations in the digital age?

Consider the case of competition among news media in the digital age. The rise of search engines, social media, news aggregators, and recommendation algorithms has fundamentally changed the way people gain access to news about friends and family, politics, the economy, culture, and leisure activities such as sports, movies, and TV shows. In 2018, two-thirds of Americans got their news through social media (Shearer and Matza 2018). As a result, the firms behind these digital technologies have become information gatekeepers. Their proprietary algorithms determine what items are most prominently displayed, based on criteria that vary across algorithms and over time within each algorithm. For instance, Facebook News first rewarded headlines that contained emotion-laden statements, then stories that users engaged with for longer periods of time, then stories with embedded videos, then stories that came from users' friends and family rather than directly from news outlets. This series of algorithmic changes created uncertainty for news outlets, which responded by imitating other news organizations that were successful at getting their stories highly ranked (Caplan and boyd 2018). Although Facebook and many of the affected news outlets are digital-age natives, the pattern uncovered in this analysis is not new to organizational scholars, nor does it require a new organizational theory to explain it. We have seen the "follow-the-leader" pattern in studies of American savings and loan associations' entry into new markets (Haveman 1993), large American corporations' choices of investment banks (Haunschild and Miner 1997), a multinational firm's choice of benchmarking targets (Still and Strang 2009), and newly founded advertising firms' symbolic efforts to gain legitimacy (Khaire 2010). Indeed, Caplan and boyd, the authors of the Facebook/digital media study, acknowledge their reliance on existing theory, citing DiMaggio and Powell (1983).

There are many other examples of how existing theories remain relevant to digital-age organizations. Relational theories of social influence explain how political "bots" spread propaganda during the run-up to elections (Woolley and Guilbeault 2017). Relational theories of interpersonal interaction explain how the online reputation system at eBay facilitates sales by engendering generalized trust (Kuwabara 2015; see also Kollock 1999). James Coleman's theory that dense social networks facilitate norm enforcement explains contributor behavior at Wikipedia (Piskorski and Gorbatâi 2017). Demographic theories of gender stereotypes and status expectations explain why women on an online peer-to-peer network who seek funding for businesses get less than otherwise similar men with similar projects, and less than otherwise similar women who seek funding for non-business projects (Kuwabara and Thébaud 2017); they also explain why women are held to a double standard in online evaluation forums (Botelho and Abraham 2017). And organizational learning theory explains why external hires in tech ventures are more valuable than people who are promoted from inside as drivers of innovation (Ng and Sherman 2021).

I have described just a small subset of organizational studies that apply existing theories to explain or interpret digital-age organizations. Yet I recognize that as our sources of data and scientific tools change, our theories may also change, because new data and tools give us opportunities to investigate new concepts and new relationships between concepts (Merton 1968). Indeed, we are likely to be able to revisit old ideas that were once thought to be impossible to study empirically: for example, connecting micro-level processes of interaction with meso-level organizational outcomes or macro-level social structures like interorganizational fields. While I cannot claim to predict how organizational theories might change beyond this general observation, I do recognize two issues that will affect the study of organizations in the digital age: new sources of data and new methods, and new ethical considerations, which I discuss below.

New Sources of Data and New Methods

"Big data" from digital sources and tools from "data science" are increasingly available to organizational scholars. These terms are fuzzy: they mean different things to different people, so let me explain what I mean by both. I focus on "bigger" data—meaning datasets that are orders of magnitude bigger than organizational scholars have had in the past (Lazer and Radford 2017). Such data are often extremely fine-grained and updated in real time. They come in many different forms: numeric, text, audio, and image. And they are digital, so they are amenable to analysis by computer systems.

"Data science" means the proliferation of new scientific tools and techniques, most notably computational statistics: statistical methods that differ from methods such as linear regression and ANOVA, in that they harness large amounts of computer memory and processing power (Wegman 1988). Although some computational methods such as principle-components analysis, multidimensional scaling, and network analysis are familiar to many organizational scholars, others such as nonparametric regression, resampling, simulations, and artificial neural networks are far less well known.[77] Nonparametric regression involves using techniques like kernel regression, splines, and smoothing (e.g., local regression) to construct the value of predictor variables from data. Resampling techniques include bootstrapping, which involves assessing the accuracy of statistical results using random sampling with replacement, and cross-validation, which involves assessing the generalizability of statistical results using samples (test or validation data) that were not used to generate estimates. Markov-chain

---

77. For a primer on network analysis, see appendix B. For mathematical details on other computationally intensive statistical techniques, like including nonparametric regression, resampling, and other Bayesian techniques, see Gelman et al. (2021). For an introduction to neural networks, see Charniak (2019).

Monte Carlo simulations involve estimating the distribution of statistics by taking random samples. And artificial neural networks involve layers of calculations between inputs and results that are "learned" by computers iteratively through forward and back propagation. In addition to the large computational resources required for these techniques, statistical analysis can also be computationally intensive if the data are "big," meaning there are many, many observations; if the data are complex, with many, many variables; and/or if the data are non-homogeneous, meaning that observations are not independent and identically distributed, are not normally distributed, and do not have constant variance, as assumed by the standard general linear model, and so require alternative, iterative estimation techniques. Finally, textual, audio, and image data must be transformed into numerical elements by complex algorithms, further increasing the computational burden.

The ability to gather and analyze far larger and more complex datasets means that we will increasingly be concerned with *the relative magnitude of associations* among variables and *the amount of variance explained*. After all, with very large datasets, p-values are likely to be excellent, because the larger the sample, the better the statistical power (Leahey 2005).[78] So substantive significance, rather than statistical significance, will be increasingly important. And rather than focus on central tendencies, we will want to assess associations among variables across the complete distribution of values—the benefit of having such large datasets is that we will have ample statistical power to do this—and so pay more attention to outliers. We will use resampling methods to conduct cross-validation. We will also make more use of non-parametric methods, such as principle-components and cluster analysis, which do not make standard assumptions about the distribution of the data or the structure of the true model. In addition, we will have to pay even more attention to the data-generating process, in order to assess sources of bias and limitations to generalization of results. This last is critical, because bigger data are on the whole not produced by and for social scientists, and the organizations that generate these data often change their procedures and coverage.

Perhaps the most extreme change may involve shifting away from hypothetico-deductive analysis toward inductive or mixed inductive-deductive analysis, conducting "computational ethnography" (McFarland, Lewis, and Goldberg 2016) or "computational grounded theory" (Nelson 2020). For example, a historical

78. Remember that the standard threshold for statistical significance, $p < 0.05$, was developed in the early twentieth century by Ronald Fisher. He was working with small random samples, however, and he described $p < 0.05$ as a convenience. That threshold has been institutionalized is no excuse for unquestioning use of it.

study of four feminist organizations first induced patterns of similarity and difference across locations and time periods using an unsupervised ML method: structural topic modeling (Nelson 2020). The author refined these patterns through deep reading of selected texts identified by the ML algorithm. Finally, she confirmed the patterns across the entire corpus, using supervised ML based on extensive human coding of random samples of observations.

Notwithstanding the advantages of "bigger" datasets, there are drawbacks. Perhaps most obvious is that such data are often not representative of the entire population that researchers want to generalize to (Lewis 2015). Sample-selection bias in big data is difficult to assess, much less correct for. A second concern is how to analyze these data—and share them so other scholars can replicate and extend your findings—while maintaining the privacy of the individuals and groups in these datasets. Relatedly, many of these data come from for-profit firms or government agencies, so they are not publicly accessible by other scholars. It is likely that scholars in some positions—especially prestigious business, law, public health, and public policy schools—will have easier access to corporate and government data sources, creating an uneven playing field in the competition for research inputs.

One of the most notable sources of bigger, richer data on organizations is text data, such as employee email exchanges, descriptions of employing organizations on GlassDoor.com, customer reviews of retail providers and products on Yelp, and messages between leaders of business, political, and civil society organizations and their followers. With these text data, we can study organizational cultures, identities, and logics in greater detail and greater scope than we have in the past. We can also trace the diffusion of organizational members' ideas and actions over time. Rather than conducting interviews or direct observations of a single organization or a few organizations, or hand-coding texts covering a small number of organizations, researchers can now analyze very large numbers of organizations using natural-language processing. For example, an unsupervised ML technique, structured topic modeling, which analyzes both data in the body of a text and the text's metadata to induce themes and calculate how much each topic is represented in each text (Roberts, Stewart, and Airoldi 2016), can be used to analyze data from employee posts on GlassDoor.com and classify employing organizations by their cultures (Schmiedel, Müller, and vom Brocke 2018).

A second notable source of bigger data involves digital traces of social networks within and between organizations, which can be observed through messages sent via electronic messaging systems, corporate social media sites, cellphone data logs, or "groupware" such as Google Docs and Google Sheets. In contrast with traditional surveys or direct observations of workplace interactions, these electronic data are both more complete (they capture all interaction partners using the focal medium or platform, not just the top few or those directly observed by researchers) *and* less complete (they generally capture interactions through only a single medium or platform). Therefore, it is critical for researchers to assess measurement validity, reliability, and generalizability when using these kinds of data. A final, more positive, point is that these data are longitudinal, which makes it easier to answer my call in chapter 6 for research into social network dynamics.

New Ethical Considerations

Studying organizations in the digital age with data-science tools and techniques raises ethical issues that are different in many ways from those that organizational scholars have faced before. Here, I focus on the two most pressing concerns: bias and opacity.

Bias can stem from the nature of the input data. All supervised ML algorithms rely on training data that are labeled by human beings. Because human beings are susceptible to biases, as a long line of research in cognitive science shows (Tversky and Kahneman 1974; Gilovich, Griffin, and Kahneman 2002), the labels supervised ML algorithms apply to data may reflect those biases. More generally, any data input into ML algorithms could reflect stereotypes and discriminatory practices. Consider, for instance, an algorithm widely used in American health care systems, but that exhibited substantial racial bias. Among patients assigned the same risk score, Black patients were far sicker (as evidenced by uncontrolled illnesses) than White patients. This happened because the algorithm's risk score incorporated historical bias in allocating health care (Obermeyer et al. 2019). The risk score from this algorithm was based on predicted health care costs, and Black patients historically received worse (less costly) care than White patients. Similarly, as explained above, ML algorithms used in the judicial system encode pre-existing racial bias. Black men are more likely than White men to be arrested, so algorithms that use criminal defendants' records to guide sentencing tend to flag far more Blacks than Whites as at high risk of recidivism, and have much lower predictive accuracy for Blacks than for Whites (Angwin et al. 2016). The use of ML "tech washes" (Brayne 2021: 6) these data, by making them seem neutral and objective. The upshot is that existing inequalities can be worsened by AI-generated predictions that disadvantaged groups, such as Black men in the American judicial system, deserve less favorable treatment (Barocas and Selbst 2016). Alas, there are no easy ways to adjust historical data to eliminate such biases.

The sources of data fed into ML algorithms may also be biased if available input data do not reflect the full range of variation. Consider, for example, facial recognition algorithms. A rigorous test of 189 commercial face recognition algorithms found that most are far more accurate when they analyze the faces of White young adult and middle-aged men than when they analyze the faces of women, people of color, the elderly, or children (Grother, Ngan, and Hanaoka 2019). This bias is due to the fact that training data contain disproportionately white young adult and middle-aged male faces; thus these algorithms have less opportunity to "learn" how to classify other kinds of faces. This bias in input data partly reflects the fact most American residents are White (U.S. Census Bureau 2020). But it also partly reflects socially derived bias: input images were drawn from websites where White men are by far the most common subjects (Buolamwini and Gebru 2018). Data from social media sites have similar issues of bias, this time in terms of disproportionately overlooking poorer people and those living in more rural areas who have more limited internet access, and thus more limited access to social media (Hargittai 2020).

Beyond problems with input data, AI algorithms can yield biased outcomes if they fall prey to the ecological fallacy (Robinson 1950)—that is, if they confuse individual-level relationships with aggregate relationships. Individual correlations are between discrete and indivisible objects such as people; aggregate or ecological correlations are between percentage figures that refer to groups of those objects. Algorithms may be biased if they make predictions based on coarse variations between groups and ignore fine-grained variation among members of a group (Barocas and Selbst 2016). For instance, resume-screening algorithms may give more weight to applicants from more prestigious colleges and universities, even though graduates from every institution vary widely and institutional prestige does not communicate much about any individual applicant's knowledge and skills. This is always troubling, but especially so when members of disadvantaged groups have less access to prestigious educational institutions.

Opacity makes it impossible adequately to investigate bias or other problems in ML algorithms. Many algorithms rely on highly complex webs of correlational inferences that are opaque, even to their architects. A kind of "magic" happens between inputting data to train, validate, and test these algorithms, and receiving the final output. The most commonly discussed example of this "magic" involves *artificial neural networks* (ANNs), ML algorithms inspired by biological neural networks, that have multiple, interconnected nodes (artificial neurons) arranged in multiple layers.[79] Humans cannot observe exactly what happens as data move between the complexly interdependent "hidden" layers of ANNs, and so cannot understand how inputs are combined to make predictions. As one analyst explained,

---

79. For a primer on ANNs, see Charniak (2019).

You can't just look inside a deep neural network to see how it works. A network's reasoning is embedded in the behavior of thousands of simulated neurons, arranged into dozens or even hundreds of intricately interconnected layers. The neurons in the first layer each receive an input, like the intensity of a pixel in an image, and then perform a calculation before outputting a new signal. These outputs are fed, in a complex web, to the neurons in the next layer, and so on, until an overall output is produced. Plus, there is a process known as back-propagation that tweaks the calculations of individual neurons in a way that lets the network learn to produce a desired output. (Knight 2017 [online])[80]

Other algorithms, including those designed to detect credit card fraud, find advertising targets, and evaluate loan applications, are opaque to outside critics because they are proprietary, developed by for-profit firms that do not allow others to observe how they are constructed (Burrell 2016).

If humans cannot understand how such black-box algorithms work, we cannot be sure they are accurate or fair. This has generated a movement by a wide array of concerned observers—computer scientists, statisticians, social scientists, policy-makers, and activists—to make such algorithms interpretable (Rudin 2019). For example, complex and uninterpretable models for predicting recidivism among convicted criminals are not more accurate than simple and interpretable models that use such obvious predictors as age, gender, and criminal history (Tollenaar and van der Heijden 2013; Angelino et al. 2018). But interpretability does not solve all ethical problems with AI systems: as I explained above, to the extent that predictors like criminal history are the product of biased policing and judicial systems, even interpretable algorithms will yield biased results.

In sum, mounting evidence about ethical issues with AI-based systems has made them controversial. Their supporters hail them as evidence-based, proactive tools that reduce costs, facilitate preventative (rather than reactive) action, and increase accuracy. In contrast, their detractors say many sources of data used in AI systems are biased or infringe on individuals' rights to privacy. Moreover, regardless of the data sources, many algorithms are opaque. It will take enormous effort for organizational scholars, as well as other social scientists, computer scientists, statisticians, ethicists, and policy scholars, to evaluate and ameliorate such ethical problems in the use of AI.

---

80. For a more extended, but still crystal-clear, explanation, see Lewis-Kraus (2016), the section beginning "To understand why scale is so important".

Conclusion

In the digital age, what organizations and organizational scholars can do has changed dramatically. As a result, how we study organizations may change. Yet our existing theories are likely to remain useful, even if new digital-age tools and data sources create opportunities to change or revisit existing theories. Finally, the rise of digital-age tools and data sources raises complex ethical issues that differ greatly from the issues organizational scholars have faced before. It's a brave new world out there, but organizational theorists have a wide array of theoretical and methodological tools to aid them as they venture forth.

9

The Impact of Organizations
on Society

ORGANIZATIONAL SCHOLARS have generally focused on the internal work-
ings of organizations, as well as the ways in which organizations are affected
by the environments in which they operate. They have focused far less on the
crucial question of how organizations affect society at large. I urge organizational scholars to turn their attention to this broad topic for several reasons.[81] Most basically, organizations are fundamental features of modern
societies (Boulding 1953; Coleman 1974, 1982; Perrow 1991), as I explained in
chapter 1. From birth to death, the lives of people in modern societies play out
in organizations. Organizations have an enormous impact on social life, wielding tremendous power over all human interests. And as I explain below, they
have a huge impact on the natural world.

Beyond the practical considerations of organizations' ubiquity and power,
we have a moral obligation to study their impact on society (Hoffman 2016).
Whether you work or study in a private or public institution, the public pays
for your salary and the infrastructure (e.g., libraries and online services) that
makes your research possible, through tax exemptions, government grants and
research contracts, public funding (for public institutions), tuition fees, and
donations. We can pay this back by diagnosing how and why organizations
affect the world we live in and figuring out how to improve the situation for
the common good. We also possess the expertise to understand organizations
in all their variety and complexity. If we don't take on this charge, who will?
Who else could do it as well as we can?

Describing and explaining the impact of organizations on society would
return the study of organizations to its roots. As I explained above, Marx and

---

81. I am not alone in this; see for example Parsons (1956); Perrow (1991, 2002), Stern and
Barley (1996), Courpasson and Clegg (2006), Riaz (2015), Greenwood (2016), and Barley (2016).

Weber were driven to understand how the rise of large organizations—mines, factories, and government bureaucracies—fundamentally shifted power upward to those who controlled them, and away from those who toiled in them (for mines and factories) or who were subject to their rules and regulations (for government bureaucracies). For his part, Durkheim was interested in modernization, including the rise of employing organizations whose workers carried out specialized tasks, and the impact of modernization and the division of labor on social solidarity. Thus, the work of Marx, Weber, and Durkheim was concerned with large-scale historical change and the state of society in general due to changes wrought by the rise of large organizations. Studying the impact of organizations on society would also resonate with the theoretical revolutions that swept our field in the 1970s, often motivated by the social upheavals of the 1960s and early 1970s. At that time, social scientists, especially young ones, were driven to study pressing social issues like inequality along ethno-racial, gender, and national lines; social cohesion and division in urban areas; how people became socialized into particular occupational or organizational cultures, often creating deep social divides; and the concentration of corporate power in a small elite. But those who followed them—and I include myself in this group—have generally taken a narrower path, focused on testing and refining theories of organizations with little concern for organizations' broader impacts.

Some scholars have complained that because organizational theory is dominated by the perspectives that were developed in the 1970s—demographic, relational, and cultural—it has grown stale (e.g., Davis 2015). I think those perspectives have continued to dominate the study of organizations (indeed, much of sociological analysis) because they provide basic insights into the interplay between social structure and agency, between the statics and dynamics of social systems. Therefore, as I argued in chapter 8, these perspectives retain considerable power to explain the new kinds of organizational systems that have developed in the digital age—even if they may need to be altered in some ways to reflect digital-age organizations' goals, structures, capabilities, norms, and interaction patterns. Yet I sympathize with the desire for a theoretical revolution. Moving to the investigation of organizations' impact on society provides us with new ways to think about reinvigorating their study. Just as in the late nineteenth and early twentieth centuries, and the 1970s and 1980s, the twenty-first century could see multiple transformations in both theories of and empirical research on organizations.

Studying the varied impacts of organizations on society will require reorienting our research and finding new dependent variables, new outcomes to explain. In this chapter, I focus on three very different outcomes that are seldom studied by organizational theorists, if not neglected altogether: societal and global inequality, politics, and environmental degradation. (At the end of the chapter, I suggest other topics to which organizational theorists should contribute.) Inequality within many societies has been rising for half a century, in some cases to levels not seen since the collapse of autocratic societies like the eighteenth-century French monarchy. Access to democratic processes is in jeopardy in many countries, including the U.S., India, and Hong Kong, with new restrictions on voting rights that often affect subordinated ethno-racial minorities (e.g., Blacks and Indigenous peoples in the U.S., and Muslims and low-caste Hindus in India). Finally, climate change has already begun to ravage the globe, with devastating effects: Pacific island nations like Nauru and Palau are sinking below rising sea levels, Southeast Asia is experiencing increased flooding, coastlines around the globe are at greater risk of more intense hurricanes and thus flooding and wind damage, the American West is ravaged by almost annual wildfire conflagrations, and Australia, the Indian subcontinent, and much of North and Central America have increasingly been suffering droughts. Even before these effects of climate change became obvious, two centuries of industrial development had produced substantial pollution of air, water, and land across the globe.

All three phenomena—societal inequality, politics, and environmental degradation—are, as I explain below, shaped by the actions of organizations. So they merit investigation by organizational theorists. This requires us to make organizational structures, interactions within and between organizations, organizational cultures and logics, and the dynamics of organizational systems the independent variables, the factors that explain these phenomena. This reorientation will take a tremendous effort, but it will broaden the audience for our work. Currently, much organizational research is conducted by faculty in professional schools, most of whom work in business schools. It is not surprising that their work tends to be concentrated on improving how organizations (mostly for-profit firms) operate, with the primary goal of benefiting managers and owners. If we follow my proposed agenda instead, we can contribute to scholarly conversations on a broad array of pressing social issues—not just in terms of societal-level inequality, politics, and environmental degradation, but also health and wellness, education, privacy, and culture and community. And we can contribute to public debates and policy design efforts to alleviate the problems we observe and help implement the solutions our analyses uncover.

Economic Inequality

Inequality has risen in many advanced industrialized nations over the past fifty years (Piketty 2014), driven in large part by gains for the wealthiest, although in some countries it peaked before the Great Recession of 2007–9 and stabilized or declined after that event (Nolan and Valenzuela 2019). For example, in the

U.S., the share of income flowing to the top 1 percent of tax units (individuals or households) rose, on average, by 3 percent per year between 1980 and 2007 (the total increase over this time period was 80 percent), but from 2007 and 2014, the upward trend slowed and the top 1 percent's share rose by only 0.23 percent per year on average. In Germany, the annual increase from 1980 to 2007 was 1.1 percent (the total increase was 28 percent), but from 2007 to 2011, the top 1 percent share actually dropped by 0.27 percent per year on average. In countries like China and India that are moving from state socialism to market capitalism, where economic growth has been extremely rapid, inequality has risen even faster. From 1990 to 2019, the share of national income flowing to the top 1 percent increased by 75 percent in India and 91 percent in China (Yang 2020).

Four types of organizations can shape societal inequality: governments, businesses, labor unions, and social movement organizations. I discuss the impact of each in turn.

Governments shape inequality. Because governments tax and spend, and because they create the rules that govern market competition, government organizations can have huge impacts on inequality.[82] Consider first taxation and spending. The American situation is complicated by federalism, a system whereby national and state governments each have supremacy in different areas of law. American states vary greatly in average income levels. In many other countries (e.g., Canada and most of the E.U.), transfers from the central government to regions are set up to reduce these inequalities, but in the U.S., such transfers often worsen them (O'Brien and Parolin 2021). There is also inequality within American states across counties, which is more marked in states where taxation and spending authority is more decentralized.

Consider one specific example of what political scientists call the "hidden welfare state" (Howard 1997), meaning tax expenditures (i.e., reductions in tax revenue through tax deductions or exemptions) that have social welfare objectives. Laws that allow people to deduct home mortgage interest and local property taxes from their income tax returns redistribute income toward wealthier people, who are far more likely to own homes, and to own a more expensive home. These laws are often touted as benefiting the social order by promoting home ownership, which is expected to stabilize social relations, but their impact in this regard is negligible: home ownership rates in Canada (66.3 percent), where no such deductions are allowed, are virtually identical to those in the U.S. (65.3 percent). These subsidies not only worsen wealth inequality; they

---

82. I focus primarily on the U.S. because I have the most knowledge of it, but the general thrust of my argument is relevant to other countries.

also worsen racial disparities, because people of color have lower average incomes and so receive far less of these tax subsidies than do Whites.[83]

Beyond tax expenditure, taxation policy has changed dramatically over the past half century, with tax rates on estates, capital gains, and top incomes falling precipitously in the U.S. during and after the Reagan administration (Piketty 2014). These changes have been compounded by cuts in funding for the Internal Revenue Service (IRS) and by shifts in IRS policies away from auditing top income earners (Johnston 2003). In 2010, the IRS budget was $13.9 billion and it received around 230 million tax returns and employed 13,879 revenue agents. Nine years later, the numbers were $11.8 billion, 253 million, and 8,526 (Horton 2018; IRS 2021). In the 1980s, the IRS budget included enough resources to audit one out of nine tax returns filed by high-income earners; by 1997, the odds had dropped to one of out sixty-six (Johnston 2003: 160). They are even lower today.

Yet all is not bad: low-income U.S. families benefit from safety-net programs like early childhood development assistance (Head Start), tax refunds (the Earned Income Credit), and food and cash assistance (the Supplemental Nutrition Assistance Program). These benefits are dwarfed, nevertheless, by benefits for wealthier people. As of 2017, households in the top quintile for earnings received 73 percent of tax deduction credits for home mortgage interest, compared to 0.1 percent for the bottom quintile, and households in the top quintile received 63 percent of tax deduction credits for employer-sponsored pension plans, compared to 0.5 percent for the bottom quintile (Urban Institute 2017). Despite the massive economic consequences of tax subsidies such as the mortgage interest tax deduction, tax breaks for pensions, and assistance for the poor, to my knowledge there is no organizational research explaining how tax subsidies come about and persist.

Sometimes governments contribute to inequality because of policy "drift," rather than policy change (Hacker and Pierson 2010). For example, consider the general partners of private equity firms and hedge funds in the U.S., whose earnings are labeled "carried interest" and taxed at the capital gains rate (currently up to 23.8 percent) rather than the higher the income tax rate (currently up to 37 percent) (Fleischer 2008). This government-sponsored benefit for people with very high incomes—their average compensation is over $2 million—is inscribed in government policies written in the early twentieth century (and rewritten in 1954) that originally covered oil- and gas-exploration projects by

83. A 2017 U.S. law reduced this subsidy for people with high home values (mostly in coastal urban areas), but that is an exception to the historical trend, motivated by the animus of the Republican-controlled government toward Democrat-leaning states.

treating the gains and losses of investors and explorers alike. Lobbying has prevented these outdated policies from changing, despite extensive criticism.

Now consider policies that shape labor and production markets. A host of
federal and state policies affect employment relations and corporate strategies.
Collectively, changes in these policies or "drift" in their effects have worsened
inequality in the U.S. over the past half century (Hacker and Pierson 2010;
Mishel and Bivens 2021). The most powerful have been (1) monetary policies
focused more on keeping inflation in check than on reducing unemployment,
benefiting those with assets over those with liabilities; (2) judicial decisions
eroding collective bargaining for workers and supporting anti-union policies;
(3) policies facilitating the globalization of trade and the offshoring of many
jobs to lower-income countries; and (4) weaker labor standards, such as declining
minimum wage levels and overtime protections. While political scientists have
done valuable work on this, organizational theorists can bring to bear theories
of organizational structure, power, culture, dynamics, and environments to generate new insights into how variation across government bureaus and their relations
with affected business organizations differentially affect inequality.

Business organizations affect inequality. Because in most countries people
work in organizations rather than for themselves or their families and because
their earnings constitute the biggest share of their incomes, much of the rise in
economic inequality is due to changes in how organizations pay their workers:
who they employ, how they structure people's jobs, and how they decide on
forms and amounts of compensation and benefits. Hence, it is not surprising
that economic inequality has long been the most-studied social impact of
organizations. Most obviously, Marx (Marx and Engels [1848] 1964; Marx
[1867] 1992), his twentieth-century followers (e.g., Blauner 1964; Braverman
1974; Burawoy 1979), and internal organizational demographers (e.g., Pfeffer
1977; Baron and Bielby 1980; Tomaskovic-Devey 1993) have examined inequality within employing organizations. More generally, the scholars who created the foundation for the study of organizations were concerned how the rise
of bureaucratic states and commercial and industrial enterprises transformed
social interaction (Weber [1927] 1981, [1968] 1978; Durkheim [1893] 1984). In
particular, they were worried about how this transformation elevated the status
and power of some individuals and groups, and lowered that of others.

Yet there has been little subsequent work by scholars of organizations examining inequality at a societal or global level—or even between organizations
within sectors like health care or finance. Instead, the vast majority of research
focuses on inequality *within* employing organizations.[84] One notable exception

---

84. For a comprehensive review, see Amis, Mair, and Munir (2020).

is work on the impact of employing organizations on societal inequality in China, both before economic reform began in 1978 (e.g., Walder 1992) and after (e.g., Bian and Logan 1996; Zhao and Zhou 2016). Under socialism, the wages and benefits Chinese employers could provide workers depended on their resources. In turn, employing organizations' resource levels depended on how much state authorities could extract from them—in other words, the strength of property rights protections against taxation (Walder 1992). Under "capitalism with Chinese characteristics," market forces first decreased then increased economic inequality; Communist Party members and workers in state-owned enterprises fared increasingly better than others, due to their connections with the state (Bian and Logan 1996).

The lessons learned from these studies can be extrapolated to capitalist societies, including former socialist ones, where state authorities levy taxes and fees on employing organizations—but those taxes and fees vary greatly across firms, affecting their resource levels. The resources available to reward employees are likely to vary by industry structure: market concentration (i.e., how much product markets are dominated by firms with large sales bases), employment concentration (i.e., how much labor markets are dominated by firms with large numbers of employees), and barriers to entry (based on regulatory, technical, or market power). We know only a little about how industry structure affects societal inequality. Perhaps surprisingly, greater employment concentration is associated with less societal inequality (Davis and Cobb 2010; Cobb and Stevens 2017), because otherwise identical workers, especially low-wage workers, are paid more by large firms (Hollister 2004). Other aspects of market structure have not been studied, due to the lack of fine-grained data on employing organizations, as I explain below. Clearly, we need more research on this topic.

We might expect inequality within employing organizations to simply aggregate to yield inequality within societies or around the world. For example, some scholars have argued that corporations' adoption of the shareholder-value logic has made them more likely to degrade the working conditions and compensation of middle- and lower-level employees, while improving the compensation (if not the working conditions) of upper-level employees (Fligstein and Shin 2004). If this pattern were to scale up to all corporations, it would contribute to societal-level inequality both directly and indirectly. Directly, corporations are among the largest employers. Indirectly, corporations are role models for many other organizations, including business partnerships and sole proprietorships. In support of this argument, consider the transition in the U.S. over the past four decades from many employing organizations offering all of their workers well-paid, stable, secure, full-time jobs with good benefits to offering increasing numbers of workers, especially those with little education and few skills, precarious jobs that are poorly paid, temporary, insecure, part-time, and without benefits like health insurance and parental leave or control over work schedules (e.g., Fligstein and Shin 2004; Kalleberg 2009, 2011, 2018; Schneider and Harknett 2019).[85] The rise of the "gig economy" has exacerbated this trend, with platforms like DoorDash, Lyft, TaskRabbit, Uber, and Upwork refusing to accept formal employer responsibility and offer benefits to workers (Griesbach et al. 2019). This trend is not limited to the for-profit sector: for example, over the past four decades, there has been a marked increase in the use of non-tenure-track faculty in non-profit American colleges and universities (American Association of University Professors 2016).

But there are reasons to question such simple aggregate effects, due to between-firm variation in employment practices. For instance, if firms outsource routine and poorly paid work like cleaning and data entry, what remains will be mostly jobs with good compensation and benefits. Outsourced jobs (whose job-holders tend to work in contract firms) tend to be less secure than the positions held by direct employees, and to offer fewer opportunities for career mobility (Davis-Blake and Broschak 2009; Kalleberg 2011). This suggests less inequality within organizations, but more inequality between organizations and within societies, if outsourced work is moved to lower-income countries. But that would increase between-country inequality. In contrast, relying more on temporary and part-time (rather than full-time) domestic employees would increase both within-organization and societal inequality. Clearly, this question merits further study.

On a global scale, complex global supply chains link organizations in richer countries to organizations in poorer ones. Such international interorganizational networks of production and payment involve organizations with very different levels of power and influence; in general, manufacturers and retailers in the Global North have much more bargaining power than manufacturers and service firms in the Global South.[86] This power differential enables firms in the Global North to pay low wages, deny basic labor rights, and take advantage of the weak labor and environmental regulations of countries in the Global South (Munir et al. 2018). This increases global inequality by trapping workers in the Global South in poorly paid jobs and transferring wealth to the owners and top employees of firms in the Global North.

85. Jobs in agriculture have always been an exception to this trend. Seventy years ago, they were usually poorly paid, temporary, insecure, and lacking in benefits. Today, they still are, despite the advances made by farm workers' unions in the 1950s and 1960s (Ganz 2000).

86. In line with the World Bank's terminology, "Global North" refers to higher-income nations, which lie predominantly but not exclusively north of the equator, while "Global South" refers to lower-income countries, which lie predominantly but not exclusively south of the equator.

Labor unions and social movement organizations can reduce inequality. Labor unions negotiate with employers over wages, benefits, and working conditions, helping reduce inequality. But they also lobby governments on behalf of their members in particular and workers in general, strengthening social welfare policies (Huber and Stephens 2009), and so reduce societal inequality. In Europe, generous social welfare policies required alliances between unions and political parties, either Christian-democratic or social-democratic (Huber and Stephens 2009). In mostly Catholic countries (e.g., Italy) and religiously mixed countries (e.g., Germany), Christian-democratic party alliances with unions led to social welfare policies that focused primarily on keeping people out of poverty through social (e.g., unemployment) insurance. In all countries, social-democratic parties' alliances with unions made it possible to create and maintain more expansive and generous social welfare policies, focused on redistribution through a wide array of policies, including not just unemployment insurance, but also public social services such as state-provided universal health care and education.

In the U.S., the United Automobile Workers' strike of 1945–46 against General Motors resulted in a new bargain: large employers would provide pensions to all workers, not just top executives, and pay for health care for employees and their families (Davis 2016; Davis and Cobb 2010; Hacker and Pierson 2010). This pattern spread to large employers in other industries, reinforcing earlier trends (Dobbin 1992). These practices, along with the increased wage rates that unions pushed for, dramatically reduced within-firm and societal inequality in the U.S. over the next three decades. But that trend has since been reversed due to the decline in unions, from covering 20.1 percent of the workforce in 1983 to 10.8 percent in 2020 (U.S. Bureau of Labor Statistics 2021b). On a more optimistic note, the recent surge in worker mobilization—the Fight for 15 seeking to raise state minimum wage levels to $15 per hour), strikes by workers in poorly paid food-service and retail jobs and by K-12 teachers (one of the most numerous of occupations, with over three million people) who seek higher pay and better benefits, and unionization drives in many low-wage occupations—coupled with the substantial recent rise in quit rates (among workers seeking better pay, working conditions, and career prospects) may portend a reversal of societal inequality. But these events are so new they have not yet been studied in detail by organizational scholars.

Overcoming obstacles to research on organizations and societal inequality. To date, research on societal inequality has generally analyzed aggregate data to show broad national trends, rather than examining the impact of the structures, policies, and practices of employing organizations. The biggest barrier to such analyses is the lack of data on employees' backgrounds, perceptions, job conditions, and rewards, on the one hand, and the structures, policies, and practices of the organizations where people work, on the other. The nationally representative surveys that have been used to study inequality do not identify employing organizations and so cannot be used to investigate differences within or between organizations, while survey and administrative data on individual organizations are usually not nationally representative. Data connecting all, or a nationally representative sample of, employing organizations to their employees are necessary, as research on within-organization inequality demonstrates that organizational hiring practices, culture, formal and informal social networks, task allocation, the structure of job ladders, performance evaluation routines, compensation practices, and promotion systems all matter. These organizational features have persistent effects on inequality because they are naturalized by three institutional myths: that organizations seek to maximize efficiency, that organizational practices are meritocratic (because that is efficient), and that globalization is a positive force (Amis, Mair, and Munir 2020). And these organizational features have very different effects on the attitudes and behavior of people in different demographic groups, based on race or ethnicity, gender, and education.

Administrative data linking employers and employees can help reveal how employing organizations shape national-level patterns of inequality. Such data exist for several European countries and, to a lesser extent, for countries in Asia and North America: see, for example, Sørensen and Sorenson (2007) on Denmark; Petersen, Penner, and Høsgnes (2014) on Norway; and Godechot and Senik (2015) on France. The most complete analysis of linked employer–employee data shows that over the past quarter-century, most of the increase in societal-level inequality across fourteen high-income countries is due to differences in wage rates *between* rather than *within* firms (Tomaskovic-Devey et al. 2020). This finding means that previous research by organizational scholars focusing on inequality within firms is missing a huge (and growing) piece of the puzzle. But research using linked employer–employee data is still hampered by the fact that these contain little or no information on employer structures, cultures, power distributions, policies, or practices. Worse: in some cases (e.g., the U.S.), they lack information on such basic things as job titles, or they are aggregated to very broad occupational categories (as in mandatory reports to the U.S. Equal Employment Opportunity Commission, which report on nine occupational categories, including professionals, office and clerical workers, and craft workers). So while such studies can suggest that rising between-employer inequality may be due to the concentration of more educated workers in a few firms or to increased outsourcing and use of temporary or contract workers, they cannot prove their case. In addition, they cannot explain why those mediating processes might have arisen in the first place, and how to alter them.

Some existing data sources can be used to connect American employing organizations to societal inequality, although they are not well known. For example, the Bureau of Labor Statistics (BLS) has collected detail survey data on (un)employment, compensation, and working conditions (https://www.bls.gov/rda/restricted-data.htm). Although access to these data is restricted to BLS sites, they are of very high quality. Recent research using these data showed increasing inequality in both wages and benefits, but more in benefits (Kristal, Cohen, and Navot 2020). It also showed that workers in non-standard positions (contract or temporary jobs) had far fewer benefits than workers in standard positions and that inequality is greater in smaller workplaces.

In addition, recent innovations in survey methods offer us hope that we can gather the necessary data (Schneider and Harknett 2022; Griesbach et al. 2019). The strategy is ingenious, if expensive. You can direct advertisements on social media platforms to specific populations—for example, employees of large retail chains like Target, Kroger, and the Gap—and offer employees prizes to complete a survey about their demographic characteristics, their jobs and working conditions, their families, and their health and wellbeing.[87] Then, you gather data from the same social media platform on the demographics of everyone who worked in the focal firms—not just the survey respondents. In pioneering studies (Schneider and Harknett 2019, 2022), estimates of education level, wages, and job tenure were close to those calculated using nationally representative surveys, so even though the data used in these studies were derived from a non-probability sample, the results are generalizable to the population at large. With large enough samples of employees in each organization, you can conduct both within- and between-firm analyses of inequality. The biggest news from this program of research is that unstable and unpredictable work schedules are more strongly associated with psychological distress, poor sleep quality, and unhappiness than is low pay, and that workers of color have more unstable and unpredictable schedules than otherwise comparable White workers.

Conclusion. Clearly, if we can find the data, there is much room to apply insights from organizational theory to explain (and, we hope, reduce) economic inequality within societies and across the globe. We can investigate a wide array of factors that drive societal and global inequality: business strategies, organizational structures, practices, cultures, and logics; power and dependence relations within and between organizations; prevailing social mores and efforts to disrupt them; new technologies; and legal institutions.

---

87. This method is expensive because you must pay for each advertisement and you need many advertisements to yield a large enough sample of employees within any set of organizations.

Politics

Formally, politics inheres in the actions of the state. Concretely, it involves electing representatives, writing and passing legislation, developing rules and regulations to carry out legislative requirements, enforcing those rules and regulations, and judging compliance with legislation, as well as the legality of legislation, rules, and regulations themselves, in the courts. Each of these processes can be shaped by the actions of organizations. Political parties endorse policy platforms and electoral candidates. Elected bodies write and pass legislation. Government bureaucracies shape and enforce rules and regulations. And courts judge actions, legislation, and regulations.

Importantly, business firms, trade and industry associations, lobbying firms, think tanks, social movement and other civil society organizations, and labor unions also shape politics. *Business firms* can shape politics directly by donating to political candidates and elected officials, or by lobbying elected officials, bureaucrats, and judges so that laws, rules, regulations, enforcement procedures, and court decisions serve business interests. They can shape politics indirectly, by funding *trade and industry associations, lobbyists, scientists,* and *think tanks,* which in turn influence political candidates, elected officials, bureaucrats, and judges. For their part, *social movement organizations, other civil society organizations,* and *labor unions* can use publicity and the power of numbers to pressure state actors, often (but certainly not always) in ways that seek to thwart the interests of business firms and their agents.

In this section, I discuss the empirical evidence on how organizations outside the formal state apparatus shape elections, laws, rules and regulations, enforcement, and court decisions. Most of my examples below involve the U.S., the country I know the most about; but I include examples from other countries where good-quality research exists on how organizations affect political processes.

Impact on elections. Most basically, business interests can help determine who is eligible to vote. Perhaps the most prominent example in the U.S. is the effort by David and Charles Koch, who run Koch Industries, a huge privately held multinational company devoted to energy and manufacturing.[88] The Koch brothers have poured hundreds of millions of dollars into the American Legislative Exchange Council (ALEC) and two related organizations, the State Policy Network and Americans for Prosperity (AfP) (Hertel-Fernandez 2019). They have been joined by several other right-wing foundations and hundreds of large manufacturing, energy, and service corporations. Together,

---

88. David Koch died in August 2019.

these organizations offer model legislation to Republican authorities to combat alleged voter fraud. This legislation emphasizes three tactics—requiring photo identification (ID), eliminating early voting and voting by mail, and removing voters from the polls—that have disproportionately targeted people of color, as well as the poor (who are disproportionately people of color), the young, and the elderly (Anderson 2019).[89] Photo IDs can be difficult for poor and elderly voters to obtain, especially after offices issuing acceptable ID cards are closed in areas that serve those populations, and the government-issued ID cards that such voters already possess (e.g., public housing IDs) are not accepted. Eliminating early voting and voting by mail depresses turnout among voters who cannot easily take time off work to vote, including most people in low-wage jobs. Removing voters from the polls has often been done without notifying those affected, which runs counter to federal law; when the affected voters have tried to vote, poll workers have been overwhelmed and unable to resolve the situation, so voters have been thwarted. This massive, business-funded effort has unfolded over the past two decades, even though voter fraud is vanishingly rare (Levitt 2007)—and it continues today. In the end, these efforts have created a "clear and present danger for democracy" (Anderson 2019: 95). Indeed, on the 2018 version of the Perceptions of Integrity Index, which is based on surveys of election experts around the world, the U.S. scored 61, far below any other wealthy industrialized nation (Norris and Grömping 2019).[90]

Lest they despair, Americans might consider instead the positive impact that some corporations and their leaders have had on electoral politics. The U.S. has seen Black corporate leaders oppose recent laws restricting voting rights in several states, starting with Georgia. It has also seen them band together to pressure other corporate leaders to follow their example. The impact of these efforts is unclear as of this writing, but certainly it merits further investigation.

89. Statistical analyses have focused on the first tactic alone. The results of such analyses are inconclusive, probably because most laws were passed recently (Highton 2017). Moreover, state laws differ greatly in detail, their on-the-ground implementation varies, and their effects depend on what other laws are in force, so using simple dummy (0, 1) variables to capture the existence of such laws masks important variation.

90. The Perceptions of Integrity Index uses expert opinions (i.e., those of political scientists who study elections) to evaluate nation-state performance in the absence of directly observable indicators of outcomes or processes. It has a theoretical range from 0 to 100. In practice, its range is narrower. The five Nordic countries scored highest (83.8 on average); several African countries scored lowest (the Democratic Republic of the Congo, Burundi, Equatorial Guinea, and Ethiopia averaged 25.25); and the other Anglo-American democracies scored moderately highly (Canada, New Zealand, Australia, and the U.K. averaged 71.5).

The global exemplar of a more benign business impact on politics is George Soros, the billionaire founder of several highly successful hedge funds, who has used the profits he earned in currency trading to launch the Open Society Foundations (OSFs), which fund civil society groups to support democracy and civil rights in over 120 countries—often in opposition to absolutist governments. OSFs seek to foster on-the-ground, publicly accountable democratic institutions, freedom of expression, and the rule of law. For example, OSFs helped launch political movements across eastern Europe before and after the fall of communism, some of which evolved into political parties espousing democracy and capitalism: for example, the Federation of Young Democrats (Fidesz) in Hungary,[91] and the Charter 77 movement in Czechoslovakia (Murphy 1993).

Impact on laws, regulations, and enforcement. For organizational scholars, perhaps the best known research on this topic is work on social movement organizations, which was inspired by the rise of the civil rights, women's, Indigenous, and anti-war movements, and their obvious impact on politics, most notably in the U.S. with respect to passage of the Civil Rights Act of 1964 and state ratification of the Equal Rights Amendment (ERA) to the U.S. Constitution (although that effort failed, it has recently been taken up again by activists and the House of Representatives). Mayer Zald and his colleagues (Zald and Ash 1966; McCarthy and Zald 1977) recognized that many social movements are formally organized; they posited that social movement organizations are more powerful when they can mobilize more resources, including money and members. Consider, for example, the women's rights movement. Demonstrating the strength of this theory, American suffragist organizations won voting rights for women in a majority of states before the passage of the Nineteenth Amendment to the U.S. Constitution in 1920, which gave women the vote; they succeeded earlier in states where they raised more funds (McCammon et al. 2001). Around the same time, federations of women's voluntary associations were successful in pressuring state legislators to enact mother's pensions—even in states where women could not yet vote (Skocpol et al. 1993). Decades later, the ERA was more likely to be ratified in states where the National Organization of Women had a larger presence, especially when Democrats dominated the state legislature, but less likely to be ratified in states where anti-ERA organizations had a larger presence, especially when Republicans dominated the state legislature (Soule and Olzak 2004).

---

91. Ironically, the liberal-democratic wing left Fidesz in 1994 and it was transformed into an authoritarian populist party led by Victor Orbán, who is now a sworn enemy of Soros.

Other social movement organizations have shaped policy outcomes: poverty reduction programs in Mississippi (Andrews 2001), concealed-carry laws (which involve licensing ordinary people to carry loaded handguns in their bags or in holsters that are hidden by coats) across U.S. states (Steidley 2018), and pro-immigrant ordinances by American municipalities (Steil and Vasi 2014). Yet, because social movement organizations usually mobilize people who have little formal political power, they are often unable to bring about policy change directly (Burstein and Linton 2002; Amenta et al. 2010). Instead, their impact is mediated by the actions of political allies, such as individual politicians and political parties sympathetic to their goals, and by how well their goals resonate with public opinion (e.g., Cress and Snow 2000; Burstein and Linton 2002; Steidley 2018).

Political-science research on the lobbying of elected officials and regulators by business organizations, pressuring legislators, staff members, and regulators to write or interpret laws favorably, has shown that lobbying in the U.S. has increased tremendously over the past half century (Drutman 2015). The vast majority of money spent on lobbying the federal government involves business interests: business outspent non-profit interest groups and labor unions by a ratio of 34:1. As a result of increased lobbying pressure, legislation does not pass (or even get onto the agenda) and regulations are not finalized until they have taken into account the interests of large firms in the affected sectors. Sometimes the impact of lobbying firms is quite direct: they share their expertise and help draft laws and regulations. Whether direct or indirect, lobbyists' influence makes many laws and regulations very long and complex: for example, the Patient Protection and Affordable Care Act of 2010 (better known as "Obamacare") was over three hundred thousand words long (over half the length of Tolstoy's opus *War and Peace*) because so many different organizational interests were taken into account, ranging from hospitals, to physicians' associations, to insurance companies, to employer groups, to labor unions. With such lengthy and complex bills and regulations, it is easy to add changes that benefit a specific firm or group of firms because no congressperson, staff member, or regulator has the time or energy to read every page.

At the state level, business lobbying organizations such as the Chamber of Commerce, the National Association of Manufacturers, ALEC, and AfP have successfully pushed state governors and legislators to enact laws weakening organized labor, holding down the minimum wage, restricting access to overtime pay, undermining occupational safety standards, and limiting unemployment insurance (Lafer 2017; Hertel-Fernandez 2019). ALEC has achieved success through the division of labor among its members, with proposals related to issues involving agriculture, finance, and health care crafted by task forces consisting of representatives from member corporations with strong economic interests in those specific sectors; ALEC has also given the most weight to the interests of the largest donors in any policy arena (Hertel-Fernandez 2019). In this way, ALEC has avoided conflicts of interest among members, which hobbles corporate influence (Schmitter and Streeck 1999; Martin 2000). ALEC's intensive lobbying efforts have been facilitated by the U.S. Supreme Court decision *Citizens United v. Federal Election Commission* (Lafer 2017), which ruled that corporations are legally people, so they have constitutional rights to free speech. As a result, corporations can legally promote their interests by funding political campaigns and mounting advertising to sway voters.

But like social movement lobbying, business lobbying does not always succeed—60 percent of U.S. business lobbying campaigns fail to change laws or regulations (Baumgartner et al. 2009)–although business lobbying tends to be more successful than social movement lobbying (Gilens and Page 2014). One common reason business lobbying fails is that business interests are not always aligned. For example, U.S. federal efforts to limit sharing of copyrighted material through the internet were supported by the film, television, and music-recording industries, but opposed by tech firms like computer and internet companies. Lobbying is most likely to yield success when it focuses on narrow, highly technical issues that do not cross partisan battle lines, when lobbyists can evade public scrutiny because they focus on issues that are not salient to the general public, and when lobbyists have long-standing relationships with legislators and their staffs (Culpepper 2010; Drutman 2015). Moreover—harking back to work on ambiguity in decision-making (March and Olsen 1976)—firms do not always establish their policy goals in advance; instead, their understandings of what policies are in their best interest depend strongly on their interactions with politicians and state officials (Woll 2008).

Sometimes the interests of big business and the people who have accumulated wealth through them involve cultural or social rather than economic issues. In the U.S., lobbyists successfully push for laws attacking public education, such as by eliminating collective bargaining for teachers, promoting charter schools, establishing school voucher programs, implementing high-stakes testing, and supporting online instruction—efforts that reduce public spending on education, thus shrinking local governments (Lafer 2017; Hertel-Fernandez 2019). Such efforts are largely social or cultural, but they do affect the bottom line. For example, many of the charter and online schools that have been replacing traditional public schools are run by for-profit corporations. Some are funded by private-equity firms, which emphasize earning huge profits through financial and operational restructuring rather than improving students' educational attainment (Wiggin 2013; Bonner, Stancill, and Raynor 2017).

Work on business lobbying has been done in many countries beyond the U.S., notably in emerging economies where formal political institutions like the rule of law are weak, leaving ample scope for agenda-setting and favor-seeking. For instance, connections between Chinese business firms and state bureaucrats, whether in the form of former bureaucrats serving as executives or board members, executives serving as elected or appointed state officials, or informal social relations between bureaucrats and corporate leaders, can benefit firms by easing access to state-controlled resources such as land and bank loans and lightening regulatory burdens, and so can help improve firm performance (e.g., Peng and Luo 2000; [Yimin] Lin 2001; Haveman et al. 2017). That may explain the rise of business lobbyists in China ([Scott] Kennedy 2005) and the rampant corruption noted by many scholars (e.g., Wedeman 2012; Pei 2016).

Impact on the courts. Organizations can directly influence judges by providing templates for compliance with government regulations. This is most likely to occur when legal mandates are ambiguous, meaning that they contain vague or contentious language, they regulate procedures rather than outcomes, or they provide weak enforcement mechanisms; in such circumstances, legal mandates give affected organizations wide latitude to interpret what compliance means on the ground (Edelman 1992). The best-documented case of legal ambiguity in the U.S. is that of equal employment opportunity and affirmative action law, which applies to most employing organizations. Ambiguous legal mandates have imbued employing organizations' compliance efforts with the power to influence legal thinking (Edelman et al. 2011). As specific structures and policies—anti-discrimination rules, affirmative action offices, grievance procedures, and training programs for women and people of color—became widespread and legitimated, they came to be accepted as indicators of compliance by judges.

Organizations must deal with many legal mandates beyond workplace civil rights, including laws governing pollution, workplace safety, criminal justice, and consumer protection. For example, one study of consumer protection law revealed that in California, courts' interpretations of laws concerning automobile warranties, like judicial interpretations of laws concerning employees' civil rights, were shaped the private grievance structures (dispute resolution venues) erected by automobile manufacturers, which ultimately weakened those laws (Talesh 2009). Clearly there is room for much more research investigating this mode of organizational influence on politics.

Conclusion. Given evidence of the substantial impact of business organizations on politics, organizational scholars have a clear mandate to jump on this topic far more than they have (for examples of role models, see Prechel [2000], Burris [2005], and Mizruchi [2013]). We should not leave it to political scientists, historians, and journalists, because they do not have the deep knowledge of ow organizations work. Future research could, for example, harness theories of organizations to investigate the flow of money and information among business firms, lobbyists, politicians and regulators, and identify the effects on voter rolls, voter turnout, election results, legislation and regulation, and appointments to the judiciary. And the impacts of social movement organizations and of labor unions on formal politics both merit further investigation by organizational scholars, as most research has been limited to demonstrating spending on lobbying or other access, and much less on actual impact.

Environmental Degradation

Organizations have obvious impacts on the physical world through their everyday activities. Mining and energy companies remove minerals and fossil fuels from the earth; forestry and agriculture businesses raise and harvest timber, food and industrial crops, and livestock; real-estate development and construction firms prepare land and erect buildings; manufacturers produce physical goods; and distributors deliver those goods to wholesalers, retailers, and end users. Service sector organizations, such as educational institutions, transportation companies, web services firms, and financial institutions, affect the physical world most obviously by consuming energy and emitting greenhouse gases, but they also produce tangible waste. For example, at the University of California Berkeley, only 52 percent of physical waste emitted in 2017–18 was reused, recycled, or composted; the rest was sent to landfills (University of California, Berkeley 2019)—despite policy goals of keeping 100 percent of waste out of landfills by 2020. More positively, non-profit conservation agencies like the Nature Conservancy buy land and environmental movement organizations like Greenpeace and the Sierra Club lobby to protect air, water, and land from degradation, and to protect wildlife.

Despite the clear impact of organizations on the physical world—as one scholar put it, "organizations are the most intensive and effective environmental destroyers" (Perrow 1997: 66)—organizational scholars have seldom studied this topic. Existing research on organizations and the natural environment is largely limited to probing the spread of sustainability goals, the logics that underpin climate change discourse, and the dynamics of activists on both sides of the climate change debate (for reviews, see Zollo, Cennamo, and Neumann 2013; Hoffman and Jennings 2018). Much research on these topics is either agenda-setting or theoretical in nature. Organizational scholars seldom study how organizations *actually* alter the natural environment: for example, by emitting greenhouse gases, cutting down forests, polluting land and water, or reducing pollution. The empirical studies that do exist have tended to use simple economistic arguments, such as positing that compensation for improvements in environmental "performance" will bear fruit, or that greenhouse gas emissions can be reduced by creating markets for carbon offsets, rather than using organizational theories that are based on more realistic behavioral factors like organizational values and norms, social-influence channels within and between organizations and vested interests within organizations, or structural factors such as organizational age, size, and technology. Only a little research applies organizational theories to explain how organizations harm the physical environment. I discuss that research here and offer suggestions for how to build on it.

Organizational characteristics. The most obvious way to start is by examining environmental degradation as a function of organizational characteristics. Consider organizational size, the most commonly studied organizational characteristic and the most readily accessible in existing data sources. On the one hand, larger manufacturing organizations may pollute less than smaller ones, because economies of scale make their operations more efficient and greater visibility makes them more hesitant to do obvious harm. On the other hand, larger organizations have more power, including the power to sway politicians through donations and lobbying efforts, and more cash to pay fines if they get caught, so they may have more leeway to pollute than do smaller organizations. One study revealed that toxic chemical emissions rates were higher for larger chemical plants, especially those embedded in multi-plant organizations (Grant, Bergesen, and Jones 2002). Subsequent research revealed positive associations between toxic chemical emissions and facilities managed by out-of-state headquarters offices; the effect was largely due to facilities located in communities with few civic associations (Grant, Jones, and Trautner 2004). Moreover, corporations with more layers of legally independent (but corporate-controlled) subsidiaries pollute more, because parent corporations are legally shielded from any liabilities that accrue due to the actions of their subsidiaries (Prechel and Zheng 2012). The implication for future research is clear: organizational structures and the nature of stakeholders matters.

Recent research extends this work to consider the locations where organizations operate. When U.S. firms increased the percentage of managers who were non-White, their toxic emissions rates fell, mostly in neighborhoods that were home to higher proportions of non-White residents (Schrage 2019). The effects were substantial: if the fraction of non-White managers in a production facility rose from 5 percent to 10 percent and the neighborhood was 60 percent non-White, toxic pollution dropped by 1.2 percent. But if the neighborhood was 90 percent non-White, toxic pollution dropped by 3 percent—2.5 times as much. This result is due to stronger race matching between managers and local activists, the greater racial salience of pollution in neighborhoods with fewer White residents, and the greater likelihood that non-White managers lived in such neighborhoods.

Other work considers the adoption of policies and practices to ameliorate climate change and reduce pollution, and the impact of those policies and practices on actual emission of toxic chemicals or greenhouse gases. For example, a study of chemical plants found that although coercive, normative, and mimetic pressures led plants to adopt such policies, adopting them did not reduce emissions, because they did not specify performance requirements and, even if they had done so, there was no enforcement mechanism (King and Lenox 2000). Another study revealed that family-owned firms polluted less than non-family-owned firms because the former were more concerned about their reputations and less about profits, and because they were more deeply embedded in their local communities (Berrone et al. 2010). Overall, the picture such studies paint is bleak: most "sustainability" and "climate" policies and practices are symbolic, not substantive (for a review, see Aragón-Correa, Marcus, and Vogel [2020]).

External influences: Social movement and business organizations. "Good" physical environments are public goods: things that everyone benefits from without payment, things whose benefits to one actor do not reduce the benefits for other actors. Their public nature demands public effort, such as pressure by social movement organizations, to preserve or improve the quality of the natural environment. Consider, for example, environmental protection campaigns such as the E.U. effort to ban single-use plastic items like straws, utensils, cups, and bags because they end up in waterways, where they constitute 80 percent of marine litter and endanger marine life. This campaign was led by organizations like Zero Waste Europe and prevailed despite strong opposition from industry groups. Yet to my knowledge, there is very little organizational research on the link between social movement activism and physical outcomes (exceptions include Grant and Vasi [2016] and Vasi and King [2019]).

We do have evidence that opposition to action on climate change comes from both firms and industry associations in the affected sectors, such as petroleum extraction and processing (e.g., the American Petroleum Institute), and from conservative think tanks (e.g., the Cato and Marshall Institutes). Conservative think tanks are central to the fight against environmental protection, because they serve as alternative sources of academic thought, employing and commissioning scientists and policy experts to write briefs and books, make media appearances, and testify to government bodies to deny human-generated climate change and other environmental degradation (Dunlap and Jacques 2013). Over 70 percent of books that deny climate change published around the world from the 1980s to 2010 were linked to conservative think tanks, including almost all of the most influential tomes.

Conclusion. We need research pinpointing the levers that business owners, managers, employees, social movements, and community members can pull to shift business firms' actions from symbolism to substance. There are only a few examples of such studies. By agitating for environmental protection policies, international environmental organizations reduced deforestation and carbon dioxide (CO_2) and chlorofluorocarbon emissions in over a hundred countries (Schofer and Hironaka 2005). Environmental movement protests reduced CO_2 emissions in American states, even after taking into consideration environmental protection policies (Muñoz, Olzak, and Soule 2018). But such macroscopic studies cannot answer the question of under what conditions governmental policies and corporate environmental sustainability pledges, policies, and practices reduce firms' emission of environmentally degrading substances, and how such reductions affect firm performance. To that end, several recent innovations pushing organizations to reduce environmental degradation are worth studying. Take, for example, the adoption of Environmental Profit and Loss statements, which cover manufacturers' and distributors' carbon emissions, water consumption and pollution, land use and pollution, air pollution, and waste—both positive actions (e.g., cleaning up rivers, using solar or wind power) and negative ones (e.g., manufacturing with dangerous chemicals, harvesting ancient forests). Other possibilities include the rise of initiatives such as the Leadership in Energy and Environmental Design certification program in the U.S. for buildings and global Cradle to Cradle certification for manufacturers of a wide array of products. We could examine the conditions under which these initiatives yield real results.

Future research could also examine interorganizational relationships and the logics organizations use to set goals and justify their actions. For example, firms' statements about climate change tend to emphasize technical problems and solutions, and to downplay emotions and conflict (Wetts 2020). This helps to explain why there has been little popular support for efforts to reduce dependence on fossil fuels or for efforts to stop deforestation and the draining of wetlands. In a very different example, distinguishing firms by sector (e.g., oil and gas, mining and smelting, manufacturing, retail sales, finance), and assessing heterogeneity across sectors with regard to the risks and benefits derived from fossil fuels as opposed to conservation and renewable energy, reveals that financial institutions such as investment banks and hedge funds perceive risks in fossil fuels and opportunities in renewables (Fligstein and Huang 2022). They use their considerable interorganizational power to fund non-governmental organizations that record greenhouse gas emissions, and push firms in which they invest to report and reduce those emissions. The firms that have been most susceptible to these influence attempts are in sectors where switching to renewable energy sources is more advantageous (e.g., manufacturing), not those (as in the oil and gas industries) that depend on fossil fuels.

Future research could also move beyond studying manufacturing facilities to studying how the consumption and transportation of goods and services degrade the environment. With regard to consumption, "fast-fashion" companies like Zara and H&M induce wasteful consumption of clothing by frequently updating their product offerings (Thomas 2019). Much of this clothing is discarded within a year. Discarded clothing made from synthetic fibers is not biodegradable, so it lingers in landfills for decades or generates noxious fumes when burned. Clothing that does biodegrade often contains chemicals that pollute soil and water. Even before clothing has reached consumers, its production generates almost 20 percent of total industrial water pollution (World Bank 1999). Indeed, textile dyeing and treatment is the tenth worst-polluting industry (Pure Earth 2016). Such wasteful and environmentally harmful production and purchasing behavior is by no means limited to fashion. Releasing new products with updated features to stimulate demand is a cornerstone of corporate strategy in many consumer industries, including automobiles and consumer electronics. With regard to transportation, the rise of online shopping for both consumers and businesses has led to an increase in small-quantity package delivery transported in trucks powered by gasoline, and to a rapidly mounting pile of packaging materials—including styrofoam inserts that will be with us for hundreds, if not millions, of years and polyethylene bags that find their way into bodies of water and the mouths of marine life, where they damage digestive systems and harm reproduction.

Organizational research on environmental degradation need not be limited to studies of for-profit organizations. Social movement organizations are an obvious force to take into consideration: public protests, corporate boycotts, and consciousness raising can all be harnessed to deter environmental degradation. Or they can be used to justify environmental degradation and cast doubt on the facts of anthropogenic climate change. For example, environmentally focused activists have mobilized to prevent high-volume hydraulic fracturing ("fracking"), which has been linked to groundwater pollution and increased seismic activity, while other activists, motivated by potential economic gain, have counter-mobilized in support of fracking (Dokshin 2016). In a different context, environmental movement organizations have supported the adoption of "green" production systems, such as wind-power plants, while counter-movements have opposed them, especially early in the history of green production systems, when they were not well established or accepted (Carlos et al. 2018). Environmental-movement organizations can also affect industry incumbents: movement organizations can stigmatize established firms for polluting, which can impel them to make their production processes more environmentally sustainable (Vasi and King 2019).

Organizational scholars could also investigate how governmental authorities counter environmental degradation by enacting and (more importantly) enforcing laws and regulations. National and subnational governments vary greatly in their stance toward environmental protection. For example, world-systems scholars have shown that the idea that countries should protect the natural environment in the same way as they protect human rights has spread through countries' ties to international non-governmental organizations (Frank, Hironaka, and Schofer 2000). This has led to a proliferation of national parks, environmental protection laws, and environment ministries, as well as increasing participation in international environmental protection organizations. Organizational scholars could dig deeper, and assess how features of national governments such as the level of conflict or consensus among elected officials (strong majority vs. coalition governments) and ruling parties' ideologies affect their willingness to protect the natural world. Moreover, we could consider subnational governments, which vary in their formal support for environmental protection, often due to receiving different levels of coercive pressure from environmental activists or corporate polluters (Vasi 2007). We could also follow the lead of political scientists, who have revealed that lobbying organizations supported by energy companies have consistently undermined efforts to increase taxes on fossil fuels, impose carbon taxes, and mandate minimum thresholds for green energy, thereby freeing corporations to continue to degrade the environment and hasten climate change (Farrell 2016; Lafer 2017: 23; Hertel-Fernandez 2019).

Causal Links between Inequality, Politics, and Environmental Degradation

Although I have so far treated these three topics as if these were independent, there are obvious causal connections between them that merit investigation by organizational scholars. First, what happens in formal political arenas such as elections, legislatures, regulatory bodies, and courts can have obvious impacts on societal inequality, as I explained above. Second, what happens in these same arenas can affect the physical environment, as when governments pass more stringent laws on pollution or greenhouse gas emissions. Third, the environmental consequences of organizational action can generate or reduce societal and global inequality. For instance, when firms choose where to locate facilities that emit air, water, or ground pollution, their choices are often biased toward locations where poorer people live, because such people have fewer economic or cultural resources to devote to opposing facility siting decisions. Fourth, inequality can increase environmental degradation. For example, the "fast fashion"

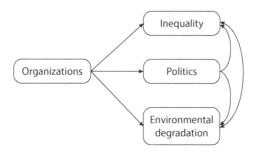

FIGURE 9.1. Connections between organizations, inequality, politics, and environmental degradation

described above, which is quickly discarded and generates long-lasting pollution, can only be sold for low prices because production is carried out in factories in low-income countries that pay very low wages (although in some cases those wages are higher than outside the textile and clothing industries) and do not regulate workplace safety. Figure 9.1 summarizes these relationships.

Conclusion

Organizations are ubiquitous and powerful elements in modern societies. As organizational scholars, we have the expertise to understand their varied forms and behaviors. That is why we must study not just organizations per se, but also their impact on society. I have sketched some things we know about organizations' impact on societal inequality, politics, and environmental degradation, based on research by journalists and by scholars in management, sociology, political science, and history. But other important topics remain for organizational scholars to investigate, including (but not limited to) health and wellness, education, privacy, and social cohesion and division.

The Covid-19 pandemic has demonstrated the weakness of many countries' public health infrastructure, the strength of international bioresearch organizations, and the unevenness in governmental and business responses around the world. But many public health issues beyond this are ripe for organizational analysis. Sociologists and policy researchers who study education have demonstrated that schools with more resources are associated with better educational attainment by their students (e.g., Gamoran 1987; Reardon 2016). But these researchers seldom engage with more nuanced theories of organizational outcomes (for exceptions, see Gamoran and Dreeben [1986] and Arum [1996]). One unhappy consequence of the digital revolution is that hacks and breaches, which result in the loss of private, personally identifiable information, are on the rise. Organizational scholars have seldom focused on these phenomena, but an obvious place to start would be the impact of data breaches on solutions—and their institutionalization in state policy and corporate practice.

In previous research, I demonstrated how media organizations (magazine publishers) supported the flourishing of nation-wide communities of faith, purpose, and practice, which bond people together or push them apart (Haveman 2015). In the same vein, others have shown that media organizations shape communities, creating and erasing social divisions. Nationwide Spanish-language television networks in the U.S. began to broadcast content that appealed to Cuban Americans, Mexican Americans, and Puerto Ricans alike, supporting the development of a pan-ethnic Hispanic ethnic community (Mora 2014). And emotionally charged statements in the news media that originated in fringe civil society organizations profoundly shaped Americans' attitudes toward Islam in the wake of the September 11, 2001 attacks (Bail 2012). In an era rife with political polarization and national (and subnational) strife, the issue of how organizations shape social cohesion and division merits further study.

If you as organizational scholars take up the challenge I pose here and study the impact of organizations on society, you will broaden the audience for our work beyond those who own and control organizations, and help engage social scientists outside of sociology departments and business schools: in political science and geography; in law, education, public health, and public policy schools; and in environmental science departments. You will also engage policy makers who can learn from your work to improve the situation. In doing this work, you may find yourselves helping to usher in a revolution in theories of organizations and empirical approaches to organizations, which will have immense impacts on the world.

Advice for PhD Students

I HAVE TAUGHT PhD students organizations, research methods, and research design for almost thirty years. To help them understand how to think and write like social scientists, I have developed a series of documents explaining the design of research projects, the logic of theory development, and scholarly writing. Here, I distill them into a single document.

Designing Research Projects

We talk about research *design* because we have to think through what we are going to do before we begin and plan our course of action. You can't just go rushing off without a plan, like Stephen Leacock's anti-hero: "Lord Ronald said nothing; he flung himself from the room, flung himself upon his horse and rode madly off in all directions" (Leacock 1911: 74). There are just too many ways to go wrong—but a lot of interesting but very different ways to go right. Designing research thoughtfully requires that you first pose research questions, taking into consideration existing knowledge, then gather and analyze data drawn from the real world, in order to draw believable (i.e., reliable and valid) descriptive and causal inferences. Plans for conducting scientific research have four components—one or more research questions, theory, data, and use of data—which I lay out serially. Of course, research involves the unexpected (that's why it's called *re*search, not search!), so any plan you make is likely to have to be revised, forcing you to iterate—to move back and forth repeatedly between components.

Research questions. You must be highly motivated to answer your research questions, because scientific research is always time-consuming, often frustrating, and sometimes expensive. As a social scientist, you should tackle a question that has important consequences for social, political, cultural, economic, or biological life. This means important to more than just you and a few of your close friends. Otherwise, why waste your time and energy? You must also contribute to one or more active scholarly literatures (also labeled theories, paradigms, perspectives, schools of thought, or traditions). Otherwise, why would any scholars (notably journal editors and reviewers) be interested in your research?

Theory. There are two complementary approaches to theory: *inductive*, where you derive new theory from data, and *deductive*, where you test existing theory on data. These approaches tend to be correlated with the nature of data: most inductive studies use qualitative data with small samples, and most deductive studies use quantitative data with large samples. This correlation is, however, changing, as scholars increasingly apply quantitative ML techniques to induce patterns from large-scale data (Nelson 2020), or apply process-tracing methods to test predictions using small-N data (Mahoney 2010). In practice, it is difficult to cleanly separate induction from deduction, since most research involves a mixture of the two analytical approaches. But you should be honest about when your argument is inductive (inspired by what you observe in your data) and when it is deductive (derived from a combination of existing theory and evidence, plus your own creative logic).

In both approaches to research, you must be able to state the theory specifically and unambiguously—not in vague or fuzzy terms. Specific and unambiguous statements of theory make it possible for you or others to confirm or disconfirm them, while vague statements make it impossible. You should be able to state the theory in hierarchical terms, so that higher-level, more abstract terms encompass lower-level, more concrete terms. For example, the abstract construct "organizational size," one of the most-studied in our field, can encompass many observable constructs, including number of employees, number of customers, assets, revenues, or scope of operations. It can also be absolute or relative; for example, market share can be conceived of in terms of sales volume (absolute) or in terms of sales rank (relative).

Data. You must clearly record the process by which you gather or generate data. There are three things to consider: the scope of the data, measurement quality, and sample representativeness. First, you should gather or generate data on as many of your theory's observable implications as possible. In inductive research, this means pulling out from your data the widest set of (logically related) conclusions and searching for or gathering more data if necessary. In deductive research, this means analyzing the widest set of logically related factors suggested by previous research and your own creative thinking. Doing this will make it easier to compare the theory to alternative explanations and discount them (Stinchcombe 1968). Second, you must develop clear logical connections between your observable variables and the unobservable constructs they represent. This is where measurement reliability (consistency of measurement over time and across observers or observations) and construct validity (accuracy in getting at abstract theoretical constructs with empirical indicators) come into play. Third, you must also be careful about how you draw data from the real world, meaning how you construct your sample. You have two options. First, you can draw representative samples using probability theory (random sampling) to avoid sample-selection bias, but this is only possible if there is a sampling frame. Second, you can draw samples using non-probability sampling, such as purposive, snowball, or quota sampling, which is especially useful for studying unusual cases or hard-to-find research subjects, and when there is no obvious sampling frame. Purposive sampling involves using your judgment to select observations. Snowball sampling involves chain referrals: ask initial research subjects to refer others, ask those subjects to refer still others, and so on. Quota sampling involves selecting cases based on particular characteristics. Non-probability sampling methods may yield richer, higher-quality data if they give you better access to data, and they may allow you to get data on outliers—cases with extreme values, deviant cases, or contrasting cases. As a result, non-probability sampling methods can make it easier to detect causal relationships in small samples—but only if you restrict the sample in ways that rule out alternative explanations.

The use of data. You should use methods of data analysis that yield unbiased inferences, meaning that your results accurately reflect the sample (and, if you used probability sampling, the population from which you drew your sample). You should also use the analytical methods that yield the most consistent inferences, meaning that the results of your analysis would be replicated if another scholar drew a similar sample from the population you studied and used similar analytical techniques. You should use the simplest possible (most efficient) analytical methods—those that require the fewest assumptions about the data while yielding the most information. Recall the sage advice attributed to Albert Einstein: "Everything should be made as simple as possible, but not one bit simpler."

Although I mentioned these components of research design in a sequence, they may occur in different orders. Indeed, you will likely have to move back and forth repeatedly among them.

My prescriptions for doing high-quality scientific research are fine, as far as they go, but they don't go far enough. You must do work that is also *interesting*. Interesting research begins (for deductive research) or ends (for inductive research) with interesting theories. Interesting theories overturn existing assumptions about the way the world works. Interesting theories do not tell people something they did not know before; rather, they tell them that something they thought they knew before was *wrong*. (Non-interesting theories fall into three categories: the obvious, the irrelevant, and the absurd.) But beware: what is considered interesting depends on what the audience knows—interest is in the minds of the observers, not in the mind of the writer.

Also recognize that interesting theories are inevitably controversial. And as two prominent sociologists of science explain, controversy spills over from the nature of the facts to the nature of the person generating and interpreting the facts:

> [S]cientific controversies . . . bring into sharp focus the competence of the protagonists. Normally in science ability is taken for granted. However, in a controversy the specific scientific issues at stake and the abilities of the scientists involved are difficult to disentangle. (Collins and Pinch 1993: 114)

So you have to be prepared to defend yourself against skeptics, which I discuss further below.

What Is Theory?

Theory is central to scientific research. But it is a confusing word, in part because it is used by social scientists in many different, often conflicting, ways. For example, most sociology PhD students take courses in classical and contemporary theory, in which they learn about the ideas that prominent nineteenth- and twentieth-century scholars had about how societies develop, are structured, and behave. Those courses focus on general theories, which seek to analyze entire societies. This book takes a narrower perspective, concentrating on middle-range theories because they are most useful for empirical research. A theory of the middle range is *a logically interconnected set of propositions, derived from assumptions about essential facts (axioms) and causal mechanisms, that yields empirically testable hypotheses and that deals with delimited aspects of social phenomena* (Merton 1968: 39–72). Merton's own words offer a powerful motivation for middle-range theories:

> Middle-range theories . . . lie between the minor but necessary working hypotheses that evolve in abundance during day-to-day research and the all-inclusive systematic efforts to develop a unified theory that will explain all the observed uniformities of social behavior, social organization and social change. Middle-range theory is principally used in sociology to guide empirical inquiry. It is intermediate to general theories of social systems which are too remote from particular classes of social behavior, organization and change to account for what is observed and those detailed orderly descriptions of particulars that are not generalized at all. Middle-range theory involves abstractions, of course, but they are close enough to observed data to be incorporated in propositions that permit empirical testing. Middle-range theories deal with delimited aspects of social phenomena, as is indicated by their labels. One speaks of a theory of reference groups, of social mobility, or role-conflict and of the formation of social

norms just as one speaks of a theory of prices, a germ theory of disease, or a kinetic theory of gases. (Merton 1968: 39–40)

Let us parse this definition to fully understand it. The object of a middle-range theory is some *delimited aspect of social life*. That the scope of analysis and application of the theory is circumscribed is what distinguishes middle-range theories from grand theories. This makes middle-range theories more tractable—easier to induce from data or deduce from prior theory and evidence, easier to confirm or disconfirm, and easier to modify in the face of disconfirmation. But it also makes scientific analysis more fragmented. There are dozens of middle-range theories of organizations floating around, and it takes a lot of squinting to piece each of these little gems into a larger mosaic, to generate a systematic understanding of organizations. Examples of middle-range theories of organizations include relationships among organizational members in terms of gender, race or ethnicity, age, or educational background; the founding of new kinds of organizations; the power of banks to control client firms; the causes of corporate mergers; the development of new administrative structures and procedures, products, or production or distribution systems; the diffusion of such innovations across organizations; and the impact of employing organizations' structures and routines on gender and ethno-racial inequality. It is because there is a bewildering array of organizational theories that I was driven to develop my trichotomous categorization scheme (demographic, relational, cultural) to help my students understand the terrain they were entering. It is because the study of organizations ranges across multiple levels of analysis, from the individual to the field, that in writing this book I subdivided research within each perspective by level of analysis.

Middle-range theories, like all scientific theories, consist of *propositions* (a.k.a. *hypotheses*), statements of association and causation that can be empirically tested. They are derived from axioms (fundamental assumptions) and from other propositions by a combination of logical deduction, operational definitions of theoretical concepts (constructs), and/or empirical evidence (that's where inductive methods come into play). Propositions, in turn, consist of *theoretical constructs* (*concepts*). There are several kinds of concepts, but all are *variables*, meaning that they can take on multiple values; they are defined so that observation will tell you which particular value a variable has when you observe a particular case.

Within each theory, we distinguish variables by their positions in propositions. *Dependent variables* are the outcomes to be explained, while *independent variables* are what explain the outcomes. We often show causal relations between concepts graphically with arrows running between concepts. For example, "women tend to earn less than otherwise comparable men" (gender [independent] → income [dependent]).[92] *Mediator variables* are literally in intermediate positions in propositions, sitting in between independent and dependent variables. For example, "women tend to earn less than men because they tend to be in less senior positions" (gender → position in hierarchy [mediator] → income). Finally, *moderator variables* literally moderate or alter relationships between two variables, sometimes by accentuating relationships, other times by attenuating them. For example, the relationship between gender and income may be weaker in larger organizations because they generally have more formal evaluation and pay policies. Here, the "thickness" of the arrow linking gender and income depends on the moderator variable "employer size."

We sometimes use complex variables: *typologies* or *taxonomies*—categorization schemes that reduce observations on multiple variables to a single variable, and thus simplify what is being studied (Bailey 1994). Typologies are derived conceptually. You begin with a theory, and derive each dimension of the typology and therefore each category in the typology. You then apply the typology to empirical data, by sorting cases into categories based on their observable characteristics—their positions along the dimensions of the typology. For example, in reference to the beer brewing industry, researchers developed a typology based on organizational size and strategy, which classified breweries into mass producers (large, seek economies of scale, and appeal to the "typical" beer drinker) and microbreweries (small, emphasize quality, authenticity, and distinctiveness) (Carroll and Swaminathan 2000). In contrast, taxonomies are derived empirically. You begin with observations of multiple variables for each case you study. You then classify cases into taxonomic categories according to how similar they are on all of those variables. Both typologies and taxonomies can simplify without losing information because many variables take on a limited number of combinations of values; that is, because they covary in a patterned way and combinations not captured in them are rare or non-existent. Typologies and taxonomies can also simplify without losing information, because they take into account the interactive effects (combinations) of all of the original variables.

What Is *Not* Theory

To fully understand what theory is, it helps to consider what theory is not. Here's a list of things that are not theory, drawn from an essay by two prominent organizational scholars (Sutton and Staw 1995), along with suggestions for how to fix your theory-in-development if it is not yet a theory.

---

92. Note the use of "tend to" to reflect the stochastic nature of propositions: not all women earn less than all otherwise comparable men. Also, the use of "otherwise-comparable" is needed to clarify that we are trying to rule out alternative explanations based on differences between men and women, such as education or work experience.

References. Simply listing references to existing theories or mentioning their names is not the same as explicating those theories' causal logic, by which I mean *explaining why* the independent variable affects the dependent variable. The remedy involves explicating which concepts and causal arguments you are adopting from cited sources and how they are linked to the theory you are developing or testing. It requires going beyond discussing observed relationships, and shifting to elucidate *causal mechanisms*, meaning the factors through which an independent variable "moves" a dependent variable (Coleman 1986; Elster 1989; Hedström and Swedberg 1998; Hedström and Ylikoski 2010).

Data. Empirical evidence does not, in and of itself, constitute theory. Empirical findings—induced from your own data, or deduced from other scholars' data—cannot substitute for causal reasoning. Data describe *which* empirical patterns you or other scholars observe; theory explains *why* you or other scholars observe (or expect to observe) those empirical patterns. Again, the remedy is to explicate causal mechanisms and relate them to the patterns you observe in your data. For example, you might show that larger organizations have more formal policies concerning the process of performance evaluation, and that such formal policies reduce gender gaps in evaluation and compensation. You would thus demonstrate empirically that the presence of formal organizational policies moderates the relationship between gender and compensation.

Variables. Lists and definitions of variables are parts of theory, but they do not in themselves constitute a complete theory. Even lists that rank variables in descending order of influence do not constitute theory. George Homans (1964: 957) likened this to "a dictionary of a language that possesses no sentences." The remedy is to put variables into sentences. This means explaining *why* particular independent variables influence the dependent variable in the way and to the extent that they do.

Diagrams. Figures that show causal relationships in a logical ordering (chains of causal processes, showing intervening factors) are not theory. They are stage props, not the performance itself. The remedy is to put words to the arrows in the diagrams and discuss these words in the text. Doing so will force you to explain the reasons for the arrows to exist and the precise nature of the arrows.

Hypotheses. As with variables, hypotheses are parts of theory, but they do not on their own constitute theory. Hypotheses are bridges between abstract theory and concrete data. Formal statements of hypotheses should not contain arguments about *why* empirically observable relationships are expected to occur; instead, they are concise statements about *what* is expected to occur. The remedy is to concentrate in the text on explaining each hypothesis.

Rhetoric

How you write is as important as what you write. What's the point of developing a beautiful new theory or conducting an elegant test of an existing theory if readers are befuddled or not convinced? This is where rhetoric—the art of using language effectively and persuasively—comes in. To begin, you should provide clear *definitions* of all variables. I urge you *not* to follow the lead of the many scholars who have long avoided clear definitions of constructs, as this lamentation from Alvin Gouldner indicates:

> The terminological disparities with respect to the definition of "status" barely fall short of being appalling. Among the varying definitions . . . are (1) "a position in the social aggregate identified with a pattern of prestige symbols" . . . ; (2) the "successful realization of claims to prestige . . . the distribution of prestige in society" . . . ; (3) "a measure of the worth or importance of the role" . . . ; (4) "the rank position with respect chiefly to income, prestige, and power—one or all of these" . . . ; (5) "a collection of rights and obligations" . . . ; (6) a "complex of mutual rights, obligations, and functions as defined by the pertinent ideal patterns" . . . ; (7) "a position in the general institutional system, recognized and supported by the entire society" . . . . One could go on. That these varying definitions are not necessarily contradictory is small consolation and certainly no guarantee that they all refer to the same things. Nowhere do these definitions become more opaque than when—as they frequently do—they refer to a status as a "position" in something. The ready familiarity of the word position seems to induce paralysis of the analytic nerve. Needless to say such terminological confusion begets efforts at neologistic clarification which may then only further becloud the field. (Gouldner 1957: 284, n. 4)

Definitions of constructs should be conceptual—abstract descriptions. You should provide concrete empirical examples to illustrate and clarify your constructs, and to distinguish them from similar ones.

Motivate your choice of explanatory and outcome variables. Why should anyone besides you care about what you're studying? Why should anyone else be interested in your particular explanation? Caring involves both *theoretical* and *substantive* interest. Motivating your study requires that you identify potential audience members and figure out what they don't know, what important gaps exist in their knowledge, and what puzzles they find interesting.

Provide a clear, logical *explanation* of why (how, and under what conditions) an explanatory variable affects the outcome variable. Your goal here should be argument (a combination of logic and empirical evidence that will convince even the most skeptical reader) rather than assertion (claims made without supporting logic or empirical evidence). Logical claims should build on each other from assumptions (axioms) toward a conclusion—a series of "if–then statements," formally termed syllogisms. Perhaps the most famous syllogism is, "All men are mortal. Socrates is a man. Therefore, Socrates is mortal." Here's another example, taken from the film *Legally Blonde*, that is almost as convincing: "Exercise gives you endorphins. Endorphins make you happy. Happy people just don't shoot their husbands, they just don't." ("Woods" 2001). Of course, in the film, Elle Woods and her colleagues prove that their client did not kill her husband.

In building your explanation, you should think about counter-arguments that skeptics could make—the opposing hypotheses they might put forward. Counter-arguments come in the following five generic forms. (1) The *direction of causality* is wrong; what you believe is the cause is actually the consequence. (2) The effect has a *different functional form* than you predict (e.g., negative instead of positive, or ∪-shaped instead of monotonically positive or negative). (3) The predicted relationship may be *contingent* on some other factor—a moderator variable. (4) The predicted relationship may be *spurious*—due to some other factor. (5) Your prediction is *obvious*. There's no reason (a priori, before examining your logic) to believe that the explanatory variable would *not* affect the outcome variable, so there's no excitement in your study—no tension in the minds of readers as they follow your argument. Many studies in sociology and management offer obvious predictions. I may be on a futile quest, given the pressure to publish, but I urge you to do better than that.

To invoke existing theory, you must provide citations. Therefore, you need to conduct a careful, up-to-date *literature review*. But this does *not* mean that you should have a section in a paper or a chapter in a book-length document entitled "Literature Review." Instead, you should tell readers a story that builds logically toward your theory. In deductive studies, you are describing empirically testable implications of existing theory, supported by logic and previous theoretical and empirical work. In inductive studies, you are describing empirically testable implications of a new theory that you generated based primarily on your own empirical work and secondarily on existing theory and empirical work. When you describe previous work, you must choose carefully; select only readings that are well designed and argued, and entirely relevant to your own research question and empirical site. You simply cannot believe everything that is published—instead, you must read critically. You must also analyze the literature deeply—go beyond surface generalities (e.g., type of organization, aspect of structure or behavior, set of explanatory variable studied) to probe the core ideas and critique the central findings. Finally, your readings must be up to date, or you risk repeating what some other scholar has done recently.

Your theory must be *coherent*—its components must hang together logically. If you have more than one outcome variable or more than one explanatory variable, you must explain how they are related. Theoretical incoherence inclines readers to perceive your theory development effort as messy and unparsimonious. If you have one outcome variable and several explanatory variables, your choice of explanatory variables should derive from a logical, empirically supported understanding of the nature and genesis of the outcome variable. If you have several outcome variables, your choice of them should also derive from a logical, empirically derived understanding of the deep connections between them—of the commonalities inherent in the phenomena you are studying.

Offer formal statements of hypotheses. This makes it easier to see what you're arguing. Hypothesis statements should be *explicitly comparative*, because both the explanatory variable (denoted by X, following standard notation) and the outcome variable (Y) vary across cases or within cases over time. Most hypotheses take one of the following forms:

- the more of X, the more [less] of Y,
- when X is large, Y is large [small],
- when X is present, Y is large [or small or present or absent],
- as X increases, Y first increases then decreases,
- as X increases up to some threshold, Y remains constant, but as X increases beyond that threshold, Y increases,
- the positive (negative) effect of X on Y will be attenuated (accentuated) when Z is large (present), or
- any observed effect of X on Y operates through a third variable, Z.

Note that none of these statements predicts a *null effect*; that is, no relationship between independent and dependent variable. Any null finding could be due to mismeasurement of constructs (bad translation of theoretical concepts into operational, empirically observable variables), a bad sampling plan, or poor analytical methods, rather than the "truth" of your theory. Note also that all hypotheses involve only *a single set of relationships*, even if they involve more than two variables. Three types of hypotheses involve three variables: *mediating effects*, where some other variable (Z) is causally intermediate, between X and Y (X → Z → Y); *moderating effects*, where the effect of X on Y depends on the value of some other variable (Z); and *spurious causation*, were X may appear to cause Y, but in actuality Z causes both X and Y. Although these types of hypotheses all involve three variables, they still involve only a single set of relationships.

In sum, your writing style greatly affects how readers understand and accept the substance of your research papers. So style is not simply a matter of readers being picky. It's a critical rhetorical tool that you need to master. Before you start to write, I strongly urge you to read Joseph Williams's *Style: Toward Clarity and Grace* (University of Chicago Press, 1990), which offers a reader-centered view of writing that is based firmly in cognitive psychology.

Finally, if you are not a native speaker of the language you are writing in, your writing style will improve greatly by taking a course on writing or having a native speaker check your grammar and syntax. I heartily recommend the amusing and educational gothic language handbooks by linguist Karen Elizabeth Gordon: for example, the *Transitive Vampire* (1984) on grammar and *The Disheveled Dictionary* (1997) on vocabulary.

How to Read Social Science

One final piece of advice takes the form of a checklist to guide your reading of journal articles, book chapters, and entire books:

- What is being explained?
- What is purported to explain that outcome?
- What is the basic argument—the reason(s) why the explanatory variable affects the outcome? What assumptions underlie the argument? What are the argument's strengths? Its weaknesses?
- What are the argument's scope conditions? Under what circumstances and to what kinds of individuals, groups, organizations, industries, or fields is it meant to apply?
- What differentiates this argument from others offered in the extant literature (or at least, in the literature you personally have read)? Can these differences be resolved through an empirical test?
- If you disagree with the argument being presented, what would it take to convince you?
- For empirical work: how, and how well, is the research designed? Consider sampling method and measurement (construct validity, internal validity, and reliability), external validity, and statistical conclusion validity (spurious causation and selection or endogeneity). What, if any, alternative explanations could account for the findings?

Conclusion

Studying organizations requires both thought and effort—thought to figure out an argument in the existing literature, to induce new arguments from empirical observations, to develop new (valid and reliable) measures of abstract concepts; and effort to read the literature, gather or generate data, and analyze data. One journalist explained, "Science is hard. It's like exploring an unknown land; we'll never know whether over the next hill lies an expansive vista or just another hill." (Prasad 2015).

To write convincing social science research papers, you need to develop arguments logically, based on a combination of ideas from earlier research, existing empirical evidence, and your own creativity. And you need to state clearly the empirical implications of those arguments—what we would expect to see in the data if your arguments were true. If you are inducing a theory from your own data, this argument and its empirical implications should be the goal, the last major section before your conclusion. If you are deducing a theory, this should be the first major section after the introduction. Logic is not enough, however; style also matters. If your writing is clear and crisp, your readers will thank you—and they will be more likely to take your idea seriously.

Formal Social Network Analysis

HERE, I PROVIDE an overview of several concepts in formal (mathematical) social network analysis. For the sake of brevity, I discuss only four key topics: graph theory applied to social networks, node characteristics, network structures, and positions and roles. For more on these and other topics, see Wasserman and Faust (1994) or Newman (2018). The former is targeted at social scientists, especially sociologists; the latter is more comprehensive and up to date.

Graph Theory Applied to Social Networks

Graphs are mathematical representations of pairwise connections between objects. In social network research, those objects are social actors— individuals, groups, or organizations. Graphs consists of social actors (*vertices*, *points*, or *nodes*) and their relationships (*lines*, *ties*, or *edges*) (Harary, Norman, and Cartwright 1965). Ties are undirected if there is no direction to the relations between nodes (think of people who are tied through being members in the same organization) and directed if there is direction to the relations (think of conversations or buyer/supplier ties). Directed ties can be unidirectional (one node sends, the other receives) or bidirectional (both nodes send and receive). To illustrate graph-theoretic concepts, Figure B.1 shows the ARPANET, the precursor to the internet, as of December 1970. It shows undirected ties, although all ties in this network were bidirectional. Figure B.1a places the nodes on a map of the forty-eight contiguous U.S. states. Figure B.1b offers a more standard depiction of the ARPANET's nodes and ties— more standard because the geographic location of the nodes generally does not matter; all that matters is which nodes are connected to which others. The thirteen nodes on the network at this point in time comprised nine universities, two non-profit research institutes (Rand and SRI), and two computing firms

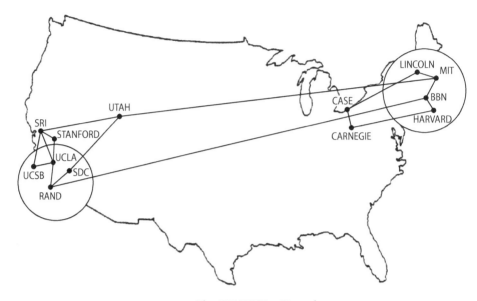

FIGURE B.1A. The ARPANET ca. December 1970
Source: Waldrup (2015). DARPA and the Internet Revolution. Arlington, VA:
US Defense Advanced Research Projects Agency.

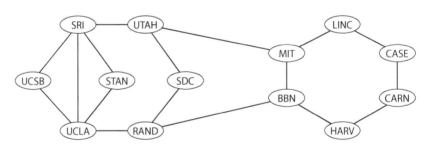

FIGURE B.1B. The ARPANET in 1970: alternative representation
Source: Easley and Kleinberg (2010: 26)

(BBN and SDC).[93] The ties were electronic connections between these organizations' mainframe computers. Graphs are *unimodal* if they connect similar objects, as in Figure B.1, or *bimodal* (a.k.a. bipartite, two-mode, or affiliation networks, which I explain below) if they connect two different kinds of objects,

93. The ARPANET continued to grow after this: by December 1972, there were 24 nodes; by June 1974, 62, including several international sites; by March 1977, 111 (https://www .livinginternet.com/i/ii_arpanet.htm; viewed March 31, 2022). The ARPANET was retired in 1990, its nodes absorbed into the much larger NSFNET. In turn, the NSFNET evolved into the internet, with its mix of commercial and noncommercial exchanges.

such as connecting corporate executives to educational institutions or corporate boards.[94]

Content—information, advice, money, material goods, social solidarity, influence, etc.—travels along the lines connecting nodes. Network ties can be *simplex* (involving a single type of relationship) or *multiplex* (involving multiple types of relationships), but scholars generally ignore the content of network ties (e.g., whether they carry information, money, friendship and social support, etc.) and treat their content as homogenous. Network scholars do, whoever, recognize variation in the structure of ties. Often their focus is on the longer *paths* content can travel: an alternating sequence of distinct nodes and lines. The length of a path is the number of steps required to move from the first node on the path to the last. For example, in Figure B.1, the shortest path from UCLA to MIT was of length three (UCLA → Rand → BBN → MIT). The longer the path, the longer it takes for exchange to occur between endpoints, or the less likely it is that exchange will occur. *Cycles* are paths that repeat nodes—for example, UCLA → Stan → SRI → UCLA in Figure B.1—which create redundancy in the network. By design, every single node in the ARPANET was part of a cycle, which meant that if an electronic connection into or out of any node failed, there would be an alternative path to reach that node.

To calculate node characteristics, attributes of network structure, and positions and roles, graphs were originally represented in matrix form, which facilitated conducting mathematical operations. One-mode networks are represented by square ("adjacency") matrices containing one row and one column for each node, as in Figure B.2. It represents the ARPANET in 1970 in matrix form. Cells note the presence (1) or absence (0) of a tie between pairs of nodes. More rarely, cells may represent the strength of a tie in terms of a continuous variable. If ties are non-directional, adjacency matrices are symmetric; if they are directional, adjacency matrices are asymmetric, as in Figure B.2.

Two-mode networks are represented two ways: (a) by rectangular matrices with one row per actor and one column for the event or organization they are connected to (rectangular because the number of actors need not equal the number of events or organizations), or (2) by square ("bi-adjacency") matrices, projections of two-mode matrices with one row and one column per actor, and cells counting the event(s) or organization(s) they have in common. Figure B.3 shows such a network. You can interpret the central panel as charting relations between individuals (dark circles) and organizations (white circles); the top panel,

<hr />

94. Such graphs are called bipartite because they contain two distinct components—two parts that involve two types of objects. Bimodal networks are the most common subset of the larger class of k-partite networks. Research on organizations and their members seldom involves networks more complex than bimodal ones.

	SRI	UCSB	UCLA	STAN	UTAH	SDC	RAND	MIT	BBN	HARV	CARN	CASE	LINC
SRI	0	1	1	1	1	0	0	0	0	0	0	0	0
UCSB	1	0	1	0	0	0	0	0	0	0	0	0	0
UCLA	1	1	0	1	0	0	1	0	0	0	0	0	0
STAN	1	0	1	0	0	0	0	0	0	0	0	0	0
UTAH	1	0	0	0	0	1	0	1	0	0	0	0	0
SDC	0	0	0	0	1	0	1	0	0	0	0	0	0
RAND	0	0	1	0	0	1	0	0	1	0	0	0	0
MIT	0	0	0	0	1	0	0	0	1	0	0	0	1
BBN	0	0	0	0	0	0	1	1	0	1	0	0	0
HARV	0	0	0	0	0	0	0	0	1	0	1	0	0
CARN	0	0	0	0	0	0	0	0	0	1	0	1	0
CASE	0	0	0	0	0	0	0	0	0	0	1	0	1
LINC	0	0	0	0	0	0	0	1	0	0	0	1	0

FIGURE B.2. The matrix projection of the ARPANET in 1970

relations between organizations projected from the central panel; and the bottom panel, relations between individuals projected from the central panel.

Node Characteristics: Egocentric Network Analysis

Much social network analysis focuses on the ties of individual nodes—egocentric networks ("ego" is the focal node, connected to "alters"). The most basic measure concerns a node's importance or *centrality*. "Importance" can have several meanings, so there are several related centrality measures: degree, closeness, betweenness (Freeman 1977, 1979), and eigenvector (Bonacich 1972, 1987). *Degree centrality* counts the number of lines connected to a node. In Figure B.1, some nodes (e.g., UCLA), had degree centrality of three, some (e.g., UCSB) two, and some (e.g., Case) one. To make this measure comparable across networks of different sizes, we normalize it by dividing it by its theoretical maximum (N-1, where N = number of nodes in the focal network). Doing that yields values ranging from $1/(N-1)$ to 1. Normalized degree centrality for

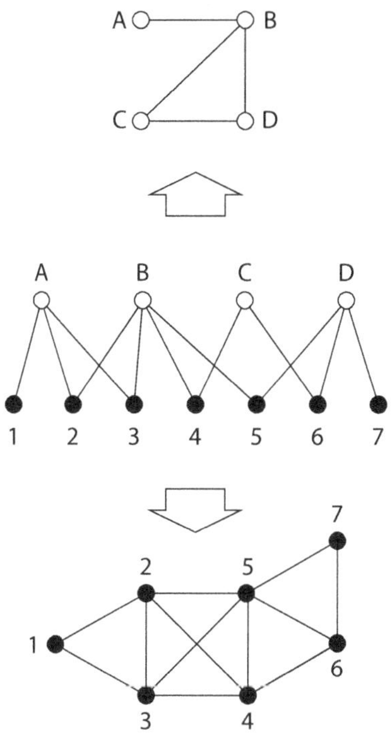

FIGURE B.3. A two-mode network and its projections

UCLA, for example, was $3/(13-1) = 0.25$. In directed graphs, where we know the direction of exchange, we can distinguish in-degree centrality (arrows pointing into ego) from out-degree centrality (arrows pointing out).

Closeness centrality is the average length of the shortest path from the focal node to all other nodes in the network.[95] In Figure B.1, UCLA's closeness centrality was 2.167 (4×1 step, 4×2 steps, 2×3 steps, 2×4 steps), while Carnegie-Mellon's was 3.25. Shorter values thus indicate more central nodes. To compare across networks and create a measure that increases rather than decreases with centrality, we divide this average into N-1. Doing that yields scores of 5.53 for UCLA and 3.29 for Carnegie-Mellon. *Betweenness centrality* counts how many times a node is present in the shortest path between two other nodes. It represents to the extent to which other actors must deal with a focal social actor in order to undertake an exchange; in other words, the extent to which the

95. A variant of closeness centrality is *k-reach*: the proportion of nodes the focal node can reach through a path length of k or less.

focal actor controls exchange flows.[96] Finally, *eigenvector centrality* captures the degree to which the focal node is connected to many nodes that themselves are connected to many other nodes (Bonacich 1972, 1987). Thus, actors with high eigenvector centrality have ties to others with high degree centrality. This differs from the other three measures in that it captures asymmetric status hierarchy (even when ties are asymmetric) rather than being in the center of the flow of exchanges (Krackhardt 1990).

In addition to centrality, network scholars analyze the *distribution* of the characteristics of ego's alters (usually this includes only 1-step ties or 1-step and 2-step ties). For non-graded characteristics like race or industry, this entails calculating *heterogeneity*; for graded characteristics like age or size, this entails calculating *inequality* or *dispersion* (Blau 1977).

Network Structure

Research on network structure shifts the level of analysis upward. Key structural elements of social networks involve connectivity and cohesion, centralization, and clustering. *Connectivity* taps into how easy it is for any node to reach any other node. The more network members interact, the more they are connected, and the more *cohesive* the focal network is. Connectivity can also involve analysis of indirect ties between nodes; for example, A is connected to C if A has a tie to B and B has a tie to C.

The simplest measure of connectivity and cohesion is *density*, the number of relations among actors in a network relative to the number that theoretically could exist.[97] As the number of actors in a network (N) increases linearly, the total possible number of ties between them (T) increases geometrically: $T = N(N-1)/2$, so for $N = 2$, $T = 1$; for $N = 3$, $T = 3$; for $N = 4$, $T = 6$; etc. Network density (D) is t/T, where t is the actual number of ties and T is the maximum possible. It ranges from zero (no ties among actors in the system) to one (a network with all actors tied to all other actors). Because the number of possible ties between network members increases geometrically with the addition of each actor, larger networks tend to be less dense. For the early ARPANET, $D = 17/[(13 \times 12)/2] = 17/78 = 0.167$, indicating that this network contains

96. Formally, betweenness centrality $= C_B(k) = 2\,\Sigma_i\,\Sigma_j\,[g_{ij}(k)/g_{ij}]$, where i, j, and k are nodes in the network, g_{ij} is the number of geodesics (i.e., shortest paths) between i and j, and $g_{ij}(k)$ is the number of geodesics between i and j that include node k.

97. However, overall network density may not accurately capture social cohesion if a network contains many cohesive (densely tied) clusters with few ties among clusters. In such circumstances, the overall network may not be cohesive, but subgroups (clusters) may (Friedkin 1981).

one-sixth of all possible ties between its thirteen member organizations. A related measure of connectivity is *average degree*, the average number of ties per node, which equals $D(N-1)$ and which is often more intuitive than density, although the two measures are highly correlated. Moreover, denser networks tend to have stronger ties, on average, because two actors who are both strongly tied to a third actor tend to be strongly tied to each other; for example, people who have friends in common tend to be friends themselves (Heider 1958).

Centralization is the extent to which one or a few nodes in a network dominate exchange (Freeman 1979). Basically, centralization captures the extent to which cohesion in a network depends on one or a few focal nodes. For example, a hub-and-spoke network is maximally centralized. In contrast, the early ARPANET was highly (although not maximally) decentralized. Centralization can be calculated based on any of the node-level measures of centrality: degree, closeness, or betweenness. You simply calculate the difference between the centrality of the most central node and all other nodes, sum those differences, and scale the sum by the same calculation done for the most centralized network (hub-and-spoke) of the same size. The resulting measure ranges from zero (a fully decentralized network) to one (for a fully centralized network).

Centralization is logically related to centrality: the former is an attribute of the entire network structure, the latter, the attribute of a focal node. Note also that density and centralization are inversely related. Maximally dense social networks have low centralization because every actor can reach every other actor through multiple paths, while maximally centralized social networks (i.e., hub-and-spoke systems) have low density. Therefore, scholars often analyze density and centralization simultaneously.

Clustering involves discovering *cohesive subgroups*, meaning sets of nodes that are more closely tied to each other than they are to nodes outside the set: *dyads* (pairs), *triads* (triplets), and *cliques* (three or more nodes, all connected to each other).[98] The early ARPANET contained cliques of size three (SRI/UCSB/UCLA and SRI/Stanford/UCLA). A less restrictive definition of cliques, *N-cliques*, includes all nodes that are connected by N steps or fewer.

---

98. To keep this appendix brief, I do not discuss other types of network subgroups, such as clans (subgroups where all ties are to other members), K-plexes (subgroups where members have ties to all but K other members), K-cores (subgroups where all members are tied to at least K other members), lambda sets (sets of ties that, if disconnected, disrupt relations among network members the most—i.e., the most important "bridges" in a network), and factions (groups whose members are connected to each other but not—or only minimally—to the members of other groups).

The early ARPANET contained a 2-clique of size four (SRI/UCSB/UCLA/ Stanford). There are also *components*: all actors in a focal component can reach all other actors, albeit through multi-step paths, but they are disconnected from actors in other components. Isolates—nodes not connected to any alter—form separate components. The early ARPANET had only a single component—by design, since the goal was to link all organizations to all others. When networks have two or more components, analysts calculate network *fragmentation*: the proportion of pairs of nodes that cannot be reached because the components they are in are disconnected. In general, cohesive subgroups can be discovered using iterative algorithms, such as multidimensional scaling or k-means, that calculate the proximity (or distance) of each node from all others.

Finally, the numbers and properties of subgroups have important implications for overall network structure. Perhaps the most prominent is *small worlds*, meaning networks in which most nodes are not connected directly to each other, but their direct connections are likely to be connected to each other (so there are a lot of cliques); as a result, most nodes in the network can be reached by any node through a few steps.[99] In formal terms, a small-world network is one in which the average path length between two nodes increases with the natural logarithm of the number of nodes (i.e., $L \propto \log[N]$, where L is the average path length and N is the number of nodes) and overall network clustering (the average probability of a direct tie between two nodes) is high (Watts and Strogatz 1998; Watts 1999). Thus, relations within clusters are dense and paths between clusters are short.

Positions and Roles

We can identify positions and roles in networks from substructures. *Positions* are sets of nodes that have similar patterns of ties (Lorrain and White 1971; White, Boorman, and Breiger 1976; Borgatti and Everett 1999), while *roles* are patterns of ties between nodes based on their respective positions (Boorman

---

99. This pattern became widely known through John Guare's play, *Six Degrees of Separation*, which is animated by the idea that everyone in the world is connected to everyone else by no more than six degrees (path length of six). That idea originated with a study by political scientist Ithiel de Sola Pool and mathematician Manfred Kochen (1978), which was circulated for decades before being published. Inspired by this work, a field experiment found the average path length between people in the U.S. to be six (Milgram 1967; Travers and Milgram 1969). Incorporating this concept, mischievous mathematicians later created the "six degrees of Paul Erdős" game (by the way, my Erdős number is four), and no less mischievous undergraduates created the "six degrees of Kevin Bacon" game.

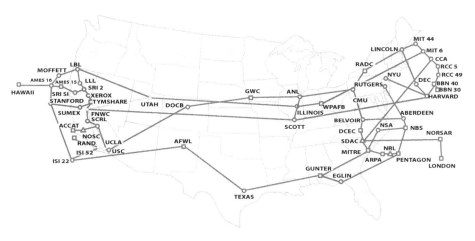

FIGURE B.4A. The (much expanded) ARPANET in July 1977
Source: National Science Foundation, n.d.

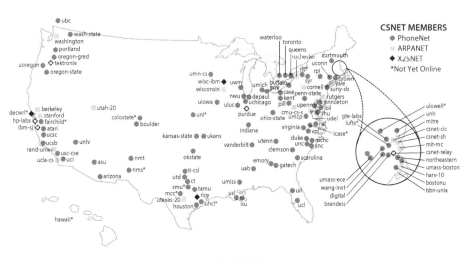

FIGURE B.4B. The CSNET in June 1984
Source: National Science Foundation, n.d.

and White 1976). Identifying roles and positions is especially valuable when analyzing networks larger than the early ARPANET, because larger network graphs are difficult to comprehend. For example, Figure B.4a shows the ARPANET in 1977, when it had over a hundred members (not all are shown), while Figure B.4b shows the much larger CSNET in 1984.

Network analysts study positions and roles in two related ways: as equivalence classes or as core versus periphery subgroups. *Equivalence classes* contain nodes that are similar to each other in terms of their relational positions—that is, their ties to other nodes. To uncover equivalence classes, we permute the rows and columns of matrix-form network data to create homogeneous equivalence classes—*"blocks"*—and generate new, simpler networks (reduced models) in which the nodes represent structural positions, rather than individual actors, and the ties between nodes represent roles. Such *block models* assume that all nodes within each block are substitutable—which they are, with regard to network ties. All nodes in a block face the same structure—ties to the same or similarly positioned alters.

There are three ways to identify blocks, in terms of structural, automorphic, and regular equivalence. To understand the differences between these, consider Figure B.5. Most strictly, *structurally equivalent* actors are connected to the exact same others, even if they are not directly connected to each other (Lorrain and White 1971; White, Boorman, and Breiger 1976). For example, in Figure B.5a, employees A and B are both supervised by store manager 1, while employees D and E are both supervised by store manager 3. Less restrictive is *automorphic equivalence*, which involves nodes that are connected to local structures that have the same pattern of ties (Pattison 1982; Winship and Mandel 1983). In Figure B.5b, store managers 1 and 3 are automorphically equivalent, because they both report to a franchise owner (the same person) and each supervises two employees. Similarly, employees A, B, D, and E are automorphically equivalent because they all have a coworker and report to a store manager, albeit different ones. Finally, *regular equivalence* (also known as *role equivalence*) stems from having the same pattern of ties to other nodes that are also regularly equivalent (Sailer 1978; Faust 1988; White and Reitz 1983). In Figure B.5c, all three store managers report to a franchise owner and all supervise employees—even if they supervise different numbers of employees. And all five employees are supervised by a store manager—even if they don't have the same number of coworkers.

In reality, it is unlikely that two nodes will be members of the exact same equivalence class. Therefore, network analysts calculate how proximate (or distant) nodes are from each other—similar to the way proximity between subgroups is calculated. Again, analysts use different algorithms to calculate proximity or distance, including correlation, Euclidean distance, hierarchical clustering, and multidimensional scaling.

To uncover *core versus periphery subgroups*, we have to distinguish between densely connected nodes in the core and sparsely connected nodes in the periphery (Borgatti and Everett 1999). To put it simply, the density of ties within the core is greater than the density of ties between the core and the periphery, which is greater than the density of ties within the periphery. You can see this clearly in Figure B.6. On the left, the dots surrounded by the dotted line are in

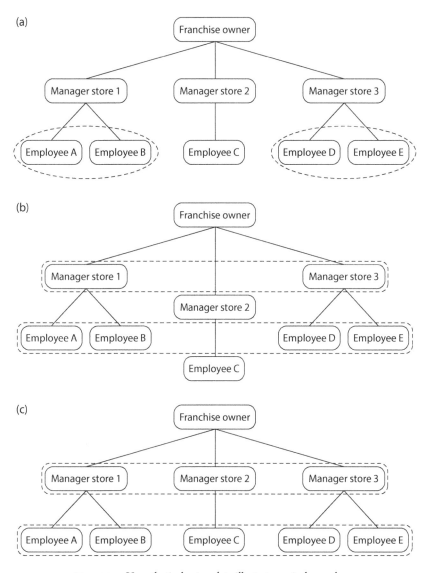

FIGURE B.5. Hypothetical network to illustrate equivalence classes.
(a) Structural equivalence, (b) Automorphic equivalence, (c) Regular equivalence

the core, the dots outside the oval are in the periphery, the lines are the ties between dyads, and the dotted line is the boundary between the core and the periphery. On the right, you see the adjacency matrix, which shows that tie density in the core is greater than between the core and the periphery, which in turn is greater than in the periphery.

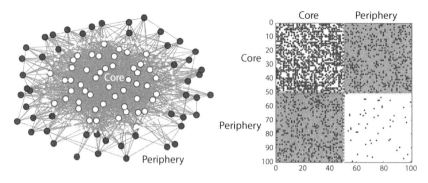

FIGURE B.6. Network core versus periphery
Source: Lee (2015)

Ties between nodes and the boundary between core and periphery can be discrete, in which case each subgroup is an equivalence class—a block. Or they can be continuous, in which case we calculate each node's proximity to the core (i.e., the centroid of the network), and tie strength based on how close dyad members are to the core. Algorithms that draw boundaries between core and periphery seek to maximize the density of the core and minimize the density of the periphery, relative to what would be expected by random assignment of nodes to each subgroup. In general, when a few nodes in the focal network have many ties and most have few ties, there is a strongly cohesive core. Core–periphery measures tend to be highly correlated with degree, closeness, and eigenvector centrality because paths through core nodes tend to be short (Rombach et al. 2017). But unlike those centrality measures, core–periphery measures take into consideration the overall pattern of ties in the network.

Note that a network may have more than one core. For example, the emerging field of data science in a prominent American university has two cores (the first in the department of electrical engineering and computer science, the second in the department of statistics) and a periphery (other engineering fields, the natural and social sciences, the humanities, and the professional schools—scholars who use tools and techniques that emerged from the two cores). Moreover, a network may have multiple layers of "coreness." For example, there may be a core, a semi-periphery, and a periphery, as has long been the case in the system of international trade, where position is defined in terms of the power to dominate or, conversely, by constraint (Wallerstein 1980, 1989). Today, the powers in this system extend beyond core nation-states to include multinational business firms such as Shell Oil and Google, and international governmental organizations such as the World Bank and the International Monetary Fund.

Conclusion

My review of formal social network analysis has necessarily been brief. I have skipped over many important concepts: for example, measures of network connectivity that take into consideration clustering. Mastery of network-analysis methods requires much deeper study. For that purpose, I recommend Wasserman and Faust (1994) and Newman (2018).

REFERENCES

Abbott, Andrew. 1988. *The System of Professions: An Essay on the Division of Expert Labor*. Chicago: University of Chicago Press.

Acker, Joan. 1990. "Hierarchies, jobs, bodies: A theory of gendered organizations." *Gender and Society* 4 (2): 139–58.

Acker, Joan and Donald R. Van Houten. 1974. "Differential recruitment and control: The sex structuring of organizations." *Administrative Science Quarterly* 19 (2): 152–63.

Adler, Paul S. 2001. "Market, hierarchy, and trust: The knowledge economy and the future of capitalism." *Organization Science* 12 (2): 215–34.

Adler, Paul S. 2009. "Marx and organization studies today." In *The Oxford Handbook of Sociology and Organization Studies: Classical Foundations*, ed. Paul S. Adler, 62–91. Oxford: Oxford University Press.

Adler, Paul S., ed. 2009. *The Oxford Handbook of Sociology and Organization Studies: Classical Foundations*. Oxford: Oxford University Press.

Adler, Paul S. and Seok-Woo Kwon. 2002. "Social capital: Prospects for a new concept." *Academy of Management Review* 27 (1): 17–40.

Ahmadjian, Christina L. and Patricia Robinson. 2001. "Safety in numbers: Downsizing and the deinstitutionalization of permanent employment in Japan." *Administrative Science Quarterly* 46 (4): 622–54.

Ahuja, Gautam. 2000. "Collaboration networks, structural holes, and innovation: A longitudinal study." *Administrative Science Quarterly* 45 (3): 425–55.

Aldrich, Howard E. 1979. *Organizations and Environments*. Englewood Cliffs, NJ: Prentice-Hall.

Aldrich, Howard E. and Ellen R. Auster. 1986. "Even dwarfs started small: Liabilities of age and size and their strategic implications." *Research in Organizational Behavior* 8: 165–98.

Aldrich, Howard E. and Martin Ruef. 2006. *Organizations Evolving*. 2nd edn. Thousand Oaks, CA: Sage.

Allison, Rachel and Margaret Ralston. 2018. "Gender, anticipated family formation, and graduate school expectations among undergraduates." *Sociological Forum* 33 (1): 95–117.

Allport, Gordon. 1954. *The Nature of Prejudice*. Reading, MA: Addison-Wesley.

Almandoz, Juan. 2014. "Founding teams as carriers of competing logics: When institutional forces predict banks' risk exposure." *Administrative Science Quarterly* 59 (3): 442–73.

Amenta, Edwin, Neal Caren, Elizabeth Chiarello, and Yang Su. 2010. "The political consequences of social movements." *Annual Review of Sociology* 36: 287–307.

American Association of University Professors. 2016. *Higher Education at a Crossroads*. Washington, DC: American Association of University Professors.

Amis, John M., Johanna Mair, and Kamal A. Munir. 2020. "The organizational reproduction of inequality." *Academy of Management Annals* 14 (1): 1–36.

Ancona, Deborah Gladstein and David F. Caldwell. 1992. "Demography and design: Predictors of new product team performance." *Organization Science* 3 (3): 321–41.

Anderson, Carol. 2019. *One Person, No Vote: How Voter Suppression Is Destroying Our Democracy*. New York: Bloomsbury Publishing.

Anderson, Perry. (1979) 2013. *Lineages of the Absolutist State*. London: New Left Books.

Andrews, Kenneth T. 2001. "Social movements and policy implementation: The Mississippi civil rights movement and the war on poverty, 1965–1971." *American Sociological Review* 66: 71–95.

Angelino, Elaine, Nicholas Larus-Stone, Daniel Alabi, Margo Seltzer, and Cynthia Rudin. 2018. "Learning certifiably optimal rule lists for categorical data." *Journal of Machine Learning Research* 18 (234): 1–78.

Angwin, Julia, Jeff Larson, Surya Mattu, and Lauren Kirchner. 2016. "Machine bias." ProPublica, https://www.propublica.org/article/machine-bias-risk-assessments-in-criminal-sentencing (viewed March 31, 2022).

Ansell, Chris. 2009. "Mary Parker Follett and pragmatist orientation." In Paul S. Adler, ed., *The Oxford Handbook of Sociology and Organization Studies: Classical Foundations*: 464–85. Oxford: Oxford University Press.

Anstey, Roger. 1975. *The Atlantic Slave Trade and British Abolition 1760–1810*. London: Macmillan.

Anteby, Michel. 2017. "Sur les traces de Michel Crozier en Amérique: Verités au pays de veritas." *French Politics, Culture & Society* 35 (3): 91–104.

Anteby, Michel and Virág Molnár. 2012. "Collective memory meets organizational identity: Remembering to forget in a firm's rhetorical history." *Academy of Management Journal*, 55 (3): 515–40.

Applebaum, Anne and Peter Pomerantsev. 2021. "The internet doesn't have to be awful." *The Atlantic*, April: 40–59.

Appleby, Joyce. 2010. *The Relentless Revolution: A History of Capitalism*. New York: W.W. Norton & Co.

Aragón-Correa, J. Alberto, Alfred A. Marcus, and David Vogel. 2020. "The effects of mandatory and voluntary regulation pressure on firms' environmental strategies: A review and recommendations for future research." *Academy of Management Annals* 14 (1): 339–65.

Argote, Linda, Brandy L. Aven, and Jonathan Kush. 2018. "The effects of communications networks and turnover on transactive memory and group performance." *Organization Science* 29 (2): 191–206.

Armstrong, Elizabeth A. 2002. *Forging Gay Identities. Organizing Sexuality in San Francisco, 1950–1994*. Chicago: University of Chicago Press.

Arthur, Michelle M. and Alison Cook. 2009. "Shareholder returns for a Catalyst award." *Group and Organization Management* 34 (4): 432–48.

Arum, Richard. 1996. "Do private schools force public schools to compete?" *American Sociological Review* 61 (1): 29–46.

Ashby, F. Gregory, and Leola A. Alfonso-Reese. 1995. "Categorization as probability density estimation." *Journal of Mathematical Psychology* 39 (2): 216–33.

Askin, Noah and Michael Mauskapf. 2017. "What makes popular culture popular? Product features and optimal differentiation in music." *American Sociological Review* 82 (5): 910–44.

Augier, Mia, James G. March, and Bilian Ni Sullivan. 2005. "Notes on the evolution of a research community: Organization studies in Anglophone North America, 1945–2000." *Organization Science* 16 (1): 85–95.

Augustine, Grace and Brayden G. King. 2019. "Worthy of debate: Discursive coherence and agreement in the formation of the field of sustainability in higher education." *Socio-Economic Review* 17 (1): 135–65.

Auslander, Leora. 1996. *Taste and Power: Furnishing Modern France.* Berkeley, CA: University of California Press.

Azoulay, Pierre, Christopher C. Liu, and Toby E. Stuart. 2017. "Social influence given (partially) deliberate matching: Career imprints in the creation of academic entrepreneurs." *American Journal of Sociology* 122 (4): 1223–71.

Bail, Christopher A. 2012. "The fringe effect: Civil society organizations and the evolution of media discourse about Islam since the September 11th attacks." *American Sociological Review* 77 (7): 855–79.

Bailey, Kenneth D. 1994. *Typologies and Taxonomies: An Introduction to Classification Techniques.* Thousand Oaks, CA: Sage.

Baker, Wayne E. 1990. "Market networks and corporate behavior." *American Journal of Sociology* 96 (3): 589–625.

Baker, Wayne E. and Robert R. Faulkner. 1991. "Role as resource in the Hollywood film industry." *American Journal of Sociology* 97 (2): 279–309.

Baker, Wayne E. and Robert R. Faulkner. 1993. "The social organization of conspiracy: Illegal networks in the heavy electrical equipment industry." *American Sociological Review* 58 (6): 837–60.

Baldassarri, Delia and Mario Diani. 2007. "The integrative power of civic networks." *American Journal of Sociology* 113 (3): 735–80.

Baldwin, Simeon E. 1901. "Private corporations, 1701–1901." In *Two Centuries Growth of American Law, 1701–1901,* 261–312. New York: Charles Scribner's Sons.

Balkundi, Prasad and David A. Harrison. 2006. "Ties, leaders, and time in teams: Strong inference about network structure's effects on team viability and performance." *Academy of Management Journal* 49 (1): 49–68.

Barach, Moshe A., Aseem Kaul, Ming D. Leung, and Sibo Lu. 2019. "Strategic redundancy in the use of big data: Evidence from a two-sided labor market." *Strategy Science* 4 (4): 298–322.

Barbulescu, Roxana and Matthew Bidwell. 2013. "Do women choose different jobs from men? Mechanisms of application segregation in the market for managerial workers." *Organization Science* 24 (3): 737–56.

Barkey, Karen. 1994. *Bandits and Bureaucrats: The Ottoman Route to State Centralization.* Ithaca, NY: Cornell University Press.

Barley, Stephen R. 1983. "Semiotics and the study of occupational and organizational cultures." *Administrative Science Quarterly* 28 (3): 393–413.

Barley, Stephen R. 1990. "The alignment of technology and structure through roles and networks." *Administrative Science Quarterly* 35 (1): 61–103.

Barley, Stephen R. 2015. "Why the internet makes buying a car less loathsome: How technologies change role relations." *Academy of Management Discoveries* 1 (1): 5–35.

Barley, Stephen R. 2016. "60th anniversary essay: Ruminations on how we became a mystery house and how we might get out of it." *Administrative Science Quarterly* 60 (1): 1–8.

Barnard, Chester I. (1938) 1968. *The Functions of the Executive*. Cambridge, MA: Harvard University Press.

Barnett, William P. and Glenn R. Carroll. 1987. "Competition and mutualism among early telephone companies." *Administrative Science Quarterly* 32 (3): 400–421.

Barnett, William P. and Glenn R. Carroll. 1995. "Modelling internal organizational change." *Annual Review of Sociology* 21: 217–36.

Barnett, William P. and Michael Woywode. 2004. "From Red Vienna to the Anschluss: Ideological competition among Viennese newspapers during the rise of National Socialism." *American Journal of Sociology* 109 (6): 1452–99.

Barocas, Solon and Andrew D. Selbst. 2016. "Big data's disparate impact." *California Law Review* 104: 671–732.

Baron, James N. and William T. Bielby. 1980. "Bringing the firms back in: Stratification, segmentation, and the organization of work." *American Sociological Review* 45 (5): 737–65.

Baron, James N., Diane Burton, and Michael T. Hannan. 1999. "Engineering bureaucracy: The genesis of formal policies, positions, and structures in high-technology firms." *Journal of Law, Economics, and Organization* 15 (1): 1–41.

Baron, James N., Alison Davis-Blake, and William T. Bielby. 1986. "The structure of opportunity: How promotion ladders vary within and among organizations." *Administrative Science Quarterly* 31 (2): 248–73.

Baron, James N., Frank R. Dobbin, and P. Devereaux Jennings. 1986. "War and peace: The evolution of modern personnel administration in U.S. industry." *American Journal of Sociology* 92 (2): 350–83.

Baron, James N., Brian S. Mittman, and Andrew E. Newman. 1991. "Targets of opportunity: Organizational and environmental determinants of gender integration within the California civil service, 1979–1985." *American Journal of Sociology* 96 (6): 1362–401.

Barron, David N., Elizabeth West, and Michael T. Hannan. 1994. "A time to grow and a time to die: Growth and mortality of credit unions in New York City, 1914–1990." *American Journal of Sociology* 100 (2): 381–421.

Barsalou, Lawrence W. 1985. "Ideals, central tendency, and frequency of instantiation as determinants of graded structure in categories." *Journal of Experimental Psychology: Learning, Memory, and Cognition* 11 (4): 629–54.

Barton, Allen H. 1968. "Bringing society back in: Survey research and macro-methodology." *American Behavioral Scientist* 12 (2): 1–9.

Basu, Onker N., Mark W. Dirsmith, and Parveen P. Gupta. 1999. "The coupling of the symbolic and the technical in an institutionalized context: The negotiated order of the GAO's audit reporting process." *American Sociological Review* 64 (4): 506–26.

Battilana, Julie and Tiziana Casciaro. 2013. "Change agents, networks, and institutions: A contingency theory of organizational change." *Academy of Management Journal* 55 (2): 381–98.

Battilana, Julie and Silvia Dorado. 2010. "Building sustainable hybrid organizations: The case of commercial microfinance organizations." *Academy of Management Journal* 53 (6): 1419–40.

Baum, Joel A. C. and Heather A. Haveman. 2020. "From the editors: The future of organizational theory." *Academy of Management Review* 45 (2): 268–72.

Baum, Joel A. C., Stan Xiao Li, and John M. Usher. 2000. "Making the next move: How experiential and vicarious learning shape the locations of chains' acquisitions." *Administrative Science Quarterly* 45 (4): 766–801.

Baum, Joel A. C., Bill McEvily, and Tim J. Rowley. 2010. "Better with age? Tie longevity and the performance implications of bridging and closure." *Organization Science* 23 (2): 529–46.

Baum, Joel A. C. and Christine Oliver. 1991. "Institutional linkages and organizational mortality." *Administrative Science Quarterly* 36 (2): 187–218.

Baum, Joel A. C. and Jitendra V. Singh. 1994. "Organizational niches and the dynamics of organizational mortality." *American Journal of Sociology* 100 (2): 346–80.

Baumgartner, Frank F., Jeffrey M. Berry, Marie Hojnacki, David C. Kimball, and Beth L. Leech. 2009. *Lobbying and Policy Change: Who Wins, Who Loses, and Why*. Chicago: University of Chicago Press.

Bavelas, Alex. 1948. "A mathematical model for small group structures." *Human Organization* 7: 16–30.

Beauvoir, Simone de. (1949) 1952. *The Second Sex*, trans. and ed. H. M. Parshley. New York: Alfred A. Knopf.

Bechky, Beth A. 2006. "Gaffers, gofers and grips: Role-based coordination in temporary organizations." *Organization Science* 17 (1): 3–31.

Beck, Nikolaus, Josef Brüderl, and Michael Woywode. 2008. "Momentum or deceleration? Theoretical and methodological reflections on the analysis of organizational change." *Academy of Management Journal* 51 (3): 413–35.

Becker, Gary S. 1957. *The Economics of Discrimination*. Chicago: University of Chicago Press.

Becker, Howard S. 1982. *Art Worlds*. Berkeley, CA: University of California Press.

Becker, Howard S., Blanche Geer, Everett C. Hughes, and Anselm L. Strauss. 1961. *Boys in White: Student Culture in Medical School*. New Brunswick, NY: Transaction Publishers.

Beckman, Christine M. and M. Diane Burton. 2007. "Leaving a legacy: Position imprints and successor turnover in young firms." *American Sociological Review* 72 (2): 239–66.

Bedeian, Arthur G. and Daniel A. Wren. 2001. "The most influential management books of the 21st century." *Organizational Dynamics* 29 (3): 221–25.

Belfanti, Carlo Marco. 1993. "Rural manufactures and rural-proto industries in the 'Italy of the Cities' from the sixteenth through the eighteenth century." *Continuity and Change* 8 (2): 253–80.

Bell, Ella L. J. Edmonson and Stella M. Nkomo. 1999. *Our Separate Ways: Black and White Women and the Struggle for Professional Identity*. Boston, MA: Harvard Business School Press.

Belliveau, Maura A., Charles A. O'Reilly III, and James B. Wade. 1996. "Social capital at the top: Effects of social similarity and status on CEO compensation." *Academy of Management Journal* 39 (6): 1568–93.

Bendix, Reinhard. 1956. *Work and Authority in Industry: Ideologies of Management in the Course of Industrialization*. Berkeley, CA: University of California Press.

Benford, Robert D. and David A. Snow. 2000. "Framing processes and social movements: An overview and assessment." *Annual Review of Sociology* 26: 611–39.

Benton, Richard A. 2016. "Corporate governance and nested authority: Cohesive network structure, actor-driven mechanisms, and the balance of power in American corporations." *American Journal of Sociology* 122 (3): 661–713.

Berger, Joseph, Susan J. Rosenholtz, and Morris Zelditch Jr. 1980. "Status organizing processes." *Annual Review of Sociology* 6: 479–508.

Berger, Peter L. and Thomas Luckmann. 1967. *The Social Construction of Reality: A Treatise in the Sociology of Knowledge*. Garden City, NY: Doubleday/Anchor Books.

Berkowitz, Stephen D., Peter J. Carrington, Yehuda Kotowitz, and Leonard Waverman. 1979. "The determination of enterprise groupings through combined ownership and directorship ties." *Social Networks* 1: 391–413.

Berle, Adolf A. and Gardner C. Means. (1932) 2001. *The Modern Corporation and Private Property*. New Brunswick, NJ: Transaction Publishers.

Berman, Elizabeth Popp. 2006. "Before the professional project: Success and failure at creating an organizational representative for English doctors." *Theory and Society* 35 (2): 157–91.

Berrone, Pascual, Cristina Cruz, Luis R. Gomez-Mejia, and Martin Larraza-Kintana. 2010. "Socioemotional wealth and corporate responses to institutional pressures: Do family-controlled firms pollute less?" *Administrative Science Quarterly* 55 (1): 82–113.

Besharov, Marya L. and Wendy K. Smith. 2014. "Multiple institutional logics in organizations: Explaining their varied nature and implications." *Academy of Management Review* 39 (3): 364–81.

Bezrukova, Katerina, Sherry M. B. Thatcher, Karen A. Jehn, and Chester S. Spell. 2012. "The effect of alignments: Examining group faultlines, organizational cultures, and performance." *Journal of Applied Psychology* 97 (1): 77–92.

Bian, Yanjie. 1997. "Bringing strong ties back in: Indirect ties, network bridges, and job searches in China." *American Sociological Review* 62 (3): 366–85.

Bian, Yanjie and John R. Logan. 1996. "Market transition and the persistence of power: The changing stratification system in urban China." *American Sociological Review* 61 (5): 739–58.

Biancini, Susan, Daniel A. McFarland, and Linus Dahlander. 2014. "The semiformal organization." *Organization Science* 25 (5): 1306–24.

Bibb, Robert and William H. Form. 1975. "The effects of industrial, occupational, and sex stratification on wages in blue-collar markets." *Social Forces* 55 (4): 974–96.

Bidwell, Matthew and Isabel Fernandez-Mateo. 2010. "Relationship duration and returns to brokering in the staffing sector." *Organization Science* 21 (6): 1141–58.

Biggart, Nicole Woolsey. 1977. "The creative-destructive process of organizational change: The case of the Post Office." *Administrative Science Quarterly* 22 (3): 410–26.

Binder, Amy. 2007. "For love and money: Organizations' creative responses to multiple environmental logics." *Theory and Society* 36 (6): 547–71.

Binder, Amy J., Daniel B. Davis, and Nick Bloom. 2016. "Career funneling: How elite students learn how to define and desire 'prestigious' jobs." *Sociology of Education* 89 (1): 20–39.

Birchall, Johnston. 1997. *The International Co-operative Movement*. Manchester: Manchester University Press.

Bird, Chloe E. 1990. "High finance, small change: Women's increased representation in bank management." In *Job Queues, Gender Queues: Explaining Women's Inroads into Male Occupations*, ed. B. Reskin and P. Roos, 145–66. Philadelphia: Temple University Press.

Bitekine, Alex and Patrick Haack. 2015. "The 'macro' and 'micro' of legitimation: Toward a mul-
tilevel theory of the legitimacy process." *Academy of Management Review* 40 (1): 49–75.

Black, Antony. 1984. *Guilds and Civil Society in European Political Thought from the Twelfth
Century to the Present.* Ithaca, NY: Cornell University Press.

Blair-Loy, Mary. 2003. *Competing Devotions: Career and Family among Women Executives.* Cambridge, MA: Harvard University Press.

Blalock, Hubert M. 1967. *Toward a Theory of Minority-Group Relations.* New York: Wiley.

Blau, Peter M. (1955) 1963. *Dynamics of Bureaucracy: A Study of Interpersonal Relations in Two
Government Agencies.* Rev. edn. Chicago: University of Chicago Press.

Blau, Peter M. (1964) 1992. *Exchange and Power in Social Life.* New Brunswick, NJ: Transaction
Publishers.

Blau, Peter M. 1970. "A formal theory of differentiation in organizations." *American Sociological
Review* 35 (2): 201–18.

Blau, Peter M. 1977. *Inequality and Heterogeneity: A Primitive Theory of Social Structure.* New
York: Free Press.

Blau, Peter M. 1994. *Structural Contexts of Opportunities.* Chicago: University of Chicago Press.

Blau, Peter M. and Otis D. Duncan. 1967. *The American Occupational Structure.* New York: Wiley.

Blau, Peter M. and Richard Schoenherr. 1971. *The Structure of Organizations.* New York: Basic
Books.

Blau, Peter M. and Joseph E. Schwartz. 1984. *Cross-cutting Social Circles.* Orlando, FL: Academic
Press.

Blauner, Robert. 1964. *Alienation and Freedom: The Factory Worker and His Industry.* Chicago:
University of Chicago Press.

Bloch, Marc. 1961. *Feudal Society,* vol. 1: *The Growth of Ties of Dependence,* trans. L. A. Manyon.
Chicago: University of Chicago Press.

Bloch, Marc. 1964. *Feudal Society,* vol. 2: *Social Classes and Political Organization,* trans L. A.
Manyon. Chicago: University of Chicago Press.

Bloch, Ruth H. and Naomi R. Lamoreaux. 2017. "Voluntary associations, corporate rights, and
the state: Legal constraints on the development of American civil society, 1750–1900." In
Organizations, Civil Society, and the Roots of Development, ed. Naomi R. Lamoreaux and John
Joseph Wallis, 231–90. Chicago: University of Chicago Press.

Block, Fred. 1987. *Revising State Theory.* Philadelphia: Temple University Press.

Bloemraad, Irene, Fabiana Silva, and Kim Voss. 2016. "Rights, economics, or family? Frame
resonance, political ideology, and the immigrant rights movement." *Social Forces* 94 (4):
1647–74.

Blommaert, Liselotte, Marcel Coenders, and Frank von Tubergen. 2014. "Discrimination of
Arabic-named applicants in the Netherlands: An internet-based field experiment examining
different phases in online recruitment procedures." *Social Forces* 92 (3): 957–82.

Blumer, Herbert. 1969. *Symbolic Interactionism: Perspective and Method.* Berkeley, CA: University
of California Press.

Boczkowski, Pablo J. 2010. *News at Work: Imitation in an Age of Information Abundance.* Chicago:
University of Chicago Press.

Bonacich, Phillip. 1972. "Factoring and weighting approaches to status scores and clique identification." *Journal of Mathematical Sociology* 2 (1): 112–20.

Bonacich, Phillip. 1987. "Power and centrality: A family of measures." *American Journal of Sociology* 92 (5): 1170–82.

Bonner, Lynn, Jane Stancill, and David Raynor. 2017. "How companies can turn a profit running charter schools." *Raleigh News and Observer*, October 12 https://www.newsobserver.com /news/local/education/article178438001.html (viewed March 31, 2022).

Boorman, Scott A. and Harrison C. White. 1976. "Social structure from multiple networks, II: Role structures." *American Journal of Sociology* 81 (6): 1384–446.

Borgatti, Stephen P. and Martin Everett. 1999. "Models of core/periphery structures." *Social Networks* 21 (4): 375–95.

Borkenhagen, Chad and John Levi Martin. 2018. "Status and career mobility in organizational fields: Chefs and restaurants in the United States, 1990–2013." *Social Forces* 97 (1): 1–26.

Börner, Stephanie. 2013. *Belonging, Solidarity, and Expansion in Social Policy*. London: Palgrave Macmillan.

Borraz, Olivier. 2011. "From risk to the government of uncertainty: The case of mobile telephony." *Journal of Risk Research* 14 (8): 969–82.

Botelho, Tristan and Mabel Abraham. 2017. "Pursuing quality: How search costs and uncertainty magnify gender-based double standards in a multistage evaluation process." *Administrative Science Quarterly* 62 (4): 698–730.

Boulding, Kenneth E. 1953. *The Organizational Revolution*. New York: Harper Brothers.

Bourdieu, Pierre. 1980. "Le capital sociale: Notes provisaires." *Actes de la recherche en sciences sociales* 31: 2–3.

Bowen, H. V. 2006. *The Business of Empire: The East India Company and Imperial Britain, 1756–1833*. Cambridge: Cambridge University Press.

Bowers, Anne. 2015. "Relative comparison and category membership: The case of equity analysts." *Organization Science* 26 (2): 571–83.

Brands, Raina A. and Isabel Fernandez-Mateo. 2017. "Leaning out: How negative recruitment experiences shape women's decisions to compete for executive roles." *Administrative Science Quarterly* 62 (3): 405–42.

Brass, Daniel J. 1984. "Being in the right place: A structural analysis of individual influence in an organization." *Administrative Science Quarterly* 29 (4): 518–39.

Brass, Daniel J. 1985. "Men's and women's networks: A study of interaction patterns and influence in an organization." *Academy of Management Journal* 28 (2): 327–43.

Brass, Daniel J. and Marlene E. Burkhardt. 1993. "Potential power and power use: An investigation of power and structure." *Academy of Management Journal* 36 (3): 441–70.

Braudel, Fernand. (1973) 1995. *The Mediterranean and the Mediterranean World in the Age of Philip II*, vol. 2, trans. Siân Reynolds. 2nd (rev.) edn. Berkeley, CA: University of California Press.

Braudel, Fernand. (1981) 1992. *Civilization and Capitalism, 15th–18th Century*, vol. 1: *The Structures of Everyday Life: The Limits of the Possible*, trans. Miriam Kochan, rev. Siân Reynolds. Berkeley, CA: University of California Press.

Braudel, Fernand. (1982) 1992. *Civilization and Capitalism, 15th–18th Century*, vol. 2: *The Wheels of Commerce*, trans. Siân Reynolds. Berkeley, CA: University of California Press.

Braudel, Fernand. (1984) 1992. *Civilization and Capitalism, 15th–18th Century*, vol. 3: *The Perspective of the World*, trans. Siân Reynolds. Berkeley, CA: University of California Press.

Braverman, Harry. 1974. *Labor and Monopoly Capital: The Degradation of Work in the Twentieth Century*. New York: Monthly Review Press.

Brayne, Sarah. 2017. "Big data surveillance: The case of policing." *American Journal of Sociology* 82 (5): 977–1088.

Brayne, Sarah. 2021. *Predict and Surveil: Data, Discretion, and the Future of Policing*. New York: Oxford University Press.

Breiger, Ronald L. 1974. "The duality of persons and groups." *Social Forces* 53 (2): 181–90.

Brenner, Robert. 1985. "Agrarian class structure and economic development in pre-industrial Europe." In *The Brenner Debate: Agrarian Class Structure and Economic Development in Pre-industrial Europe*, ed. T. H. Aston and C.H.E. Philpin, 10–63. Cambridge: Cambridge University Press.

Brentano, Luigi. 1890. *On the History and Development of the Gilds, and the Origin of Trade-Unions*. London: Trübner & Co.

Brewer, Alexandra, Melissa Osborne, Anna S. Mueller, Daniel M. O'Connor, Arjun Dayal, and Vineet M. Arora. 2020. "Who gets the benefit of the doubt? Performance evaluations, medical errors, and the production of gender inequality in emergency medical education." *American Sociological Review* 85 (2): 247–70.

Brint, Steven. 1992. "Hidden meanings: Cultural content and context in Harrison White's structural sociology." *Sociological Theory* 10 (2): 194–208.

Brinton, Mary C. and Victor Nee, eds. 1998. *The New Institutionalism in Sociology*. New York: Russell Sage Foundation.

Briscoe, Forrest and Michelle Rogan. 2016. "Coordinating complex work: Knowledge networks, partner departures, and client relationship performance in a law firm." *Management Science* 62 (8): 2392–411.

Briscoe, Forrest and Wenpin Tsai. 2011. "Overcoming relational inertia: How organizational members respond to acquisition events in a law firm." *Administrative Science Quarterly* 56 (3): 408–40.

Britton, Dana M. 2000. "The epistemology of the gendered organization." *Gender and Society* 14 (3): 418–34.

Broschak, Joseph P. 2004. "Managers' mobility and market interface: The effect of managers' career mobility on the dissolution of market ties." *Administrative Science Quarterly* 49 (4): 608–40.

Brodman, James. 2009. *Charity and Religion in Medieval Europe*. Washington, DC: Catholic University of America Press.

Bromley, Patricia and John W. Meyer. 2015. *Hyper-Organization: Global Organizational Expansion*. Oxford: Oxford University Press.

Brown, Elizabeth A. R. 1974. "The tyranny of a construct: Feudalism and historians of medieval Europe." *American Historical Review* 79 (4): 1063–88.

Brüderl, Josef and Rudolf Schüssler. 1990. "Organizational mortality: The liabilities of newness and smallness." *Administrative Science Quarterly* 35 (3): 530–47.

Brynjolfsson Erik and Kristina McElheran. 2016. "The rapid adoption of data driven decision-making." *American Economic Review* 106 (5): 133–39.

Brynjolfsson Erik and Tom Mitchell. 2017. "What can machine learning do? Workforce implications." *Science* 358 (6370): 1530–34.

Buchmann, Claudia, Thomas A. DiPrete, and Anne McDaniel. 2008. "Gender inequalities in education." *Annual Review of Sociology* 34: 319–37.

Budig, Michelle J. 2002. "Male advantage and the gender composition of jobs: Who rides the glass escalator?" *Social Problems* 49 (2): 258–77.

Buolamwini, Joy and Timmit Gebru. 2018. "Gender shades: Intersectional accuracy disparities in commercial gender classification." *Proceedings of Machine Learning Research* 81: 1–15.

Burawoy, Michael. 1977. "Social structure, homogenization, and 'The process of status attainment in the United States and Great Britain.'" *American Journal of Sociology* 82 (5): 1031–42.

Burawoy, Michael. 1979. *Manufacturing Consent: Changes in the Labor Process under Monopoly Capitalism.* Chicago: University of Chicago Press.

Burkov, Andriy. 2019. *The Hundred-Page Machine Learning Book.* Available for download on a "read first, buy later" basis via http://themlbook.com/ (viewed March 31, 2022).

Burns, Tom and George M. Stalker. (1961) 1994. *The Management of Innovation.* 3rd edn. Oxford: Oxford University Press.

Burrell, Jenna. 2016. "How the machine 'thinks': Understanding opacity in machine learning algorithms." *Big Data and Society* 3 (1): 1–12.

Burris, Val. 2005. "Interlocking directorates and political cohesion among corporate elites." *American Journal of Sociology* 111 (1): 249–83.

Burstein Paul and April Linton. 2002. "The impact of political parties, interest groups, and social movement organizations on public policy: Some recent evidence and theoretical concerns." *Social Forces* 81 (2): 380–408.

Burt, Ronald S. 1983. *Corporate Profits and Co-optation: Networks of Market Constraints and Directorate Ties in the American Economy.* New York: Academic Press.

Burt, Ronald S. 1992. *Structural Holes: The Social Structure of Competition.* Cambridge, MA: Harvard University Press.

Burt, Ronald S. 1998. "The gender of social capital." *Rationality and Society* 10 (1): 5–46.

Burt, Ronald S. 2005. *Brokerage and Closure.* New York: Oxford University Press.

Burt, Ronald S. and Ilan Talmud. 1993. "Market niche." *Social Networks* 15 (2): 133–49.

Cameron, Rondo E. 1961. *France and the Economic Development of Europe, 1800–1914.* Princeton, NJ: Princeton University Press.

Caplan, Robyn, and danah boyd. 2018. "Isomorphism through algorithms: Institutional dependencies in the case of Facebook." *Big Data and Society* 5 (1): 1–12.

Carley, Kathleen and Michael Palmquist. 1992. "Extracting, representing, and analyzing mental models." *Social Forces* 70 (3): 601–36.

Carlos, W. Chad, Wesley D. Sine, Brandon H. Lee, and Heather A. Haveman. 2018. "Gone with the wind: Industry development and the evolution of social movement influence." *Sustainability, Stakeholder Governance, and Corporate Social Responsibility* (Advances in Strategic Management 38), ed., 339–65. Bingley: Emerald Publishing Limited.

Carnabuci, Gianluca, Cécile Emery, and David Brinberg. 2018. "Emergent leadership structures in informal groups: A dynamic, cognitively informed network model." *Organization Science* 29 (1): 118–33.

Carney, William J. 1995. "Limited liability companies: Origins and antecedents." *University of Colorado Law Review* 66 (4): 855–80.

Carroll, Glenn R. 1985. "Concentration and specialization: Dynamics of niche width in populations of organizations." *American Journal of Sociology* 90 (6): 1262–83.

Carroll, Glenn R., Stanislav D. Dobrev, and Anand Swaminathan. 2002. "Organizational processes of resource partitioning." *Research in Organizational Behavior* 24: 1–40.

Carroll, Glenn R., and Michael T. Hannan. 2000. *The Demography of Corporations and Industries*. Princeton, NJ: Princeton University Press.

Carroll, Glenn R., and Anand Swaminathan. 2000. "Why the microbrewery movement? Organizational dynamics of resource partitioning in the American brewing industry after Prohibition." *American Journal of Sociology* 106 (3): 715–62.

Carruthers, Bruce G. 2013. "From uncertainty toward risk: The case of credit ratings." *Socio-Economic Review* 11 (3): 525–51.

Casciaro, Tiziana, Francesca Gino, and Maryam Kouchaki. 2014. "The contaminating effects of building instrumental ties: How networking can make us feel dirty." *Administrative Science Quarterly* 59 (4): 705–35.

Casciaro, Tiziana and Mikolaj Jan Piskorski. 2005. "Power imbalance, mutual dependence, and constraint absorption: A closer look at resource dependence theory." *Administrative Science Quarterly* 50 (3): 167–99.

Castilla, Emilio J. 2008. "Gender, race, and meritocracy in organizational careers." *American Journal of Sociology* 113 (6): 1479–527.

Castilla, Emilio J. 2015. "Accounting for the gap: A firm study manipulating organizational accountability and transparency in pay decisions." *Organization Science* 26 (2): 311–33.

Cattani, Gino, Simone Ferriani, and Paul D. Allison. 2014. "Insiders, outsiders, and the struggle for consecration in organizational fields: A cross-periphery perspective." *American Sociological Review* 79 (2): 258–81.

Cech, Erin. 2013. "Ideological wage inequalities? The technical/social dualism and the gender wage gap in engineering." *Social Forces* 91 (4): 1147–82.

Cech, Erin. 2014. "The self-expressive edge of occupational sex segregation." *American Journal of Sociology* 119 (3): 747–89.

Chan, Curtis K. and Michel Anteby. 2016. "Task segregation as a mechanism for within-job inequality: Women and men of the Transportation Security Administration." *Administrative Science Quarterly* 61 (2): 184–216.

Chandler, Alfred D., Jr. 1977. *The Visible Hand: The Managerial Revolution in American Business*. Cambridge, MA: Belknap Press of Harvard University Press.

Chandler, Alfred D., Jr. 1990. *Scale and Scope: The Dynamics of Industrial Capitalism*. Cambridge, MA: Belknap Press of Harvard University Press.

Chappelle, Olivier, Bernard Schölkopf, and Alexander Zien. 2006. *Semi-Supervised Learning*. Cambridge, MA: MIT Press.

Charles, Maria and Karen Bradley. 2009. "Indulging our gendered selves? Sex segregation by field of study in 44 countries." *American Journal of Sociology* 114 (4): 924–76.

Charniak, Eugene. 2019. *Introduction to Deep Learning*. Cambridge, MA: MIT Press.

Chatman, Jennifer A. 1991. "Matching people and organizations: Selection and socialization in public accounting firms." *Administrative Science Quarterly* 36 (3): 459–84.

Chatman, Jennifer A. and Francis J. Flynn. 2001. "The influence of demographic heterogeneity on the emergence and consequences of cooperative norms in work teams." *Academy of Management Journal* 44 (5): 956–74.

Chatman, Jennifer A. and Charles A. O'Reilly. 2016. "Paradigm lost: Reinvigorating the study of organizational culture." *Research in Organizational Behavior* 36 (supplement C): 199–224.

Chatman, Jennifer A., Jeffrey T. Polzer, Sigal G. Barsade, and Margaret A. Neale. 1998. "Being different yet feeling similar: The influence of demographic composition and organizational culture on work processes and outcomes." *Administrative Science Quarterly* 43 (4): 749–80.

Chattopadhyay, Prithviraj. 1999. "Beyond direct and symmetrical effects: The influence of demographic dissimilarity on organizational citizenship behavior." *Academy of Management Journal* 42 (3): 273–87.

Chaves, Mark. 1997. *Ordaining Women: Culture and Conflict in Religious Organizations*. Cambridge, MA: Harvard University Press.

Cherlin, Andrew J. 2012. "Goode's *World Revolution and Family Patterns*: A reconsideration at fifty years." *Population and Development Review* 38 (4): 577–607.

Child, John. 1972. "Organizational structure, environment and performance: The role of strategic choice." *Sociology* 6 (1): 1–22.

Childress, Clayton. 2017. *Under the Cover: The Creation, Production, and Reception of a Novel*. Princeton, NJ: Princeton University Press.

Christin, Angèle. 2020. *Metrics at Work: Journalism and the Contested Meaning of Algorithms*. Princeton, NJ: Princeton University Press.

Chu, Johan C. and Gerald F. Davis. 2016. "Who killed the inner circle? The decline of the American corporate interlock network." *American Journal of Sociology* 122 (3): 714–54.

Clark, Burton R. 1970. *The Distinctive College: Antioch, Reed, and Swarthmore*. Chicago: Aldine.

Clark, Peter. 2000. *British Clubs and Societies 1580–1800*. Oxford: Oxford University Press.

Clawson, Dan. 1980. *Bureaucracy and the Labor Process*. New York: Monthly Review Press.

Cleary, Esmond John. 1965. *The Building Society Movement*. London: Elek Books.

Clegg, Stewart and Michael Lounsbury. 2009. "Sintering the iron cage: Translation, domination, and rationality." In *The Oxford Handbook of Sociology and Organization Studies: Classical Foundations*, ed. Paul S. Adler, 118–45. Oxford: Oxford University Press.

Clemens, Elisabeth S. 1997. *The People's Lobby: Organizational Innovation and the Rise of Interest Group Politics in the United States, 1890–1925*. Chicago: University of Chicago Press.

Clemens, Elisabeth S. and James M. Cook. 1999. "Politics and institutionalism: Explaining durability and change." *Annual Review of Sociology* 25: 441–66.

Cobb, J. Adam and Flannery G. Stevens. 2017. "These unequal states: Corporate organization and income inequality in the United States." *Administrative Science Quarterly* 62 (2): 304–40.

Coffin, Judith G. 1994. "Gender and the guild order: The garment trades in eighteenth-century Paris." *Journal of Economic History* 54 (4): 768–93.

Cohen, Lisa E. 2013. "Assembling jobs: A model of how tasks are bundled into and across jobs." *Organization Science* 24 (2): 432–54.

Cohen, Lisa E., Joseph P. Broschak, and Heather A. Haveman. 1998. "And then there were more? The effect of organizational sex composition on the hiring and promotion of managers." *American Sociological Review* 63 (5): 711–27.

Cohen, Michael D., James G. March, and Johan P. Olsen. 1972. "A garbage can model of organizational choice." *Administrative Science Quarterly* 17 (1): 1–25.

Cohen, Philip N. and Matt L. Huffman. 2007. "Working for the woman? Female managers and the gender wage gap." *American Sociological Review* 72 (5): 681–703.

Cohen, Wesley M. and Daniel A. Levinthal. 1990. "Absorptive capacity: A new perspective on learning and innovation." *Administrative Science Quarterly* 35 (1): 128–52.

Coleman, James S. 1974. *Power and the Structure of Society*. New York: W.W. Norton & Co.

Coleman, James S. 1982. *The Asymmetric Society*. Syracuse, NY: Syracuse University Press.

Coleman, James S. 1986. "Social theory, social research, and a theory of action." *American Journal of Sociology* 91 (6): 1309–35.

Coleman, James S. 1988. "Social capital in the creation of human capital." *American Journal of Sociology* 94 (supplement): S95–S120.

Coleman, James S., Elihu Katz, and Herbert Menzel. 1957. "The diffusion of an innovation among physicians." *Sociometry*, 20 (4): 253–70.

Collins, Harry and Trevor Pinch. 1993. *The Golem: What Everyone Should Know about Science*. Cambridge: Cambridge University Press.

Cooley, Charles Horton. 1902. *Human Nature and the Social Order*. New York: Charles Scribner's Sons.

Cooley, Charles Horton. 1909. *Social Organization: A Study of the Larger Mind*. New York: Charles Scribner's Sons.

Coons, Arthur G., Arthur D. Browne, Howard A. Campion, Glenn S. Dumke, Thomas C. Holy, Dean E. McHenry, Henry T. Tyler, Robert J. Wert, and Keith Sexton (consultant), with the assistance of the Technical Committees, the Joint Advisory Committee, and the representatives of the Legislature and other state agencies. 1960. *A Master Plan for Higher Education in California, 1960–1976*. Sacramento, CA: Regents of the University of California.

Corbo, Leonardo, Raffaele Corrado, and Simone Ferriani. 2016. "A new order of things: Network mechanisms of field evolution in the aftermath of an exogenous shock." *Organization Studies* 37 (3): 323–48.

Cordery, Simon. 2003. *British Friendly Societies, 1750–1914*. London: Palgrave Macmillan.

Correll, Shelley J. 2001. "Gender and the career choice process: The role of biased self-assessments." *American Journal of Sociology* 106 (6): 1691–730.

Correll, Shelley J., Stephen Benard, and In Paik. 2007. "Getting a job: Is there a motherhood penalty?" *American Journal of Sociology*, 112 (5): 1297–338.

Coser, Lewis A., Charles Kadushin, and Walter W. Powell. 1982. *Books: The Culture and Commerce of Publishing*. New York: Basic Books.

Cottrell, P. L. 1980. *Industrial Finance 1830–1914: The Finance and Organization of English Manufacturing Industry*. London: Methuen.

Courpasson, David and Stewart R. Clegg. 2006. "Dissolving the iron cages? Tocqueville, Michels, bureaucracy and the perpetuation of elite power." *Organization* 13 (3): 319–43.

Creighton, Andrew L. 1996. "Inventing the common corporation: The development of legal governance structures for U.S. corporations in the early nineteenth century." Working paper, University of California, Berkeley.

Cress, Dan and David A. Snow. 2000. "The outcomes of homeless mobilization: The influence of organization, disruption, political mediation, and framing." *American Journal of Sociology* 105 (4): 1063–104.

Crilly, Donal, Morten Hansen, and Maurizio Zollo. 2016. "The grammar of decoupling: A cognitive-linguistic perspective on firms' sustainability claims and stakeholders' interpretation." *Academy of Management Journal* 59 (2): 705–29.

Cross, Rob and Jonathan N. Cummings. 2004. "Tie and network correlates of individual performance in knowledge-intensive work." *Academy of Management Journal* 47 (6): 928–37.

Crowston, Clare Haru and Claire LeMercier. 2019. "Surviving the end of the guilds: Apprenticeship in eighteenth and nineteenth-century France." In *Apprenticeship in Early Modern Europe*,
ed. Maarten Prak and Patrick Wallis, 282–308. Cambridge: Cambridge University Press.

Crozier, Michel. 1964. *The Bureaucratic Phenomenon*. Chicago: University of Chicago Press.

Culpepper, Pepper D. 2010. *Quiet Politics and Business Power: Corporate Control in Europe and
Japan*. Cambridge: Cambridge University Press.

Cummings, Jonathon N. and Robb Cross. 2003. "Structural properties of work groups and their
consequences for performance." *Social Networks* 25 (3): 197–210.

Cyert, Richard M. and James G. March. (1963) 1992. *A Behavioral Theory of the Firm*. 2nd edn.
Cambridge, MA: Blackwell.

Czopp, Alexander M., Aaron C. Kay, and Sapna Cheryan. 2015. "Positive stereotypes are perva-
sive and powerful." *Perspectives on Psychological Science* 10 (4): 451–63.

Dacin, M. Tina, Kamal Munir, and Paul Tracey. 2010. "Formal dining at Cambridge colleges:
Linking ritual performance and institutional maintenance." *Academy of Management Journal*
53 (6): 1393–418.

Dahl, Robert A. 1957. "The concept of power." *Behavioral Science* 2 (3): 201–15.

Dahlin, Kristina B., Laurie R. Weingart, and Pamela J. Hinds. 2005. "Team diversity and information use." *Academy of Management Journal* 48 (6): 1107–23.

David, Robert J., Wesley D. Sine, and Heather A. Haveman. 2013. "Seizing opportunity in emerging fields: How entrepreneurs legitimated the professional form of management consulting."
Organization Science 24 (2): 356–77.

Davis, Gerald F. 2009. "The rise and fall of finance and the end of the society of organizations."
Academy of Management Perspectives 23 (3): 27–44.

Davis, Gerald F. 2015. "Celebrating organizational theory: The after-party." *Journal of Management Studies* 52 (2): 309–19.

Davis, Gerald F. 2016. *The Vanishing American Corporation: Navigating the Hazards of a New
Economy*. Oakland, CA: Berrett-Koehler.

Davis, Gerald F. and J. Adam Cobb. 2010. "Resource dependence theory: Past and future." In
Stanford's Organizational Theory Renaissance, 1970–2000 (Research in the Sociology of
Organizations 28), ed. Claudia Bird Schoonhoven and Frank Dobbin, 21–42. Bingley: Em-
erald Publishing Limited.

Davis, Gerald F., Kristina A. Diekmann, and Catherine H. Tinsley. 1994. "The decline and fall
of the conglomerate firm in the 1980s: The deinstitutionalization of an organizational form."
American Sociological Review 59 (4): 547–70.

Davis, Gerald F., Mina Yoo, and Wayne E. Baker. 2003. "The small world of the American corporate elite, 1991–1999." *Strategic Organization* 1 (3): 301–26.

Davis, Natalie Zemon. 1982. "Women in the crafts in sixteenth-century Lyon." *Feminist Studies*
8 (1): 46–80.

Davis-Blake, Alison. 1992. "The consequences of organizational demography: Beyond social
integration effects." In *Research in the Sociology of Organizations*, vol. 10, ed. Pamela Tolbert
and Samuel B. Bacharach: 175–97. Greenwich, CT: JAI Press.

Davis-Blake, Alison and Joseph P. Broschak. 2009. "Outsourcing and the changing nature of
work." *Annual Review of Sociology* 35: 321–40.

de Figueiredo, Rui J. P., Evan Rawley, and Christopher I. Rider. 2015. "Why are firms rigid? A general framework and empirical evidence." *Organization Science* 26 (5): 1502–19.

de Sola Pool, Ithiel and Manfred Kochen. 1978. "Contacts and influence." *Social Networks* 1 (1): 5–51.

de Vries, Jan. 2008. *The Industrious Revolution: Consumer Behavior and the Household Economy, 1650 to the Present.* Cambridge: Cambridge University Press.

Deephouse, David L. 1996. "Does isomorphism legitimate?" *Academy of Management Journal* 39 (4): 1024–39.

DeJordy, Rich, Maureen Scully, Marc Ventresca, and W. E. Douglas Creed. 2020. "Inhabited ecosystems: Propelling transformative social change between and through organizations." *Administrative Science Quarterly* 65 (4): 931–71.

Dezső, Cristian L. and David Gaddis Ross. 2012. "Does female representation in top management improve firm performance? A panel data investigation." *Strategic Management Journal* 33 (9): 1072–89.

DiBenigno, Julia and Katherine C. Kellogg. 2014. "Beyond occupational differences: The importance of cross-cutting demographics and cultural toolkits for collaboration in a U.S. hospital." *Administrative Science Quarterly* 59 (3): 375–408.

Dickson, Bruce J. 2003. *Red Capitalists in China: The Party, Private Entrepreneurs, and Prospects for Political Change.* Cambridge: Cambridge University Press.

DiMaggio, Paul. 1982a. "Cultural entrepreneurship in nineteenth-century Boston: The creation of an organizational base for high culture in America." *Media, Culture, and Society* 4 (1): 33–50.

DiMaggio, Paul. 1982b. Cultural entrepreneurship in nineteenth-century Boston, part II: The classification and framing of American art. *Media, Culture, and Society* 4 (4): 303–22.

DiMaggio, Paul J. 1986. "Structural analysis of organizational fields: A blockmodel approach." *Research in Organizational Behavior* 8: 335–70.

DiMaggio, Paul J. 1988. "Interest and agency in institutional theory." In *Institutional Patterns and Organizations: Culture and Environment*, ed. Lynne G. Zucker, 3–21. Cambridge, MA: Ballinger.

DiMaggio, Paul J. 1991. "Constructing an organizational field as a professional project: U.S. art museums, 1920–1940." In *The New Institutionalism in Organizational Analysis*, ed. Walter W. Powell and Paul J. DiMaggio, 267–92. Chicago: University of Chicago Press.

DiMaggio, Paul J. and Walter W. Powell. 1983. "The iron cage revisited: Institutional isomorphism and collective rationality in organizational fields." *American Sociological Review* 48 (2): 147–60.

Dioun, Cyrus. 2018. "Negotiating moral boundaries: Social movements and the strategic (re)definition of the medical in marijuana markets." In *Social Movements, Stakeholders and Non-Market Strategy* (Research in the Sociology of Organizations 56), ed. Forest Briscoe, Brayden G. King, and Jocelyn Leitzinger, 53–82. Bingley: Emerald Publishing Limited.

DiTomaso, Nancy, Corinne Post, and Rochelle Parks-Yancy. 2007. "Workforce diversity and inequality: Power, status, and numbers." *Annual Review of Sociology* 33: 473–501.

Djelic, Marie-Laure. 1998. *Exporting the American Model: The Postwar Transformation of European Business.* Oxford: Oxford University Press.

Dobbin, Frank R. 1992. "The origins of private social insurance: Public policy and fringe benefits in America, 1920–1950." *American Journal of Sociology* 97 (5): 1416–50.

Dobbin, Frank. 2009. "How Durkheim's theory of meaning-making influenced organizational sociology." In *The Oxford Handbook of Sociology and Organization Studies: Classical Foundations*, ed. Paul S. Adler, 201–22. Oxford: Oxford University Press.

Dobbin, Frank R. and Timothy Dowd. 1997. "How policy shapes competition: Early railroad foundings in Massachusetts." *Administrative Science Quarterly* 42 (3): 501–29.

Dobbin, Frank R., Daniel Schrage, and Alexandra Kalev. 2015. "Rage against the iron cage: The varied effects of bureaucratic personnel reforms on diversity." *American Sociological Review* 80 (5): 1014–44.

Dobbin, Frank R., and John R. Sutton. 1998. "The strength of a weak state: The employment rights revolution and the rise of human resources management divisions." *American Journal of Sociology* 104 (2): 441–76.

Dobbin, Frank R., John R. Sutton, John W. Meyer, and W. Richard Scott. 1993. "Equal opportunity law and the construction of internal labor markets." *American Journal of Sociology* 99 (2): 396–427.

Doering, Laura. 2018. "Risks, returns, and relational lending: Personal ties in microfinance." *American Journal of Sociology* 123 (5): 1341–81.

Doeringer, Peter B. and Michael J. Piore. 1971. *Internal Labor Markets and Manpower Analysis*. Lexington, MA: Heath.

Dokshin, Fedor. 2016. "Whose backyard and what's at issue? Spatial and ideological dynamics of local opposition to fracking in New York State, 2010 to 2013." *American Sociological Review* 81 (5): 921–48.

Domhoff, G. William. 1983. *Who Rules America Now?* Englewood Cliffs, NJ: Prentice-Hall.

Douglas, Mary. 1966. *Purity and Danger: An Analysis of the Conceptions of Pollution and Taboo*. London: Routledge and Kegan Paul.

Douglas, Mary. 1986. *How Institutions Think*. Syracuse, NY: Syracuse University Press.

Drescher, Seymour. 2010. *Econoside: British Slavery in the Era of Abolition*. 2nd edn. Chapel Hill, NC: University of North Carolina Press.

Driver, Harold E. 1961. *Indians of North America*. Chicago: University of Chicago Press.

Drutman, Lee. 2015. *The Business of America is Lobbying: How Corporations Became More Politicized and Politics Became More Corporate*. Oxford: Oxford University Press.

Duffy, Brooke Erin. 2017. *(Not) Getting Paid to Do What You Love: Gender, Media, and Aspirational Work*. New Haven, CT: Yale University Press.

Dumas, Tracy L., Katherine W. Phillips, and Nancy P. Rothbard. 2013. "Getting closer at the company party: Integration experiences, racial dissimilarity, and workplace relations." *Organization Science* 24 (5): 1377–401.

Dunlap, Riley E., and Peter J. Jacques. 2013. Climate change denial books and conservative think tanks: Exploring the connection. *American Behavioral Scientist* 57 (6): 699–731.

Dunn, Mary B. and Candace Jones. 2010. "Institutional logics and institutional pluralism: The contestation of care and science logics in medical education, 1967–2005." *Administrative Science Quarterly* 55 (1): 114–49.

Durand, Rodolphe, Nina Granqvist, and Anna Tyllström. 2017. "From categories to categorization: A social perspective on market categorization." In *From Categories to Categorization: Studies in Sociology, Organizations and Strategy at the Crossroads* (Research in the Sociology of Organizations 51), ed. Rodolphe Durand, Nina Granqvist, and Anna Tyllström, 3–30. Bingley: Emerald Publishing Limited.

Durkheim, Émile. (1893) 1984. *The Division of Labor in Society*, trans. W. D. Halls, with an introduction by Lewis Coser. New York: Free Press.

Durkheim, Émile. (1897) 1951. *Suicide: A Study in Sociology*, transl. John A. Spauling and George Simpson; ed. with an introduction by George Simpson. New York: Free Press.

Durkheim, Émile. (1982) 1995. *The Rules of Sociological Method and Selected Texts on Sociology and its Method*, ed. Steve Lukes, trans W. D. Halls. New York: Free Press.

Durkheim, Émile. (1912) 1996. *Elementary Forms of Religious Life*, trans. Karen Fields. New York: Free Press.

Durkheim, Émile and Marcel Mauss. (1903) 1963. *Primitive Classification*, trans. and with an introduction by Rodney Needham. Chicago: University of Chicago Press.

Dutton, Jane E. and Janet M. Dukerich. 1991. "Keeping an eye on the mirror: Image and identity in organizational adaptation." *Academy of Management Journal* 34 (3): 517–44.

Eagly, Alice H. and Amanda B. Diekman. 1997. "The accuracy of gender stereotypes: A dilemma for feminism." *Revue internationale de psychologie sociale/International Review of Social Psychology* 10: 11–30.

Easley, David, and Jon Kleinberg. 2010. *Networks, Crowds, and Markets: Reasoning about at Highly Connected World*. Cambridge: Cambridge University Press.

Eaton, Charlie, Jacob Habinek, Adam Goldstein, Cyrus Dioun, Daniela García Santibáñez Godoy, and Robert Osley-Thomas. 2016. "The financialization of US higher education." *Socio-Economic Review* 14 (3): 507–35.

Economist. 2017. "Automatic for the people: How Germany's Otto is using artificial intelligence." *The Economist*, April 15.

Economist. 2021. "The other tech giant: Wikipedia is 20, and its reputation has never been higher." *The Economist*, January 7.

Edelman, Lauren B. 1990. "Legal environments and organizational governance: The expansion of due process in the American workplace." *American Journal of Sociology* 95 (6): 1401–40.

Edelman, Lauren B. 1992. "Legal ambiguity and symbolic structures: Organizational mediation of civil rights law." *American Journal of Sociology* 97 (6): 1531–76.

Edelman, Lauren B., Linda H. Krieger, Scott R. Eliason, Catherine R. Albiston, and Virginia Mellema. 2011. "When organizations rule: Judicial deference to institutionalized employment structures." *American Journal of Sociology* 117 (3): 888–954.

Edwards, Richard. 1979. *Contested Terrain: The Transformation of the Workplace in the Twentieth Century*. New York: Basic Books.

Elfenbein, Daniel W. and Todd R. Zenger. 2011. "What's a relationship worth? Repeated exchange the the development and deployment of relational capital." *Organization Science* 25 (1): 222–44.

Elias, Norbert. (1939) 1982. *Power and Civility: The Civilizing Process*, vol. 2, trans. Edmund Jephcott, with some notes and revisions by the author. New York: Pantheon Books.

Elliott, James R. and Ryan A. Smith. 2004. "Race, gender, and workplace power." *American Sociological Review* 69 (3): 365–86.

Elsbach, Kimberly D. 1994. "Managing organizational legitimacy in the California cattle industry: The construction and effectiveness of verbal accounts." *Administrative Science Quarterly* 39 (1): 57–88.

Elster, Jon. 1989. *Nuts and Bolts for the Social Sciences*. Cambridge: Cambridge University Press.

Elul, Yonaton, Aviv A. Rosenberg, Assaf Schuster, Alex M. Bronstein, and Yael Yaniv. 2021. "Meeting the unmet needs of clinicians from AI systems showcased for cardiology with deep-learning-based ECG analysis." *Proceedings of the National Academy of Science* 118 (24): e2020620118.

Elvira, Marta and Mary E. Graham. 2002. "Not just a formality: Pay system formalization and sex-related earnings effects." *Organization Science* 13 (6): 601–17.

Ely, Robin J. 1995. "The power in demography: Women's social constructions of gender identity at work." *Academy of Management Journal* 38 (3): 589–634.

Ely, Robin J. and David A. Thomas. 2001. "Cultural diversity at work: The effect of diversity perspectives on work group processes and outcomes." *Administrative Science Quarterly* 46 (2): 229–73.

Emerson, Richard M. 1962. "Power-dependence relations." *American Sociological Review* 27 (1): 31–41.

Emirbayer, Mustafa. 1997. "Manifesto for a relational sociology." *American Journal of Sociology* 103 (2): 281–312.

Emirbayer, Mustafa and Ann Mische. 1998. "What is agency?" *American Journal of Sociology* 103 (4): 962–1023.

Epstein, Cynthia Fuchs. 1971. *Woman's Place: Options and Limits in Professional Careers*. Berkeley, CA: University of California Press.

Epstein, Cynthia Fuchs. 1981. *Women in Law*. New York: Basic Books.

Espeland, Wendy Nelson and Michael Sauder. 2016. *Engines of Anxiety: Academic Rankings, Reputation, and Accountability*. New York: Russell Sage Foundation.

Espeland, Wendy N. and Mitchell L. Stevens. 1998. "Commensuration as a social process." *Annual Review of Sociology* 24 (1): 313–43.

Erikson, Emily. 2014. *Between Monopoly and Free Trade: The British East India Company, 1600–1757*. Princeton, NJ: Princeton University Press.

Eurostat. 2019. "E-commerce statistics." Eurostat: Statistics Explained, https://ec.europa.eu /eurostat/statistics-explained/index.php/E-commerce_statistics (viewed March 31, 2022).

Fairbairn, Brett. 1994. "History from the ecological perspective: Gaia theory and the problem of cooperatives in turn-of-the-century Germany." *American Historical Review* 99 (4): 1203–39.

Farber, Henry S., Daniel Herbst, Iliyana Kuziemko, and Suresh Naidu. 2018. "Unions and inequality over the twentieth century: New evidence from survey data." NBER working paper 24587.

Farrell, Justin. 2016. "Corporate funding and ideological polarization about climate change." *Proceedings of the National Academy of Science* 113 (1): 92–97.

Faulkner, Robert R. 1983. *Music on Demand: Composers and Careers in the Hollywood Film Industry*. New Brunswick, NJ: Transaction Books.

Faust, Katherine. 1988. "Comparison of methods for positional analysis: Structural and general equivalences." *Social Networks* 10 (4): 313–41.

Fayol, Henri. (1916) 1930. *Industrial and General Administration*, trans. J. A. Coubrough. London: Sir Isaac Pitman & Sons.

Featherman, David L. and Robert M. Hauser. 1976. "Sexual inequalities and socioeconomic achievement in the U.S., 1962–1973." *American Sociological Review* 41 (3): 462–83.

Featherman, David L. and Robert M. Hauser. 1978. *Change and Opportunity*. New York: Academic Press.

Feldman, Martha S. 2000. "Organizational routines as a source of continuous change." *Organization Science* 11 (6): 611–29.

Feldman, Naomi H., Thomas L. Griffiths, and James J. Morgan. 2009. "The influence of categories on perception: Explaining the perceptual magnet effect as optimal statistical inference." *Psychological Review* 116 (4): 752–82.

Ferguson, John-Paul and Rembrand Koning. 2018. "Firm turnover and the return of racial establishment segregation." *American Sociological Review* 83 (3): 445–74.

Fernandez, Roberto M., Emilio J. Castilla, and Paul Moore. 2000. "Social capital at work: Networks and employment at a phone center." *American Journal of Sociology* 105 (5): 1288–356.

Fernandez, Roberto M. and Isabel Fernandez-Mateo. 2006. "Networks, race, and hiring." *American Sociological Review* 71 (1): 42–71.

Fernandez, Roberto M. and Roman V. Galperin. 2014. "The causal status of social capital in labor markets." In *Contemporary Perspectives on Organizational Social Networks* (Research in the Sociology of Organizations 40), ed. Daniel J. Brass, Giuseppe Labianca, Ajay Mehra, Daniel S. Halgin, and Stephen P. Borgatti, 445–62. Bingley: Emerald Publishing Limited.

Fernandez, Roberto M. and M. Lourdes Sosa. 2005. "Gendering the job: Networks and recruiting at a call center." *American Journal of Sociology* 111 (3): 859–904.

Festinger, Leon, Stanley Schachter, and Kurt Back. 1950. "The Spatial Ecology of Group Formation." In *Social Pressures in Informal Groups: A Study of Human Factors in Housing*, 33–59. New York: Harper.

Fine, Gary Alan. 1996. *Kitchens: The Culture of Restaurant Work*. Berkeley, CA: University of California Press.

Finke, Roger and Rodney Stark. 1992. *The Churching of America 1776–1990: Winners and Losers in our Religious Economy*. New Brunswick, NJ: Rutgers University Press.

Fiol, C. Marlene. 2002. "Capitalizing on paradox: The role of language in transforming organizational identities." *Organization Science* 13 (6): 653–66.

Fischer, Claude S. 2005. "*Bowling Alone*: What's the score?" *Social Networks* 27 (2): 155–67.

Fleischer, Victor. 2008. "Two and twenty: Taxing private partnership profits in private equity firms." *NYU Law Review* 83 (1): 1–59.

Fleming, Lee, Santiago Mingo, and David Chen. 2007. "Collaborative brokerage, generative creativity, and creative success." *Administrative Science Quarterly* 52 (3): 443–75.

Fligstein, Neil. 1990. *The Transformation of Corporate Control*. Cambridge, MA: Harvard University Press.

Fligstein, Neil. 1997. "Social skill and institutional theory." *American Behavioral Scientist* 40: 397–405.

Fligstein, Neil. 2001. *The Architecture of Markets: An Economic Sociology of Twenty-First-Century Capitalist Societies*. Princeton, NJ: Princeton University Press.

Fligstein, Neil and Janna Huang. 2022. "Finance in global capitalism's response to climate change." Working paper, University of California, Berkeley.

Fligstein, Neil and Doug McAdam. 2012. *A Theory of Fields*. New York: Oxford University Press.

Fligstein, Neil and Taekjin Shin. 2004. "The shareholder value society: A review of the changes in working conditions and inequality in the United States, 1976 to 2000." In *Social Inequality*, ed. Kathy Neckerman, 401–32. New York: Russell Sage Foundation Press.

Fligstein, Neil, Jonah Stuart Brundage, and Michael Schultz. 2016. "Seeing like the Fed: The roles of culture, cognition, and framing in the failure to anticipate the financial crisis of 2008." *American Sociological Review* 82 (5): 879–909.

Floge, Lilianne and Deborah M. Merrill. 1986. "Tokenism reconsidered: Male nurses and female physicians in a hospital setting." *Social Forces* 64 (4): 925–47.

Fohlen, Claude. 2008. "Entrepreneurship and management in France in the nineteenth century." In *The Cambridge Economic History of Europe, Vol. 7: The Industrial Economies: Britain, France, Germany, and Scandinavia*, ed. Peter Mathias and M. M. Posten, 347–81. Cambridge: Cambridge University Press.

Follett, Mary Parker. (1927) 1941. *Dynamic Administration: The Collected Papers of Mary Parker Follett*, ed. Henry C. Metcalf and L. Urwick. New York: Harper Brothers.

Frank, David John, Ann Hironaka, and Evan Schofer. 2000. "The nation-state and the natural environment over the twentieth century." *American Sociological Review* 65 (1): 96–116.

Franke, Richard H., and J. D. Kaul. 1978. "The Hawthorne experiments: First statistical interpretation." *American Sociological Review* 43 (5): 623–43.

Freedeman, Charles. 1979. *Joint-Stock Enterprise in France 1807–1867: From Privileged Company to Modern Corporation*. Chapel Hill, NC: University of North Carolina Press.

Freedeman, Charles. 1988. "Cartels and the law in France before 1914." *French Historical Studies* 15 (3): 462–78.

Freedeman, Charles. 1993. *The Triumph of Corporate Capitalism in France, 1867–1913*. Rochester, NY: University of Rochester Press.

Freeman, Linton C. 1977. "A set of measures of centrality based on betweenness." *Sociometry* 40 (1): 35–41.

Freeman, Linton C. 1979. "Centrality in social networks: Conceptual clarification." *Social Networks* 1 (3): 215–39.

Freeman, Linton C. 2004. *The Development of Social Network Analysis*. Vancouver, BC: Empirical Press.

Freeman, Richard B. and James L. Medoff. 1984. *What Do Unions Do?* New York: Basic Books.

Freyer, Tony. 1992. *Regulating Big Business: Antitrust in Great Britain and America, 1880–1990*. Cambridge: Cambridge University Press.

Friedan, Betty. 1963. *The Feminine Mystique*. New York: W.W. Norton & Co.

Friedberg, Erhardt. 1997. *Local Orders: The Dynamics of Organized Action*, trans. Emoretta Yang. Greenwich, CT: JAI Press.

Friedkin, Noah E. 1981. "The development of structure in random networks: An analysis of the effects of increasing network density on five measures of structure." *Social Networks* 3 (1): 41–45.

Friedland, Roger and Robert R. Alford. 1991. "Bringing society back in: Symbols, practices, and institutional contradictions." In *The New Institutionalism in Organizational Analysis*, ed. Walter W. Powell and Paul J. DiMaggio, 232–63. Chicago: University of Chicago Press.

Furlough, Ellen and Carl Strikwerda, eds. 1999. *Consumers against Capitalism? Consumer Cooperation in Europe, North America, and Japan, 1840–1990*. Lanham, MD: Rowman & Littlefield.

Gaddis, S. Michael. 2015. "Discrimination in the credential society: An audit study of race and college selectivity in the labor market." *Social Forces* 93 (4): 1451–79.

Galaskiewicz, Joseph and Ronald S. Burt. 1991. "Interorganizational contagion in corporate philanthropy." *Administrative Science Quarterly* 36 (1): 88–105.

Galaskiewicz, Joseph and Stanley S. Wasserman. 1981. "A dynamic study of change in a regional corporate network." *American Sociological Review* 46 (4): 475–84.

Galbraith, Jay R. 1973. *Designing Complex Organizations*. Reading, MA: Addison-Wesley.

Gamoran, Adam. 1987. "The stratification of high-school learning opportunities." *Sociology of Education* 60 (3): 135–55.

Gamoran, Adam. 2001. "American schooling and educational inequality: A forecast for the 21st century." *Sociology of Education* 74 (extra issue): 135–53.

Gamoran, Adam and Robert Dreeben. 1986. "Coupling and control in educational organizations." *Administrative Science Quarterly* 31 (4): 612–32.

Gantt, Henry Laurence. 1916. *Industrial Leadership*. New Haven, CT: Yale University Press.

Ganz, Marshall. 2000. "Resources and resourcefulness: Strategic capacity in the unionization of California agriculture, 1955–1966." *American Journal of Sociology* 105 (4): 1003–62.

Gärdenfors, Peter. 2014. *The Geometry of Meaning: Semantics Based on Conceptual Spaces*. Cambridge, MA: MIT Press.

Gargiulo, Martin. 1993. "Two-step leverage: Managing constraint in organizational politics." *Administrative Science Quarterly* 38 (1): 1–19.

Gavetti, Giovanni, Daniel Levinthal, and Willie Ocasio. 2007. "Neo-Carnegie: The Carnegie school's past, present, and reconstructing for the future." *Organization Science* 18 (3): 523–36.

Geertz, Clifford. 1973. *The Interpretation of Cultures*. New York: Basic Books.

Gehman, Joel, Matthew Grimes, and Ke Cao. 2019. "Why we care about certified B corporations: From valuing growth to certifying values practices." *Academy of Management Discoveries* 5 (1): 97–101.

Gelman, Andrew, John Carlin, Hal Stern, David Dunson, Aki Vehtari, and Donald Rubin. 2021. *Bayesian Data Analysis*. 3rd edn. Available for download from http://www.stat.columbia.edu /~gelman/book (viewed March 31, 2022).

Gibson, Christina B. and Jennifer L. Gibbs. 2006. "Unpacking the concept of virtuality: The effects of geographic dispersion, electronic dependence, dynamic structure, and national diversity on team innovation." *Administrative Science Quarterly* 51 (3): 451–95.

Giddens, Anthony. 1984. *The Constitution of Society: Outline of the Theory of Structuration*. Berkeley, CA: University of California Press.

Gilbreth, Frank B. and Lillian M. Gilbreth. 1917. *Applied Motion Study: A Collection of Papers on the Efficient Method to Industrial Preparedness*. New York: Sturgis and Walton.

Gilens, Martin and Benjamin I. Page. 2014. "Testing theories of American politics: Elites, interest groups, and average citizens." *Perspectives on Politics* 12 (3): 564–81.

Gilovich, Thomas, Dale Griffin, and Daniel Kahneman. 2002. *Heuristics and Biases: The Psychology of Intuitive Judgment*. New York: Cambridge University Press.

Gioia, Dennis A., Kristin N. Price, Aimee L. Hamilton, and James B. Thomas. 2010. "Forging an identity: An insider-outsider study of the processes involved in the formation of organizational identity." *Administrative Science Quarterly* 55 (1): 1–46.

Gispen, C.W.R. 1988. "German engineers and American social theory: Historical perspectives on professions." *Comparative Studies in Society and History* 30 (3): 550–74.

Godart, Frédéric C. and Charles Galunic. 2019. "Explaining the popularity of cultural elements: Networks, culture, and the structural embeddedness of high fashion trends." *Organization Science* 30 (1): 151–68.

Godechot, Olivier and Claudia Senik. 2015. "Wage comparisons in and out of the firm: Evidence from a matched employer-employee French database." *Journal of Economic Behavior and Organization* 117 (C): 395–410.

Goffman, Erving. 1959. *The Presentation of Self in Everyday Life*. Garden City, NY: Doubleday Anchor.

Goffman, Erving. 1961. *Asylums: Essays on the Social Situation of Mental Patients and Other Inmates*. New York: Doubleday Anchor.

Goffman, Erving. 1974. *Frame Analysis: An Essay on the Organization of Experience*. New York: Harper & Row.

Goldberg, Amir, Sameer B. Srivastava, V. Govind Manian, William Monroe, and Christopher Potts. 2016. "Fitting in or standing out? The tradeoffs of structural and cultural embeddedness." *American Sociological Review* 81 (6): 1190–222.

Goldin Claudia and Cecilia Rouse. 2000. "Orchestrating impartiality: The impact of 'blind' auditions on female musicians." *American Economic Review* 90 (4): 715–41.

Goldstein, Adam. 2012. "Revenge of the managers: Labor cost-cutting and the paradoxical resurgence of managerialism in the shareholder value era, 1984 to 2001." *American Sociological Review* 77 (2): 268–94.

Goode, William J. 1963. *World Revolution and Family Patterns*. Glencoe, IL: Free Press.

Gordon, George G. and Nancy DiTomaso. 1992. "Predicting corporate performance from organizational culture." *Journal of Management Studies* 29 (6): 783–98.

Gordon, Karen Elizabeth. 1984. *The Transitive Vampire: A Handbook of Grammar for the Innocent, the Eager, and the Damned*. New York: Times Books.

Gordon, Karen Elizabeth. 1997. *The Disheveled Dictionary: A Curious Caper through Our Sumptuous Lexicon*. New York: Houghton-Mifflin.

Gorman, Elizabeth H. 2005. "Gender stereotypes, same-gender preference, and organizational variation in the hiring of women: Evidence from law firms." *American Sociological Review* 70 (4): 702–28.

Gorman, Elizabeth H. and Julie A. Kmec. 2009. "Hierarchical rank and women's occupational mobility: Glass ceilings in corporate law firms." *American Journal of Sociology* 114 (5): 1428–74.

Gosden, P.H.J.H. 1961. *The Friendly Societies in England, 1815–1875*. Manchester: Manchester University Press.

Gouldner, Alvin W. 1954. *Patterns of Industrial Bureaucracy*. New York: Free Press.

Gouldner, Alvin W. 1957. "Cosmopolitans and locals: Toward an analysis of latent social roles I." *Administrative Science Quarterly* 2 (3): 281–306.

Granovetter, Mark. 1973. "The strength of weak ties." *American Journal of Sociology* 78 (6): 1360–80.

Granovetter, Mark S. 1985. "Economic action and social structure: The problem of embeddedness." *American Journal of Sociology* 91: 481–510.

Granovetter, Mark S. (1974) 1995. *Getting a Job: A Study of Contacts and Careers.* Chicago: University of Chicago Press.

Grant, Don Sherman II, Albert J. Bergesen, and Andrew W. Jones. 2002. "Organizational size and pollution: The case of the U.S. chemical industry." *American Sociological Review* 67 (3): 389–407.

Grant, Don Sherman II, Andrew W. Jones, and Mary Nell Trautner. 2004. "Do facilities with distant headquarters pollute more? How civic engagement conditions the environmental performance of absentee-managed plants." *Social Forces* 83 (1): 189–214.

Grant, Don Sherman II, and Ion Bogdan Vasi. 2016. "Civil society in an age of environmental anxiety: How local environmental nongovernmental organizations reduce U.S. power plants' carbon dioxide emissions." *Sociological Forum* 32 (1): 94–115.

Gray, Garry C. and Susan S. Silbey. 2014. "Governing inside the organization: Interpreting regulation and compliance." *American Journal of Sociology* 120 (1): 96–145.

Greenwood, Royston. 2016. "OMT, then and now." *Journal of Management Inquiry* 26 (10): 27–33.

Greenwood, Royston, Amalia Magán Díaz, Stan Xaio Li, and José Céspedes Lorente. 2010. "The multiplicity of institutional logics and the heterogeneity of organizational responses." *Organization Science* 21 (2): 521–39.

Greenwood, Royston, Roy Suddaby, and C. R. Hinings. 2002. "Theorizing change: The role of professional associations in the transformation of institutionalized fields." *Academy of Management Journal* 45 (1): 58–80.

Greve, Henrich R. 1995. "Jumping ship: The diffusion of strategy abandonment." *Administrative Science Quarterly* 40: 444–73.

Greve, Henrich R. 1998. "Performance, aspirations, and risky organizational change." *Administrative Science Quarterly* 43 (1): 58–86.

Greve, Henrich R. 1999. "The effect of change on performance: Inertia and regression to the mean." *Administrative Science Quarterly* 44 (3): 590–614.

Greve, Henrich R., and Hayagreeva Rao. 2012. "Echoes of the past: Organizational foundings as sources of an institutional legacy of mutualism." *American Journal of Sociology* 118 (3): 635–75.

Greve, Henrich R., and Cyndi Man Zhang. 2017. "Institutional logics and power sources: Merger and acquisition decisions." *Academy of Management Journal* 60 (2): 671–94.

Griesbach, Kathleen, Adam Reich, Luke Elliott-Negri, and Ruther Milkman. 2019. "Algorithmic control in platform food delivery work." *Socius* 5: 1–15.

Grother, Patrick, Mei Ngan, and Kayee Hanaoka. 2019. *Face Recognition Vendor Test. Part 3: Demographic Effects.* Washington, DC: National Institute of Standards and Technology.

Gualtieri, Gillian. 2020. "Symbolic compliance and student concerns: Legal endogeneity and Title IX at American colleges and universities." *Sociological Forum* 35 (1): 207–28.

Guillaume, Yves R. F., Jeremy F. Dawson, Ilian Otaye-Ebede, Stephen A. Woods, and Michael A. West. 2017. "Harnessing demographic differences in organizations: What moderates the effect of workforce diversity?" *Journal of Organizational Behavior* 38 (2): 276–303.

Guillén, Mauro F. 1994. *Models of Management: Work, Authority, and Organization in a Comparative Perspective.* Chicago: University of Chicago Press.

Guinnane, Timothy W. 2001. "Cooperatives as information machines: German rural credit cooperatives, 1883–1914." *Journal of Economic History* 61 (2): 366–89.

Guinnane, Timothy W., Ron Harris, Naomi R. Lamoreaux, and Jean-Laurent Rosenthal. 2007. "Putting the corporation in its place." *Enterprise and Society* 8 (3): 687–729.

Guinnane, Timothy W., Ron Harris, Naomi R. Lamoreaux, and Jean-Laurent Rosenthal. 2008. "Pouvoir et propriété dans l'enterprise: Pour une histoire internationale des sociétés à responsibilité limitée." *Annales: Histoire, Sciences Sociales* 63: 73–110.

Gulati, Ranjay and Martin Gargiulo. 1999. "Where do interorganizational networks come from?" *American Journal of Sociology* 104 (5): 1439–93.

Gulati, Ranjay and Maxime Sytch. 2007. "Dependence asymmetry and joint dependence in interorganizational relationships: Effects of embeddedness on a manufacturer's performance in procurement relationships." *Administrative Science Quarterly* 52 (1): 32–69.

Gulati, Ranjay, Maxime Sytch, and Adam Tatarynowicz. 2012. "The rise and fall of small worlds: Exploring the dynamics of social structure." *Organization Science* 23 (2): 449–71.

Guler, Isin, Mauro F. Guillén, and John Muir Macpherson. 2002. "Global competition, institutions, and the diffusion of organizational practices: The international spread of ISO 9000 quality certificates." *Administrative Science Quarterly* 47 (2): 207–32.

Gulick, Luther H. and Lyndall Urwick. 1937. *Papers on the Science of Administration*. New York: Columbia University Institute of Public Administration.

Gusfield, Joseph R. 1963. *Symbolic Crusade: Status Politics and the American Temperance Movement*. Urbana-Champaign, IL: University of Illinois Press.

Guthrie, Douglas. 1999. *Dragon in a Three-Piece Suit: The Emergence of Capitalism in China*. Princeton, NJ: Princeton University Press.

Guthrie, Douglas and Louise Marie Roth. 1999. "The state, courts, and equal opportunities for female CEOs in U.S. organizations: Specifying institutional mechanisms." *Social Forces* 78 (2): 511–42.

Haber, Samuel. 1991. *The Quest for Authority and Honor in the American Professions, 1750–1900*. Chicago: University of Chicago Press.

Habermas, Jürgen. (1962) 1991. *The Structural Transformation of the Public Sphere: An Introduction into a Category of Bourgeois Society*, trans. Thomas Burger with Frederick Lawrence. Cambridge, MA: MIT Press.

Hacker, Jacob S. and Paul Pierson. 2020. "Winner-take-all politics: Public policy, political organization, and the precipitous rise of top incomes in the United States." *Politics and Society* 38 (2): 152–204.

Hallett, Timothy. 2010. "The myth incarnate: Recoupling processes, turmoil, and inhabited institutions in an urban elementary school." *American Sociological Review* 75 (1): 52–74.

Hampton, James A. 1998. "Similarity-based categorization and fuzziness of natural categories." *Cognition* 65 (2–3): 137–65.

Han, Shin-Kap. 1994. "Mimetic isomorphism and its effect on the audit services market." *Social Forces* 73 (2): 637–63.

Hannah, Leslie. 1976. *The Rise of the Corporate Economy*. Baltimore: Johns Hopkins University Press.

Hannan, Michael T. 1998. "Rethinking age dependence in organizational mortality: Logical formalizations." *American Journal of Sociology* 104 (1): 126–64.

Hannan, Michael T. and John Freeman. 1989. *Organizational Ecology*. Cambridge, MA: Harvard University Press.

Hannan, Michael T., Gaël Le Mens, Greta Hsu, Balázs Kovács, Giacomo Negro, László Pólos, Elizabeth Pontikes, and Amanda Sharkey. 2019. *Concepts and Categories: Foundations for Sociological and Cultural Analysis*. New York: Columbia University Press.

Hannan, Michael T., László Pólos, and Glenn R. Carroll. 2007. *Logics of Organizational Theory: Audiences, Codes, and Ecologies*. Princeton, NJ: Princeton University Press.

Hannon, John M. and George T. Milkovich. 1996. "The effect of human resource reputation signals on share prices: An event study." *Human Resource Management* 35 (3): 405–24.

Hansen, Morton T. 1999. "The search-transfer problem: The role of weak ties in sharing knowledge across organizational subunits." *Administrative Science Quarterly* 44 (1): 82–111.

Harary, Frank, Robert Zane Norman, and Dorwin Cartwright. 1965. *Structural Models: An Introduction to the Theory of Directed Graphs*. New York: Wiley.

Hargittai, Eszter. 2020. "Potential bias in big data: Omitted voices on social media." *Social Science Computer Review* 38 (1): 10–34.

Harris, Ron. 2000. *Industrializing English Law: Entrepreneurship and Business Organisation, 1720–1844*. Cambridge: Cambridge University Press.

Harris, Ron. 2008. "The institutional dynamics of early modern Eurasian trade: The commenda and the corporation." *Journal of Economic Behavior and Organization* 71: 606–22.

Harrison, David A., Kenneth H. Price, Joanne H. Gavin, and Anna T. Florey. 2002. "Time, teams, and task performance: Changing effects of surface- and deep-level diversity on group functioning." *Academy of Management Journal* 45 (5): 1029–45.

Haunschild, Pamela R. and Anne S. Miner. 1997. "Modes of interorganizational imitation: The effects of outcome salience and uncertainty." *Administrative Science Quarterly* 42 (3): 472–500.

Haveman, Heather A. 1992. "Between a rock and a hard place: Organizational change and performance under conditions of fundamental environmental transformation." *Administrative Science Quarterly* 37 (1): 48–75.

Haveman, Heather A. 1993. "Follow the leader: Mimetic isomorphism and entry into new markets." *Administrative Science Quarterly* 38 (4): 593–627.

Haveman, Heather A. 2000. "The future of organizational sociology: Forging ties between paradigms." *Contemporary Sociology* 29 (3): 476–86.

Haveman, Heather A. 2009. "The Columbia school and the study of bureaucracies: Why organizations have lives of their own." In *The Oxford Handbook of Sociology and Organization Studies: Classical Foundations*, ed. Paul S. Adler, 585–606. Oxford: Oxford University Press.

Haveman, Heather A. and Lisa E. Cohen. 1994. "The ecological dynamics of careers: The impact of organizational founding, dissolution, and merger on job mobility." *American Journal of Sociology* 100 (1): 104–52.

Haveman, Heather A. and Robert J. David. 2008. "Organizational ecologists and institutionalists: Friends or foes?" In *The SAGE Handbook of Organizational Institutionalism*, ed. Royston Greenwood, Christine Oliver, Kerstin Sahlin, and Roy Suddaby, 571–93. Thousand Oaks, CA: Sage.

Haveman, Heather A. and Gillian Gualtieri. 2017. "Institutional logics." In *Oxford Research Encyclopedia of Business and Management*, ed. R. Aldag. New York: Oxford University Press.

Haveman, Heather A., Jacob Habinek, and Leo A. Goodman. 2012. "How entrepreneurship evolves: The founders of new magazines in America, 1741–1860." *Administrative Science Quarterly* 57 (4): 585–624.

Haveman, Heather A., Nan Jia, Jing Shi, and Yongxiang Wang. 2017. "The dynamics of political embeddedness in China." *Administrative Science Quarterly* 62 (1): 67–104.

Haveman, Heather A. and Nataliya Nedzhvetskaya. 2022. "Community, self-help, and enterprise: The coevolution of capitalism and non-profit and for-profit businesses in Britain and Germany." In *The Corporation: Rethinking the Iconic Form of Business Organization* (Research in the Sociology of Organizations 78), ed. Renate E. Meyer, Stephan Leixnering, and Jeroen Veldman, 121–71. Bingley: Emerald Publishing Limited.

Haveman, Heather A. and Hayagreeva Rao. 1997. "Structuring a theory of moral sentiments: Institutional and organizational coevolution in the early thrift industry." *American Journal of Sociology* 102 (6): 1606–51.

Haveman, Heather A. and Rachel Wetts. 2019a. "Organizational theory: From classical sociology to the 1970s." *Sociology Compass* 13 (3): e12627.

Haveman, Heather A. and Rachel Wetts. 2019b. "Contemporary organizational theory: The demographic, relational, and cultural perspectives." *Sociology Compass* 13 (3): e12664.

Hawley, Amos H. 1950. *Human Ecology: A Theory of Human Structure*. New York: The Ronald Press Co.

Hawley, Amos H. 1968. *Human Ecology: A Theoretical Essay*. Chicago: University of Chicago Press.

Hayes, Rutherford B. 1922. *The Diary and Letters of Rutherford B. Hayes, Nineteenth President of the United States*, ed. Charles Richard Williams. Columbus, OH: Ohio State Archaeological and Historical Society.

Heaney, Michael T. and Fabio Rojas. 2014. "Hybrid activism: Social movement mobilization in a multimovement environment." *American Journal of Sociology* 119 (4): 1047–103.

Hedström, Peter. 1992. "Is organizational ecology at an impasse?" *Contemporary Sociology* 21 (6): 751–53.

Hedström, Peter and Richard Swedberg. 1998. *Social Mechanisms: An Analytical Approach to Social Theory*. Cambridge, MA: Cambridge University Press.

Hedström, Peter and Petri Ylikoski. 2010. "Causal mechanisms in the social sciences." *Annual Review of Sociology* 36: 49–67.

Heider, Fritz. 1958. *The Psychology of Interpersonal Relations*. New York: John Wiley & Son.

Heilman, Madeline. 2012. "Gender stereotypes and workplace bias." *Research in Organizational Behavior* 32: 113–35.

Heimer, Carol A. and Mitchell L. Stevens. 1997. "Caring for the organization: Social workers as frontline risk managers in neonatal intensive care units." *Work and Occupations* 24 (2): 133–63.

Heinze, Katherine L. and Klaus Weber. 2016. "Toward organizational pluralism: Institutional intrapreneurship in integrative medicine." *Organization Science* 27 (1): 157–72.

Helfen, Markus and Jörg Sydow. 2013. "Negotiating as institutional work: The case of labour standards and international framework agreements." *Organization Studies* 34 (8): 1073–98.

Henderson, Rebecca M. and Kim B. Clark. 1990. "Architectural innovation: The reconfiguration of existing product technologies and the failure of established firms." *Administrative Science Quarterly* 35 (1): 9–30.

Henderson, William O. 1975. *The Rise of German Industrial Power, 1834–1914*. London: Temple Smith.

Herlihy, David. 1997. *The Black Death and the Transformation of the West*, ed. and with an introduction by Samuel K. Cohn Jr. Cambridge, MA: Harvard University Press.

Herring, Cedric. 2009. "Does diversity pay? Race, gender, and the business case for diversity." *American Sociological Review* 74 (2): 208–24.

Hertel-Fernandez, Alexander. 2019. *State Capture: How Conservative Activists, Big Business, and Wealthy Donors Reshaped the American State—and the Nation*. Oxford: Oxford University Press.

Hiatt, Shon R., Wesley D. Sine, and Pamela S. Tolbert. 2009. "From Pabst to Pepsi: The deinstitutionalization of social practices and the creation of entrepreneurial opportunities." *Administrative Science Quarterly* 54 (4): 635–67.

Hickey, Daniel. 1997. *Local Hospitals in Ancien Régime France: Rationalization, Resistance, Renewal 1530–1789*. Montreal: McGill-Queens University Press.

Hickson, David J., C. Robin Hinings, C. A. Lee, R. E. Schneck, and Johannes M. Pennings. 1971. "A strategic contingencies' theory of intraorganizational power." *Administrative Science Quarterly* 16 (2): 216–29.

Highton, David. 2017. "Voter identification laws and turnout in the United States." *Annual Review of Political Science* 20: 149–67.

Hinings, Bob and Renate E. Meyer. 2018. *Starting Points*. Cambridge: Cambridge University Press.

Hirsch, Paul M. 1975. "Organizational effectiveness and the institutional environment." *Administrative Science Quarterly* 20 (3): 327–44.

Hirsch, Paul M. 1986. "From ambushes to golden parachutes: Corporate takeovers as an instance of cultural framing and institutional integration." *American Journal of Sociology* 91 (4): 800–37.

Hirsch, Paul M. 1997. "Sociology without social structure: Neoinstitutionalist theory meets brave new world." *American Journal of Sociology* 102 (6): 1702–23.

Hirschman, Dan and Ellen Berrey. 2017. "The partial deinstitutionalization of affirmative action in U.S. higher education, 1988 to 2014." *Sociological Science* 4 (18): 449–68.

Ho, Karen. 2009. *Liquidated: An Ethnography of Wall Street*. Durham, NC: Duke University Press.

Hochschild, Arlie Russell. (1983) 2003. *The Managed Heart: Commercialization of Human Feeling*. Berkeley, CA: University of California Press.

Hodges, Richard. 1982. *Dark Age Economics: The Origins of Towns and Trade A.D. 600–1000*. New York: St. Martin's Press.

Hodges, Richard. 2012. *Dark Age Economics: A New Audit*. London: Bristol Classical Press.

Hoffman, Andrew J. 2016. "Reflections: Academia's emerging crisis of relevance and the consequent role of the scholar." *Journal of Change Management* 16 (2): 77–96.

Hoffman, Andrew J. and P. Devereaux Jennings. 2018. *Re-engaging with Sustainability in the Anthropocene Era*. Oxford: Oxford University Press.

Hoffmann, Stefan-Ludwig. 2003. "Democracy and associations in the long nineteenth century: Toward a transnational perspective." *Journal of Modern History* 75 (2): 269–99.

Hofstede, Geert. 1980. *Culture's Consequences: International Differences in Work-Related Values*. Beverly Hills, CA: Sage.

Hollister, Matissa N. 2004. "Does firm size matter anymore? The new economy and firm size wage effects." *American Sociological Review* 69 (5): 659–76.

Holm, Peter. 1995. "The dynamics of institutionalization: Transformation processes in Norwegian fisheries." *Administrative Science Quarterly* 40 (3): 398–422.

Homans, George C. 1950. *The Human Group.* New York: Harcourt, Brace, Jovanovich.

Homans, George C. 1964. "Contemporary theory." In *Handbook of Modern Sociology,* ed. R.E.L. Faris, 951–77. Chicago: Rand-McNally.

Horton, Emily. 2018. 2018. "Funding Bill Falls Short for the IRS." Center on Budget and Policy Priorities, *Off the Charts* (blog), March 23, https://www.cbpp.org/blog/2018-funding-bill -falls-short-for-the-irs (viewed March 31, 2022).

House, Robert J. 1977. "A 1976 theory of charismatic leadership." In *Leadership: The Cutting Edge,* ed. James G. Hunt and Lars L. Larson, 189–207. Carbondale, IL: Southern Illinois Press.

Howard, Christopher. 1997. *The Hidden Welfare State: Tax Expenditures and Social Policy in the United States.* Princeton, NJ: Princeton University Press.

Hsu, Greta. 2006. "Jacks of all trades and masters of none: Audiences' reactions to spanning genres in feature film marketing." *Administrative Science Quarterly* 51 (3): 420–50.

Hsu, Greta and Stine Grodal. 2015. "Category taken-for-grantedness as a strategic opportunity: The case of light cigarettes, 1964 to 1993." *American Sociological Review* 80 (1): 28–62.

Huber, Evelyne and John D. Stephens. 2009. *Development and Crisis of the Welfare State: Parties and Politics in Global Markets.* Chicago: University of Chicago Press.

Huffman, Matt L., Philip N. Cohen, and Jessica Pearlman. 2010. "Engendering change: Organizational dynamics and workplace gender desegregation, 1975–2005." *Administrative Science Quarterly* 55 (2): 255–77.

Hughes, Diane Owen. 1973. "On voluntary associations in history: Medieval Europe." *American Anthropologist* 76 (2): 333–34.

Hultin, Mia. 2003. "Some take the glass escalator, some hit the glass ceiling? Career consequences of occupational sex segregation." *Work and Occupations* 30 (1): 30–61.

Huy, Quy Nguyen, Kevin G. Corley, and Matthew S. Kraatz. 2014. "From support to mutiny: Shifting legitimacy judgments and emotional reaction impacting the implementation of radical change." *Academy of Management Journal* 57 (6): 1650–80.

Hyde, Janet Shibley. 2014. "Gender similarities and differences." *Annual Review of Psychology* 65: 373–98.

Hyman, Richard. 1975. *Industrial Relations: A Marxist Introduction.* London: Macmillan.

Hymer, Stephen. 1972. "The multinational corporation and the law of uneven development." In *Economics and World Order,* ed. Jagdish Bhagwati, 113–40. New York: Macmillan.

Ibarra, Herminia. 1992. "Homophily and differential returns: Sex differences in network structure and access in an advertising firm." *Administrative Science Quarterly* 37 (3): 422–47.

Ibarra, Herminia. 1995. "Race, opportunity, and diversity of social circles in managerial networks." *Academy of Management Journal* 38 (3): 673–703.

Ingram, Paul and Karen Clay. 2000. "The choice-within-constraints new institutionalism and implications for sociology." *Annual Review of Sociology* 27: 525–46.

Ingram, Paul and Magnus Thor Torafson. 2010. "Organizing the in-between: The population dynamics of network-weaving organizations in the global interstate network." *Administrative Science Quarterly* 55 (4): 577–605.

IRS. 2021. "IRS Budget and Workforce," https://www.irs.gov/statistics/irs-budget-and -workforce (viewed March 31, 2022).

Isaac, Larry W. and Larry J. Griffin. 1989. "Ahistoricism in time-series analyses of historical process: Critique, redirection, and illustrations from U.S. labor history." *American Sociological Review* 54 (6): 873–90.

Jacoby, Henry. 1973. *The Bureaucratization of the World*, trans. Eveline L. Kanes. Berkeley, CA: University of California Press.

James, Erika Hayes. 2000. "Race-related difference in promotion and support: Underlying effects of human and social capital." *Organization Science* 11 (5): 493–508.

Janis, Irving L. 1982. *Groupthink: Psychological Studies of Policy Decisions and Fiascoes*. Boston, MA: Houghton Mifflin.

Jansen, Marius and Gilbert Rozman, eds. 1986. *Japan in Transition: From Tokugawa to Meiji*. Princeton, NJ: Princeton University Press.

Jarausch, Konrad H. 1990. "The German professions in history and theory." In *German Professions, 1800–1950*, ed. Geoffrey Cocks and Konrad H. Jarausch, 9–14. New York: Oxford University Press.

Jay, Jason. 2013. "Navigating paradox as a mechanism of change and innovation in hybrid organizations." *Academy of Management Journal* 56 (1): 137–59.

Jehn, Karen A., Gregory B. Northcraft, and Margaret A. Neale. 1999. "Why differences make a difference: A field study of diversity, conflict, and performance in workgroups." *Administrative Science Quarterly* 44: 741–63.

Jensen, Michael. 2006. "Should we stay or should we go? Accountability, status anxiety, and client defections." *Administrative Science Quarterly* 51: 97–128.

Jepperson, Ronald L. 1991. "Institutions, institutional effects, and institutionalization." In *The New Institutionalism in Organizational Analysis*, ed. Walter W. Powell and Paul J. DiMaggio, 143–63. Chicago: University of Chicago Press.

Johnson, Paul. 2010. *Making the Market: Victorian Origins of Corporate Capitalism*. Cambridge: Cambridge University Press.

Johnson, Victoria. 2007. "What is organizational imprinting? Cultural entrepreneurship in the founding of the Paris Opera." *American Journal of Sociology* 113: 97–127.

Johnston, David Cay. 2003. *Perfectly Legal: The Secret Campaign to Rig our Tax System to Benefit the Super Rich—and Cheat Everybody Else*. New York: Portfolio.

Jones, Candace, Massimo Maoret, Felipe G. Massa, and Silviya Svejenova. 2012. "Rebels with a cause: Formation, contestation, and expansion of the de novo category 'modern architecture,' 1870–1975." *Organization Science* 23 (6): 1523–45.

Jones, Colin. 1989. *The Charitable Imperative: Hospitals and Nursing in Ancien Regime and Revolutionary France*. London: Routledge.

Jonsson, Stefan, Henrich R. Greve, and Takako Fujiwara-Greve. 2009. "Undeserved loss: The spread of legitimacy loss to innocent organizations in response to reported corporate deviance." *Administrative Science Quarterly* 54 (2): 195–228.

Jordan, Michael I. and Tom M. Mitchell. 2015. "Machine learning: Trends, perspectives, and prospects." *Science* 349 (6245): 255–60.

Joshi, Aparna, Hui Liao, and Susan E. Jackson. 2006. "Cross-level effects of workplace diversity on sales performance and pay." *Academy of Management Journal* 49 (3): 459–81.

Jung, Jiwook. 2016. "Through the contested terrain: Implementation of downsizing decisions by large U.S. firms, 1984 to 2005." *American Sociological Review* 81 (2): 347–73.

Jung, Jiwook and Taekjin Shin. 2019. "Learning not to diversify: The transformation of graduate business education and the decline of diversifying acquisitions." *Administrative Science Quarterly* 64 (2): 337–69.

Jurafsky, Daniel and James H. Martin. 2021. *Speech and Language Processing.* 3rd edn draft book manuscript, available at https://web.stanford.edu/~jurafsky/slp3 (viewed March 31, 2022).

Jussim, Lee, Jarret T. Crawford, and Rachel S. Rubenstein. 2015. "Stereotype (in)accuracy in perceptions of groups and individuals." *Current Directions in Psychological Science* 24 (6): 490–97.

Kabo, Felichism W., Natalie Cotton-Nessler, Yongha Hwang, Margaret C. Levinstein, and Jason Owen-Smith. 2014. "Proximity effects on the dynamics and outcomes of scientific collaborations." *Research Policy* 43 (9): 1469–85.

Kacperczyk, Aleksandra J. and Peter Younkin. 2017. "The paradox of breadth: The tension between experience and legitimacy in the transition to entrepreneurship." *Administrative Science Quarterly* 62 (4): 731–64.

Kalev, Alexandra. 2009. "Cracking the glass cages? Restructuring and ascriptive inequality at work." *American Journal of Sociology* 114: 1591–643.

Kalleberg, Arne L. 2009. "Precarious work, insecure workers: Employment relations in transition." *American Sociological Review* 74 (1): 1–22.

Kalleberg, Arne L. 2011. *Good Jobs, Bad Jobs: The Rise of Polarized and Precarious Employment Systems in the United States, 1970s to 2000s.* New York: Russell Sage Foundation.

Kalleberg, Arne L. 2018. *Precarious Lives: Job Insecurity and Well-Being in Rich Democracies.* Cambridge: Polity.

Kanter, Rosabeth Moss. 1977. *Men and Women of the Corporation.* New York: Basic Books.

Kanter, Rosabeth Moss and Rakesh Khurana. 2009. Types and positions: The significance of Georg Simmel's sturctural theories for organizational behavior. In *The Oxford Handbook of Sociology and Organization Studies: Classical Foundations,* ed. Paul S. Adler, 291–306. Oxford: Oxford University Press.

Kaplan, Benjamin J. 2007. *Divided by Faith: Religious Conflict and the Practice of Toleration in Early Modern Europe.* Cambridge, MA: Belknap Press of Harvard University Press.

Karabel, Jerome. 2005. *The Chosen: The Hidden History of Admission and Exclusion at Harvard, Yale, and Princeton.* New York: Houghton Mifflin.

Karim, Fazida, Azeezat A. Oyewande, Lamis F. Abdalla, Reem Chaudry Ehsanullah, and Safeera Khan. 2020. "Social media use and its connection to mental health: A systematic review." *Cureus* 12 (6): e8627.

Katila, Riitta, Jeff D. Rosenberger, and Kathleen M. Eisenhardt. 2008. "Swimming with sharks: Technology ventures, defense mechanisms and corporate relationships." *Administrative Science Quarterly* 53 (2): 295–332.

Kaufman, Jason. 2008. "Corporate law and the sovereignty of states." *American Sociological Review* 73 (3): 402–25.

Kellogg, Katherine C., Melissa A. Valentine, and Angèle Christin. 2020. "Algorithms at work: The new contested terrain of control." *Academy of Management Annals* 14 (1): 366–410.

Kelly, Dawn and Terry L. Amburgey. 1991. "Organizational inertia and momentum: A dynamic model of strategic change." *Academy of Management Journal* 34 (3): 591–612.

Kelly, Erin L. 2003. "The strange history of employer-sponsored child care: Interested actors, uncertainty, and the transformation of law in organizational fields." *American Journal of Sociology* 109 (3): 606–49.

Kelly, Erin and Frank Dobbin. 1998. "How affirmative action became diversity management: Employer responses to antidiscrimination law, 1961–1996." *American Behavioral Scientist* 41 (7): 960–84.

Keltner, Dacher, Deborah H. Gruenfeld, and Cameron Anderson. 2003. "Power, approach, and inhibition." *Psychological Review* 110 (2): 265–84.

Kemp, Simon. 2020. "Digital 2020: 3.8 billion people use social media." *Digital 2020 Global Digital Overview*, https://wearesocial.com/blog/2020/01/digital-2020-3-8-billion-people-use-social-media (viewed May 20, 2020).

Kennedy, Mark Thomas. 2005. "Behind the one-way mirror: Refraction in the construction of product market categories." *Poetics* 33 (3–4): 201–26.

Kennedy, Mark Thomas. 2008. "Getting counted: Markets, media, and reality." *American Sociological Review* 73 (2): 270–95.

Kennedy, Scott. 2005. *The Business of Lobbying in China.* Cambridge, MA: Harvard University Press.

Keyfitz, Nathan. 1977. *Applied Mathematical Demography.* New York: Wiley.

Khaire, Mukti. 2010. "Young and no money? Never mind: The material impact of social resources on new venture growth." *Organization Science* 21 (1): 168–85.

Khaire, Mukti and R. Daniel Wadhwani. 2010. "Changing landscapes: The construction of meaning and value in a new market category: Modern Indian art." *Academy of Management Journal* 53 (6): 1281–304.

Khanna, Vikramaditya. 2005. "The economic history of the corporate form in ancient India." Working paper, University of Michigan Law School.

Kieser, Alfred. 1989. "Organizational, institutional, and societal evolution: Medieval craft guilds and the genesis of formal organizations." *Administrative Science Quarterly* 34 (4): 540–64.

Kim, Eun-Mee. 1996. "The industrial organization of the *chaebol.*" In *Asian Business Networks*, ed. Gary G. Hamilton, 231–52. New York: Walter de Gruyter.

Kindleberger, Charles. 1993. *A Financial History of Western Europe.* Oxford: Oxford University Press.

King, Andrew A. and Michael J. Lenox. 2000. "Industry self-regulation without sanctions: The chemical industry's responsible care program." *Academy of Management Journal* 43 (4): 698–716.

King, Brayden G., Teppo Felin, and David G. Whetten. 2010. "Finding the organization in organization science: A meta-theory of the organization as a social actor." *Organization Science* 21 (1): 290–305.

Klarner, Patricia and Sebastian Raisch. 2013. "Move to the beat: Rhythms of change and performance." *Academy of Management Journal* 56 (1): 160–84.

Kloppenborg, J. S. and S. G. Wilson, eds. 1996. *Voluntary Associations in the Greco-Roman World.* New York: Routledge.

Kluegel, James R. 1978. "The causes and cost of racial exclusion from job authority." *American Sociological Review* 43 (3): 285–301.

Knight, Will. 2017. "The dark secret at the heart of AI." *MIT Technology Review* online, https://www.technologyreview.com/s/604087/the-dark-secret-at-the-heart-of-ai (viewed March 31, 2022).

Kochan, Thomas, Katerina Bezrukova, Robin Ely, Susan Jackson, Aparna Joshi, Karen Jehn, Jonathan Leonard, David Levine, and David Thomas. 2003. "The effects of diversity of business performance: Report of the diversity research network." *Human Resource Management* 42 (1): 3–21.

Kogut, Bruce and Gordon Walker. 2001. "The small world of Germany and the durability of national networks." *American Sociological Review* 66 (3): 317–35.

Kollock, Peter. 1999. "The production of trust in online markets." In *Advances in Group Processes*, vol.16, ed. E. J. Lawler, M. Macy, S. Thyne, and H. A. Walker, 99–123. Greenwich, CT: JAI Press.

Kovács, Balázs, Glenn R. Carroll, and David W. Lehman. 2017. "The perils of proclaiming an authentic organizational identity." *Sociological Science* 4 (4): 80–106.

Krackhardt, David. 1990. "Assessing the political landscape: Structure, cognition, and power in organizations." *Administrative Science Quarterly* 35 (2): 342–69.

Krackhardt, David and Lyman W. Porter. 1986. "The Snowball effect: Turnover embedded in communication networks." *Journal of Applied Psychology* 71 (1): 50–55.

Krause, Elliott A. 1996. *Death of the Guilds: Professions, States, and the Advance of Capitalism, 1930 to the Present*. New Haven, CT: Yale University Press.

Krippner, Greta. 2005. "The financialization of the American economy." *Socio-Economic Review* 3 (2): 173–208.

Kristal, Tali, Yinon Cohen, and Edo Navot. 2020. "Workplace compensation practices and the rise in benefits inequality." *American Sociological Review* 85 (2): 271–97.

Kroezen, Jochem J. and Pursey P.M.A.R. Heugens. 2019. "What is dead may never die: Institutional regeneration through logic reemergence in Dutch brewing." *Administrative Science Quarterly* 64 (4): 976–1019.

Kunda, Gideon. 1992. *Engineering Culture: Control and Commitment in a High-Tech Corporation*. Philadelphia: Temple University Press.

Kurzweil, Ray. 2017. "The singularity is near," http://www.singularity.com/charts (viewed March 31, 2022).

Kuwabara, Ko. 2015. "Do reputation and systems undermine trust? Divergent effects of enforcement type on generalized trust and trustworthiness." *American Journal of Sociology* 120 (5): 1390–428.

Kuwabara, Ko and Sarah Thébaud. 2017. "When beauty doesn't pay: Gender and beauty biases in a peer-to-peer lending market." *Social Forces* 95 (4): 1371–98.

Lafer, Gordon. 2017. *The One Percent Solution: How Corporations Are Remaking American One State at a Time*. Ithaca, NY: Cornell University Press.

Lamont, Michèle and Virág Molnár. 2002. "The study of boundaries in the social sciences." *Annual Review of Sociology* 28: 167–95.

Lamoreaux, Naomi R. and Jean-Laurent Rosenthal. 2005. "Legal regime and contract flexibility: A comparison of business organization's choices in France and the United States during the era of industrialization." *American Law and Economics Review* 7 (1): 28–61.

Land, Kenneth C., Glenn Deane, and Judith R. Blau. 1991. "Religious pluralism and church membership: A spatial diffusion model." *American Sociological Review* 56: 237–49.

Lang, Robert, and Elizabeth Carrott Minnaugh. 2010. "The L^{3}C, history, basic construct, and legal history." *Vermont Law Review* 35 (1): 15–30.

Lange, Matthew. 2009. *Lineages of Despotism and Democracy: British Colonialism and State Power*. Chicago: University of Chicago Press.

Larson, Magali S. 1977. *The Rise of Professionalism*. Berkeley, CA: University of California Press.

Lau, Dora C. and J. Keith Murnighan. 1998. "Demographic diversity and faultlines: The compositional dynamics of organizational groups." *Academy of Management Review* 23 (2): 325–40.

Laumann, Edward O. and David Knoke. 1987. *The Organizational State: Social Change in National Policy Domains*. Madison, WI: University of Wisconsin Press.

Laurison, Daniel and S. Friedman. 2016. "The class pay gap in higher professional and managerial occupations." *American Sociological Review* 81 (4): 668–95.

Lawrence, Barbara. 1997. "The black box of organizational demography." *Organization Science* 8 (1): 1–22.

Lawrence, Megan. 2018. "Taking stock of the ability to change: The effect of prior experience." *Organization Science* 29 (3): 489–506.

Lawrence, Paul D. and Jay W. Lorsch. 1967. *Organizations and Environments: Managing Differentiation and Integration*. Boston, MA: Harvard Business School Press.

Lawrence, Thomas B. and Roy Suddaby. 2006. "Institutions and institutional work." In *Sage Handbook of Organization Studies*, ed. Stewart R. Clegg, Cynthia Hardy, Thomas B. Lawrence, and Walter R. Nord, 2nd edn, 215–54. London: Sage.

Laybourn, Keith. 1991. *British Trade Unionism, c. 1770–1990: A Reader in History*. Wolfeboro Falls, NJ: Alan Sutton.

Lazer, David and Jason Radford. 2017. "Data ex machina: Introduction to big data." *Annual Review of Sociology* 43: 1–18.

Le Mens, Gaël, Michael T. Hannan, and László Pólos. 2011. "Founding conditions, learning, and organizational life chances: Age dependence revisited." *Administrative Science Quarterly* 56 (1): 95–126.

Leacock, Stephen. 1911. *Nonsense Novels*. Toronto: McClelland and Stewart.

Leahey, Erin. 2005. "Alphas and asterisks: The development of statistical significance testing standards in sociology." *Social Forces* 84 (1): 1–24.

Lee, Sang Hoon. 2015. "Core–periphery structures in networks." Slides from the 18th Statistical Physics Workshop, Chonbuk National University.

Leicht, Kevin. 1989. "On the estimation of the union threat effect." *American Sociological Review* 54 (6): 1035–57.

Leixnering, Stephan, Renate E. Meyer, and Peter Doralt. 2022. "The past as prologue: Purpose dynamics in the history of the *Aktiengesellschaft*." In *The Corporation: Rethinking the Iconic Form of Business Organization* (Research in the Sociology of Organizations 78),, ed. Renate E. Meyer, Stephan Leixnering, and Jeroen Veldman, 97–120. Bingley: Emerald Publishing Limited.

Lepore, Jill. 2009. "Not so fast." *The New Yorker*, October 5.

Levi, Margaret, Tanio Melo, Barry R. Weingast, and Frances Zlotnick. 2017. "Opening access, ending the violence trap: Labor, business, government, and the National Labor Relations Act." In *Organizations, Civil Society, and the Roots of Development*, ed. Naomi R. Lamoreaux and John Joseph Wallis, 331–66. Chicago: University of Chicago Press.

Levillain, Kevin and Blanche Segrestin. 2019. "From primacy to purpose commitment: How emerging profit-with-purpose corporations open new corporate governance avenues." *European Management Review* 37 (5): 637–47.

Levins, Richard. 1968. *Evolution in a Changing Landscape: Some Theoretical Explorations*. Princeton, NJ: Princeton University Press.

Levinthal, Daniel A. 1991. "Random walks and organizational mortality." *Administrative Science Quarterly* 36 (3): 397–420.

Levitt, Barbara and James G. March. 1988. "Organizational learning." *Annual Review of Sociology* 14 (1): 319–40.

Levitt, Justin. 2007. *The Truth about Voter Fraud*. New York: Brennan Center for Justice.

Levy, Adalbert Béla. 1950. *Private Corporations and their Control: Part One*. London: Routledge & Kegan Paul.

Lewin, Kurt. 1947. "Frontiers of group dynamics: Concept, method and reality in social science, social equilibria, and social change." *Human Relations* 1: 5–41.

Lewis, Kevin. 2015. "Three fallacies of digital footprints." *Big Data & Society* 2 (2): 1–4.

Lewis-Kraus, Gideon. 2016. "The great A.I. awakening." *The New York Times Magazine*, December 18.

Likert, Rensis. 1967. *The Human Organization*. New York: McGraw-Hill.

Lim, Vivien K. G., Thompson S. H. Teo, and Geok Leng Loo. 2002. "How do I loaf here? Let me count the ways." *Proceedings of the ACM* 45 (1): 66–70.

Lin, Nan. 1999. "Social networks and status attainment." *Annual Review of Sociology* 25: 467–87.

Lin, Nan. 2001. *Social Capital: A Theory of Social Structure and Action*. Cambridge: Cambridge University Press.

Lin, Yimin. 2001. *Between Politics and Markets: Firms, Competition, and Institutional Change in Post-Mao China*. Cambridge: Cambridge University Press.

Lincoln, James R., Michael L. Gerlach, and Christina L. Ahmadjian. 1996. "Keiretsu networks and corporate performance in Japan." *American Sociological Review* 61 (1): 67–88.

Lincoln, James R., Michael L. Gerlach, and Christina L. Ahmadjian. 1998. "Evolving patterns of Keiretsu organization and action in Japan." *Research in Organizational Behavior* 20: 303–45.

Lincoln, James R., and Jon Miller. 1979. "Work and friendship ties in organizations: A comparative analysis of relational networks." *Administrative Science Quarterly* 24 (2): 181–99.

Lindebaum, Dirk, Mikko Vesa, and Frank den Hond. 2020. "Insights from 'The Machine Stops' to better understand rational assumptions in algorithmic decision making and its implications for organizations." *Academy of Management Review* 45 (1): 247–63.

Lipset, Seymour Martin. 1950. *Agrarian Socialism: The Cooperative Commonwealth Federation in Saskatchewan*. Berkeley, CA: University of California Press.

Lipset, Seymour Martin, Martin A. Trow, and James S. Coleman. 1956. *Union Democracy: The Internal Politics of the International Typographical Union*. New York: Free Press.

Lis, Catharina and Hugo Soly. 1994. "'An irresistible phalanx': Journeymen's associations in Western Europe, 1300–1800." *International Review of Social History* 39 (supplement 2): 11–52.

Liu, Christopher C. and Sameer B. Srivastava. 2015. "Pulling closer and moving apart: Interaction, identity, and influence in the U.S. senate, 1973 to 2009." *American Sociological Review* 80 (1): 192–217.

Liu, Christopher C., Sameer B. Srivastava, and Toby E. Stuart. 2016. "An intraorganizational ecology of individual attainment." *Organization Science* 27 (1): 90–105.

Liu, Min and Filippo Carlo Wezel. 2014. "Davids against Goliath? Collective identities and the market success of peripheral organizations during resource partitioning." *Organization Science* 26 (1): 293–309.

Liu, Sida and Hongqi Wu. 2016. "The ecology of organizational growth: Chinese law firms in the age of globalization." *American Journal of Sociology* 122 (3): 798–827.

Lloyd, Stephen. 2010. "Transcript: Creating the CIC." *Vermont Law Review* 35: 31–43.

Lom, Stacy E. 2016. "Changing rules, changing practices: The direct and indirect effects of tight coupling in figure skating." *Organization Science* 27 (1): 36–52.

Lorrain, François P., and Harrison C. White. 1971. "Structural equivalence of individuals in social networks." *Journal of Mathematical Sociology* 1 (1): 49–80.

Lorwin, Val R. 1954. *The French Labor Movement.* Cambridge, MA: Harvard University Press.

Lounsbury, Michael. 2001. "Institutional sources of practice variation: Staffing college and university recycling programs." *Administrative Science Quarterly* 46 (1): 29–56.

Lowie, Robert H. 1948. *Primitive Societies.* New York: Rinehart & Co.

Luo, Xueming, Marco Shaojun Qin, Zheng Fang, and Zhe Qu. 2021. "Artificial intelligence coaches for sales agents: Caveats and solutions." *Journal of Marketing* 85 (2): 14–32.

Lutter, Mark. 2015. "Do women suffer from network closure? The moderating effect of social capital on gender inequality in a project-based labor market, 1929 to 2010." *American Sociological Review* 80 (2): 329–58.

MacIver, R. M. 1917. *Community: A Sociological Study.* London: Macmillan & Co.

Mackie, Brendan. 2021. "Everyday corporations: Clubs and civil society 1688–1800." Unpublished dissertation, University of California, Berkeley.

Magee, Joe C. and Adam D. Galinsky. 2008. "Social hierarchy: The self-reinforcing nature of power and status." *Academy of Management Annals* 2 (1): 351–98.

Maguire, Steve, Cynthia Hardy, and Thomas B. Lawrence. 2004. "Institutional entrepreneurship in emerging fields: HIV/AIDS treatment advocacy in Canada." *Academy of Management Journal* 47 (5): 657–79.

Mahoney, James. 2000. "Path dependence in historical sociology." *Theory and Society* 29 (4): 507–48.

Mahoney, James. 2010. "After KKV: The new methodology of qualitative research." *World Politics* 62 (1): 120–47.

Malter, Daniel. 2014. "On the causality and cause of returns to organizational status: Evidence from the grands crus classés of the Médoc." *Administrative Science Quarterly* 59 (2): 271–300.

March, James G. and Johan P. Olsen, eds. 1976. *Ambiguity and Choice in Organizations.* Bergen: Universitetsforlaget.

March, James G. and Herbert A. Simon. (1958) 1993. *Organizations.* Cambridge, MA: Blackwell.

Markham, Tanya M., and Eden S. Blair. 2019. "The value of values: An update on the L3C entity, its uses, and purposes." *UMKC Law Review* 88: 927–53.

Marquis, Christopher. 2003. "The pressure of the past: Network imprinting in intercorporate communities." *Administrative Science Quarterly* 48 (4): 655–89.

Marquis, Christopher and Michael Lounsbury. 2007. "Vive la résistance: Competing logics and the consolidation of U.S. community banking." *Academy of Management Journal* 50 (4): 799–820.

Marquis, Christopher and András Tilcsik. 2013. "Imprinting: Toward a multi-level theory." *Academy of Management Annals* 7 (1): 193–243.

Martin, Cathie Jo. 2000. *Stuck in Neutral: Business and the Politics of Human Capital Investment Policy*. Princeton, NJ: Princeton University Press.

Marx, Karl. (1844) 1993. *The Economic and Philosophical Manuscripts*. Marx/Engels Internet Archive, https://archive.org/details/economicphilosop00kmar (viewed March 31, 2022).

Marx, Karl. (1852) 2005. *The Eighteenth Brumaire of Louis Bonaparte*, trans. Daniel de Leon. Project Gutenberg.

Marx, Karl. (1867) 1992. *Capital: A Critique of Political Economy*, vol. 1, trans. Ben Fowkes. Harmondsworth: Penguin Books.

Marx, Karl and Friedrich Engels. (1932) 1947. *The German Ideology*, ed. Roy Pascal. New York: International Publishers.

Marx, Karl and Friedrich Engels. (1848) 1964. *The Communist Manifesto*, trans. Samuel Moore. New York: Washington Square Press.

Maschke, Erich. 1969. "Outline of the history of German cartels from 1873 to 1914." In *Essays in European Economic History, 1789–1914*, ed. François Crouzet, W. H. Chaloner, and W. M. Stern, 226–58. London: Edward Arnold.

Maslow, Abraham H. 1943. A theory of human motivation. *Psychological Review* 50 (4): 370–96.

May, Robert M. 1973. *Stability and Complexity in Model Ecosystems*. Princeton, NJ: Princeton University Press.

Mayo, G. Elton. 1945. *The Social Problems of an Industrial Civilization*. Boston, MA: Harvard Graduate School of Business Administration.

Mayo, G. Elton. (1933) 1960. *Human Problems of Industrial Civilization*. New York: Viking.

McAdam, Doug. 1988. *Freedom Summer*. New York: Oxford University Press.

McCain, Bruce E., Charles A. O'Reilly III, and Jeffrey Pfeffer. 1983. "The effects of departmental demography on turnover: The case of a university." *Academy of Management Journal* 26 (4): 626–41.

McCammon, Holly J., Karen E. Campbell, Ellen M. Granberg, and Christine Mowery. 2001. "How movements win: Gendered opportunity structures and U.S. women's suffrage movements, 1866–1919." *American Sociological Review* 66 (1): 49–70.

McCarthy, John D. and Mayer N. Zald. 1977. "Resource mobilization and social movements: A partial theory." *American Journal of Sociology* 82 (6): 1212–41.

McClelland, Charles E. 1991. *The German Experience of Professionalization: Modern Learned Professions and their Organization from the Early Nineteenth Century to the Hitler Era*. Cambridge: Cambridge University Press.

McDonald, Steve. 2011. "What's in the 'old boys' network? Accessing social capital in gendered and racialized networks." *Social Networks* 33 (4): 317–30.

McFarland, Daniel A., Kevin Lewis, and Amir Goldberg. 2016. "Sociology in the era of big data: The ascent of forensic social science." *American Sociologist* 47 (1): 12–35.

McFayden, M. Ann, Matthew Semadeni, and Albert A. Cannella Jr. 2009. "The value of strong ties disconnected to others: Examining knowledge creation in biomedicine." *Organization Science* 20 (3): 552–64.

McGinn, Kathleen L. and Katherine L. Milkman. 2013. "Looking up and looking out: Career mobility effects of demographic similarity among professionals." *Organization Science* 24 (4): 1041–60.

McGuire, Gail M. 2000. "Gender, race, ethnicity, and networks: The factors affecting the status of employees' network members." *Work and Occupations* 27 (4): 501–23.

McKendrick, David G. and James B. Wade. 2010. "Frequent incremental change, organizational size, and mortality in high-technology competition." *Industrial and Corporate Change* 19 (3): 613–39.

McKendrick, Neil M., John Brewer, and J. H. Plumb. 1982. *The Birth of a Consumer Society: The Commercialization of Eighteenth-Century England*. Bloomington, IN: Indiana University Press.

McKenzie, Roderick D. 1926. "The scope of human ecology." *The American Journal of Sociology* 32 (1): 141–54.

McPherson, Chad Michael and Michael Sauder. 2013. "Logics in action: Managing institutional complexity in a drug court." *Administrative Science Quarterly* 58 (2): 165–96.

McPherson, J. Miller. 1983. "An ecology of affiliation." *American Sociological Review* 48 (4): 519–32.

McPherson, J. Miller and James R. Ranger-Moore. 1991. "Evolution on a dancing landscape: Organizations and networks in dynamic Blau space." *Social Forces* 70 (1): 19–42.

McPherson, J. Miller, Lynn Smith-Lovin, and James M. Cook. 2001. "Birds of a feather: Homophily in social networks." *Annual Review of Sociology* 27: 415–44.

Mead, George Herbert. 1934. *Mind, Self, and Society from the Standpoint of a Social Behaviorist*, ed. and with an introduction by Charles W. Morris. Chicago: University of Chicago Press.

Mechanic, David. 1962. "Sources of power of lower participants in complex organizations." *Administrative Science Quarterly* 7 (3): 349–64.

Mehra, Ajay, Martin Kilduff, and Daniel J. Brass. 2001. "The social networks of high and low self-monitors: Implications for workplace performance." *Administrative Science Quarterly* 46 (1): 121–46.

Mercer, Helen. 1995. *Constructing a Competitive Order: The Hidden History of British Antitrust Policies*. Cambridge: Cambridge University Press.

Merluzzi, Jennifer and Adina D. Sterling. 2017. "Lasting effects? Referrals and career mobility of demographic groups in organizations." *Industrial and Labor Relations Review* 70 (1): 105–31.

Merton, Robert K. 1936. "The unanticipated consequences of purposive social action." *American Sociological Review* 1 (6): 894–904.

Merton, Robert K. 1940. "Bureaucratic structure and personality." *Social Forces* 18 (4): 560–68.

Merton, Robert K. 1968. *Social Theory and Social Structure*. Enlarged edn. New York: Free Press.

Meyer, John W. 1977. "The effects of education as an institution." *American Journal of Sociology* 83 (1): 53–77.

Meyer, John W., John Boli, George M. Thomas, and Francisco O. Ramirez. 1997. "World society and the nation-state." *American Journal of Sociology* 103 (1): 144–81.

Meyer, John W., and Brian Rowan. 1977. "Institutionalized organizations: Formal structure as myth and ceremony." *American Journal of Sociology* 83 (2): 340–63.

Mezias, John M. and Stephen J. Mezias. 2000. "Resource partitioning, the founding of specialist firms, and innovation: The American feature film industry, 1912–1929." *Organization Science* 11 (3): 306–22.

Michels, Robert. (1915) 1958. *Political Parties: A Sociological Study of the Oligarchical Tendencies of Modern Democracy*, trans. Eden Paul and Cedar Paul. Glencoe, IL: Free Press.

Milgram, Stanley. 1967. "The small world problem." *Psychology Today* 2: 60–67.

Mills, C. Wright. 1956. *The Power Elite*. London: Oxford University Press.

Mills, C. Wright. 1959. *The Sociological Imagination*. London: Oxford University Press.

Miner, Anne S. 1990. "Structural evolution through idiosyncratic jobs: The potential for unplanned learning." *Organization Science* 1 (2): 195–210.

Miner, Anne S. and Pamela R. Haunschild. 1996. "Population-level learning." *Research in Organizational Behavior* 17: 115–67.

Minkoff, Debra C. 1999. "Bending with the wind: Strategic change and adaptation by women's and racial minority organizations." *American Journal of Sociology* 104 (6): 1666–703.

Mintz, Steven. 1995. *Moralists and Modernizers: America's Pre–Civil War Reformers*. Baltimore: Johns Hopkins University Press.

Mintz, Beth and Michael Schwartz. 1985. *The Power Structure of American Business*. Chicago: University of Chicago Press.

Mishel, Lawrence and Josh Bivens. 2021. "Identifying policy levers generating wage suppression and wage inequality." Working paper, Economic Policy Institute.

Mizruchi, Mark S. 1982. *The American Corporate Network, 1904–1974*. Beverly Hills, CA: Sage.

Mizruchi, Mark S. 1992. *The Structure of Corporate Political Action: Interfirm Relations and their Consequences*. Cambridge, MA: Harvard University Press.

Mizruchi, Mark S. 1996. "What do interlocks do? An analysis, critique, and assessment of research on interlocking directorates." *Annual Review of Sociology* 22: 271–98.

Mizruchi, Mark S. 2013. *The Fracturing of the American Corporate Elite*. Cambridge, MA: Harvard University Press.

Mizruchi, Mark S. and Lisa C. Fein. 1999. "The social construction of organizational knowledge: A study of the uses of coercive, mimetic, and normative isomorphism." *Administrative Science Quarterly* 44 (4): 653–83.

Mizruchi, Mark S. and Linda Brewster Stearns. 1988. "A longitudinal study of the formation of interlocking directorates." *Administrative Science Quarterly* 33 (2): 194–210.

Mizruchi, Mark S. and Linda Brewster Stearns. 2001. "Getting deals done: The use of social networks in bank decision-making." *American Sociological Review* 66 (5): 647–71.

Mobasseri, Sanaz. 2019. "Race, place, and crime: How violent crime events affect employer discrimination." *American Journal of Sociology* 125 (1): 63–104.

Moen, Phyllis, Erin L. Kelly, Wen Fan, Shi-Rong Lee, David Almeida, Ellen Ernst Kossek, and Orfeu M. Buxton. 2016. "Does a flexibility/support organizational initiative improve high-tech employees' well-being? Evidence from the work, family, and health network." *American Sociological Review* 81 (1): 134–64.

Mohr, John W. 1998. "Measuring meaning structures." *Annual Review of Sociology* 24: 345–70.

Mohr, John W. and Vincent Duquenne. 1997. "The duality of culture and practice: Poverty relief in New York City, 1888–1917." *Theory and Society* 26 (2–3): 305–56.

Mollat, Michel. 1986. *The Poor in the Middle Ages: An Essay in Social History*. New Haven, CT: Yale University Press.

Moody, James. 2004. "The structure of a social science collaboration network: Disciplinary cohesion from 1963 to 1999." *American Sociological Review* 69 (2): 213–38.

Moody, James and Douglas R. White. 2003. "Structural cohesion and embeddedness: A hierarchical concept of social groups." *American Sociological Review* 68 (1): 103–27.

Moody, J. Carroll and Gilbert C. Fite. 1984. *The Credit Union Movement: Origins and Development 1850 to 1980.* Dubuque, IA: Kendall/Hunt Publishing Co.

Mora, G. Cristina. 2014. *Making Hispanics: How Activists, Bureaucrats, and Media Constructed a New American.* Chicago: University of Chicago Press.

Moreno, Jacob L. 1932. *Application of the Group Method to Classification.* New York: National Committee on Prisons and Prison Labor.

Moreno, Jacob L. 1934. *Who Shall Survive?* Washington, DC: Nervous and Mental Disease Publishing Company.

Morrill, Calvin. 1991. "Conflict management, honor, and organizational change." *American Journal of Sociology* 97 (3): 585–621.

Morris, Aldon D. 1984. *The Origins of the Civil Rights Movement: Black Communities Organizing for Change.* New York: Free Press.

Morris, R. J. 1983. "Voluntary societies and British urban elites, 1780–1985: An analysis." *Historical Journal* 26 (1): 95–118.

Morton, Graeme, Boudien de Vries, and R. J. Morris. 2006. *Civil Society, Associations, and Urban Places: Class, Nation and Culture in Nineteenth Century Europe.* Aldershot: Ashgate.

Mouw, Ted. 2003. "Social capital and finding a job: Do contacts matter?" *American Sociological Review* 68 (6): 868–98.

Mueller, Charles W., Ashley Finley, Roderick D. Iverson, and James L. Price. 1999. "The effects of group racial composition on job satisfaction." *Work and Occupations* 26 (2): 187–219.

Mun, Eunmi. 2016. "Negative compliance as an organizational response to legal pressure: The case of Japanese equal employment opportunity." *Social Forces* 94 (4): 1409–37.

Munir, Kamal, Muhammad Ayaz, David L. Levy, and Hugh Willmott. 2018. "The role of global intermediaries in governance of global production networks: Restructuring work relations in Pakistan's apparel industry." *Human Relations* 71 (4): 560–83.

Muñoz, John, Susan Olzak, and Sarah A. Soule. 2018. "Going green: Environmental protest, policy, and CO_2 emissions in U.S. states, 1990–2007." *Sociological Forum* 33 (2): 403–21.

Murphy, Antoin. 2005. "Corporate ownership in France: The importance of history." In *The History of Corporate Governance around the World,* ed. Randall K. Morck, 185–222. Chicago: University of Chicago Press.

Murphy, Brendan. 1993. "A profile of financier George Soros." *The Atlantic,* July.

Murray, Joshua. 2017. "Interlock globally, act domestically: Corporate political unity in the 21st century." *American Journal of Sociology* 122 (6): 1617–23.

Musselin, Christine. 2001. *The Long March of French Universities.* New York: Routledge.

Nadel, Siegfried F. 1957. *The Theory of Social Structure.* Glencoe, IL: Free Press.

National Science Foundation. n.d. *NSF and the Birth of the Internet:* Illustrations: "Maps of Internet Growth 1960s through 1990s," https://nsf.gov/news/special_reports/nsf-net/resources.jsp (viewed April 2, 2022).

Negro, Giacomo, Özgecan Koçak, and Greta Hsu. 2010. "Research on categories in the sociology of organizations." In *Categories in Markets: Origins and Evolution* (Research in the Sociology of Organizations 31), ed. Greta Hsu, Giacomo Negro, and Özgecan Koçak, 3–35. Bingley: Emerald Publishing Limited.

Negro, Giacomo, Fabiana Visentin, and Anand Swaminathan. 2014. "Resource partitioning and the organizational dynamics of 'fringe banking.'" *American Sociological Review* 79 (5): 680–704.

Nelson, Jennifer L. 2019. "How organizational minorities form and use social ties: Evidence from teachers in majority-white and majority-black schools." *American Journal of Sociology* 125 (2): 382–430.

Nelson, Laura K. 2020. "Computational grounded theory." *Sociological Methods and Research* 49 (1): 3–42.

Nelson, Richard R. and Sidney G. Winter. 1982. *An Evolutionary Theory of Economic Change.* Cambridge, MA: Belknap Press of Harvard University Press.

Neufeld, Michael J. 1986. "German artisans and political repression: The fall of journeymen's associations in Nuremberg, 1806–1868." *Journal of Social History* 19 (3): 491–502.

Newman, Mark. 2018. *Networks.* 2nd edn. New York: Oxford University Press.

Ng, Weiyi and Eliot L. Sherman. 2021. "In search of inspiration: External mobility and the emergence of technology intrapreneurs." *Organization Science,* https://doi: 10.1287/orsc.2021.1530.

Nolan, Brian and Luis Valenzuela. 2019. "Inequality and its discontents." *Oxford Review of Economic Policy* 35 (3): 396–430.

Norris, Pippa and Max Grömping. 2019. *Electoral Integrity Worldwide.* Sydney: The Electoral Integrity Project.

North, Douglass C. and Robert Paul Thomas. 1973. *The Rise of the Western World: A New Economic History.* New York: Cambridge University Press.

O'Brien, Rourke D. and Zachary Parolin. 2021. "Fiscal regimes and inequality." Working paper, Yale Center for Empirical Research on Stratification and Inequality.

O'Mahony, Siobhán. 2003. "Guarding the commons: How community managed software projects protect their work." *Research Policy* 32 (7): 1179–98.

O'Reilly, Charles A., David F. Caldwell, and William P. Barnett. 1989. "Work group demography, social integration, and turnover." *Administrative Science Quarterly* 34 (1): 21–37.

Obermeyer, Ziad, Brian Powers, Christine Vogeli, and Sendhil Mullainathan. 2019. "Dissecting racial bias in an algorithm used to manage the health of populations." *Science* 366 (6464): 447–53.

Obstfeld, David. 2005. "Social networks, the tertius lungens orientation, and involvement in innovation." *Administrative Science Quarterly* 50 (1): 100–130.

Ody-Brasier, Amandine and Isabel Fernandez-Mateo. 2017. "When being in the minority pays off: Relationships among sellers and price setting in the Champagne industry." *Administrative Science Quarterly* 82 (1): 147–78.

Ody-Brasier, Amandine and Freek Vermeulen. 2014. "The price you pay: Price-setting as a response to norm violation in the market for Champagne grapes." *Administrative Science Quarterly* 59 (1): 109–44.

Okazaki, Tetsuji. 2001. "The role of holding companies in pre-war Japanese economic development: Rethinking *zaibatsu* in perspectives on corporate governance." *Social Science Japan Journal* 4 (2): 243–68.

Oliver, Christine. 1991. "Strategic responses to institutional processes." *Academy of Management Review* 16 (1): 145–79.

Oliver, Christine. 1992. "The antecedents of deinstitutionalization." *Organization Studies* 13 (4): 563–88.

Olzak, Susan. 2016. "The effect of category spanning on the lethality and longevity of terrorist organizations." *Social Forces* 95 (2): 559–84.

Orlikowski, Wanda J. and Susan V. Scott. 2014. "What happens when evaluation goes online? Exploring apparatuses of valuation in the travel sector." *Organization Science* 25 (3): 868–91.

Orme, Nicholas and Margaret Elise Graham Webster. 1995. *The English Hospital 1070–1570*. New Haven, CT: Yale University Press.

Owen-Smith, Jason and Walter W. Powell. 2004. "Knowledge networks as channels and conduits: The effects of spillovers in the Boston biotechnology community." *Organization Science* 15 (1): 5–21.

Padgett, John F. and Christopher K. Ansell. 1993. "Robust action and the rise of the Medici, 1400–1434." *American Journal of Sociology* 98 (6): 1259–319.

Page, Scott E. 2007. *The Difference: How the Power of Diversity Creates Better Groups, Firms, Schools, and Societies*. Princeton, NJ: Princeton University Press.

Pager, Devah. 2003. "The mark of a criminal record." *American Journal of Sociology* 108 (5): 937–75.

Palmer, Donald. 1983. "Broken ties: Interlocking directorates and intercorporate co-ordination." *Administrative Science Quarterly* 28 (1): 40–55.

Park, Robert E. 1936. "Human ecology." *American Journal of Sociology* 42 (1): 1–15.

Parsons, Talcott. 1956. "Suggestions for a sociological approach to the study of organizations." *Administrative Science Quarterly* 1 (1): 63–85.

Pattison, Philippa E. 1982. "The analysis of semigroups of multirelational systems." *Journal of Mathematical Psychology* 25 (2): 87–118.

Payne, P. L. 1967. "The emergence of the large-scale company in Great Britain, 1870–1914." *Economic Journal* 20 (3): 519–42.

Pearce, Jone L. and Qiumei Jane Xu. 2012. "Rating performance or contesting status: Evidence against the homophily explanation for supervisor demographic skew in performance ratings." *Organization Science* 23 (2): 373–85.

Pedulla, David S. 2014. "The positive consequences of negative stereotypes: Race, sexual orientation, and the job application process." *Social Psychology Quarterly* 77 (1): 75–94.

Pedulla, David S. and Sarah Thébaud. 2015. "Can we finish the revolution? Gender, work–family ideals, and institutional constraint." *American Sociological Review* 80 (1): 116–39.

Pei, Minxin. 2016. *China's Crony Capitalism: The Dynamics of Regime Decay*. Cambridge, MA: Harvard University Press.

Peng, Mike W. and Yadong Luo. 2000. "Managerial ties and firm performance in a transition economy: The nature of a micro–macro link." *Academy of Management Journal* 43 (3): 486–501.

Penner, Andrew M. 2008. "Gender differences in extreme mathematical achievement: An international perspective on biological and social factors." *American Journal of Sociology* 114 (supplement): S138–S170.

Pentland, Brian T. and Henry H. Rueter. 1994. "Organizational routines as grammars of action." *Administrative Science Quarterly* 39 (3): 484–510.

Perlow, Leslie A., Jody Hoffer Gittell, and Nancy Katz. 2020. "Contextualizing patterns of work group interaction: Toward a nested theory of structuration." *Organization Science* 15 (5): 520–36.

Pernell-Gallagher, Kim. 2015. "Learning from performance: Banks, collateralized debt obligations, and the credit crisis." *Social Forces* 94 (1): 31–59.

Perrault, Raymond (coordinator), Yoav Shoham, Erik Brynjolfsson, Jack Clark, John Etchemendy, Barbara Grosz, Terah Lyons, James Manyika, and Juan Carlos Niebles, with Saurabh Mishra (project manager). 2019. *The AI Index 2019 Annual Report*, Human-Centered AI Institute, Stanford University, https://hai.stanford.edu/ai-index-2019 (viewed March 31, 2022).

Perrow, Charles. 1961. "The analysis of goals in complex organizations." *American Sociological Review* 26 (6): 854–66.

Perrow, Charles. 1986. *Complex Organizations: A Critical Essay.* 3rd edn. Glenview, IL: Scott Foresman.

Perrow, Charles. 1991. "A society of organizations." *Theory and Society* 20 (6): 725–62.

Perrow, Charles. 1997. "Organizing for environmental destruction." *Organization and Environment* 10 (1): 66–72.

Perrow, Charles. 2002. *Organizing America: Wealth, Power, and the Origins of Corporate Capitalism.* Princeton, NJ: Princeton University Press.

Perry-Smith, Jill E. 2006. "Social yet creative: The role of social relationships in facilitating individual creativity." *Academy of Management Journal* 49 (1): 85–101.

Petersen, Trond and Laurie A. Morgan. 1995. "Separate and unequal: Occupation-establishment sex segregation and the gender wage gap." *American Journal of Sociology* 101 (2): 329–65.

Petersen, Trond, Andrew M. Penner, and Geir Høsgnes. 2014. "From motherhood penalties to fatherhood premia: The new challenge for gender equality and family policy, lessons from Norway." *American Journal of Sociology* 119 (5): 1434–72.

Petersen, Trond, Ishak Saporta, and Marc-David Seidel. 2000. "Offering a job: Meritocracy and social networks." *American Journal of Sociology* 106 (3): 763–816.

Pettigrew, Andrew M. 1979. "On studying organizational cultures." *Administrative Science Quarterly* 24 (4): 570–81.

Pfeffer, Jeffrey. 1972. "Merger as a response to organizational interdependence." *Administrative Science Quarterly* 17 (3): 382–94.

Pfeffer, Jeffrey. 1977. "Toward an examination of stratification in organizations." *Administrative Science Quarterly* 22 (4): 553–67.

Pfeffer, Jeffrey. 1981. *Power in Organizations.* Cambridge, MA: Ballinger.

Pfeffer, Jeffrey. 1982. *Organizations and Organizational Theory.* New York: Pitman.

Pfeffer, Jeffrey. 1983. "Organizational demography." In *Research in Organizational Behavior* 5: 299–357

Pfeffer, Jeffrey. 1993. "Barriers to the advancement of organizational science: Paradigm development as a dependent variable." *Academy of Management Review* 18 (4): 599–620.

Pfeffer, Jeffrey. 1997. *New Directions for Organizational Theory.* New York: Oxford University Press.

Pfeffer, Jeffrey and Alison Davis-Blake. 1987. "The effect of the proportion of women on salaries: The case of college administrators." *Administrative Science Quarterly* 32 (1): 1–24.

Pfeffer, Jeffrey and Gerald R. Salancik. 1978. *The External Control of Organizations: A Resource Dependence Perspective*. New York: Harper & Row.

Phillips, Damon J. 2005. "Organizational genealogies and the persistence of gender inequality: The case of Silicon Valley law firms." *Administrative Science Quarterly* 50 (3): 440–72.

Phillips, Damon J. 2013. *Shaping Jazz: Cities, Labels, and Global Emergence of an Art Form*. Princeton, NJ: Princeton University Press.

Phillips, Damon J. and Ezra W. Zuckerman. 2001. "Middle-status conformity: Theoretical restatement and empirical demonstration in two markets." *American Journal of Sociology* 107 (2): 379–429.

Pierson, Paul. 2004. *Politics in Time: History, Institutions, and Social Analysis*. Princeton, NJ: Princeton University Press.

Piketty, Thomas. 2014. *Capital in the Twenty-First Century*, trans. Arthur Goldhammer. Cambridge, MA: Belknap Press of Harvard University Press.

Pirenne, Henri. (1925) 2014. *Medieval Cities: Their Origins and the Revival of Trade*, trans. Frank D. Halsey, with a new introduction by Michael McCormick. Princeton, NJ: Princeton University Press.

Piskorski, Mikołaj Jan and Andreea Gorbatâi. 2017. "Testing Coleman's social-norm enforcement mechanism: Evidence from Wikipedia." *American Journal of Sociology* 122 (4): 1183–222.

Podolny, Joel M. 1993. "A status-based model of market competition." *American Journal of Sociology* 98 (4): 829–72.

Podolny, Joel M. 2001. "Networks as pipes and prisms of the market." *American Journal of Sociology* 107 (1): 33–60.

Podolny, Joel M. and James N. Baron. 1997. "Resources and relationships: Social networks and mobility in the workplace." *American Sociological Review* 62 (5): 673–93.

Podolny, Joel M. and Toby E. Stuart. 1995. "A role-based ecology of technological change." *American Journal of Sociology* 100 (5): 1224–60.

Poggi, Gianfranco. 1978. *The Development of the Modern State*. Palo Alto, CA: Stanford University Press.

Polanyi, Karl. 1944. *The Great Transformation: The Political and Economic Origins of Our Time*. Boston, MA: Beacon Press.

Porac, Joseph F., Howard Thomas, and Charles Baden-Fuller. 1989. "Competitive groups as cognitive communities: The case of Scottish knitwear manufacturers." *Journal of Management Studies* 26 (4): 397–416.

Portes, Alejandro. 1998. "Social capital: Its origins and applications in modern sociology." *Annual Review of Sociology* 24: 1–24.

Portes, Alejandro and Julia Sensenbrenner. 1993. "Embeddedness and immigration: Notes on the social determinants of economic action." *American Journal of Sociology* 98 (6): 1320–50.

Posen, Hart E., Thomas Keil, Sangyun Kim, and Felix D. Meissner. 2018. "Renewing research on problemistic search: A review and research agenda." *Academy of Management Annals* 12 (1): 208–51.

Powell, Walter W. 1985. *Getting into Print: The Decision-Making Process in Scholarly Publishing*. Chicago: University of Chicago Press.

Powell, Walter W., Aaron Horvath, and Christof Brandtner. 2016. "Click and mortar: Organizations on the web." *Research in Organizational Behavior* 36: 101–20.

Powell, Walter W., Kenneth W. Koput, and Laurel Smith-Doerr. 1996. "Interorganizational collaboration and the locus of innovation: Networks of learning in biotechnology." *Administrative Science Quarterly* 41 (1): 116–45.

Prasad, Vinay. 2015. "The folly of big science awards." *The New York Times*, October 4.

Prechel, Harland. 2000. *Big Business and the State: Historical Transitions and Corporate Transformations, 1880s-1990s*. Albany, NY: State University of New York Press

Prechel, Harland and Lu Zheng. 2012. "Corporate characteristics, political embeddedness, and environmental pollution by large U.S. corporations." *Social Forces* 90 (3): 947–70.

Price, Seymour J. 1958. *Building Societies: Their Origins and History*. London: Franey & Co.

Provan, Keith G. and Juliann G. Sebastian. 1998. "Networks within networks: Service link overlap, organizational cliques, and network effectiveness." *Academy of Management Journal* 41 (4): 453–63.

Pugh, Derek S., David J. Hickson, and C. Robin Hinings. 1969. "An empirical taxonomy of structures of work organizations." *Administrative Science Quarterly* 14 (1): 115–26.

Pugh, Derek S., David J. Hickson, C. Robin Hinings, and C. Turner. 1968. "Dimensions of organizational structure." *Administrative Science Quarterly* 13 (1): 65–105.

Pure Earth. 2016. *2016 World's Worst Pollution Problems*. New York: Pure Earth.

Rafaeli, Anat and Michael G. Pratt. 1993. "Tailored meanings: A look at dress." *Academy of Management Review* 18 (1): 32–55.

Randel, Amy E. and P. Christopher Earley. 2009. "Organizational culture and similarity among team members' salience of multiple diversity characteristics." *Journal of Applied Psychology* 39 (4): 804–33.

Ranganathan, Aruna and Alan Benson. 2020. "A numbers game: Quantification of work, autogamification, and worker productivity." *American Sociological Review* 85 (4): 573–609.

Rao, Hayagreeva. 1998. "Caveat emptor: The construction of non-profit consumer watchdog organizations." *American Journal of Sociology* 103 (4): 912–61.

Rao, Hayagreeva, Philippe Monin, and Rodolphe Durand. 2003. "Institutional change in Tocque Ville: Nouvelle cuisine as an identity movement in French gastronomy." *American Journal of Sociology* 108 (4): 795–843.

Rao, Hayagreeva, Philippe Monin, and Rodolphe Durand. 2005. "Border crossing: Bricolage and the erosion of categorical boundaries in French gastronomy." *American Sociological Review* 70 (6): 968–91.

Raymond, Eric S. 2001. *The Cathedral and the Bazaar: Musings on Open Source by an Accidental Revolutionary*. Sebastopol, CA: O'Reilly Media.

Raynard, Mia, Fangmei Lu, and Runtian Jing. 2019. "Reinventing the state-owned enterprise? Negotiating change during profound environmental upheaval." *Academy of Management Journal* 63 (4): 1300–1335.

Reagans, Ray. 2005. "Preferences, identity, and competition: Predicting tie strength from demographic data." *Management Science* 51 (9): 1374–83.

Reagans, Ray. 2011. "Close encounters: Analyzing how social similarity and propinquity contribute to strong network connections." *Organization Science* 22 (4): 835–49.

Reagans, Ray and Bill McEvily. 2003. "Network structure and knowledge transfer: The effects of cohesion and range." *Administrative Science Quarterly* 48 (2): 240–67.

Reagans, Ray E., Ezra W. Zuckerman, and Bill McEvily. 2004. "How to make the team: Social networks vs. demography as criteria for designing effective projects in a contract R&D firm." *Administrative Science Quarterly* 49 (1): 101–33.

Reardon, Sean F. 2016. "School segregation and racial achievement gaps." *RSF: The Russell Sage Journal of the Social Sciences* 2 (5): 34–57.

Reed, Mike. 2009. "Bureaucratic theory and intellectual renewal in contemporary organization studies." In *The Oxford Handbook of Sociology and Organization Studies: Classical Foundations*, ed. Paul S. Adler, 559–84. Oxford: Oxford University Press.

Ren, Hong, Barbara Gray, and David A. Harrison. 2015. "Triggering faultline effects in teams: The importance of bridging friendship ties and breaching animosity ties." *Organization Science* 26 (2): 390–404.

Rendall, Jane. 1984. *The Origins of Modern Feminism: Women in Britain, France, and the United States, 1780–1860*. New York: Schocken.

Reskin, Barbara F. and Debra Branch McBrier. 2000. "Why not ascription? Organizations' employment of male and female managers." *American Sociological Review* 65 (2): 210–33.

Reynolds, Susan. 1994. *Fiefs and Vassals: The Medieval Evidence Reinterpreted*. Oxford: Oxford University Press.

Rex, Simon. 2017. *The History of Building Societies*. Building Society Association, https://www.bsa.org.uk/information/consumer-factsheets/general/the-history-of-building-societies (viewed March 31, 2022).

Riaz, Suhaib. 2015. "Bringing inequality back in: The economic inequality footprint of management and organizational practices." *Human Relations* 68 (7): 1085–97.

Rider, Christopher I. 2012. "How employees' prior affiliations constrain organizational network change: A study of U.S. venture capital and private equity." *Administrative Science Quarterly* 57 (3): 453–83.

Rider, Christopher I. and David Tan. 2014. "Labor market advantages of organizational status: A study of lateral partner hiring by large U.S. law firms." *Organization Science* 26 (2): 356–72.

Ridgeway, Cecilia. 1991. "The social construction of status value: Gender and other nominal characteristics." *Social Forces* 70 (2): 367–86.

Ridgeway, Cecilia, Elizabeth Boyle, Kathy Kuipers, and Dawn Robinson. 1998. "How do status beliefs develop? The role of resources and interaction." *American Sociological Review* 63 (3): 331–50.

Risse, Guenter B. 1999. *Mending Bodies, Saving Souls: A History of Hospitals*. New York: Oxford University Press.

Rivera, Lauren A. 2012. "Hiring as cultural matching: The case of elite professional service firms." *American Sociological Review* 77 (6): 999–1022.

Rivera, Lauren A. 2017. "When two bodies are (not) a problem: Gender and relationship status discrimination in academic hiring." *American Sociological Review* 82 (6): 1111–38.

Roberts, Margaret E., Brandon M. Stewart, and Edoardo M. Airoldi. 2016. "A model of text for experimentation in the social sciences." *Journal of the American Statistical Association* 111 (515): 988–1003.

Roberts, M.J.D. 2004. *Making English Morals: Voluntary Association and Moral Reform in England, 1767–1886*. Cambridge: Cambridge University Press.

Robinson, W. S. 1950. Ecological correlations and the behavior of individuals. *American Sociological Review* 15 (3): 351–57.

Roethlisberger, Fritz Jules and W. J. Dickson. 1939 (with Harold A. Wright and Carl Pforzheimer). *Management and the Worker: An Account of a Research Program Conducted by the Western Electric Company, Hawthorne Works, Chicago*. Cambridge, MA: Harvard University Press.

Rogan, Michelle. 2014. "Executive losses without client departures: The role of multiplex ties in exchange partner retention." *Academy of Management Journal* 57 (2): 563–84.

Rombach, Puck, Mason A. Porter, James H. Fowler, and Peter J. Mucha. 2017. "Core–periphery structures in networks (revised)." *SIAM Review* 59 (3): 619–46.

Rosch, Eleanor H. 1973. "Natural categories." *Cognitive Psychology* 4 (3): 328–50.

Rosch, Eleanor H. 1975. "Cognitive representations of semantic categories." *Journal of Experimental Psychology: General* 104 (3): 192–233.

Rosenberg, Hans. 1958. *Bureaucracy, Aristocracy, and Autocracy: The Prussian Experience, 1660–1815*. Cambridge, MA: Harvard University Press.

Rosenberg, Nathan and L. E. Birdzell Jr. 1986. *How the West Grew Rich: The Economic Transformation of the Industrial World*. New York: Basic Books.

Roth, Louise Marie. 2004. "The social psychology of tokenism: Status and homophily processes on Wall Street." *Sociological Perspectives* 47 (2): 189–214.

Roy, Donald. 1952. "Quota restriction and goldbricking in a machine shop." *American Journal of Sociology* 57 (5): 427–42.

Roy, William G. 1997. *Socializing Capital: The Rise of the Large Industrial Corporation in America*. Princeton, NJ: Princeton University Press.

Rudin, Cynthia. 2019. "Stop explaining black box models for high stakes decisions and use interpretable models instead." *Nature Machine Intelligence* 1 (5): 206–15.

Ruef, Martin. 1999. Social ontology and the dynamics of organizational forms: Creating market actors in the healthcare field, 1966–1994. *Social Forces* 77 (4): 1403–32.

Ruef, Martin and Kelly Patterson. 2009. "Credit and classification: The impact of industry boundaries in nineteenth-century America." *Administrative Science Quarterly* 54 (3): 486–520.

Ryder, Norman B. 1965. "The cohort as a concept in the study of social change." *American Sociological Review* 30 (6): 843–61.

Sailer, Lee Douglas. 1978. "Structural equivalence: Meaning and definition, computation and application." *Social Networks* 1 (1): 73–90.

Sailer, Kerstin and Ian McCulloh. 2012. "Social networks and spatial configuration: How office layouts drive social interaction." *Social Networks* 34 (1): 47–58.

Salzinger Leslie. 2001. *Genders in Production: Making Workers in Mexico's Global Factories*. Berkeley, CA: University of California Press.

Sampson, Anthony. 1995. *Company Man: The Rise and Fall of Corporate Life*. New York: Times Business.

Saxenian, Annalee. 1994. *Regional Advantage: Culture and Competition in Silicon Valley and Route 128*. Cambridge, MA: Harvard University Press.

Schalk, Ruben. 2019. "Apprenticeships with and without guilds: The northern Netherlands." In *Apprenticeship in Early Modern Europe*, ed. Maarten Prak and Patrick Wallis, 187–216. Cambridge: Cambridge University Press.

Schein, Edgar H. 1996. "Culture: The missing concept in organization studies." *Administrative Science Quarterly* 41 (2): 229–40.

Schilling, Melissa A. and Corey C. Phelps. 2007. "Interfirm collaboration networks: The impact of large-scale network structure on firm innovation." *Organization Science* 53 (7): 1113–26.

Schlesinger, Arthur M. 1944. "Biography of a nation of joiners." *American Historical Review* 50 (1): 15–16.

Schmiedel, Theresa, Oliver Müller, and Jan vom Brocke. 2019. "Topic modeling as a strategy of inquiry in organizational research: A tutorial with an application example on organizational culture." *Organizational Research Methods* 22 (4): 941–68.

Schmitter, Phillippe C. and Wolfgang Streeck. 1999. *The Organization of Business Interests.* Cologne: Max Planck Institute for the Study of Societies.

Schneiberg, Marc and Elisabeth S. Clemens. 2006. "The typical tools for the job: Research strategies in institutional analysis." *Sociological Theory* 24 (3): 195–227.

Schneiberg, Marc, Marissa D. King, and Thomas Smith. 2008. "Social movements and organizational form: Cooperative alternatives to corporations in the American insurance, dairy, and grain industries." *American Sociological Review* 73 (4): 635–67.

Schneider, Daniel and Kristen Harknett. 2019. "Consequences of routine work-schedule instability for worker health and well-being." *American Sociological Review* 84 (1): 82–114.

Schneider, Daniel and Kristen Harknett. 2022. "What's to like? Facebook as a tool for survey data collection." *Sociological Methods and Research* 51 (1): 108–40.

Schofer, Evan and Ann Hironaka. 2005. "The effects of world society on environmental protection outcomes." *Social Forces* 84 (1): 25–47.

Schoonhoven, Claudia Bird. 1981. "Problems with contingency theory: Testing assumptions hidden within the language of contingency 'theory.'" *Administrative Science Quarterly* 26 (3): 349–77.

Schor, Juliet B. and William Attwood-Charles. 2017. "The 'sharing' economy: Labor, inequality, and social connection on for-profit platforms." *Sociology Compass* 11 (8): e12493.

Schrage, Dan. 2019. "Organizing pollution: Organizational demography, neighborhoods, and racial inequality in exposure to toxic chemicals, 1987–2012." Working paper, University of Southern California.

Schwartz, Michael. 2008. "A postscript to 'Catnets.'" *Sociologica*, May–June, https://www.rivisteweb.it/doi/10.2383/26577 (viewed March 31, 2022).

Scott, John. 1987. "Intercorporate structures in Western Europe: A comparative historical analysis." In *Intercorporate Relations: The Structural Analysis of Business*, ed. Mark S. Mizruchi and Michael Schwartz, 219–32. Cambridge: Cambridge University Press.

Scott, John C. 2006. "The mission of the university: Medieval to modern transitions." *Journal of Higher Education* 77 (1): 1–39.

Scott, W. Richard. 2003. *Organizations: Rational, Natural, and Open Systems.* 6th edn. Upper Saddle River, NJ: Prentice-Hall.

Scott, W. Richard. 2014. *Institutions and Organizations.* 4th edn. Thousand Oaks, CA: Sage.

Scott, W. Richard and Gerald F. Davis. 2007. *Organizations and Organizing: Rational, Natural, and Open Systems Perspectives.* Upper Saddle River, NJ: Prentice-Hall.

Scott, W. Richard, Martin Ruef, Peter J. Mendel, and Carol A. Caronna. 2000. *Institutional Change and Healthcare Organizations: From Professional Dominance to Managed Care.* Chicago: University of Chicago Press.

Scully, Maureen and W. E. Douglas Creed. 1997. "Stealth legitimacy: Employee activism and corporate response during the diffusion of domestic partner benefits." Paper presented at the Academy of Management Meetings, Boston, MA.

Seavoy, Ronald E. 1982. *The Origins of the American Business Corporation, 1784–1855*. Westport, CT: Greenwood Press.

Segal, David. 2011. "Is law school a losing game?" *The New York Times*, January 8: Business Section, 1.Selznick, Philip. 1949. *TVA and the Grassroots*. Berkeley, CA: University of California Press.

Selznick, Philip. 1957. *Leadership in Administration: A Sociological Interpretation*. Berkeley, CA: University of California Press.

Selznick, Philip. 1996. "Institutionalism 'old' and 'new.'" *Administrative Science Quarterly* 41 (2): 270–77.

Sewell, William H., Jr. 1980. *Work and Revolution in France: The Language of Labor from the Old Regime to 1848*. Cambridge: Cambridge University Press.

Sewell, William H., Jr. 1992. "A theory of structure: Duality, agency, and transformation." *American Journal of Sociology* 98 (1): 1–29.

Shearer, Elisa and Katerina Eva Matsa. 2018. "News use across social media platforms 2018." Pew Research Center, September 10, https://www.journalism.org/2018/09/10/news-use-across -social-media-platforms-2018 (viewed March 31, 2022).

Shenhav, Yehouda. 1999. *Manufacturing Rationality: The Engineering Foundations of the Managerial Revolution*. New York: Oxford University Press.

Shenhav, Yehouda and Yitchak Haberfeld. 1992. "Organizational demography and inequality." *Social Forces* 71 (1): 123–43.

Shibagaki, Kazuo. 1966. "The early history of the *zaibatsu*." *The Developing Economies* 4 (4): 535–66.

Shin, Taekjin. 2009. "Earnings inequality within organizations." *Social Science Research* 38 (1): 225–38.

Shore, Jesse, Ethan Bernstein, and David Lazer. 2015. "Facts and figuring: An experimental investigation of network structure and performance in information and solution spaces." *Management Science* 26 (5): 1432–46.

Shryock, Henry S. and Jacob S. Siegel. 1971. *The Methods and Materials of Demography*. Washington, DC: U.S. Bureau of the Census.

Siggelkow, Nikolaj. 2002. "Evolution toward fit." *Administrative Science Quarterly* 47 (1): 125–59.

Sills, David L. 1957. *The Volunteers: Means and Ends in a National Organization*. Glencoe, IL: Free Press.

Silva, Fabiana. 2018. "The strength of whites' ties: How employers reward the referrals of black and white jobseekers." *Social Forces* 97 (2): 741–68.

Simmel, Georg. 1950. *The Sociology of Georg Simmel*, trans. and ed. Kurt H. Wolff. New York: Free Press.

Simmel, Georg. 1955. *Conflict and the Web of Group-Affiliations*, trans. Kurt H. Wolff and Reinhard Bendix. New York: Free Press.

Simon, Herbert A. (1947) 1976. *Administrative Behavior: A Study of Decision-Making Processes in Administrative Organization*. 3rd edn. New York: Free Press.

Simon, Herbert A. 1955. "A behavioral model of rational choice." *Quarterly Journal of Economics* 69 (1): 99–118.

Simons, Tal, Patrick A. M. Vermeulen, and Joris Knoben. 2016. "There's no beer without a smoke: Community cohesion and neighboring communities' effects on organizational resistance to antismoking regulations in the Dutch hospitality industry." *Academy of Management Journal* 59 (2): 545–78.

Sine, Wesley D., Heather A. Haveman, and Pamela S. Tolbert. 2005. "Risky business? Entrepreneurship in the new independent-power sector." *Administrative Science Quarterly* 50 (2): 200–232.

Sine, Wesley D. and Brandon H. Lee. 2009. "Tilting at windmills? The environmental movement and the emergence of the U.S. wind energy sector." *Administrative Science Quarterly* 54 (1): 123–55.

Skaggs, Sheryl. 2008. "Producing change or bagging opportunity? The effects of discrimination litigation on female representation in supermarket management." *American Journal of Sociology* 113 (4): 1148–82.

Skocpol, Theda. 1997. "The Tocqueville problem: Civic engagement in American democracy." *Social Science History* 21 (4): 455–79.

Skocpol, Theda, Marjorie Abend-Wein, Christopher Howard, and Susan Goodrich Lehmann. 1993. "Women's associations and the enactment of women's pensions in the United States." *American Political Science Review* 87 (3): 686–701.

Skocpol, Theda, Marshall Ganz, and Ziad Munson. 2000. "A nation of organizers: The institutional origins of civic voluntarism in the United States." *American Political Science Review* 94 (3): 527–46.

Skowronek, Stephen. 1982. *Building a New American State: The Expansion of National Administrative Capacities, 1877–1920.* Cambridge: Cambridge University Press.

Sloan, Alfred P., Jr. 1963. *My Years with General Motors.* Garden City, NY: Anchor Books.

Smircich, Linda. 1983. "Concepts of culture and organizational analysis." *Administrative Science Quarterly* 28 (3): 339–58.

Smith, Adam. (1776) 1981. *An Inquiry into the Nature and Causes of the Wealth of Nations*, vols 1 & 2, ed. R. H. Campbell and A. S. Skinner (gen. eds); W. B. Todd (text ed.). Indianapolis: Liberty Prints.

Smith, Edward E., Edward J. Shoben, and Lance J. Rips. 1974. "Structure and process in semantic memory: A featural model for semantic decisions." *Psychological Review* 81 (3): 214–41.

Smith, Ken G., Ken A. Smith, Judy D. Olian, Henry P. Sims Jr., Douglas P. O'Bannon, and Judith A. Scully. 1994. "Top management team demography and process: The role of social integration and communication." *Administrative Science Quarterly* 39 (3): 412–38.

Smith, S. D. 2005. "Women's admission to guilds in early-modern England: The case of the York merchant tailors' company, 1693–1776." *Gender and History* 17 (1): 99–126.

Smith, Sandra S. 2005. "'Don't put my name on it': Social capital activation and job-finding assistance among the black urban poor." *American Journal of Sociology* 111 (1): 1–57.

Snijders, Tom A. B. 2001. "The statistical evaluation of social network dynamics." *Sociological Methodology* 31 (1): 361–95.

Snijders, Tom A. B. 2017. "Stochastic actor-oriented models for network dynamics." *Annual Review of Statistics and Its Application* 4: 343–63.

Snow, David A., E. Burke Rochford, Steven K. Worden, and Robert D. Benford. 1986. "Frame alignment processes, micromobilization, and movement participation." *American Sociological Review* 51 (4): 464–81.

Soener, Matthew and Michael Nau. 2019. "Citadels of privilege: The rise of LLCs, LPs and the perpetuation of elite power in America." *Economy and Society* 48 (3): 399–425.

Solal, Isabelle and Kaisa Snellman. 2019. "Women don't mean business? Gender penalty in board composition." *Organization Science* 30 (6): 1270–88.

Sørensen, Jesper B. 2002. "The strength of corporate culture and the reliability of firm performance." *Administrative Science Quarterly* 47 (1): 70–91.

Sørensen, Jesper B. 2004. "Recruitment-based competition between industries: A community ecology." *Industrial and Corporate Change* 13 (1): 149–70.

Sørensen, Jesper B. and Olav Sorenson. 2007. Corporate demography and income inequality. *American Sociological Review* 72 (5): 766–783.

Sorenson, Olav, Valentina Assenova, Guan-Cheng Li, Jason Boada, and Lee Fleming. 2016. "Expand innovation finance via crowdfunding." *Science* 354 (639): 1526–28.

Sorenson, Olav and Michelle Rogan. 2014. "(When) do organizations have social capital?" *Annual Review of Sociology* 40: 261–80.

Soule, Sarah A. and Susan Olzak. 2004. "When do social movements matter? The politics of contingency and the Equal Rights Amendment." *American Sociological Review* 69 (4): 473–97.

South, Scott J., Charles M. Bonjean, William T. Markham, and Judy Corder. 1982. "Social structure and intergroup interaction: Men and women of the federal bureaucracy." *American Sociological Review* 47 (5): 587–99.

Srivastava, Sameer B. 2015. "Network intervention: Assessing the effects of formal mentoring on workplace networks." *Social Forces* 94 (1): 427–52.

Stainback, Kevin, Thomas N. Ratliff, and Vincent J. Roscigno. 2011. "The context of workplace sex discrimination: Sex composition, workplace culture, and relative power." *Social Forces* 89 (4): 1165–88.

Stainback, Kevin and Donald Tomaskovic-Devey. 2009. "Intersections of power and privilege: Long-term trends in managerial representation." *American Sociological Review* 74 (5): 800–820.

Starkey, Ken. 1992. "Durkheim and organizational analysis: Two legacies." *Organizational Studies* 13 (4): 627–42.

Steidley, Trent. 2018. "Big guns or big talk? How the National Rifle Association matters for conceal carry weapons laws." *Mobilization* 23 (1): 101–25.

Steil, Justin Peter and Ion Bogdan Vasi. 2014. "The new immigration contestation: Social movements and local immigration policy making in the United States, 2000–2011." *American Journal of Sociology* 119 (4): 1104–55.

Sterling, Adina D. 2015. "Preentry contacts and the generation of nascent networks in organizations." *Organization Science* 26 (3): 650–67.

Stern, Robert N. and Stephen R. Barley. 1996. "Organizations and social systems: Organizational theory's neglected mandate." *Administrative Science Quarterly* 41 (1): 146–52.

Stewart, Matthew. 2006. "The management myth." *The Atlantic*, June.

Still, Mary C. and David Strang. 2009. "Who does an elite organization emulate?" *Administrative Science Quarterly* 54 (1): 58–89.

Stinchcombe, Arthur L. 1959. "Bureaucratic and craft administration of production: A comparative study." *Administrative Science Quarterly* 4 (2): 168–87.

Stinchcombe, Arthur L. 1965. "Social structure and organizations." In *Handbook of Organizations*, ed. J. March, 142–93. Chicago: Rand-McNally.

Stinchcombe, Arthur L. 1968. *Constructing Social Theories*. Chicago: University of Chicago Press.

Stogdill, R. M. 1948. "Personal factors associated with leadership." *Journal of Psychology* 25 (1): 35–71.

Stokman, Frans N., Rolf Ziegler, and John Scott, eds. 1985. *Networks of Corporate Power: A Comparative Analysis of Ten Countries*. London: Polity Press.

Stolzenberg, Ross M. 1975. "Occupations, labor markets, and the process of wage attainment." *American Sociological Review* 40 (5): 645–65.

Stolzenberg, Ross M. 1978. "Bringing the boss back in: Employer size, employee schooling, and socioeconomic achievement." *American Sociological Review* 43 (6): 813–28.

Stovel, Katherine W. and Michael Savage. 2006. "Mergers and mobility: Organizational growth and the origins of career migration at Lloyds Bank." *American Journal of Sociology* 111 (4): 1080–121.

Stovel, Katherine W. and Lynette Shaw. 2012. "Brokerage." *Annual Review of Sociology* 38: 139–58.

Strang, David and John W. Meyer. 1993. "Institutional conditions for diffusion." *Theory and Society* 22 (4): 487–511.

Strang, David and Mary C. Still. 2004. "In search of the élite: Revising a model of adaptive emulation with evidence from benchmarking teams." *Industrial and Corporate Change* 13 (2): 309–33.

Strang, David and Nancy Brandon Tuma. 1993. "Spatial and temporal heterogeneity in diffusion." *American Journal of Sociology* 99: 614–39.

Strayer, Joseph R. (1970) 2005. *On the Medieval Origins of the Modern State*. Princeton, NJ: Princeton University Press.

Stuart, Toby E., Ha Hoang, and Ralph C. Hybels. 1999. "Interorganizational endorsements and the performance of entrepreneurial ventures." *Administrative Science Quarterly* 44 (2): 315–49.

Suchman, Mark C. 1995. "Managing legitimacy: Strategic and institutional approaches." *Academy of Management Review* 20 (3): 571–610.

Sutton, Robert I. and Barry M. Staw. 1995. "What a theory is not." *Administrative Science Quarterly* 40 (3): 371–84.

Swidler, Ann. 1986. "Culture in action: Symbols and strategies." *American Sociological Review* 51 (2): 273–86.

Tajfel, Henri. 1982. "Social psychology of intergroup relations." *Annual Review of Psychology* 33: 1–39.

Tajfel, Henri and John C. Turner. 1979. "An integrative theory of intergroup conflict." In *The Social Psychology of Intergroup Relations*, ed. S. Worchel and L. W. Austin, 33–37. Monterey, CA: Brooks/Cole.

Tajfel, Henri and John C. Turner. 1986. "The social identity theory of intergroup behavior." In *Psychology of Intergroup Relations*, ed. S. Worchel and L. W. Austin, 7–24. Chicago: Nelson-Hall.

Talesh, Shauhin A. 2009. "The privatization of public legal rights: How manufacturers construct the meaning of consumer law." *Law and Society Review* 43 (3): 527–61.

Taylor, Frederick Winslow. 1911. *The Principles of Scientific Management*. New York: W. W. Norton & Co.

Taylor, James. 2006. *Creating Capitalism: Joint-Stock Enterprise in British Politics and Culture, 1800–1870.* Haworth, NJ: Woodbridge.

Terkel, Studs. 1972. *Working: People Talk about What They Do All Day and How They Feel about What They Do.* New York: Avon Books.

Thaplyal, Kiran Kumar. 2001. "Guilds in ancient India." In *Life Thoughts and Culture in India*, ed. G. C. Pande, 995–1006. Delhi: Munshiram Manoharlal Publishers Pvt. Ltd.

Thébaud, Sarah and Amanda J. Sharkey. 2016. "Unequal hard times: The influence of the Great Recession on gender bias in entrepreneurial financing." *Sociological Science* 3 (1): 1–31.

Thirsk, Joan. 1978. *Economic Policy and Projects: Development of a Consumer Society in Early Modern England.* Oxford: Clarendon Press.

Thomas, Dana. 2019. *Fashionopolis: The Price of Fast Fashion—and the Future of Clothes.* New York: Penguin Press.

Thomas, David and John J. Gabarro. 1999. *Breaking Through: The Making of Minority Executives in Corporate America.* Boston, MA: Harvard Business School Press.

Thomas, Kyla. 2018. "The labor market value of taste: an experimental study of class bias in U.S. employment." *Sociological Science* 5 (24): 562–97.

Thompson, James D. 1967. *Organizations in Action.* New York: McGraw-Hill.

Thornton, Alex. 2019. "Gender Equality in STEM is possible: These countries prove it." World Economic Forum (blog), https://www.weforum.org/agenda/2019/03/gender-equality-in -stem-is-possible (viewed March 31, 2022).

Thornton, Patricia H. and William Ocasio. 1999. "Institutional logics and the historical contingency of power in organizations: Executive succession in the higher education publishing industry, 1958 to 1990." *American Journal of Sociology* 105 (3): 801–43.

Thornton, Patricia H., William Ocasio, and Michael Lounsbury. 2012. *The Institutional Logics Perspective: A New Approach to Culture, Structure and Process.* Oxford: Oxford University Press.

Tilcsik, András. 2011. "Pride and prejudice: Employment discrimination against openly gay men in the United States." *American Journal of Sociology* 117 (2): 586–626.

Tilly, Charles. 1990. *Coercion, Capital, and European States 1000–1990 AD.* Oxford: Blackwell.

Tilly, Richard H. 1966. *Financial Institutions and Industrialization in the Rhineland, 1815–1870.* Madison, WI: University of Wisconsin Press.

Tocqueville, Alexis de. (1848) 2000. *Democracy in America*, trans. and ed. Harvey C. Mansfield and Delba Winthrop. Chicago: University of Chicago Press.

Tolbert, Pamela S. and Lynne G. Zucker. 1983. "Institutional sources of change in the formal structure of organizations: The diffusion of civil service reform, 1880–1935." *Administrative Science Quarterly* 28 (1): 22–39.

Tolbert, Pamela S. and Lynne G. Zucker. 1996. "The institutionalization of institutional theory." In *Handbook of Organization Studies*, ed. S. Clegg, C. Hardy, and W. Nord, 175–190. Thousand Oaks, CA: Sage.

Tollenaar, Nikolaj and P.G.M. van der Heijden. 2013. "Which method predicts recidivism best? A comparison of statistical, machine learning, and data mining predictive models." *Journal of the Royal Statistical Society*, series A: 2013 (176, Part 2): 565–84.

Tomaskovic-Devey, Donald. 1993. *Gender and Racial Inequality at Work: The Sources and Consequences of Job Segregation.* Ithaca, NY: ILR Press.

Tomaskovic-Devey, Donald and Sheryl Skaggs. 2002. "Sex segregation, labor process organization, and gender earnings inequality." *American Journal of Sociology* 108 (1): 102–28.

Tomaskovic-Devey, Donald, Anthony Rainey, Dustin Avent-Holt, Nina Bandelj, István Boza, David Cort, Olivier Godechot et al. 2020. "Rising between-workplace inequalities in high-income countries." *Proceedings of the National Academy of Science* 117 (17): 9277–83.

Tönnies, Ferdinand. (1887) 1957. *Community and Society*, trans. Charles P. Loomis. New Brunswick, NJ: Transaction Publishers.

Townley, Barbara. 2002. "The role of competing rationalities in institutional change." *Academy of Management Journal* 45 (1): 163–79.

Trasolini, Roberto P. and Michael F. Byrne. 2021. "Accurate measurement of colonic polyps: In the 'AI' of the beholder?" *European Journal of Gastroenterology and Hepatology* 33 (6): 773–74.

Travers, Jeffrey and Stanley Milgram. 1969. "An experimental study of the small-world problem." *Sociometry* 32 (4): 425–43.

Trice, Harrison M. and Janice M. Beyer. 1984. "Studying organizational culture through rites and ceremonies." *Academy of Management Review* 9 (4): 653–69.

Tripsas, Mary. 2009. "Technology, identity, and inertia through the lens of 'The Digital Photography Company.'" *Organization Science* 20 (2): 441–60.

Tsai, Wenpin. 2001. "Knowledge transfer and intraorganizational networks: Effects of network position and absorptive capacity on business unit innovation and performance." *Organization Science* 44 (5): 996–1004.

Tsai, Wenpin. 2002. "Social structure of 'coopetition' within a multiunit organization: Coordination, competition, and intraorganizational knowledge sharing." *Organization Science* 13 (2): 179–90.

Tsui, Anne S., Terri D. Egan, and Charles A. O'Reilly III. 1992. "Being different: Relational demography and organizational attachment." *Administrative Science Quarterly* 37 (4): 549–79.

Turco, Catherine J. 2010. "Cultural foundations of tokenism: Evidence from the leveraged buyout industry." *American Sociological Review* 75 (6): 894–913.

Tversky, Amos and Daniel Kahneman. 1974. "Judgment under uncertainty: Heuristics and biases." *Science* 185 (4157): 1121–31.

Tyler, Alice Felt. 1944. *Freedom's Ferment: Phases of American Social History from the Colonial Period to the Outbreak of the Civil War.* New York: Harper Torchbooks.

University of California, Berkeley. 2019. *UC Berkeley Zero Waste Plan.* Berkeley, CA: University of California.

Urban Institute. 2017. "Nine charts about wealth inequality in America (updated)," https://apps.urban.org/features/wealth-inequality-charts (viewed March 31, 2022).

Useem, Michael. 1984. *The Inner Circle: Large Corporations and the Rise of Business Political Activity in the U.S. and U.K.* New York: Oxford University Press.

U.S. Bureau of Labor Statistics. 2021a. "Labor productivity and costs." Washington, DC: Bureau of Labor Statistics, Labour Costs Annual Series, https://www.bls.gov/lpc/#tables (viewed March 31, 2022).

U.S. Bureau of Labor Statistics. 2021b. "News Release: Union Members—2020." Washington, DC: Bureau of Labor Statistics.

U.S. Census Bureau. 2020. "Population estimates as of July 1, 2019." QuickFacts: United States, https://www.census.gov/quickfacts/fact/table/US/PST045219 (viewed March 31, 2022).

U.S. Census Bureau. 2021. "Quarterly retail e-commerce sales: 4th quarter 2021." U.S. Census Bureau News, https://www.census.gov/retail/mrts/www/data/pdf/ec_current.pdf (viewed March 31, 2022).

U.S. Supreme Court. 1992. *Quill Corp. v. North Dakota*, 504 U.S. 298 1992.

U.S. Supreme Court. 2018. *South Dakota v. Wayfair Inc.*, 585 U.S., ___ 138 S. Ct. 2080 (2018).

Uzzi, Brian. 1996. "The sources and consequences of embeddedness for the economic performance of organizations: The network effect." *American Sociological Review* 61 (4): 674–98.

Uzzi, Brian. 1999. "Embeddedness in the making of financial capital: How social relations and networks benefit firms seeking capital." *American Sociological Review* 64 (4): 481–505.

Uzzi, Brian and Jarrett Spiro. 2005. "Collaboration and creativity: The small world problem." *American Journal of Sociology* 111 (2): 447–504.

Vaisey, Stephen. 2009. "Motivation and justification: A dual-process model of culture in action." *American Journal of Sociology* 114 (6): 1675–715.

Van den Steen, Eric. 2010. "Culture clash: The costs and benefits of homogeneity." *Management Science* 56 (10): 1718–38.

van der Linden, Marcel. 1996. *Social Security Mutualism: The Comparative History of Mutual Benefit Societies*. New York: Peter Lang.

van Dijk, Hans, Marloes L. van Engen, and Daan van Knippenberg. 2011. "Defying conventional wisdom: A meta-analytical examination of the differences between demographic and job-related diversity relationships with performance." *Organizational Behavior and Human Decision Processes* 119 (1): 38–53.

van Knippenberg, Daan and Michaéla Schippers. 2007. "Work group diversity." *Annual Review of Psychology* 58: 515–41.

Van Maanen, John. 1973. "Observations on the making of policeman." *Human Organization* 32 (4): 407–18.

Van Maanen, John. 1991. "The smile factory: Work at Disneyland." In *Reframing Organizational Culture*, ed. Craig C. Lundberg, Joanne Martin, Larry F. Moore, Meryl Reis Louis, and Peter J. Frost, 58–76. Newbury Park, CA: Sage.

Van Maanen, John and Edgar H. Schein. 1979. "Toward of theory of organizational socialization." *Research in Organizational Behavior* 1: 209–64.

Vasi, Ion Bogdan. 2007. "Thinking globally, planning nationally, acting locally: Nested organizational fields and the adoption of environmental practices." *Social Forces* 86 (1): 113–37.

Vasi, Ion Bogdan and Brayden G. King. 2019. "Technology stigma and secondary stakeholder activism: The adoption and growth of clean power programs in the U.S. utility sector." *Socio-Economic Review* 17 (1): 37–61.

Vasi, Ion Bogdan, Edward T. Walker, John S. Johnson, and Hui Fen Ten. 2015. "'No fracking way!' Documentary film, discursive opportunity, and local opposition against hydraulic fracturing in the United States, 2010 to 2013." *American Sociological Review* 80 (5): 934–59.

Vogel, David. 1989. *Fluctuating Fortunes: The Political Power of Business in America*. New York: Basic Books.

von Hippel, Eric. 2005. *Democratizing Innovation*. Cambridge, MA: MIT Press.

von Krogh, Georg, Sebastian Spaeth, and Karim R. Lakhani. 2003. "Community, joining, and specialization in open source software innovation: A case study." *Research Policy* 32 (7): 1217–41.

Voshoughi, Soroush, Deb Roy, and Sinan Aral. 2018. "The spread of true and false news online." *Science* 359 (6380): 1146–51.

Walder, Andrew G. 1992. "Property rights and stratification in socialist redistributive economies." *American Sociological Review* 57 (4): 524–39.

Walder, Andrew G. 1995. "Local governments as industrial firms: An organizational analysis of China's transitional economy." *American Journal of Sociology* 101 (2): 263–301.

Waldrup, Mitchell. 2015. "DARPA and the Internet Revolution." Arlington, VA: US Defense Advanced Research Projects Agency.

Wallace, Jean E. and Fiona M. Kay. 2012. "Tokenism, organizational segregation, and coworker relations in law firms." *Social Problems* 59 (3): 389–410.

Wallerstein, Immanuel. 1974. *The Modern World-System I: Capitalist Agriculture and the Origins of the European World-Economy in the Sixteenth Century*. San Diego, CA: Academic Press.

Wallerstein, Immanuel. 1980. *The Modern World-System II: Mercantilism and the Consolidation of the European World-Economy, 1600–1750*. San Diego, CA: Academic Press.

Wallerstein, Immanuel. 1989. *The Modern World-System III: The Second Era of Great Expansion of the Capitalist World-Economy, 1730–1840s*. San Diego, CA: Academic Press.

Wang, Daniel J. and Sarah A. Soule. 2012. "Social movement organizational collaboration: Networks of learning and the diffusion of protest tactics, 1960–1995." *American Journal of Sociology* 117 (6): 1674–722.

Wasserman, Stanley and Katherine Faust. 1994. *Social Network Analysis: Methods and Applications*. Cambridge: Cambridge University Press.

Watts, Duncan J. 1999. *Small Worlds: The Dynamics of Networks between Order and Randomness*. Princeton, NJ: Princeton University Press.

Watts, Duncan J. and Steven H. Strogatz. 1998. "Collective dynamics of 'small-world' networks." *Nature* 393 (6684): 440–42.

Webb, Sidney and Beatrice Webb. 1920. *The History of Trade Unionism*. Rev. edn (extended to 1920). New York: Longmans, Green, & Co.

Weber, Klaus, Gerald F. Davis, and Michael Lounsbury. 2009. "Policy as myth and ceremony: The global spread of stock exchanges, 1980–2005." *Academy of Management Journal* 52 (6): 1319–47.

Weber, Klaus, Kathryn L. Heinsze, and Michaela DeSoucey. 2008. "Forage for thought: Mobilizing codes in the movement for grass-fed meat and dairy products." *Administrative Science Quarterly* 53 (3): 529–67.

Weber, Max. (1889) 2003. *The History of Commercial Partnerships in the Middle Ages*, trans. and with an introduction by Lutz Kaebler; foreword by Charles Lemert. Lanham, MD: Rowman & Littlefield.

Weber, Max. (1904–5) 1958. *The Protestant Ethic and the Spirit of Capitalism*, trans. Talcott Parsons. New York: Charles Scribners' Sons.

Weber, Max. (1927) 1981. *General Economic History*, trans. Frank H. Knight; with a new introduction by Ira J. Cohen. New Brunswick, NJ: Transaction Publishers.

Weber, Max. 1958. *The City*, trans. and ed. Don Martindale and Gertrud Neuwirth. New York: Free Press.

Weber, Max. (1968) 1978. *Economy and Society: An Outline of Interpretive Sociology*, trans. and ed. Guenther Roth and Claus Wittich. Berkeley, CA: University of California Press.

Weber, Steve. 2004. *The Success of Open Source*. Cambridge, MA: Harvard University Press.

Wedeman, Andrew. 2012. *Double Paradox: Rapid Growth and Rising Corruption in China*. Ithaca, NY: Cornell University Press.

Wegman, Edward J. 1988. "Computational statistics: A new agenda for statistical theory and practice." *Journal of the Washington Academy of Sciences* 78 (4): 310–22.

Weick, Karl E. 1976. "Educational organizations as loosely coupled systems." *Administrative Science Quarterly* 21 (1): 1–19.

Weick, Karl E. 1995. *Sensemaking in Organizations*. Thousand Oaks, CA: Sage.

Weisshaar, Katherine. 2018. "From opt out to blocked out: The challenges for labor market re-entry after family-related employment lapses." *American Sociological Review* 83 (1): 34–60.

Wells, Georgia, Jeff Horwitz, and Deepa Seetharaman. 2021. "Facebook knows Instagram is toxic for teen girls, company documents show." *The Wall Street Journal*, September 14, https://www.wsj.com/articles/facebook-knows-instagram-is-toxic-for-teen-girls-company-documents-show-11631620739 (viewed March 31, 2022).

Wensky, Margret. 1982. "Women's guilds in Cologne in the later Middle Ages." *Journal of European Economic History* 11 (3): 631–50.

Western, Bruce and Jake Rosenfeld. 2011. "Unions, norms, and the rise of U.S. wage inequality." *American Sociological Review* 76 (4): 513–37.

Westney, D. Eleanor. 1987. *Imitation and Innovation: The Transfer of Western Organizational Patterns to Meiji Japan*. Cambridge, MA: Harvard University Press.

Westphal, James D., Ranjay Gulati, and Stephen M. Shortell. 1997. "Customization or conformity: An institutional and network perspective on the content and consequences of TQM adoption." *Administrative Science Quarterly* 42 (2): 366–94.

Westphal, James D. and Edward J. Zajac. 1994. "Explaining institutional decoupling: The case of stock repurchase programs." *Administrative Science Quarterly* 46 (2): 202–28.

Wetts, Rachel. 2020. "Models and morals: Elite-oriented and value-neutral discourse dominates American organizations' framing of climate change." *Social Forces* 98 (3): 1339–69.

Whetten, David A. and Paul C. Godfrey, eds. 1998. *Identity in Organizations: Building Theory through Conversations*. Thousand Oaks, CA: Sage

Wharton, Amy S., Sharon R. Bird, and Thomas Rotolo. 2000. "Social context at work: A multi-level analysis of job satisfaction." *Sociological Forum* 15 (1): 65–90.

White, Douglas R. and Karl P. Reitz. 1983. "Graph and semigroup homomorphisms on networks of relations." *Social Networks* 5 (2): 193–234.

White, Harrison C. 1970. *Chains of Opportunity: System Models of Mobility in Organizations*. Cambridge, MA: Harvard University Press.

White, Harrison C., Scott A. Boorman, and Ronald L. Breiger. 1976. "Social structure from multiple networks I: Block models of roles and positions." *American Journal of Sociology* 81 (4): 730–80.

Whyte, William H., Jr. 1956. *The Organization Man*. New York: Simon and Schuster.

Wiebe, Robert H. 1967. *The Search for Order, 1877–1920*. New York: Hill and Wang.

Widdows, Dominic. 2004. *Geometry and Meaning*. Stanford, CA: Stanford University Press.

Wiersema, Margarethe F. and Karen A. Bantel. 1992. "Top management team demography and corporate strategic change." *Academy of Management Journal* 35 (1): 91–121.

Wiggin, Addison. 2013. "Charter school gravy train runs express to fat city." *Forbes*, September 10, https://www.forbes.com/sites/greatspeculations/2013/09/10/charter-school-gravy-train -runs-express-to-fat-city/#14e2d1d82be8 (viewed March 31, 2022).

Wilentz, Sean. 1984. "Against exceptionalism: Class consciousness and the American labor movement, 1790–1920." *International Labor and Working Class History* 26: 1–24.

Williams, Christine L. 1989. *Gender Differences at Work: Women and Men in Nontraditional Occupations*. Berkeley, CA: University of California Press.

Williams, Christine L. 1995. *Still a Man's World: Men Who Do Women's Work*. Berkeley, CA: University of California Press.

Williams, Joseph M. 1990. *Style: Toward Clarity and Grace*. Chicago: University of Chicago Press.

Williamson, Oliver E. 1975. *Markets and Hierarchies: Analysis and Antitrust Implications*. New York: Free Press.

Wilmers, Nathan. 2020. "Job turf or variety: Task structure as a source of organizational inequality." *Administrative Science Quarterly* 65 (4): 1018–57.

Winkler, Adam. 2018. *We the Corporations: How American Businesses Won Their Civil Rights*. New York: Liveright Publishing Corporation.

Winship, Christopher and Michael Mandel. 1983. "Roles and positions: A critique and extension of the blockmodeling approach." In *Sociological Methodology 1983–1984*, ed. S. Leinhardt, 314–45. San Francisco: Jossey-Bass.

Wiswall, Matthew and Basit Zafar. 2018. "Preference for the workplace, investment in human capital, and gender." *Quarterly Journal of Economics* 113 (1): 457–507.

Withers, Michael, Ji Youn (Rose) Kim, and Michael Howard. 2018. "The evolution of the board interlock network following Sarbanes-Oxley." *Social Networks* 52: 56–67.

Wolf, Wendy C. and Neil D. Fligstein. 1979. "Sex and authority in the workplace: The causes of sexual inequality." *American Sociological Review* 44: 235–52.

Woll, Cornelia. 2008. *Firm Interests: How Governments Shape Business Lobbying on International Trade*. Ithaca, NY: Cornell University Press.

Wong, Julia. 2017. "Former Facebook executive: Social media is ripping our society apart." *The Guardian*, https://www.theguardian.com/technology/2017/dec/11/facebook-former -executive-ripping-society-apart (viewed March 31, 2022).

"Woods, Elle." 2001. In *Legally Blonde* (dir. Robert Luketic). Quoted at: http://www.imdb.com /title/tt0250494/quotes (viewed March 31, 2022).

Woodward, Joanne. (1965) 1994. *Industrial Organization: Theory and Practice*. 2nd edn. Oxford: Oxford University Press.

Woolley, Samuel C. and Douglas R. Guilbeault. 2017. "Computational propaganda in the United States: Manufacturing consensus online." Working paper, University of Oxford.

World Bank. 1999. *Pollution Prevention and Abatement Handbook 1998*. Washington, DC: World Bank.

World Population Review. 2022. "States with internet sales tax." World Population Review, http://worldpopulationreview.com/states/states-with-internet-sales-tax (viewed March 31, 2022).

Wry, Tyler, J. Adam Cobb, and Howard E. Aldrich. 2013. "More than a metaphor: Assessing the historical legacy of resource dependence and its contemporary promise as a theory of environmental complexity." *Academy of Management Annals* 7 (1): 439–86.

Xiao, Zhixing and Anne S. Tsui. 2007. "When brokers may not work: The cultural contingency of social capital in Chinese high-tech firms." *Administrative Science Quarterly* 52 (1): 1–31.

Yakubovich, Valery. 2005. "Weak ties, information, and influence: How workers find jobs in a local Russian labor market." *American Sociological Review* 70 (3): 408–21.

Yang, Li. 2020. *What's New about Income Inequality in Asia?* World Inequality Lab Issue Brief, available at https://wid.world/wp-content/uploads/2020/11/WorldInequalityLab _IssueBrief_2020_08_IncomeInequalityAsia.pdf (viewed March 31, 2022).

Yang, Tiantian and Howard E. Aldrich. 2014. "Who's the boss? Explaining gender inequality in entrepreneurial teams." *American Sociological Review* 79 (2): 303–27.

Yates, JoAnn and Craig N. Murphy. 2019. *Engineering Rules: Global Standard Setting since 1880.* Baltimore: Johns Hopkins University Press.

Yenkey, Christopher B. 2018. "The outsider's advantage: Distrust as a deterrent to exploitation." *American Journal of Sociology* 124 (3): 613–63.

Younkin, Peter and Venkat Kuppuswamy. 2018. "The colorblind crowd? Founder race and performance in crowdfunding." *Management Science* 64 (7): 3269–87.

Yu, Wei-shin. 2013. "It's who you work with: Effects of workplace shares of nonstandard employees and women in Japan." *Social Forces* 92 (1): 25–57.

Zald, Mayer and Roberta Ash. 1966. "Social movement organizations: Growth, decay, and change." *Social Forces* 44 (3): 327–40.

Zald, Mayer N. and Patricia Denton. 1963. "From evangelism to general service: The transformation of the YMCA." *Administrative Science Quarterly* 8 (2): 214–34.

Zatzick, Christopher D., Marta M. Elvira, and Lisa E. Cohen. 2003. "When is more better? The effects of racial composition on voluntary turnover." *Organization Science* 14 (5): 483–96.

Zeitlin, Maurice. 1974. "Corporate ownership and control: The large corporation and the capitalist class." *American Journal of Sociology* 79 (5): 1073–119.

Zenger, Todd R. and Barbara S. Lawrence. 1989. "Organizational demography: The differential effects of age and tenure distributions on technical communication." *Academy of Management Journal* 32 (2): 353–76.

Zerubavel, Eviatar. 1991. *The Fine Line: Making Distinctions in Everyday Life.* Chicago: University of Chicago Press.

Zhang, Letian. 2017. "A fair game? Racial bias and repeated interaction between NBA coaches and players." *Administrative Science Quarterly* 62 (4): 603–25.

Zhao, Wei and Xueguang Zhou. 2017. "From institutional segmentation to market fragmentation: Institutional transformation and the shifting stratification order in China." *Social Science Research* 63: 19–35.

Zilber, Tammar B. 2002. "Institutionalization as an interplay between actions, meanings and actors: The case of a rape crisis center in Israel." *Academy of Management Journal* 45 (1): 234–54.

Zollo, Maurizio. 2009. "Superstitious learning with rare strategic decisions: Theory and evidence from corporate acquisitions." *Organization Science* 20 (5): 894–908.

Zollo, Maurizio, Carmelo Cennamo, and Kerstin Neumann. 2013. "Beyond what and why: Understanding organizational evolution toward sustainable enterprise models." *Organization and Environment* 26 (3): 241–59.

Zucker, Lynne G. 1977. "The role of institutionalization in cultural persistence." *American Sociological Review* 42 (5): 726–43.

Zucker, Lynne G. 1983. "Organizations as institutions." In *Research in the Sociology of Organizations*, vol. 2, ed. Sam Bacharach, 1–47. Greenwich, CT: JAI Press.

Zucker, Lynne G. 1988. "Where do institutional patterns come from? Organizations as actors in social systems." In *Institutional Patterns and Organizations: Culture and Environment*, ed. Lynne G. Zucker, 23–49. Cambridge, MA: Ballinger.

Zuckerman, Ezra W. 1999. "The categorical imperative: Securities analysts and the legitimacy discount." *American Journal of Sociology* 104 (5): 1398–438.

INDEX

Page indicators in italics refer to figures and tables.

A NOTE ON THE TYPE

This book has been composed in Arno, an Old-style serif typeface in the classic Venetian tradition, designed by Robert Slimbach at Adobe.

CPSIA information can be obtained
at www.ICGtesting.com
Printed in the USA
JSHW062350011122
31720JS00002BE/2